AVANT GARDE THEATRE

Examining the development of avant garde theatre from its inception in the 1890s right up to the present day, Christopher Innes exposes a central paradox of modern theatre; that the motivating force of theatrical experimentation is primitivism. What links the works of Strindberg, Artaud, Brook and Mnouchkine is an idealisation of the elemental and a desire to find ritual in archaic traditions. This widespread primitivism is the key to understanding both the political and aesthetic aspects of modern theatre and provides fresh insights into contemporary social trends.

The original text, first published in 1981 as *Holy Theatre*, has been fully revised and up-dated to take account of the most recent theoretical developments in anthropology, critical theory and psychotherapy. New sections on Heiner Müller, Robert Wilson, Eugenio Barba, Ariane Mnouchkine and Sam Shepard have been added. As a result, the book now deals with all the major avant garde theatre practitioners, in Europe and North America. Essential reading for anyone attempting to understand contemporary drama.

Christopher Innes is Professor of English at York University, Ontario.

AVANT GARDE THEATRE

1892–1992

Christopher Innes

London and New York

First published 1993
by Routledge
11 New Fetter Lane, London EC4P 4EE

Simultaneously published in the USA and Canada
by Routledge
29 West 35th Street, New York, NY 10001

Reprinted 1994

Typeset in Linotron 10 on 12 point Baskerville by
Intype, London
Printed and bound in Great Britain by
Butler & Tanner Ltd, Frome and London

A catalogue record for this book is available from the British Library

Library of Congress Cataloging in Publication Data
Innes, C. D.
Avant garde theatre/Christopher Innes.
p.   cm.
Rev. and updated ed. of: Holy theatre. 1981.
Includes bibliographical references and index.
1. Drama – 20th century – History and criticism.   2. Experimental
theater.   I. Innes, C. D. Holy theatre.   II. Title.
PN1861.15   1993   92–16204
809.2′04 – dc20

ISBN 0–415–06517–8   ISBN 0–415–06518–6   (pbk)

CONTENTS

ILLUSTRATIONS

ACKNOWLEDGEMENTS

I should like to thank the following individuals and institutions for providing illustrative material and for permission to reproduce the various sketches and photographs: Akademie der Künste (West Berlin), Chris J. Arthurs, Agence de Presse Photographique Bernand, Zoë Dominic, Ed Ellis and The Banff Centre for the Arts, Adolf u. Luisa Haeuser-Stiftung, Stadt u. Universitäts Bibliothek Frankfurt am Main, Ted Hughes, Lindsay Kemp, Lipnitzki Viollet, Theatermuseum des Institutes für Theaterwissenschaft der Universität Köln, Museum of the Performing Arts, New York Public Library at Lincoln Center, Theatre Museum Collection Victoria and Albert Museum, Max Waldman, and Richard Feldman.

I wish to express my deep appreciation to those who helped me to define the avant garde line of development by responding to my questions and providing information so generously: in particular Roger Blin, Joe Chaikin, Lindsay Kemp, Charles Marowitz and Richard Schechner; members of Jean-Louis Barrault's company at the Gare d'Orsay and of the Théâtre du Soleil, as well as staff at the National Theatre and Arthur Holmberg of ART. In addition I would like to thank Edward Bond for persuading me that, despite similarities in a play like *Early Morning*, his work had no place in this study, and Ann Saddlemyer for her helpful criticism of the first version of this study.

My thanks are also due to York University for the research fellowship that allowed me to complete the 1981 edition – originally published by Cambridge University Press under the title of *Holy Theatre*. This completely revised and updated version has been supported both by a grant from the Faculty of Arts at York University, and by the Social Sciences and Humanities Research Council of Canada, to whom I am most grateful. I would also like to acknowledge the help of Marion Jaeckel and Alyson McMackon, who provided bibliographical assistance.

Last, but by no means least, my wife's unflagging interest and encouragement has been invaluable, both then and now.

1

INTRODUCTION

THEMES AND DEFINITIONS

'Avant garde' has become a ubiquitous label, eclectically applied to any type of art that is anti-traditional in form. At its simplest, the term is sometimes taken to describe what is new at any given time: the leading edge of artistic experiment, which is continually outdated by the next step forward. But 'avant garde' is by no means value-neutral, as such usage implies. For Marxist critics like George Lukács it became synonymous with decadence, a cultural symptom of the malaise engendered by bourgeois society; for apologists it is the defining imperative in all art of our time, and 'the modern genius is essentially avant-gardistic'.[1]

Borrowed from military terminology by Bakunin, who titled the short-lived anarchist journal he published in Switzerland in 1878 *L'Avant-Garde*, the label was first applied to art by his followers. Their aim in revolutionizing aesthetics was to prefigure social revolution; and avant garde art is still characterized by a radical political posture. Envisioning a revolutionary future, it has been equally hostile to artistic tradition, sometimes including its immediate predecessors, as to contemporary civilization. Indeed, on the surface the avant garde as a whole seems united primarily in terms of what they are against: the rejection of social institutions and established artistic conventions, or antagonism towards the public (as representative of the existing order). By contrast any positive programme tends to be claimed as exclusive property by isolated and even mutually antagonistic sub-groups. So modern art appears fragmented and sectarian, defined as much by manifestos as imaginative work, and representing the amorphous complexity of post-industrial society in a multiplicity of dynamic but unstable movements focused on philosophic abstractions. Hence the use of '-isms' to describe them: symbolism, futurism, expressionism, formalism, surrealism.

However, beneath this diversity there is a clearly identifiable unity of purpose and interest (at least in the theatre) which has all the characteristics of a coherent trend, since its principles can be shown to be shared

1

quite independent of direct influence. For example, there are striking similarities between the work of Antonin Artaud in the 1930s and of Jerzy
Grotowski in the 1960s, even though Grotowski knew nothing of the 'theatre of cruelty' when he developed his concept of 'poor theatre'. At the
same time one can trace all the network of cross-fertilization that normally
defines a single artistic movement, signalled equally by the continuing
influence of a precursor (Alfred Jarry, August Strindberg) or shared
vocabulary (for instance 'theatre laboratory'), as by co-operation and imitation.

Thus Artaud and Roger Vitrac named their theatre after Jarry, and
Eugène Ionesco was a member of the Collège de Pataphysique, an anti-
establishment group devoted to Jarry's ideas. He included the figure of
Jarry in one of his plays, while Jean-Louis Barrault based one of his last
major productions on Jarry's life. Jarry's *Ubu* plays have been performed
by Peter Brook, Joe Chaikin and the Becks' Living Theatre, while a
'Savage God' theatre company (named after W.B. Yeats' disapproving
response to the first performance of *Ubu roi*) was founded in Canada by
John Juliani. Similarly the whole German expressionist movement derived
from Strindberg, and one of Artaud's earliest productions was Strindberg's
Dream Play, which also influenced Fernando Arrabal. Artaud worked both
with Roger Blin, who directed all Genet's major plays, and with Barrault,
who was responsible for establishing Brook's Centre for International Theatre Research in Paris, one of the many 'theatre laboratories' that –
following Grotowski's lead – were established in Belgium, Denmark and
the United States in the 1960s. It was specifically Artaud's influence that
led Brook to branch out from the traditional theatre, and Artaud's *The
Theatre and its Double* had an almost immediate impact on the American
counter-culture theatre groups when finally translated into English. Ariane
Mnouchkine is consciously paralleling both Artaud and Brook. Eugenio
Barba was trained by Grotowski, and Chaikin by the Becks, while Grotowski, Brook and Chaikin have co-operated on joint projects. Brook worked
with Charles Marowitz, whose Open Space theatre produced Sam
Shepard's first major play; and Shepard later collaborated with Chaikin.
Heiner Müller, whose early work has links with Artaud as well as the
expressionists, joined forces with the neo-surrealist Robert Wilson in the
1980s. These interconnections chart the mainline avant garde movement,
although there are many other names that could be mentioned.[2]

For contemporary observers in the 1920s, or even in the 1960s, what is
central was often obscured by the rhetoric of manifestos claiming unique-
ness for different aspects of the general movement. But from today's perspective shared concerns stand out clearly because they recur. And this
recurrence is even more significant since, although it is obviously a response
to the ethics of the age, it by no means reflects popularly accepted ideas
or the dominant ideological assumptions.

Perhaps paradoxically, what defines this avant garde movement is not overtly modern qualities, such as the 1920s romance of technology – Georges Antheil's 'aeroplane sonata', Corrado Govoni's 'poésie elettriche' or Enrico Prampolini's 'theatre of mechanics' – but primitivism. This has two complementary facets: the exploration of dream states or the instinctive and subconscious levels of the psyche; and the quasi-religious focus on myth and magic, which in the theatre leads to experiments with ritual and the ritualistic patterning of performance. These are integrated not only by the Jungian concept that all figures of myth are contained in the unconscious as expressions of psychological archetypes, but also by the idea that symbolic or mythopoeic thinking precedes language and discursive reason, revealing fundamental aspects of reality that are unknowable by any other means.[3] Both are variations of the same aim: to return to man's 'roots', whether in the psyche or prehistory. In theatrical terms this is reflected by a reversion to 'original' forms: the Dionysian rituals of ancient Greece, shamanistic performances, the Balinese dance-drama. Along with anti-materialism and revolutionary politics, the hallmark of avant garde drama is an aspiration to transcendence, to the spiritual in its widest sense. Antonin Artaud's pretentious claim to a 'Holy Theatre' – picked up by various avant garde artists, most recently Murray Shafer – is revealing.

Even for anthropologists or ethnographers, the primitive is almost always seen through a western, contemporary prism; and creative artists freely reinterpret primitive models to serve aims that would be alien to the original culture. However, this is far more than a cult of the superficially exotic and barbaric. In avant garde drama, as the widespread use of a term like 'theatre laboratory' in the 1960s and 1970s indicates, primitivism goes hand in hand with aesthetic experimentation designed to advance the technical progress of the art itself by exploring fundamental questions: 'The questions are: What is a theatre? What is a play? What is an actor? What is a spectator? What is the relation between them all? What conditions serve this best?'[4] On this level, the scientific ethos of the modern age parallels the return to 'primal' forms, equally signalling an attempt to replace the dominant modes of drama – and by extension the society of which these are the expression – by rebuilding from first principles.

The idealization of the primitive and elemental in theatre, together with the rediscovery and adapting of remote or archaic models, could be seen as an extension of the medievalism and orientalism of the nineteenth-century romantics. It parallels the borrowings from African sculpture or pre-Columbian Indian artifacts in the visual arts from Post-Impressionism on, and can be found in many other aspects of modern culture. It is echoed in Freud's 'primal' therapy and his 'attempt in *Totem and Taboo* to exploit the newly won analytic insights for an investigation of the origins of religion and morality', or in the anthropological value placed on the primitive state by Lévi-Strauss.[5] It is expressed in Conrad's fascination with 'the heart of darkness', or in D.H. Lawrence's primitivism, as in the popular escapism of Edgar Rice Burroughs' *Tarzan* series that were as much in vogue during the 1960s and 1970s, as they had been when first published between 1912 and 1936. It also conditions critical theories such as Mikhail Bakhtin's ideal of 'carnivalesque' literature, which proposes artistic forms that embody the anarchic and grotesque, inherently revolutionary energies of the Roman Saturnalia and medieval popular carnivals as an alternative to the 'limited and reduced aesthetic stereotypes of modern times'.[6]

Indeed aspects of primitivism – ranging from ritualistic techniques, or borrowing from archaic and oriental traditions, to the presentation of dream states and surrealistic images, or an attempt to tap the spectators' subconscious – have been so widespread in twentieth-century theatre that the boundaries of the avant garde are amorphous. In part the movement is hard to distinguish because its influence has been so pervasive. It can be traced in an official institution like Vilar's Théâtre National Populaire, which also searched for 'ceremonial subjects' to establish a communion between actors and spectators comparable with the mass enthusiasm evoked by medieval mysteries. It surfaces in the Nazi *'Thingspiel'*, and in rock festivals, where the rhythms and psychedelic lights urge a similar surrender to the instinctive id that in the right conditions resembles a Dionysiac revel.

Avant garde elements also appear in other types of experimental theatre. Some of W.B. Yeats' comments seem to echo exactly the same concerns: 'I have always felt that my work is not drama but the ritual of a lost faith' – 'drama which would give direct expression to reverie, to the speech of the soul with itself'. And his borrowing from Japanese Nōh theatre, or his use of incantation and ritualized movement, is typical. Even his Rosicrucian mysticism has its counterparts. Yet his poetic aims are traditional, appealing 'to the eye of the mind' – the conscious imagination – and relying on 'the ancient sovereignty of words', while the avant garde moved in exactly the opposite direction.[7] Similarly, Samuel Beckett's work is related in its use of symbolism and psychodrama, as in its stripping away of worn-out theatrical idioms to create minimalist images – but despite early interest in the surrealists, his existential vision is quite distinct from the avant garde stress on liberating the primitive side of the psyche.

The mainstream of the avant garde is not simply defined by shared stylistic qualities, although these may be what is most immediately obvious. Rather, the avant garde is essentially a philosophical grouping. Its members are linked by a specific attitude to western society, a particular aesthetic approach, and the aim of transforming the nature of theatrical performance: all of which add up to a distinctive ideology. Although there may be stylistic similarities in the work of a symbolist like Yeats, or an existentialist like Beckett – as in surrealists like Cocteau and Breton, an absurdist such as Adamov, or a religious dramatist like T.S. Eliot – the essential basis of their art is antithetical to the anarchic primitivism and radical politics of the avant garde.

2

THE POLITICS OF PRIMITIVISM

BAKUNIN – BAKHTIN

The identifying signature of avant garde art, all the way back to Bakunin and his anarchist journal *L'Avant-Garde* in 1878, has been an unremitting hostility to contemporary civilization. Its most obvious aspect has been negative: the rejection of social organization and artistic conventions, aesthetic values and materialistic ideals, syntactical structure and logic, as well as everything associated with the bourgeoisie. But this apparent nihilism always implied a utopian alternative to the *status quo*, which has three aspects. Broadly speaking these can be called the philosophical, the populist and the primitive – although such avant garde categories are often inseparable, equally political and tend to be expressed in psychological terms.

As a philosophy, the avant garde corresponds to anarchism, which also has its nihilistic side. Although its public image became misleadingly associated with bearded, bomb-throwing terrorists, the basic principle of the turn-of-the-century anarchist movement could be best described as extreme individualism. For Bakunin and his followers, personal rights totally superseded those of the state, which by definition were coercive; egalitarian communes would be the only valid form of social organization; and all set rules that prescribed behaviour ('being') had to be discarded for a fluid sense of individual fulfilment ('becoming'). In general terms these remain the ideals of the avant garde, even if their source frequently went unrecognized, while translating them into theatrical practice tended to disguise the link with Bakunin's ideas. Thus the anarchist battle against political hierarchies turned into an attack on the cultural hegemony of the establishment (which was sometimes little more than *épater les bourgeois*). Personal liberation came to be conceived psychologically or even spiritually, rather than as an external condition, although the route to its achievement was frequently physical – freeing the mind through assaulting the senses – and had strong political overtones. The commune was identified with the acting group: again, in a sense, an internalization of the

6

anarchist aim. And an emphasis on artistic creation as 'process', in place of presenting a theatrical 'product', substituted for the notion of 'becoming' versus 'being'.

Exactly the same anti-hierarchical ethos characterizes the populist aspect of anarchism, which is perhaps best defined in Mikhail Bakhtin's work. Despite being isolated from avant garde developments in Stalinist Russia and restricted to literary theory, his path-breaking studies of Dostoevsky and particularly Rabelais are not only representative, but also offer a critical tool for analysing avant garde work. By contrast to classical and mimetic literature – seen as inherently authoritarian and logocentric in its 'monologism' (his term for Aristotelian unity and the separation of genres, in which aesthetic harmony is achieved by a singleness of voice and perspective) – Bakhtin traces a counter-culture archetype to popular street carnivals. All of what has been defined as 'great literature' since the Renaissance is considered an aberration in the context of this much longer 'folk tradition', which incorporates contradictory elements, combining the comic and tragic with the grotesque, to create a multi-tonal or 'dialogic' model that is intrinsically revolutionary.[1] Derived from the Russian Formalist school of linguistics, Bakhtin's literary sociology parallels anarchism but gives it a Marxist gloss.

As exemplified in the Roman Saturnalia, the medieval 'Feast of Fools', or the modern Mardi Gras, for Bakhtin the essence of carnival was that it both comprised 'the people as a whole' and made them 'aware of their sensual, material bodily unity and community', as well as being 'outside of and contrary to all existing forms of the coercive socioeconomic and political organization, which is suspended for the time of the festival'. An antidote to the 'official' culture (whether ecclesiastic or feudal) that promotes an abstract spirituality at the expense of the physical, and is characterized by rigidity and intellectual seriousness, the carnival spirit asserts the biological basis of life, the oneness of human existence with the earth. It exalts all 'lower' elements: those that are denigrated or denied by the official value system, whether 'vulgar' bodily functions, 'crude'/'impure' aesthetic categories, or social inferiors. Breaking taboos to signal 'the defeat . . . of the earthly upper classes, of all that oppresses and restricts', it dissolves the concept of an atomized bourgeois individuality by making each festive participant conscious of 'being a member of a continually growing and renewed people'.[2] This utopian ideal of community (and by extension Communism) is both generated and affirmed by laughter. It is also presented as nothing less than a 'cosmic principle', one of Bakhtin's recurring labels for the carnevalesque.

Translated into literary terms (with Rabelais as the archetypal exemplar, from whom Bakhtin derives a radical theory of humour), this carnival spirit is expressed in gargantuan themes of physical appetite and excremental or genital imagery, corrosive parody, and abusive language, together with violent shifts of tone or the juxtaposition of contradictory fragments, inversion and materialistic hyperbole. Its indispensable traits are the grotesque and ambivalence, which are seen as being integrally connected. On the thematic level a deliberate stressing of the ugly or monstrous, the half-formed or incomplete, and the unity of opposites (body and spirit, monkey and man, copulation and dismemberment) goes along with verbal puns, multiple viewpoints and switches in consciousness on a stylistic level. Artistic forms qualify as carnevalesque if they release imaginative and sexual energies by subverting social, moral and aesthetic categories, norms and prohibitions. Both the grotesque and ambivalence intrinsically display 'the potentiality of an entirely different world, of another order, another way of life'; and this is associated with irrationality or madness, which by definition offers an 'abnormal' viewpoint that is free from conventional ideas and official 'truths'.[3] It also relates to the kind of psychological universe created by Dostoevsky, where the disruption of cause-and-effect literary logic, together with temporal and spatial distortions, draw a reader inside the divided consciousness of an outcast whose pathological mentality casts doubt on standard concepts of reality.

Bakhtin himself pointed out the correspondence between the 'dialogizing' of consciousness in Dostoevsky, and expressionist drama with its distorted perspectives and subjectivity. But the parallels between his ideas and avant garde theatre are far wider. Abusive parody, combined with the focus on physical ugliness and moral monstrosity are the hallmarks of Alfred Jarry's fragmented plays. The positive function of madness, the inversion of moral categories and the grotesque in all its aspects are central to Antonin Artaud's work. An ambivalent attack on the sacred, the breaking of taboos and the exaltation of the body characterize Jerzy Grotowski's theatre, leading to a search for primal relationships between man and the natural world. Sexual liberation and social revolution formed the core of the Living Theatre, revolving around a universal ideal of community that was represented as a cosmic principle. Indeed, Jarry and Jean-Louis Barrault both created dramas based on Rabelais: one right at the start of the avant garde movement, the other as a direct response to the student revolution of 1968. In a sense, through Jarry, the roots of avant garde theatre lie in the type of radical laughter that Bakhtin saw as fundamental to the carnival spirit, which is also evident in the dark expressionist depictions of urban existence and the surrealist portrayals of the bourgeoisie, although comedy is signally absent from Artaud and most later manifestations of the avant garde.

This tendency to quasi-religious seriousness, which all too often led to inflated self-pretension, is the antithesis of Bakhtin's carnival spirit. But carnevalesque qualities are the defining marks of avant garde drama: in particular the emphasis on stage production as process in opposition to the fixed art-product of classical aesthetics; and the fusion of actors and audience, breaking down the barriers between performance and reality to create a comm-union of (in theory at least) equal participants. As Bakhtin puts it, 'Carnival was . . . the feast of becoming, change and renewal. It was hostile to all that was immortalized and completed' – both in society and art – while a telling passage uses the stage as a metaphor:

> Carnival does not know footlights, in the sense that it does not acknowledge any distinction between actors and spectators. Footlights would destroy a carnival, as the absence of footlights would destroy a theatrical performance.

Perhaps even more centrally, the same uniting of opposites such as death and birth or dismemberment and copulation in carnival has been seen as typical – in artistic terms – of the avant garde, which being 'the experimental edge of modernity, has historically given itself a double task: to destroy and to invent'.[4] Such parallels are the more striking and significant since there can be no question of influence. Bakhtin himself was cut off from artistic developments in Europe, and shows a very limited knowledge even of early expressionist theatre, while his study of Rabelais was only written in 1940, remained unpublished until 1965, and first became available to the West (in an English translation from the Russian) in 1968, some months after Barrault's production of *Rabelais*.

THE CULT OF THE PRIMITIVE

The thrust of Bakhtin's work is also regressive – finding its ideals in the return to a medieval survival of traditions from prehistory, already marginalized in Rabelais' time and increasingly effaced by social developments that were the opposite of all they stood for – and this links carnevalesque populism with the third aspect of the avant garde: primitivism. In the theatre this primitivism has taken two highly productive forms, apparently contradictory but actually complementary. On the one hand there is the transformation of the stage into a laboratory for exploring fundamental questions about the nature of performance and the relationship between actor and audience. On the other, the exploitation of irrationality, the exploration of dream states, the borrowing of archaic dramatic models, mythological material or tribal rituals. What unites the scientific with the quasi-mythical is that stripping down drama to the naked actor on a bare stage also ultimately leads to an interior focus on the psyche and to experiments with subliminal or direct physical communication. Both are returning to the 'roots' of theatre – whether in its primitive origins or by divesting it of scenic or illusionistic 'accretions' – as much as to the psychological or prehistoric 'roots' of man.

This atavism itself is a symptom of the avant garde hostility to modern society and all the artistic forms that reflect its assumptions. The point of borrowing from African sculpture or Balinese dance is that, in being 'primitive', it embodies an alternative value scale. In the same way the point of exalting the unconscious and emotional side of human nature is to provide an antidote to a civilization that almost exclusively emphasizes the rational and intellectual. The conviction that bourgeois society destroys the artistic individual led expressionists like Toller, surrealists like Breton or absurdists like Adamov to join the Communist Party. Quite rightly, however, their motives were questioned by other communists. In the totalitarian state to which they were committed, their artistic approach would be impossible, as the suicide of Mayakovsky had already demonstrated. Yet it was no coincidence that Artaud described the 'social suicide' of Van Gogh as a prototype for the modern artist, and defined an incoherent scream of protest as the official voice of the avant garde.

Artaud's call for consciously suicidal protest might seem completely apolitical, just as primitivism could be seen simply as escapism, or the value put on the subconscious as retreat from reality. Indeed the misconception that ritualistic, mythical theatre and political theatre are mutually exclusive opposites – epitomized in the Tynan/Ionesco controversy (*The Observer*, 1958) – is far too commonly accepted. Perhaps this is because at its extreme the avant garde repudiation of society either harks back to a 'mystic in the state of savagery' stance (as Paul Claudel tellingly described Rimbaud) or alternatively expresses itself obliquely in a movement towards abstraction which, in defining itself as 'anti-theatre', rejects thematic meanings, logical structures and anything that might be identified as an ideological position or 'message'. This tends to be justified – misleadingly and paradoxically – as 'theatre of pure form' (Witkiewicz, 1921), or as drama 'that cannot serve any other kind of truth but its own' and therefore has the sole function of revealing 'the fundamental laws of [dramatic] construction' (Ionesco, 1958). On one level such claims are an attempt to align the stage with advances in other art forms. As the expressionist director Jessner put it: 'Just as there is a pure (absolute) music and a pure (absolute) painting, we must have pure theatre.'[5] But emphasizing stylistic exploration at the expense of statement does not really rule out commitment, despite some avant garde claims that any drama 'fixated on politics' is outdated and irrelevant since

> the most advanced phenomena are neither literary nor political, but formal. If the middle of the twentieth century is going to be remembered, it will be for the ensembles of the Living Theatre, the Open Theatre, Café la Mama and Grotowski, whose common factor is a physical, unnaturalistic theatre-language, spiritually revolutionary and standing in opposition to . . . psychological realism, Aristotelian time structure.[6]

Leaving aside the incorrect assertion that ideological commitment automatically rules out stylistic advances, which is clearly contradicted by the work of ideological artists like Bertolt Brecht, what is significant is the stress on spiritual revolution. In the conventional Marxist view (Brecht's *Man is Man* being a representative example), an individual's personality is determined by environmental conditions, and therefore social change must precede any alteration in consciousness. The avant garde reverses the process, seeing a fundamental change in human nature as the prerequisite for social alteration. As Eugenio Barba put it, 'Our craft is the possibility of changing ourselves, and thus changing society' – while the links to primitivism are clear in Richard Schechner's assertion that 'the ambition to make theatre into ritual is nothing other than a wish to make performance efficacious, to use [theatrical] events to change people'.[7]

Naturally in light of this political intention, the most appropriate – and in fact the most frequently used – ritual forms were the 'rites of passage', analysed by anthropologists like Van Gennep as early as 1908. The basic pattern here is the separation of participants from their previous environment, frequently through sensory deprivation and disorientation: an action that symbolizes a change in their nature, and their physical integration into a new group. And recognition of this type of ritual is the key to understanding the treatment of the audience in Grotowski's 'paratheatrical' projects or in the Living Theatre.

This borrowing of ritual forms to manipulate the audience is what distinguishes avant garde aims most clearly from social or politically committed drama. Both kinds of theatre may repudiate existing social conditions and work for change. But commitment uses logical structures – whether 'dialectical' as in Brecht or the conventional cause-and-effect of Bernard Shaw – since its aim is to promote a future programme (class revolution/eugenic evolution) through a conscious awareness of specific issues. Shaw's desire for a 'pit of philosophers' is as typical as Brecht's attempts to instil the 'smoking-observing' attitude of 'experts' in his audience, and emotional responses are secondary, evoked only as a technique of positive reinforcement for the intellectual message. The essence of a rite of passage, by contrast, is that it requires physical and emotional involvement in a present action, and seeks to change the nature of the participants directly by irrational, often highly disturbing means: 'In philosophical terms, initiation is equivalent to a basic change in existential condition; the novice emerges from his ordeal endowed with a totally different being from that which he possessed before his initiation; he has become *another*.'[8]

This may seem an unrealistic expectation for the modern theatre with an audience who are not only self-aware but are also aware of the make-believe and pretence inherent in stage performance. Yet, in the political sphere, images are all too often taken for reality, while the concept of a ceremonial action changing one's existential nature is the basis of the major surviving rituals of our secularized society. Baptism literally gives anonymous babies a spiritual and social identity, a name and a place in the group; marriage transforms two individuals into 'one flesh' legally as well as figuratively; the funeral service marks the transition from mortal clay to an unknown spiritual state. On the other hand there are still existing models in certain highly traditional/primitive cultures, which offer a graphic demonstration of tantalizing possibilities not only by presenting ritual in what is clearly a form of theatre, but also by apparently inducing a change in the participants that is not merely symbolic but actual.

BALI AND CULTURAL COLONIALISM

The best-documented example is the Balinese dance-drama, and it is no coincidence that this was the model Artaud chose for his ideal theatre after seeing a single performance by a Balinese troupe in 1931. Their programme was a medley of musical pieces (Gong; Lasem), a dynamic sitting dance by a single male (Keybar) and a court dance for pre-pubescent girls (Legong), solo displays interspersed with group formation dances (Djanger), a warrior dance and an ogre dance (Baris; Rakshasa) – and one theatrical performance, a Barong drama in which some sort of mythic animal appears.[9] There is no record of what the story line was on that occasion, or of how it was presented.[10] However, if it corresponded to Margaret Mead's pathbreaking anthropological film of *Trance and Dance in Bali*, shot only six years later, it epitomized many of the qualities that the expressionists and surrealists had been working towards, but in an authentic mythic and ritual form. As such it was a logical extension of the experimentation that Artaud had already begun in his Théâtre Alfred Jarry.

The film records the dramatized re-enaction of a myth. Masked actors represent supernatural beings – a hieratically stylized dragon and a nightmarish but grotesquely human witch. Their conflict symbolizes a quintessential spiritual opposition, in which the protective deity – as a flying creature of light, the principle of life itself – wars with chaos, night and death in the form of evil magic embodying the plague (the image that Artaud took to define the ideal effect of his theatre). This clash of symbols is the centre of the drama, and the two 'Gods' are the only figures with prescribed speeches. But the focus of the performance is on the choruses of warriors and maidens, who stand for the human population, are unmasked, and wear traditional folk dress rather than 'costumes'. Their dances have been elaborated during the annual repetition of the spectacle from time immemorial, until these form the theatrical action – while the original sacred play has become reduced to a thematic prologue defining the issues at stake. However, the climax of their dance is psychological rather than dramatic. It is marked by a shift from acted-out pretence to actuality at the point where the dancers enter a state of trance and turn the swords, with which they had unsuccessfully (in dramatic terms)

Figure 1a Balinese Maiden's chorus: formalized postures and archaic gestures.

Figure 1b Balinese dancers in different degrees of trance, tension and invulnerability. Note the force needed to bend the kris and the use of incense.

attempted to attack the witch, against their own breasts. But being literally 'possessed', their skin remains unpierced – or in another variation such trance dancers can thread long skewers through cheeks and arms, with no pain or bleeding, and without leaving any scars. So although unable to kill death itself in the symbol of the witch, they achieve victory by the dominance of spirit over body in proving their flesh (in reality) invulnerable to the razor-sharp sword points which they thrust and stab against themselves with all their strength.

Artaud was correct in describing all the elements of the Balinese performance he witnessed as 'calculated':

> Nothing is left to chance or personal initiative . . . everything is thus regulated and impersonal; not a movement of the muscles, not the rolling of an eye but seem to belong to a kind of reflective mathematics which controls everything and by means of which everything happens.[11]

But he was quite wrong in attributing this to 'the absolute preponderance of the director (*metteur en scène*) whose creative power *eliminates words*'.[12] Each step in the dance, bend of the torso, toss of the hair or flex of the fingers, like the flattening of individuality in the dancers' facial rigidity, is as fixed by custom and prescribed by immemorial tradition as the sequence of events in the mythical history. Postures and formalized hand attitudes found in the dancing figures of twelfth-century Hindu-Javanese religious monuments are still retained with amazing precision in the Balinese performance; and these are clearly archaic survivals, not consciously adopted forms.

Apart from shading the eyes with the hand, fingers curled back and body drooping to indicate despair, or first and second fingers pointing at the end of a rigidly extended arm to embody anger, few of the gestures have dramatic meaning. On one level, like the hypnotic monotone musical accompaniment with its strongly stressed rhythms, all the stylized movements of the dance can be seen as techniques designed to induce the trance which is the justification for the performance. As anthropologists noted, the length of a performance and the number of times sequences of movement are repeated or elaborated in different permutations are determined by the difficulty the dancers find in entering a trance, and by the intensity of what can only be called mass self-hypnosis.[13] Another aspect that observers have commented on is the contagious nature of this delirium. Once one dancer achieves it, others succumb almost immediately; and Margaret Mead's film records the instance of an elderly woman in the audience being unwillingly but irresistibly sucked into the trance state, in spite of her earlier declaration that she would not participate. For Artaud the conjunction of trance and fixed, depersonalized gestures expressed 'the automatism of the liberated unconscious'.[14] And certainly, if we are to believe our eyes and the camera, this type of communicative delirium is real and in no way pretended. Indeed, the final event in this particular Balinese performance was a ceremony of exorcism. The dancers apparently could not return to their 'right minds' without the aid of a priest.

This in fact is a common element in much primitive drama. The actor becomes 'possessed' by the spirit he impersonates and has to be 'released' from his role by a member of the audience who removes his head-dress, his make-up or his mask so that he reverts to his everyday face underneath, or by a priest who burns incense under his nose. Clearly this type of performance draws on areas of the mind that our intellectual western tradition represses or ignores, and – quite apart from discrediting the rationalistic nineteenth-century definition of myth as a fictitious narrative, since those re-enacting a myth have no conscious control over their actions once they have fully entered their 'role' and so do not function as 'story-tellers' in any usual sense – its psychological effectiveness made it a natural model for the avant garde.

There are other ways too in which the Balinese model was significant. Like all early dramatic forms, it is closely linked with religion. In addition to its ritual context, being preceded by the ceremonial purification of the dancers as well as followed by exorcism, the type of performance documented by the film was performed in temple precincts during a religious festival – an aspect that Artaud was able to ignore since the performance he attended was in the artificial setting of a colonial exhibition. Hence his assertion that this was a 'purely popular' rather than sacred theatre, which reflected his own opposition to socially ratified religion (and particularly Christianity). More to the point, being an immediately transferrable technique, was a particular use of language. What little dialogue the Balinese spectacle contained was in an archaic tongue that apparently neither performers, the Balinese audience (let alone the French spectators), nor even priests understood. It thus became an incantation. The only other vocal communication was on the level of pure sound, expressive of general emotional states, so that meaning was transmitted on a physical level through attitudes which, while not directly allegorical, had an intrinsically symbolic effect through their highly formalized codification.[15] These aspects gave Artaud a working example of the 'concrete language, intended for the senses and independent of speech', which has been such an influential concept in avant garde theatre.

As a re-enaction of myth, however, the Balinese dance represents only one aspect of primitive drama. The other primary form, traditionally dismissed as superstition and only recently recognized as a valid object for analysis through the work of anthropologists, is the shamanistic performance. This typically contains the same rhythmic use of music and a similar stylized level of mime. But the performer is a single expert (the shaman), in contrast to the Balinese model where all members of the social group participate; and it relies more on illusion for its effect, being usually conducted in a darkened space and frequently involving sleight of hand or ventriloquism. The basis of the performance is the same: a self-induced trance in which the physical and spiritual worlds are assumed to interpenetrate. But here the functional focus is on the spectator, not the actor.

In one general pattern of shamanistic seance the witch doctor goes into a trance by a sick man's bedside, and mimes a journey to the spirit world and a struggle to rescue the invalid's soul, which is assumed to have been stolen by demons and only has to be returned to restore physical health. Obviously, in this faith-healing process it is the level of belief that can be generated which is the healing agent; and in a description of a typical performance

> the Shaman went further and further into a state of ecstasy, and finally, throwing the drum into the hands of his assistant . . . began the shamanistic dance – a pantomime illustrating how the khargi [spirit guide], accompanied by the group of spirits, rushed on his dangerous journey fulfilling the Shaman's commands . . . Under the hypnotic influence of the shamanistic ecstasy, those present often fell into a state of mystical hallucination feeling themselves active participants in the Shaman's performance.[16]

Avant garde drama generally shares this kind of quasi-mystical therapeutic aim, whether in the expressionist form of emotional inspiration that supposedly 'transfigured' the spectators so that they 'rose up New Men'; or in Artaud's 'exorcism', which was intended both to strip away the constraints of civilization, restoring the natural relationship to the spiritual universe, and to purge the audience of violence by indulging them (against all psychiatric principles) in images of 'gratuitous crime' and cruelty; or in Grotowski's 'paratheatrical' projects and the Living Theatre's political psychotherapy, where both these approaches are combined.

In its own way, Artaud's view of the Balinese dance-drama is of course colonialist in prizing it as alien, exotic and 'other'. Such a performance embodies values very different from those of western society. Yet they are by no means 'natural' or uncivilized. The whole concept of 'the primitive' assumes a privileged observer, who assigns significance to 'primitive' art or life in so far as it appears to be the opposite of the present, or of industrial urban civilization. If the present is seen as too sophisticated, rational, materialistic, technological, or repressively Christian, then 'the primitive mind' is taken to exemplify the naive, the irrational or sexuality. It embodies the spiritual, in harmony with nature, or representative of pagan freedom. Ignoring the diversity of native cultures, 'the primitive' is generally imagined as a universal quality: the quintessentially human from which European history has deviated. It has also tended to be interpreted in terms of European political ideology, as a left-wing ideal of pre-capitalist economic and social relations in the 1960s – or, interchangeably, as the Fascist ideal of 'blood' and 'folk' in the 1930s. To the Victorians, labelling a people as 'primitive' (with connotations of 'dark', cruel, backward, child-like) affirmed their own moral superiority and right to imperial conquest. The revolution in consciousness represented by modernism simply inverted this, making 'primitive' a synonym for utopian. All are equally imaginary projections, reflecting the needs or desires of the observer.[17]

This was true of most ethnographers; and it applied even more to avant garde artists who in general had little opportunity of experiencing African or Oriental cultures except out of context. The Balinese performance that Artaud saw was framed by the 'Colonial Exhibition' at which it was presented in France; Nigerian masks or Polynesian carvings automatically change their significance when displayed as art objects in a western house or museum. And the few artists who went in search of 'the primitive' on its home ground had already formulated their ideas, which inevitably conditioned what they found. Artaud returned from Mexico with a drug-induced fantasy of Cortez and Montezuma: colonialism inflated into existential archetype. Peter Brook's theatrical travels in Africa consistently misinterpreted the reactions of the native audience, and his trip to India was a pilgrimage. Traditional religious rituals observed 'on location', like those that Richard Schechner transplanted to New York, became transformed into counter-culture, sexual rites. In their native context the effective agent was long-established familiarity – for a Parisian or Off-Off-Broadway audience they had imaginative power in direct relation to their strangeness and unconventionality.

Any object changes its significance when switched to different surroundings, or divorced from its original function; and the metamorphosis is even more extreme in the case of artistic expression or theatrical performance styles, let alone the culturally determined behaviour patterns of ritual. At the same time, the key factor in the artistic explosion over the last century – the development of new forms, alternative visions, unprecedented ways of relating to the public – has been the discovery of different cultures that came from colonization. From the vogue for 'Japonisme' in the 1890s and the influence of Nōh drama on Gordon Craig and Yeats, or of Chinese acting on Brecht, Asian models have been an essential stimulus for western artistic innovation. Asian influence defines much of modern dance from Maurice Béjart to Meredith Monk, and appears in the work of such mainstream dramatists as Eugene O'Neill, Thornton Wilder and Paul Goodman in America, or Andre Obey in France. It has even made its mark on opera through Andrei Serban, or on the American musical with Hal Prince; and it is still more central to the avant garde theatre. Indeed, there is hardly a single significant avant garde figure who has not experimented with Asian models.

The impact of Bali on Artaud is characteristic. Strindberg was influenced

17

by eastern mysticism; Barrault by Nōh and Kabuki performance styles through Claudel; Brook borrows eclectically from a range of non-European sources – Sufi, Nōh, Kathakali – and the line runs through Grotowski (who has acknowledged the influence of Nōh acting techniques) and Tadeusz Kantor, Richard Schechner and Joe Chaikin, to Richard Forman and contemporary US experimental groups who have adapted Javanese shadow puppets, Indian Kathakali, or even produced a cowboy-Kabuki. Ariane Mnouchkine mixes Greek and Shakespearean traditions with Balinese theatre, Kathakali dance and Kabuki staging, while Robert Wilson has updated a symbolist opera by Gabriele D'Annunzio and Claude Debussy, both of whom were influenced by the turn-of-the-century vogue for 'Japonisme' – *The Martydom of St Sebastian* (1988) originally staged in Paris in 1911 – to create an equivalent of traditional Nōh drama. Conversely, standard European models ranging from Ibsen to Beckett have had just as much impact on the development of modern Chinese drama, or Japanese experimental theatre.

The value of this cross-cultural impetus for western modern and post-modernist art can hardly be overstated. Yet deriving, as it does, from nineteenth-century imperialism makes the nature of this stimulus deeply questionable; and the whole artistic enterprise of interculturalism remains inherently problematic, even where it is more than superficial exoticism. However, the attempt to reproduce the effects of 'primitive' or ritual theatre helps to explain avant garde elements that might otherwise seem puzzling, such as the apparent incompatibility of stressing emotional authenticity and using stylized movement or unnatural gesture to express it. At the same time, the spectacular and rhetorical nature of ritual action is inherently theatrical, and has helped to disguise some of the philosophical problems in this return to 'roots'.

But all this did not happen at once. Initially the avant garde concentrated on adapting symbolic structures from the familiar Christian tradition or attempting to reproduce dream states. It was really only in the 'theatre laboratories' of the 1960s that models from outside the European cultural heritage were applied in anything more than a superficial way, or that ritual was consciously explored in terms of its reciprocal effect on the actor and onlooker. Nevertheless, the principles of these later experiments were already formulated by the symbolists and expressionists.

3

DREAMS, ARCHETYPES AND THE IRRATIONAL

SYMBOLISM AND ALFRED JARRY

From the first this atavistic trend in avant garde drama was very much a child of its time, reflecting a general intellectual climate that had been produced by literary movements earlier in the nineteenth century. The seeds can be found in the late romantic fascination for the 'night side of nature', out of which came two related positions, both equally antagonistic to the rationalistic and factual documentation of naturalism. One is well represented by Rimbaud's notorious claim that 'One must be a visionary . . . The poet makes himself a visionary through a long, immense and reasoned derangement of the senses.' The other can be characterized by the symbolist stress on 'suggestive indefiniteness of vague and therefore spiritual effect' (Poe).

In the theatre, the most noticeable effect of symbolist theories was an undramatic progression into abstraction and stasis, a withdrawal from the audience epitomized by the number of plays that followed Maeterlinck's *Pelléas and Mélisande* (1892) in being performed behind gauzes.[1] But certain aspects of their work do anticipate subsequent productive developments. Thematically a great many symbolist plays were associated with religious revivalism of the time, whether in the traditional terms of Edmond Harancourt's updated mystery play, *La Passion* (performed on Good Friday 1890, in Holy Week 1891 and at Easter 1892), or in the esoteric and occult Babylonian spectacles of Joséphin Péladan's Théâtre de la Rose Croix. Technically their more interesting devices were attempts to find symbolic 'correspondences' between colours and sounds which led to multi-level, synaesthetic productions, plus an emphasis on expressive tone and pitch in speaking, rather than on the sense of what was said, together with the development of mime to portray psychological states in immediate, physical terms, instead of describing these in dialogue.

The aim was to reach a deeper level of reality than deceptive surface appearances – to embody the inner nature of archetypal man in concrete symbols, in contrast to the naturalistic depiction of socially defined individuals.

The key figure here was Maurice Maeterlinck, whose plays produced at the Théâtre d'Art set the standards for symbolist theatre. Already in his first play, *The Wicked Princess* (1889), Maeterlinck concentrated on the atmospheric evocation of subliminal images, using details of the setting – which were typically indistinct and impressionistic: rustling leaves, moonlit reflections in water, shadows on a wall – solely for their symbolic value, rather than as representations of a social context to authenticate the dramatic situation. External reality had become a psychic projection of the characters. This was the hallmark of symbolist drama, and it reached its fullest expression in the cavern scene of *Pelléas and Mélisande*. Here Golaud, having caught Pelléas caressing Mélisande's long blonde tresses, leads him into the subterranean vaults beneath the castle; and it is immediately clear that this is a descent into the abysses of the subconscious mind. The characters are revealed as elements of the psyche, the castle itself as the intellect, and the relative valuation of conscious versus subconscious is typical. The apparently massive, impregnable edifice of rationalism is seen as precariously perched on unstable foundations, an artificial construction beneath which are dark caverns filled with stagnant pools where 'strange lizards' live. Representing the house of intellect as a castle stresses its defensive, repressive aspect, but belief in its permanence can only be maintained by a deliberate refusal to see what it covers. As Golaud says, implicitly attacking nineteenth-century rationalistic attitudes:

> There are hidden workings here which no one suspects, and the whole castle will be engulfed one of these nights if we don't watch out. But what can one do? There's no one who wants to come down here.[2]

This negative value placed on rational structures of thought was what led the symbolists to attempt to find direct, as opposed to discursive ways of communicating – a language, at once sensual and subliminal – and it is this linking of apparent opposites that has become a basic characteristic of all avant garde drama, leading straight to Artaud's ideal of 'directly affecting the organism' of the spectator by creating a 'concrete language, intended for the senses and independent of speech', which would give a 'physical knowledge of images' in a manner comparable to acupuncture.[3] Following this symbolist line, Maeterlinck worked towards a 'theatre of silence', implicitly dismissing the discussion basis of Pineroesque or Ibsenite problem plays. Words (in an argument that strikingly anticipates Samuel Beckett) automatically substitute habitual reactions for existential awareness; verbalizing emotion deprives it of authenticity; and 'static drama' replaces external conflict, which by definition is superficial. By the 1920s a school of silence was building on these ideas in plays (like those of Jean-Jacques Bernard) where characters only speak past each other in overlapping monologues while the action is located and developed on a wordless, sub-textual level that bears little relationship to the direction of the spoken dialogue. As a result the psychological incomprehensibility of the figures becomes a claim to authenticity: 'We have progressed beyond the explanatory drama . . . Let the characters speak for themselves, their inconsistencies and illogicalities express their essential humanity. We [authors] have no better claim than anyone else to be able to explain them' (Denys Amiel, 1923). This was a principle that Harold Pinter was later to repeat almost word for word, and the premise that 'the more acute the experience the less articulate the expression' is typical.[4] On another level Maeterlinck's ideal of musically structured gesture and movement, intuitively expressing the nuances of internal states in plastic form, was equally significant; and its influence can be seen in the high development of mime in French theatre, represented by the art of Decroux, Barrault and Marceau.

For critics at the turn of the century the mime artist automatically presented 'a hieratic image of life'. His silence, which led to stylized, exaggerated gestures and the transformation of his face into a mask, gained resonance from its distance to the everyday – and, precisely because 'mute and representing symbols, gave a more powerful impression of [psychological] reality and consequently generated a much more intense emotional field than conventional actors with their vocal imitations'.[5] A natural extension of this interest led the symbolists to explore the possibilities of puppet theatre, which until then had been associated primarily with crude and popular entertainment. Gordon Craig's vision of the ideal actor as an 'übermarionette' was paralleled by Maeterlinck's belief that puppets would be the most suitable performers for his early plays, or by Lugné-Poe's original intention of founding his Théâtre de l'Oeuvre as a puppet theatre.

Indeed there is a natural symbolist aspect to marionettes. Their abstraction of the human form represents emotions on a general level, and simplifies a sequence of actions to its essentials. Individual experience never obtrudes, as it inevitably does to some extent with an actor's personality. The particular value of this is that a puppet stands in the same relationship to reality as a national flag does to a nation, so that the complete vision reaches full expression in the spectator's mind and not on the stage – subjectively realized instead of being presented as something objective, external – and in the typical symbolist view 'impersonal puppets, beings of wood and cardboard, possess a pure and mysterious life. Their aspect of truth catches us unawares, disquiets. Their elemental gestures contain the complete expression of human feelings.'[6]

Elements of symbolist staging have become an accepted part of the modern theatre's technical repertoire, and even the theory of 'correspondences' was taken up by the expressionists, as in Kandinsky's scenario *The*

Yellow Sound (1909). But most of the general concepts of symbolist drama have dated badly because their viewpoint was basically conventional. Their choice of subject matter tended toward traditional legend and artificial medievalism, while the religious aspect of their work remained within the socially accepted limits of catholicism and their attempts to explore the subconscious appear facile in the light of Freud and Jung. Yet out of this context comes one of the key works of modern drama, which has had a decisive influence on avant garde theatre: Alfred Jarry's *Ubu* trilogy. And it is no accident that *Ubu roi* (1896) was originally conceived as a puppet play and first performed by Lugné-Poe's Théâtre de l'Oeuvre, where the same year Jarry had played the role of the Old Man of the Mountains in Lugné-Poe's symbolist production of *Peer Gynt*. At the same time the more obvious superficial aspects of the play, the scatological obscenity, the deliberate crudeness of dialogue and presentation, the grotesque farce, all make a statement that is fundamentally opposed to symbolist principles, as W.B. Yeats, whose French was too limited to understand any of Jarry's deeper intentions, was quick to see:

> I go to the first performance of Alfred Jarry's *Ubu roi* . . . and [my friend] explains to me what is happening on the stage. The players are supposed to be dolls, toys, marionettes, and now they are all hopping like wooden frogs, and I can see for myself that the chief personage, who is some kind of King, carries for Sceptre a brush of the kind that we use to clean a [water] closet. Feeling bound to support the most spirited party, we have shouted for the play, but that night at the Hotel Corneille I am very sad . . . I say 'After Stéphane Mallarmé, after Paul Verlaine, after Gustav Moreau, after Puvis de Chavannes, after our own verse, after all our subtle colours and nervous rhythm, after the faint mixed tints of Conder, what more is possible? After us the Savage God.'[7]

The uproar at that first performance was so violent after Gémier uttered Ubu's first word, the infamous '*merdre*', that the action was brought to a complete halt; and it continued throughout, with catcalls and vociferous arguments between rioting factions in the audience making the dialogue almost entirely inaudible.[8] It is therefore hardly surprising that the initial reactions to the play concentrated on those elements designed to insult the audience's sensibilities: the flouting of moral taboos, the anarchic attack on social institutions or the provocative parody of all the turn-of-the-century thematic and stylistic expectations of serious drama. What primarily came across was the deliberate childishness of plot and characterization. On this level the monstrous figure of Ubu seems to sum up Jarry's intentions, a grotesquely ugly embodiment of our most despicable instincts, whose involvement in any situation reveals his own amoral and anti-social qualities in all the participants – exposing the rapacity, avarice, self-serving

Figure 2 Jarry's figure of Ubu, the monstrous puppet image of the bourgeois, on which all subsequent productions of the plays have been based.

treachery and ingratitude, conceit, cowardice and simple greed that he epitomizes to be at the root of all human activities, and particularly those that are conventionally valued as honourable, heroic, altruistic, patriotic, idealistic or in any way socially respected. Thus Ubu reduces kingship to gorging oneself on sausages and wearing an immense hat; economic competition to a kicking, struggling race; social reform to slaughter motivated solely by envious cupidity; battle royal to boastful brawling; or religious faith to fearful superstition, manipulated by the unscrupulous for their own benefit. In other words, a figure symbolizing all that bourgeois morality condemns is claimed to be representative of the real basis of bourgeois society, which then stands condemned by its own principles.

To attack society for its hypocrisy, even when this aroused vehement indignation on the part of 'right-minded' critics, as with Ibsen's *A Doll's House* or *Ghosts*, was intellectually acceptable. But here the satiric style of presentation undermined the social commentary. The characters, 'depersonalized' by masks and grotesque costumes or represented by life-size dressmaker's dummies (there were forty of these, outnumbering the actors), lacked any of the psychological depth associated with serious drama. Their motivations were inconsistent, their inner natures openly expressed in the simplest terms – so removing any suspicion that they might have a three-dimensional core of individuality. And their lines were delivered in an artificial singsong voice with exaggerated articulation. Similarly, instead of a setting which either documented a specific social environment natural-istically, or even served as a symbolic projection of emotional states, Jarry's scene, with its centrepiece of a marble fireplace incongruously set in a landscape, where tropical foliage arbitrarily mixed with arctic snow, was explicitly 'supposed to represent Nowhere'. This had a poetry of its own, related both to a primitive like Gauguin and to the later surrealists, but the overall effect hardly corresponded to conventional notions of the poetic. The execution was crude, like Ubu's mask which was obviously cardboard, or the costumes which were deliberately 'shoddy'.

The plot is equally paltry. Ubu leads a palace revolution, murders the King of Poland (who is too stupid to take even elementary precautions) and all the royal family except the queen and Bougrelas, the crown prince. The queen promptly dies of 'misfortunes' and the ghost of the dead king demands that Bougrelas avenge him, while Ubu works his way through the population, starting with the aristocracy and moving down through judges and financiers, massacring everyone and expropriating their money. His henchman and co-conspirator, thrown into prison for demanding the reward Ubu had promised him, escapes to Russia and persuades the Tsar to declare war on Ubu, who by now is slaughtering even the peasants for their petty cash. While Ubu marches off fearfully to meet the Russian invasion, his equally repulsive wife tries to rob him of the accumulated treasure he has buried in the palace, is driven out by Bougrelas at the head of a popular revolt and flees to Ubu, who has been defeated by the Tsar and attacked by a bear. She pretends to be a supernatural apparition, the archangel Gabriel, to frighten him into forgiving her for stealing his loot, and in the ensuing marital quarrel she is saved from being torn to pieces only by the entry of the pursuing Bougrelas. Knocking down their attackers with the dead bear, the Ubus take to their heels and set sail for France.

In his epigraph to the play Jarry refers to Shakespeare – singled out undoubtedly because the romantics had elevated him to practically divine status as the proponent of heroic individualism – and the action is clearly a farrago of Shakespearean situations: the bloody murder of a good king, and the flight of his son from *Macbeth*; the father's ghost, and Fortinbras leading a revolt against the palace from *Hamlet*; Buckingham, whose reward for helping a usurper is refused, from *Richard III*; and the bear from *The Winter's Tale*. At first sight this seems no more than frivolity, literary parody without a point. But it ties in with Jarry's rejection of art as 'a stuffed crocodile' and gains thematic relevance in the context of his exploration of 'the power of the base appetites'.[9] Shakespeare can be seen as representing the ideals of western culture, which are thus shown to be fake. *Ubu roi* undermines the very concept of man's nobility by treating as ludicrous the images that were held up to every schoolboy as models of human, as well as dramatic excellence (remembering that Jarry was still at school when he wrote the first version of the play), reducing heroic actions to burlesque and fine sentiments to pastiche.

The other plays in the trilogy attack equally basic aspects of 'civilized man'. *Ubu Cuckolded* (unpublished until 1944) dismisses the moral nature of the individual, with Ubu flushing the toilet on the shapeless figure of his conscience, which he carries around in a suitcase and only consults to discover if the innocent are helpless enough to be victimized without personal danger; while *Ubu Enchained* (published in 1900 but unperformed until 1937) discredits the notion of individuality *per se*. Here it is the national motto of 'liberty, equality, fraternity' itself that is under attack with 'free men' being drilled in 'blind and unwavering indiscipline', demonstrating their liberty by such consistent disobedience that they can be controlled by simply being ordered to do the opposite of what is required. Individualism is presented as such rigid conformity that paradoxically the only possibility of asserting free will, which by definition must be the opposite of orthodoxy, lies in following orders, and Ubu decides to become a slave. He progressively 'promotes' himself to lower and lower forms of servitude, from a domineering servant to a serf who can be whipped, from a gaoler to a galley slave. Finally the whole population emulates him, storming the prisons to win the deepest dungeons for themselves, stealing his fetters and rushing to the Turkish galleys in a wild competition for the most absolute form of 'freedom'. So, left with no one to act as his master or gaoler, Ubu determines that 'from now on I shall be the slave of my Strumpot', or base instincts and physical appetites – which is indeed the point at which liberty (to indulge one's desires) and slavery (to one's 'lower' nature) become inseparable.

This attack on the fundamental concepts of western civilization is accompanied by the satiric denigration of everything bourgeois, ranging from snobbery and artistic salons to rent collection and academic pedantry. But the satire is curiously unfocused, and the constant descent into nonsense undermines any conventionally serious point Jarry might be making. The nihilism is so anarchic that it discredits itself – and the surprising thing is that recent commentators, like the critics in that first audience (who at least had the justification that the uproar prevented any of the play's subtler aspects from coming across), continue to see the primary intention of *Ubu roi* in purely negative protest and shock effect.[10] If this were its real value, Artaud would hardly have named his theatre after Jarry.

As Jarry's friend Apollinaire pointed out, his satire 'operates upon reality in such a way that it totally destroys its object and rises completely above it', becoming a form of poetic vision in which the comprehensiveness of the negation itself becomes creative.[11] The *Ubu* plays in fact are exercises in Jarry's theory of 'pataphysics', a 'science of imaginary solutions'. This bears much the same relationship to science, the rational way of analysing and describing the world, as Jarry's anti-theatre does to conventional drama. Its premise is that what we perceive as our world is no more than a mental construct, and that therefore there is no true distinction between perception and hallucination. What has the status of reality is simply whatever exerts the most powerful hold on the imagination, and in Jarry's view the accepted laws of physics, being based on observed norms, are 'correlations of . . . accidental data which, reduced to the status of unexceptional exceptions, possess no longer even the virtue of originality'. As such, these are imaginatively inferior to 'the laws governing exceptions'. So pataphysics deals with the particular instead of the general. It also works on the principle of the identity of opposites, defines external form as essence in a true symbolist way, and so becomes a way of describing 'a universe which can be – and perhaps should be – envisaged in the place of the traditional one'.[12] It is in this sense that the staging for *Ubu roi* should be understood: a contradictory synthesis of incongruities, liberating the imagination by the unusual juxtaposition of everyday objects, and simultaneously offering an alternative universe in which anything is possible:

> Just as a play can be set in Eternity by, say, letting people fire revolvers in the year one thousand or thereabouts, so you will see doors opening onto snow-covered plains under blue skies, mantelpieces with clocks on them swinging open to turn into doorways, and palm trees flourishing at the foot of beds so that little elephants perching on book shelves can graze on them . . . A set which is supposed to represent Nowhere . . . and the action takes place in Poland, a country so legendary, so dismembered that it is well qualified to be this particular Nowhere, or, in terms of a putative Franco-Greek etymology, a distantly interrogative somewhere.[13]

However, Jarry's intention is not simply to present his audience with a surrogate world, but also to force each spectator to imagine his own reality; and all the elements in this comedy of total warfare, quite apart from their thematic significance, can be seen as hallucinatory techniques. Beneath the crudely insulting and childishly simple surface is a sophisticated manipulation of vision. The inversion of norms, exaggeration and oversimplification undermine our everyday frame of reference, as do the fusion of the inflated and prosaic or the tone of grandiose banality. The scatological obscenity and gratuitous violence are shock effects to make normal reactions seem obsessive or inappropriate. Thus, try as we may to apply socially approved feelings to Jarry's mass demolition of characters (who are literally chopped to mincemeat, torn to pieces, stuffed into sewers, impaled or exploded), we can only find the violence and death funny. Such extreme and wholesale slaughter discredits or deadens conventional responses – particularly if there is no relation between cause and effect, as when one character is chopped in two and both halves continue to function as before, or another's hair is set on fire and his only comment is 'what a night, I've got hair ache'. Similarly, the distortions of perspective in the setting overload the audience's capacity to rationalize the picture presented to them, as does the syllogistic logic demonstrating the identity of opposites (which is particularly obvious in *Ubu Enchained*) or the transformations and multiplications of characters (like Achras and Rebontier in *Ubu Cuckolded* who have a crocodile and monkey as their doubles, while the crocodile, whistling like a steam engine, is defined as a snake).

Where Rimbaud had advocated a 'reasoned derangement of the senses' for the poet, Jarry applies it to the audience. Habitual assumptions about reality and socially learned responses are called into question, cutting the ground from under our mental feet. At the same time our imagination is challenged, both by the extravagance of the dramatic world and by the self-parodying theatricality of the presentation, where single characters stand for a whole army, but puppet qualities and unnatural voices exaggerate their symbolic nature into artificiality – or where placards announce changes of scene, but without any of the unobtrusiveness of Shakespearean staging, being carried in by a man in full evening dress who trots across the stage on the points of his toes to underline the irrelevance of specifying place in a setting that is 'Nowhere'.

As Jarry put it in the epigraph to *Ubu Enchained*: 'We shall not have succeeded in demolishing everything unless we demolish the ruins as well. But the only way I can see of doing that is to use them to put up a lot of fine, well-designed buildings.'[14] The 'ruins' stand for traditional concepts, the nationalisms and rationalisms of post-industrial society, and these can only be abolished effectively by restructuring the bricks into alternate visions. Hence the extra letter in Ubu's notorious opening expletive, which illustrates Jarry's method in miniature. Transforming *'merde'* into *'merdre'* makes the familiar strange. The scatologically shocking becomes simultaneously hallucinatory; and (in one of Jarry's typical puns) a fundamental aspect of reality is subtly distorted, in order to challenge and liberate the spectator's imagination.

Jarry's approach is too confused, his techniques – drawn from *grand guignol* puppet theatre, symbolist abstraction and Shakespeare – too diversified for the full impact of his drama to be realized. On the one hand his intention is satiric protest, confronting the public 'like the exaggerating mirror in the stories of Madame Leprince de Beaumont, in which the depraved saw themselves with dragons' bodies, or bulls' horns, or whatever corresponded to their particular vice'. On the other he is trying to create 'an ABSTRACT theatre', with masks replacing the psychological portrayal of

27

an individual by 'the effigy of the CHARACTER', and with 'universal gesture' achieving 'essential expression'.[15] The contradictions are too extreme. Ubu is not only an antisocial force capable of devastating the bourgeois *Weltanschauung*, a wish-fulfilment figure, destructive to the point of self-destruction – hence Jarry's own identification with his character, signing himself 'Ubu' and speaking in a Ubuesque 'special voice' that reduced the semantic content of his words to nonsense by giving equal weight to each syllable. Ubu also epitomizes the qualities of the bourgeoisie, whom Jarry despised. Negative and positive elements are superimposed, self-cancelling. As a result his plays had little immediate effect. After the initial shock, Jarry's work rapidly became accepted as 'art'. He was taken up by Ambroise Vollard, the impresario of symbolist and Post-Impressionist painting, who popularized Jarry along with Cézanne, Chagall and Odilon Redon, as well as Bonnard and Rouault, both of whom illustrated the 'further adventures' of Père Ubu that Vollard wrote; and when Gémier played the role again in 1908 it was 'before a completely calm, one might almost say indifferent audience . . . neither amused, nor scandalized, nor surprised'.[16]

This performance was prefaced by an academic lecture appraising Jarry's literary significance. The effect was judged to be 'very spiritual'; and Gémier planned to found a 'Théâtre Ubu', creating new plays around Jarry's characters. The most dispiriting thing for an artist who aims to *épater les bourgeois* is the capacity of society to absorb irritants, like an oyster seeing dirt thrown into the works only as a potential pearl. And by the 1920s the academic industry had made Jarry's anarchism harmlessly respectable with pedantic essays such as 'Brahma and Ubu, or the historical spirit'.[17] But his true significance lies in the appeal to the irrational and (through the elements of deliberate naivety and the primitive, child's convention in stage presentation) the pre-social level of the mind. This was picked up by Artaud and by the 'College of Pataphysics', founded in 1948 and including Eugene Ionesco, Boris Vian and René Clair among its members.

AUGUST STRINDBERG

By the turn of the century another anti-naturalistic movement was taking shape, which shared many of the symbolist premises and in particular the concept of the world as a dynamic projection of the human mind, while avoiding both the Maeterlinckian retreat into lyrical, indefinite stasis and Jarry's extreme of satiric irrationalism. The initial impetus came from Strindberg, whose most influential work after his 'inferno' period of psychological crisis was largely autobiographical and attempted to transcribe subjective experience directly into stage terms.

The key plays were *To Damascus* (1898–1904), *A Dream Play* (1902) and *The Ghost Sonata* (1907). Strindberg's subjective involvement was strong even in his early naturalistic drama; and already by 1888 in the preface to *Miss Julie* one can see him breaking out of the naturalist format. Here the concept of the individualized character, determined by hereditary attributes and environmental influences, is already in the opening stages of dispersal. People are presented as 'conglomerations of past and present stages of civilization', a fragmentary patchwork of contradictory and transient elements; and they are referred to as 'souls', not self-aware personalities. Minor figures are already thought of as 'abstract . . . without individuality', the setting is designed to produce 'unfamiliar perspectives' and the principles of composition are defined by musical analogy instead of as patterns of cause and effect: 'the dialogue wanders gathering in the opening scenes material which is later picked up, worked over, repeated, expounded and developed like the theme in a musical composition'.[18] Here Strindberg could still give such elements a naturalistic rationale, but they point straight to the new dramatic form that he developed in *To Damascus* with its unitary characterization and contrapuntal structure.

These qualities can be seen clearly in the first part of this monumental trilogy of spiritual exploration, the tone of which echoes an early letter of Strindberg's, where he confesses:

> It seems to me that I am walking about in my sleep, as though fiction and life were blended . . . Through much writing my life has become a shadow of life. I no longer seem to be treading on earth but rather to be hovering without weight in an atmosphere not of air but of darkness . . . all concepts of right, wrong, true, false, disappear; and whatever happens, no matter how unusual it is, strikes me as quite fitting.[19]

This is repeated in the opening scene by the clearly autobiographical central figure of the Unknown (or the Stranger): an author who also doubts whether his life has any more reality than his own writings. On the surface the dramatic conflict is presented as a Promethean challenge to God, with the Unknown defying the 'Invisible One', daring 'unseen powers' to strike him down with a bolt of lightning, and working to free mankind from 'suffering'. But the sufferings are in fact psychological repressions; and the human beings to be saved, as well as those characters who represent the 'unseen powers' he struggles against, are all projections of his own mind. The Lady, for instance, on one level clearly modelled on Strindberg's wives (Frieda Uhl in parts I and II, Harriet Bosse in part III), not only represents all women, the quintessential female – for Strindberg at once redemptive and destructive of the male spirit, and christened 'Eve' by the Unknown. She is also an integral part of his own psyche. She appears each time in answer to an unspoken 'call', responding to a subconscious wish of the Unknown who sees her as 'impersonal, nameless'; and the Mother, whom he acknowledges to be only echoing his own thoughts, tells him that he has made her in his own image. If there is any solution in the drama it is in this recognition by the Unknown that his antagonist is an aspect of himself. Other characters clearly represent alternate or auxiliary egos. Like the Unknown, on his forehead the Beggar carries the scar of a blow from his brother's axe, simultaneously Cain and Abel. Both of them fit the description of a wanted criminal and, when pallbearers describe the Dead Man in the coffin they are carrying, he too resembles the Unknown. Finally, in the central scene, all the figures are refracted yet again in an asylum where the Unknown recognizes the Beggar, the Lady and the Mother in different lunatics, and himself in the figure of a megalomaniac who believes himself to be Caesar.

In this world of self-reflections any extension is merely a regression into more and more distorted mirror images, from the Beggar's appearance, which is 'very strange', to the inmates of the asylum: now at several removes from the 'reality' of the central ego, and therefore presented as spectres, whose faces are death's-heads with waxen skin and crumbling features. As a mental universe, the world of the play is self-enclosed, and there can be no escape from this terrifying vision. The deformation of the figures represents the guilt of the Unknown – the psychological effect of breaking 'the Commandments'. But these nightmares also occur because the Unknown is 'bankrupt', having 'lost the power to create',[20] and – significantly – the solution therefore lies in the will, the ability to transform this internal world through the poetic imagination:

> This is life . . . I feel myself swell and stretch, rarefy, become boundless; I am everywhere, in the sea which is my blood, in the mountains which are my skeleton, in the trees, in the flowers. And my head reaches to heaven. I look out over the Universe which is, and I feel the strength of the Creator within me, for I am the Creator. I should like to take this globe into my hand and knead it into something completer, more lasting, more beautiful. I should like to see all creation happy . . .[21]

As a 'deliverer', therefore, the Unknown has to free himself; and the God he wrestles with is his conscious intellect, which represses and restrains. So that, as in the title image of Saul of Tarsus, the spiritual illumination on the road to Damascus brings him to terms with the creative elements of his psyche that his rational mind had denied. Hence what he has learned by the end of the trilogy is to marry thesis (assent) with antithesis (dissent) in an affirmative Hegelian synthesis of 'Don't say: Either – Or. Say: Both – And', uniting not only opposed attitudes to life but also the different parts of a divided personality. In Hegelian terms each synthesis is the formation of a fresh thesis, repeating the pattern of antithesis and synthesis on a higher level, and it is in this sense that the Unknown is said to 'rise from the dead, having renounced your old name'.[22] He has become the expressionist New Man. 'Like a little new-born child', however, his baptism will still consecrate him to a saga of suffering on this higher spiritual plane of existence.

Conventional plot construction – based on a linear sequence of cause and effect, in which the characters are independent entities, while the conflict rises out of mutually exclusive personal motivations and can be resolved only in terms of action – is clearly inappropriate to this type of thematic pattern and internalized characterization. Instead Strindberg developed what has been called a 'polyphonic form' for *To Damascus*. The structure in part I is geometrical, rather than being built up out of rising climaxes as in a conventional dramatic action. It begins and ends on the same street corner, moving inward through different levels of memory and hallucination to the 'fever' vision of the ninth scene in the asylum, then repeating the same sequence of eight scenes in reverse order to return the Unknown to the everyday awareness of ordinary experience. Within this formal progression and inversion, associative links determine the transition from one stage to another, not causality, while varying degrees of intensity are created by repetitions. Phrases recur: 'life's fool', 'my liberator/the liberator', 'the changeling'. Concepts resurface continually: Bluebeard's castle, the mill grinding souls, the Curse of Deuteronomy. Mendelssohn's 'Funeral March' follows the Unknown everywhere: theme and variation. This enables Strindberg to break out of the conventional framework of time, which here becomes a measure of subjective experience, expanding and contracting. Thus the last scene, in which the Unknown receives money by post, follows on directly from the first scene, where he is waiting for the post office to open. It also allows symbolic relationships to be substituted for temporal sequences.

It seems to have become almost obligatory to identify *To Damascus* as the source of much that is experimental in modern theatre. Yet although poets on the path of self-discovery, 'strangers' even, and the division of scenes into seven steps on a road to Calvary (following the pattern that Strindberg outlined in the Mother's advice to 'plant a cross at every station, but stop at the seventh. You don't have to suffer fourteen, like Him')[23] are among the platitudes of German expressionist drama, this is not precisely accurate. Strindberg admired Maeterlinck, and some of the play's dream effects can be traced back to his work. But quite apart from that, it strains the credulity to see how *To Damascus* could have had much direct influence, given its stage history (or rather lack of it). Not surprisingly when one takes the 250-page length with its forty-five speaking parts plus additional Shadows, Sisters of Mercy, Musicians, Monks, Venus Worshippers, Witnesses and Whores into account, the trilogy has never been staged in its entirety. And even the first and most easily performable part has had relatively few productions, only reaching the English stage for example in 1937.

Figure 3 Scene design for *To Damascus*. Stations of the Cross and the subconscious world.

In fact *To Damascus* must be seen as a seriously flawed work. The symbolism is obvious and overexplicit, therefore limiting connotations instead of acting as a nexus for meanings. There is an uneasy mixture of purely personal references and universal imagery. The characters are not so much paradigmatic, as unconvincing abstractions; and their dialogue is too often leaden with stilted and sententious phrasing. In short the general stylistic effect is one of pretentious imprecision while, as Eric Bentley has put it, the thematic tone is 'unconvincing religiosity'. It is rather *A Dream Play* – given striking productions in Germany by the expressionist director Rudolph Bernauer (1916) and by Max Reinhardt (1921), and in France by Antonin Artaud (1928) – or *The Ghost Sonata*, which Artaud also worked on, that were directly influential.

In these plays the same qualities that made *To Damascus* so innovative recur, but in progressively subtler and better-integrated forms. In writing *A Dream Play* Strindberg's ideas were modified by *The Philosophy of the Unconscious* by Eduard von Hartmann (a forerunner of Freud whose *Interpretation of Dreams*, though apparently unknown to Strindberg, had been published the year before in 1901); and the structure is far closer to the workings of the subconscious mind than the mathematically balanced, schematic patterning of the earlier play, with its intellectualized correspondence to the Stations of the Cross.

There is the same fluidity of scene in *A Dream Play*. But the transitions are motivated by the action and occur in response to the characters' desires or fears, rather than simply representing the central figure's states of mind in visual terms, as in the earlier play with its schematic stage directions like:

> *The scene grows dark. A medley of décors ensues – a landscape, a palace and a room descend and come forward, while the characters and furniture disappear. At length the* STRANGER, *who has been standing as though paralysed and asleep, also vanishes and out of the confusion emerges a prison cell . . .*[24]

There is an equivalent development in the way repetition and variation are used. But only one phrase 'Alas for mankind . . .' is reiterated, and its simplicity as well as its frequency gives it the emotive focus of a leitmotif. Instead of abstract concepts recurring, physical objects are reused from scene to scene: the doorkeeper's shawl or the secret door. And these expand in meaning with each change in their function or shape, taking on continually new symbolic connotations, like the castle that grows, blooms and bursts into flames. Although scenes are again repeated and inverted, there is no sense of an artificial and superimposed geometry. The Fairhaven/Foulstrand reversal has an internal logic, based on the identity of opposites, with misery being the common denominator. Similarly the repetition of the scene outside the theatre, with the Officer waiting hopelessly for the singer he loves, is justified by the emotive force of the characters' desires, not by an abstract pattern, and becomes a way of embodying one of the major themes:

POET: I think I have seen this before . . .
                       Perhaps I dreamed it?
                       . . . Or wrote it.
DAUGHTER: Then you know what poetry is.
POET: Then I know what dreaming is.
DAUGHTER: I feel we stood somewhere else and spoke these words.
POET: Then you can soon work out what reality is.
DAUGHTER: Or dreaming.
POET: Or poetry.[25]

The only other repeated scene serves a comparable framing function to the street corner in *To Damascus* – except that here the return to the opening measures a decisive change in perception, with the forest of gigantic and colourful hollyhocks on the backcloth being transformed into a wall of enquiring and agonized human faces by the illumination of the burning castle, while flowers spring from the manure and the chrysanthemum-bud blooms in a symbol of spiritual transcendence. Again this return is designed to create a double time, in which the action of the play seems to take place in a limbo of the mind and therefore outside temporal or spatial laws, since the final tableau follows straight on the opening lines, where the chrysanthemum is described as already beginning to unfold:

DAUGHTER: Won't it flower soon? We're past midsummer.
GLAZIER: Don't you see the flower up there?[26]

Unlike *To Damascus*, where this underlines the essentially rational image of a circle, here the effect is elliptical, a hallucinatory foreshortening designed to follow our experience of dreams.

The extent to which Strindberg's ability to depict the workings of the subconscious has progressed in *A Dream Play* is indicated by the well-known Author's note, which is frequently referred to as a concise synopsis of his stylistic aims:

> In this dream play the author has, as in his former dream play, TO DAMASCUS, attempted to imitate the inconsequent yet transparently logical shape of a dream. Everything can happen, everything is possible and probable. Time and place do not exist; on an insignificant basis of reality the imagination spins, weaving new patterns; a mixture of memories, experiences, free fancies, incongruities and improvisations. The characters split, double, multiply, evaporate, condense, disperse, assemble. But one consciousness rules over them all, that of the dreamer; for him there are no secrets, no illogicalities, no scruples, no laws. He neither acquits nor condemns, but merely relates . . .

The approach described here – with its echoes of Strindberg's letter of 1887, referring to his inability to distinguish life from imagination and his automatic acceptance of whatever presented itself to his mind, however unusual or immoral by conscious standards – is clearly derived from his personal dream experiences. As an outline of the way autobiographical elements have been transmuted into symbols through the prism of subliminal contrasts and connections in the play, this is accurate enough; and it illuminates the principles of intensification and condensation on which the 'new patterns' (by implication superior to the logical perceptions of the waking world) have been created. But it is not simply a straight transcription of Strindberg's working method here, although it could indeed be applied directly to his previous play.

This becomes clear as soon as one asks who the dreamer is and sees that, unlike *To Damascus* there is no dominating 'consciousness' in the play itself. The 'Author's note', in fact, has more relevance to the theme of *A Dream Play*, than to its form. As the Daughter reveals, repeating the entry in Strindberg's diary for the day when he finished writing the play, it is 'the divine primal force', a spiritual essence divided between all men, that is assumed to have created the vision. Life itself is therefore an illusory dream in which men, as physical entities, are no more than phantoms; and, as the final image of fire and flower clearly affirms, 'death really is the awakening'.[27] One of the draft titles, *Prisoners*, referred overtly to the idea of mankind as spirits locked in bodies, serving the life sentence of a materialistic definition of existence. The secret of the door is the 'nothingness' to which, as the opposite of physical 'being', the spiritual nature of man aspires, and suffering becomes the catalyst that liberates the spirit by making daily life unendurable: a remarkable transformation in which the suffering and humiliations, that Strindberg had earlier raged against as meaningless and totally evil, become positive values.

At the same time, unlike Rimbaud or the surrealists – for whom the function of poetry is to transcribe the subconscious, since dreams are revelations of reality *per se* – Strindberg's prefatory note explicitly states that what *A Dream Play* reproduces is the structure of dreaming, but not the actual content of a dream. His theme presupposes that dreams are false (the dream of life being unreal), although the dream state (an awareness that life is a dream) is true perception. What Strindberg in fact seems to be attempting is the creation of a myth. The story of the daughter of a god, whose descent to earth and involvement in all possible variations of imperfect human love reveals the spiritual meaning of existence, corresponds closely to Eliade's definition of myth as a 'primordial revelation, exemplary model' that 'gives meaning and value to life' by narrating 'how . . . a reality came into existence'.[28] In light of this, Strindberg's use of the dream form to present a myth has additional significance in anticipating the association between dreams and myths noted by Otto Rank in *The Myth of the Birth of the Hero* (1909) and picked up by Jung, who saw myths as embodying the collective dreams of the tribe.[29]

4

THERAPY AND SUBLIMINAL
THEATRE

GERMAN EXPRESSIONISM

As might be expected, staging is a major problem in Strindberg's dream plays. They demanded technical resources that did not exist at the beginning of the century; and even Strindberg's own Intimate Theatre never produced *A Dream Play*, although the original intention in founding it was to provide suitable performance conditions for precisely this, following what Strindberg felt was the failure of the play's first production six months earlier (April 1907). 'The whole performance became "a phenomenon of materialization" instead of the intended dematerialization'[1] – a problem that equally affected Reinhardt's 1921 production, which presented a tableau of suffering human faces by rows of real actors, clothed in black and with whitened, staring features.

Strindberg himself moved away from any attempt to realize his vision in physical terms. His proposals to August Falck, the director of the Intimate Theatre, reveal symbolist influence – neutral drapes taking on different nuances of colour from the lighting to reflect changing moods, with simple 'allegorical' objects to evoke imaginative echoes for the location of each scene: sea shells for Fingal's Cave, signal flags for Foulstrand, a number-board for songs representing the church – and his thoughts on his 'chamber plays' show him working towards a theatre of the mind, independent of the stage or physical representation:

> If Shakespeare's highly sophisticated contemporaries could do without scenery, we too should be able to imagine walls and trees . . . everything is make-believe on the stage.
>
> The poet's vision is profaned through the written word; the written drama is profane in a definite way when it is materialized through performance.[2]

It is this concept of a theatre of the mind, in which the stage ceases to be a physical representation of the world and becomes a projection of myth or the author's inner self, that struck the German expressionists with such force. Elsewhere in Europe Strindberg's main impact seems to have been as an example of drama in revolt. The obsessional qualities in his work were valued primarily as a form of subversive anarchy, irrationality being antisocial; and when Lugné-Poe produced *The Ghost Sonata*, he stressed 'this stifling atmosphere of agony and madness'.[3] Conservative critics rejected Strindberg as 'one of the most execrated and execrable writers of our time' whose 'work is nothing but a series of pamphlets against religion, the monarchy, science'.[4] So productions of his plays became a natural focus for avant garde rejections of society. It was certainly in this spirit that Artaud, who (like Jarry) had begun his career as an actor under Lugné-Poe, staged *A Dream Play*. When his surrealist ex-colleagues disrupted the one and only performance, his defence – in a speech from the stage that only added to the uproar by alienating his Swedish supporters who had financed this production – was to claim that 'Strindberg is a renegade, just like Jarry, like Lautréamont, like Breton, like me. We are presenting this play because it vomits on its fatherland, on all nations, on society.'[5] By contrast, in Germany Strindberg's drama was more easily accepted – between 1913 and 1915 there were more than a thousand performances of twenty-four of his plays in sixty-two cities – partly perhaps because dramatists like Wedekind had already surpassed the level of social revolt in his work (*Spring's Awakening*, 1891; *Erdgeist*, 1895, best known today in Berg's operatic version, *Lulu*). As a result Strindberg's primary influence there was as a stylistic model.

Since the term 'expressionism' was first appropriated for the drama by Walter Hasenclever in a series of essays on 'The theatre of tomorrow . . . the call for a spiritual stage',[6] it seems appropriate to use one of his plays as an example of expressionist drama. *Humanity* (1918) is representative of the way the structural qualities of Strindberg's dream plays were developed.

The title itself underlines the abstract nature of the characterization. Only the protagonist, Alexander, who is simultaneously a murderer and the murderer's victim (carrying his own decapitated head around with him in a sack), and the two figures symbolizing the dual nature of woman, Lissi and Agathe, demonic sexuality and purifying spiritual love, have proper names. The other characters are described simply in generic human terms as the sufferers from whom regeneration might come – The Youth, The Girl, The Mother – or defined by social function as representatives of the corrupt and repressive materialistic world of society – Doctor, Banker, Whores, Beggar. Like *To Damascus*, Hasenclever's play contains an obligatory asylum scene and begins and ends on the same spot, though here the 'framing scene' is loaded with symbolic connotations. Instead of an everyday street corner, the opening is a cemetery at sunset; and the first image sets the action firmly in the spiritual sphere. A stone cross topples over as the protagonist rises from the grave; and what follows is clearly signposted as a dream, since everything takes place during the course of the night, with the ending at dawn.

This is, perhaps rather over-obviously, the dark night of the soul in which daily existence is seen as a nightmare. The stock market is presented as a demonic roulette game where only the number thirteen comes up, the bankrupted losers are pushed down through a trap door by masked men, and the table collapses under the weight of the stakes. Social revolution is rejected as a solution, since the workers are defined as brutally material- istic; and the question 'Human beings?' only brings the response 'Slaves.'[7] The conventional alternatives of romantic love, or hope for the future in a new generation are also dismissed, because sexual constancy is imposs- ible. Even before the first words of the play, The Girl has already deceived her lover, who is seduced by Lissi and dies of syphilis.

Against this nightmare world of whores and death (no less than ten of the main figures are stabbed, throttled, strangled, literally disintegrate with syphilis or commit suicide) is set the possibility of transformation or spiri- tual renewal through a Christ-like love of mankind. Lissi's nihilistic 'Dead is dead!' is balanced by Alexander's cry of 'Resurrection'.[8]

On the other side we are shown images of an alternate, spiritual reality in the progress of Alexander, who gives everything to the poor. He brings The Girl back to life, when she slashes open her wrists after her abortion, by drinking her blood as it flows from her veins. He embraces all sinners as his 'family', and buries the abandoned corpse of the dead woman with his own hands. And in typical expressionist fashion Alexander's pilgrimage in search of himself repeats Christ's Passion, betrayed by an obvious Judas- figure, a mock crown set on his head. As in Toller's play *Transfiguration* (1919) – where the 'caricatures of humanity', who have let mechanical institutions enslave them out of fear, need nothing but the revelation that 'you could . . . still be human, if only you had faith in yourselves and in humanity, if only you would grant that spirit its fulfilment', in order to leap up from their crawling prostration transformed into 'unconditioned new men'[9] – so here the ending is emblematic of renewal and hope achieved. Agathe releases Alexander from the condemned cell by taking his chains on herself, 'the sky appears, chorals are sung from spires', and the murderer, who epitomizes the 'hatred' that explicitly dominates the nightmare world where 'HUMAN BEINGS in the shape of beasts . . . crawl about', is transfigured into an *Ecce Homo*:

The sun rises.
THE MURDERER, *spreading out his arms*: I love![10]

The main problem here, one that Toller and other expressionists share, is that this humanist ecstasy is so vague. The pictures of social evil and deformed humanity are graphic, imaginatively convincing in spite of their one-sided extremism. Yet the transformation is so sudden that it appears

Figure 4 Apotheosis in *Transfiguration*. Stylized revelation – the rhetoric of salvation.

unmotivated; and the images of salvation, of the apotheosis of reborn man are merely rhetorical.

The structure of *Humanity* is also typical of expressionist drama; and its qualities can perhaps be seen most clearly by analogy to the paintings of the *fauves*, where autonomous structure (or in Kandinsky's terms 'internal necessity') was substituted for composition after nature (or 'external necessity'). The free associations of images replaced logical organizations of mimetic shapes, with the 'arc' of discontinuous scenes (*Bilderbogen*) in plays patterned on the Stations of the Cross (*Stationendrama*) being in many ways equivalent to the visual artists' preference for curvilinear forms. Time and space do not exist as categories for organizing experience, or rather the attempt to give the action immediacy and direct relevance to all spectators leads to abstract universalization. So Hasenclever specifies the time as 'today' and the scene as 'the world'. Hence too the cemetery, a setting in a sense outside time, which had already been used in another play, Fritz von Unruh's *A Family* (1916), where 'the tragedy is not confined to any temporal straitjacket [*Zeitkostüm*] – its action plays inside and in front of a church and on a mountain peak'.[11]

Unlike such plays as Toller's *Masses and Man* or *Transfiguration* – in which key episodes 'are to be imagined as a shadowy reality, played out in the distant interior of a dream'[12] – Hasenclever has extended Strindberg's principles for reproducing the internal logic, rather than the visual impression of a dream. The scenes in *Humanity* are not only linked by

Figure 5 The prison of psychological repression in *Masses and Man*. Free association of images, dream states and emotional intensity.

associations, rather than cause and effect. They also become almost independent moments – a montage of single images, each making a specific impression, out of which a composite picture emerges.

There is a corresponding development in the use of language. Where Strindberg's dialogue tended to the poetic or metaphoric, Hasenclever's characters are reduced to emotionally charged and evocative single words. Already in Wedekind or Sternheim speech had been condensed to a staccato telegraphese, intended to express emotional intensity. Here this has become the full-blown expressionist '*Schrei*'. The intellectual, denotative quality of language has been excluded by removing practically all grammatical structures and connectives. Assertion takes the place of discursive argument, and there is no room for a character's utterances to express personality or indicate motivation. This of course reinforces the status of the figures as archetypes. Either they represent caricatured aspects of external society versus intrinsic moral qualities, as in *Humanity*, or they become projections of the protagonist-poet's spiritual struggle, as in Sorge's *The Beggar* (1912). But, as a perceptive critic like Brecht immediately realized, this is a form of inflation that devalues its own symbolic currency;

and a figure like Hasenclever's Alexander at times appears almost a parody, Strindberg's Unknown reduced to an algebraic lowest common denominator:

THE FATHER: Who are you?
ALEXANDER: I seek myself.
THE FATHER: A Man!![13]

At the same time this type of dialogue must be seen as an attempt to reflect the uncontrolled emotional depths of the subconscious in such a way as to appeal directly to the same pre-rational levels in the spectators' minds. Strindberg's images are intellectually formulated and interpretable as allegory. This expressionist simplicity is designed to reach a more basic stratum of awareness, on which men are united by instinctive and emotional qualities shared by all. So the appropriate verbal forms are assumed to be the spontaneous cry or unpremeditated image. There are obvious parallels to Nietzsche's concept of tragedy, in which the 'spirit of music' liberates man from individuality and reunites the Dionysiac audience with the universal will in a 'collective ecstasy'.

Ultimately then, what is significant is a particular expressive quality – the means rather than the meaning – as the self-adopted label of 'expressionism' indicates. The structures of action and dialogue are not only intended to embody the fundamental operations of the mind through intensification and condensation, but also to speak directly to the audience's collective subconscious. Hasenclever's use of isolated key words – Life, Death, Love, Brother, Money, Syphilis, Atonement, Sunrise and Resurrection, always capitalized and followed by two, sometimes three exclamation marks – is the equivalent of a painter like Franz Marc's belief that certain colours automatically trigger specific emotional associations. Responses are to be subliminal, almost Pavlovian; and the essential criteria are therefore directness, immediacy, intensity. In short, the expressionist play or painting should ideally be a transparent conductor, transferring the artist's subjective vision to the spectator's mind without being filtered through the intellect or socially conditioned perspectives, so that it is experienced as 'lived truth'. In no sense is the artistic process intended to create an objective reality that an audience, as observers, could consider critically or react to individually.

The world only exists on stage as a vehicle for the soul, or a reflection of the will. So objects and figures can be transformed to correspond to the emotional state of the dreaming or visionary mind. There can be oppositions, contrasts, but no real conflict; and many expressionist plays literally culminate in monologues. This subjectivity carries over into the form. The climax is introspective, the crisis being the point at which feeling ('*Seele*') becomes so forceful that it bursts through the dramatic structure into incoherence, not by the decisive nature of physical action (death, marriage, etc.). Drama becomes concentrated to a point of 'pure' emotion; and the ending of one monologue, the 1,000-line declamation in the final act of *The Beggar*, is worth quoting because it is particularly revealing about the expressionist author's intentions:

> Oh tears! Tears! . . . Joy! . . . ETERNAL LIFE!!! And not to be able to live it! Indeed I know I can't live it – oh curses! Curses! To be condemned to words! Yes, I am damned by words! I must become a sculptor of symbols, must renounce the priesthood . . . Poet . . . Holy only on the surface . . . Hypocrite . . . Think . . . Think . . . Symbols . . . *Leaps impetuously upward with hands outstretched.* Oh consoling lightning . . . Illumination . . . Agonizing consolation of the lightning . . . SYMBOLS OF ETERNITY . . . End! End! Goal and end! If the blood, the sum of unreality, of tumult, of the desire for tumult in me . . . in my blood, if this is condemned to speak in symbols, then so be it: SPEAK THROUGH SYMBOLS OF ETERNITY. *Exhaustion.*[14]

Speech is at several removes from spiritual reality. To find a frequency that avoids the noisy static of daily life, the artist must use symbols. But conventional symbolism is too limiting because of its intellectual connotations, and as a result the pauses on an expressionist's page are made to carry more meaning than what is said. Visual images, keyed in by emotionally charged words and accompanied by suggestive vocal sounds, become the primary means of communication, comparable to Artaud's 'hieroglyphs'.

The problem (for the expressionists) is that the attempt to short-circuit the twin gaps between external representation and internal states, and between expression and reception, leads to a form of vacuum. Particularly when read as a text and divorced from performance, expressionist dialogue seems loaded with more weight of emotion than the words can bear. Pathos has been exaggerated to the point where it turns into bathos; and symbolic meaning is so inflated that it loses contact with the particular, becoming emptied of significance. Theatrical conventions are only effective when they appear the natural form for a particular concept of existence, when the medium is so well integrated with the message that it goes unnoticed. By contrast these techniques tend to attract attention to themselves and, partly because of the expressionist fixation on emotional absolutes, frequently seem to be used with all the subtlety of sledgehammers. Paradoxically then, the attempt to abolish form, to turn it into a transparent conductor, makes the formal elements obtrusive.

At the same time the most frequent criticism of the expressionist approach is its undramatic abstraction.[15] This negative evaluation is mainly based on reading the plays in literary form. But with their relegation of dialogue to a minor role, these are not so much texts as deliberately incomplete scripts. They should be seen as a framework for mime accompanied by exclamations; and if the stage directions are too abbreviated to give more than bare indications of the desired effect, this is because the expressionists were writing for a recognized style of presentation that had developed in response to their requirements.

EXPRESSIONIST STAGING

Obviously, expressionist figures not being naturalistic individuals in the context of a specific social environment, the mimetic approach to acting was inappropriate. Instead the effects aimed at by the expressionists were artificial, exaggerated and rhetorical. But at the same time the expressionist actor was to be an example of 'the new man' for the audience, revealing his innermost being directly in movement, gesture and facial expression. Kornfeld's 'Epilogue to the Actor' (1913) shows the dual requirement clearly. Not only is the actor to create 'his characters from his [own] experience of the emotion or fate he has to portray . . . and not from his recollections of human beings he has seen filled with these emotions or victims of this fate', he is also not to conceal 'the fact that he is acting. Let him not deny the theatre or try to feign reality.'[16] This basic antithesis remained unresolved, perhaps because it corresponded to the contradiction inherent in expressionist characterization: as the 'self' is made the subject of analysis it becomes increasingly elusive and ambiguous, escaping into role playing where the face dissolves into multiple masks.

On one level the actor searches for absolute emotional truth, which only subjective experience can guarantee, and which any element of pretence or illusion discredits. 'Not counterfeit thoughts, but his emotions alone lead and guide him. Only then can he advance and approach absolute ecstasy': an emotional transcendence which is to be achieved through trance states and self-hypnosis.[17] Again the principles are those of spontaneity and immediacy, ruling out the prior selection of feelings to be exhibited, since these would have been distorted by the process of intellectual reflection. Behind this is the expressionist concept of humanity. If the opinions and behaviour patterns that define individuality are associated with the conscious, rational side of the mind, then the essential qualities of a human being are universal, relating to the idea of a 'collective soul'. So the aim of the actor becomes to divest himself of personality. He presents 'nothing but the most sublime and the most miserable: HE BECOMES MAN . . . not a puppet dangling on the strings of a psychological philosophy of life'.[18]

Following this line, techniques were developed to project archetypal emotions directly in physical terms through rhythms of movement, posture and symbolic gesture. In an approach Grotowski was to develop to its limits in the 1960s, the actor's body becomes an expressive instrument, literally incarnating his spiritual being – at least according to one of the

Figure 6 Fritz Kortner as Richard III. Ecstatic acting – facial 'masking' and exaggerated gestures.

leading expressionist exponents, Erwin Kalser, who had made his name as the Student in Falckenberg's 1915 production of *The Ghost Sonata*. This was a classic example of the 'ecstatic' acting style, where the actor playing the Old Man came to blows with Kalser during the dress rehearsal because of the hate built up by their roles, a telling symptom of the extreme emotional states and degree of involvement in expressionist acting. And while performing the part of the Cashier in Kaiser's *From Morn to Midnight* (1916) Kalser commented:

> Of what else does the actor's training consist, but removing the obstinacy of the body, which he himself resists, to make it completely and totally the organ of the soul? The soul must reach deep into the hidden core of the body, so that nothing is impossible for him; he can completely forget himself in his soul . . . The actor who is conscious of his inner strength goes onto the stage as someone sleepwalking.[19]

On this level the actor always plays himself, though trying to reach beneath the merely personal, and came to be compared with shamans and mystics, paralleling Strindberg's claim that the actor should function as a spiritualist medium in a trance – a transformation from within that actors themselves believed they achieved, referring to 'tremendous spiritual ecstasies' experienced when they were able to reach a semi-unconscious dream state in performance.[20]

On the other level, expressionist actors clearly conformed to a highly rhetorical style. Their exaggerated gesticulations show the influence of the traditional series of six distorted hand gestures developed by Hans Sachs to depict character in the medieval German Passion Play – a deliberate return to the archaic which indicates the expressionist concern with the primitive. Their faces were transformed into 'masks' (again with all the primitive connotations) by the rigid tension of facial muscles. Hands became stretched into talons, arms curved sinuously as swans' necks to form exterior 'signs' of psychological states. Movement swung between an almost epileptic dynamism and cataleptic stasis, creating driving rhythms in which rapid and highly patterned moves continually froze into a series of emblematic positions comparable to the schemata of classical Greek theatre. Voices were harsh, emphatic, staccato, matching the compression of dialogue into isolated nouns or telegraphic phrases. The whole surface effect was angular, corresponding to the crooked arches and oblique perspectives of the expressionist sets in which the actors were framed. It was grotesque, gothic and sharply conventionalized.

However the expressionists themselves saw no contradiction between rigid stylization and subjectivity, contemporaneity and archaism. For them what provided a synthesis was the concept of the universality of emotion; the continued presence of atavistic instincts in modern man beneath the surface of superficial rationalism imposed by western civilization; and the belief that personal emotion, if intense enough and expressed in archetypal forms, would release primitive responses and automatically evoke the same emotional state in the spectators. As Stefan Zweig commented, announcing 'the New Pathos' in 1909, 'technical proficiency' must 'no longer be an end in itself, but only a means of inspiring pathos'. And this would only be achieved by 'a return to the origins' of art, since primitive poetry was idealized as 'a scarcely verbalized cry' that expressed 'the excess of a sensation – full of pathos because it arose out of passion – solely with the aim of generating passion'.[21]

This ecstatic style was undoubtedly powerful. When rhetorically exaggerated gestures, originally designed for mass spectacles in gigantic staging areas like Max Reinhardt's 'theatre of the 5,000', were transformed unchanged to smaller stages like the intimate Kammerspiele (where Falckenberg's production of *The Ghost Sonata* was performed on an acting area barely 26 ft wide and without depth), the emotional projection would have been overpowering. And it is hardly surprising that Fritz Kortner – whose performances in Karl Heinz Martin's production of *Transfiguration* and Leopold Jessner's of *Wilhelm Tell* (both in 1919) set the standards for expressionist acting – had gone through an apprenticeship with Reinhardt, and had been the leader of the chorus in his monumental version of *Oedipus Rex*.

In light of this impassioned presentation, the number of insane characters and madhouse scenes in expressionist drama is hardly coincidental. It corresponds to the image of the ecstatic actor as 'a man possessed', even if this tended only too literally to mean bared teeth and rolling eyes. In addition to this over-obviousness, as Zweig's stress on 'the excess of sensation' implies, plays like *Humanity* require a performance to start on such a high level of intensity that it leaves little room for building to any crescendo. As a result, the aggressive emphasis and sustained emotional pitch could become a form of overkill, exhausting the spectator's ability to respond by its unremitting violence. At the same time the schemata that are intended to crystallize meaning become clichés through repetition, the clearest example being the Christ image which recurs at the climax of so many expressionist plays. Indeed this was effectively emptied of meaning through being used to signal a whole range of emotive states from ecstatic transfiguration (as in *Humanity*), to the agony of sacrifice (as in *From Morn to Midnight*, where Kaiser's dying Cashier stands 'with outstretched arms slumping against the cross sewn on the curtains. His gasp sobs like an *Ecce* – his expiring breath sighs like a *Homo*').[22]

Despite such flaws, this ritualistic style of performance had a wider currency than is generally realized. In particular it provides a working model for visualizing what Artaud intended when he described his ideal actor as 'signalling through the flames': creating 'violent physical images' of 'energy in the unconscious', which 'crush and hypnotize the sensibility of the spectator'. In fact, Artaud's description of the qualities he admired in Lugné-Poe's acting could be applied word for word to the expressionists:

> his surprising changes of voice, his fingers which became rigid points, his inflamed glances evoked thoughts of a tradition now lost to the theatre. One would have said we were in the presence of an actor from the mystery plays of medieval France.[23]

Significantly too, bearing in mind the expressionist rejection of discursive language, and their reduction of dialogue to rhythmic exclamation, this style of acting carried over into silent film and had strong affinities with contemporary dance. Indeed some of the aims of expressionism can be seen more clearly in some para-theatrical forms developed at the time, because here the essential qualities are presented independent of the traditional dramaturgical elements of characterization and plot still retained in the plays.

EURYTHMICS AND PSYCHODRAMA

The work of Dalcroze and Laban is mainly discussed today in terms of time-and-motion study. But their techniques were worked out and displayed in wordless performances based on archetypal concepts, or mythological stories: *Titan, Prometheus, Echo and Narcissus*. 'Eurythmics', Dalcroze's system of movement training, focused on the emotions aroused by musical rhythms and translated these into attitude and gesture, while Laban's theory of 'eukinetics' reduced all movements to opposed pairs of stylized 'shapes' – for instance centripedal or scooping versus centrifugal or 'scattering'. Being distilled to their essential elements, such movements held strong psychological associations. And the dance-drama group that Laban established to demonstrate his ideas repeated variations of these 'pure shapes' to express clearly defined emotions such as anger, joy, love or fear, until all the dancers reached a 'universal celebratory state'. Dalcroze went even further, collaborating with Adolphe Appia on various experimental pieces and festival productions at Hellerau, which culminated in a startling performance of Gluck's *Orfeo and Eurydice* at Geneva in 1914.

Appia specifically saw Dalcroze's theories as the source for a radically new concept of theatre, which – significantly – would restore a primal unity:

> The point of contact between body and mind, which alone can create harmony has become lost: eurythmics will try to find it again. This is its great significance for the theatre . . . The awakening of rhythm

Figure 7 Rudolf van Laban, *Titan*. Musical rhythms and archetypal movements.

in ourselves, in our own flesh, is the death-knell of a great part of our contemporary art, particularly the scenic art.

To develop the relationship between movement of the human body through time, the spatial context it occupied, and music, he designed 'rhythmic spaces', in which architectural shapes combined with varying light to express emotions. These were elaborated into starkly simple settings of multi-level platforms, steps and columns, in which the choreographed patterns of choral dance exposed 'the eternal drama hidden beneath historical customs, events, and costumes . . . purely human Expression, stripped of all historic pomp, presenting a sacred commentary on – and a transfigured realization of – the events'.[24] Hellerau was an educational institute; and Dalcroze's system of physical exercises evolved as a tool for fostering musical awareness in his students. Even when applied to opera by Appia, eurythmics retained its educational basis, extending to the audience on a psychological level. The great hall at Hellerau, built in 1911 to house the festival performances, was consciously designed to break down the standard separation between spectators and performers – the earliest example of this characteristic avant garde principle. Although photos show audiences massed at one end of the floor and at some distance from the action, their raked seats echoed the flights of steps (the trademark of Appia's Hellerau settings) at the other end, and the system of diffused lighting embraced the whole area. An arrangement of several hundred white and coloured spotlights, set behind the translucent linen screens that covered all the walls and the ceiling of the hall, and controlled from a single console (the 'light organ'), this served as an emotional intensifier. Merged with the mood of the piece – transmitted through their senses by light and music, together with the spatial integration – the spectators were to share the vision of communal harmony embodied in the students' dancing.

The Hellerau experiment and the idealistic hopes of its community came to a premature end in 1914, swept away by the cataclysm of the First World War, although Dalcroze and Appia collaborated on the revival of one of the earliest pieces in 1920. But their work provided a wide, if diffuse, stimulus for the avant garde movement. Among the leading theatrical figures who responded enthusiastically to the Appia/Dalcroze *Orfeo* at Hellerau (in addition to such representatives of conventional drama as Shaw and Stanislavski) were Max Reinhardt, Leopold Jessner, Sergei Diaghilev, Paul Claudel and Georges Pitoëff. Both the stress on performance as therapy for the performer and the abstraction of physical expression to universal shapes were carried over into the ecstatic style of expressionist acting in the use of repeated and rhythmic movement for hypnotic effect, heightening emotional states to the point where the subjective turns into the archetypal. Jessner adopted Appia's flights of steps and emotive lighting (drenching the stage in a blood-red glare for *Richard III* in 1920). Claudel's first play to reach the stage – *Tidings Brought to Mary*, written in 1892 – which was produced by Lugné-Poe in 1912, had been performed with Appia's settings and Dalcroze's collaboration in the same summer festival at Hellerau; and Claudel in particular admired the 'union of music, the plastic sense, and light [in *Orfeo*], the like of which I have never seen'.[25] Through Claudel, the line from Hellerau merges with the post-Artaudian avant garde theatre in France. He sought to gain the same quality in his own dramas, which Jean-Louis Barrault (the most successful of Artaud's disciples) was later to direct.

One other example of Hellerau's legacy should be mentioned, since it links up with the Jungian aspect of expressionism, and the search for ritualistic or mythical archetypes to incarnate emotions so deeply felt that they become universal and transfigure the individual by a return to the roots of human nature. Diaghilev, impressed by the potential of eurythmics for ballet, hired Marie Rambert, a pupil of Dalcroze, to assist in the Nijinski production of Stravinsky's *Rite of Spring* (1913). Set in prehistoric Russia and depicting a pagan ritual of mating and human sacrifice, in which a virgin possessed by ancestral spirits dances in an ecstasy to music of increasing violence and volume until she falls lifeless to the ground, this ballet brings together all the primitive and mythic tendencies we have noted in expressionism. It also preserves the intended effect of ecstatic acting in musical terms, with atavistic rhythms, rapidly changing metres and conflicting polytonal chords which produce a febrile and unsettling restlessness, and ostinatos (the constant repetition of melodic figures) building in intensity to create overpowering dissonances.

If the experiments of Laban or Appia and Dalcroze had a significant influence on stage technique, and helped to shape the search for new modes of theatrical expression, the work of Jakob Moreno brings out the complementary effect of theatre on other areas of social activity. Where the dance-drama grew out of pedagogy, and related to Jungian archetypes, Moreno demonstrates the Freudian aspect of subjectivism: theatre as therapy.

Moreno, the Viennese founder of group psychotherapy, did little more than extend current expressionist practice when he drew up his plans for a 'theatre without spectators' in 1923. The architectural design for his ideal theatre gives a quasi-religious impression that accurately reflected the expressionist belief in the divinity of man, and the realization of God in every individual through the full release of human potential (however odd this may seem from the standpoint of psychiatry today). The shape was that of a circular basilica with a stage in the centre and broad steps rising like terraces in concentric circles up to the outside wall, where there were four equidistant semi-circular 'chapels', each with its own stage and surrounding steps. This was the prototype of the egg-shaped Bauhaus design for a 'total theatre' by Walter Gropius (1928), and both were architectural attempts to integrate the audience in stage action. But Gropius' spectators were to be passive, involved only imaginatively and emotionally, although totally encompassed with external activity, scenes being played out around them on the perimeter, between them in broad aisles, in the middle of them on a central stage and extending above them by unbroken cinema projection over the curving ceiling. Moreno's concept was far more radical. His public were not spectators but active participants. There were no seats. Standing encouraged more overt responses and allowed free movement from one centre of action to another or even onto one of the stages, making a constant interchange possible between reacting and enacting. And since the focus of this psychodrama was the relationship of the individual to the group, those participants less directly involved acted as both the antagonist and the setting. Instead of an audience there was a responsive environment literally standing for society as the wider, normative context within which the individual moves.

There were no scripts, no professional performers, no aesthetic appreciation, no scenery. Ordinary members of the public led others in improvised 'scenarios' dealing with personal psychiatric problems of general relevance to the group, and modified their actions following suggestions or alternatives demonstrated by those surrounding them. In practice Moreno gathered a nucleus of particularly interesting 'case histories', who reappeared to act out the on-going saga of their personal and sexual relationships night after night. In theory, however, this was 'Theatre for everybody . . . not an expert actor surrounded by an open-mouthed attentive mass; all must play with it . . . must make the stride from awareness to improvisation'.[26] And the structure Moreno developed reflected these desired elements of spontaneity and equality. First a preparatory phase, releasing inhibitions, finding a common problem and discovering the most suitable exponent, who would function as a protagonist for the group. Then a series of situations acted out impromptu following (ideally) 'the free play of the subconscious', with the protagonists playing the role of the 'self', others co-opted as 'auxiliary egos' or antagonists, and the mass giving 'resonance' through comparisons and corrections. This was followed by discussion.

Moreno's 'theatre of improvisation' developed from his work with children, which led him to conclude: first, that megalomania was normal, since the self is inevitably a central concern for the individual; and second, that spontaneity is the ultimate basic human trait, even prior to sexuality or other drives. The form of his theatre reflected his belief that blocks and repressions were created by the distorting pressures of an unhealthy social environment – not as in Freudian theory by infantile traumas. And performances were based on the premise that 'acting is healthier than speaking', which gave a therapeutic rationale for replacing 'the logical/verbal emphasis of traditional theatre' by 'improvisational situations'. In short Moreno's theatre offered a psychological value for the egoistic focus of expressionism and its elevation of '*Seele*' (Soul) – the uncontrolled emotional aspect of the subconscious that was expressed by the '*Schrei*' (Cry) – to the essential constituent of art. It also held out a justifiable rationale for the expressionist repudiation of society, one which – being psychological – was more consistent than the sort of ideological rejection that led various artists to a communist position.

Equally significantly, Moreno's psychodrama also gives a rationale for elements in expressionist plays which otherwise might appear arbitrary stylistic devices, for example the structure of short, independent tableaux and the substitution of montage for temporal sequence:

> Scenarios only radiate magical influence when they are performed with a special tempo and in a foreshortened perspective . . . The foreshortening of the play is essential because intensity can only be held for a brief time. Tension is followed by release. An improvisation must not be carried on past the player's moment of release . . . The performance progresses in upward spiralling leaps with interpolated pauses. In the improvised theatre the 'drama' is not decided by the totality of the whole but by the scenic atoms . . . 'Time' is not pre-sented but moments. The acts of a play are loosed from one another; they form a chain of independent, illuminating impulses.[27]

EXPRESSIONIST INFLUENCES AND ARTAUDIAN PRECURSORS

The stylistic characteristics of expressionism are generally dismissed today as outdated, the thematic aspirations as inflated and pretentious. But much of the subsequent avant garde development either repeats or derives from their experiments.

The symbolists' exploration of 'correspondences' between colours and sounds, or the expressionists' appeal to the pre-rational, primitive levels of the mind, lead directly to all the varied attempts to create a 'total theatre'. These take four main directions. The most traditional is Wagner's symphonic *Gesamtkunstwerk*, in which all the other elements of drama were subordinated to the romantic absolutes of idealism and emotion in the music: paralleling symbolism, it led directly to Appia's concepts and the attempt to make spectators direct participants in the stage action. Alterna-tively there is the example of Charles Dullin's work at L'Atelier, uniting a multiplicity of theatrical styles to create a specifically theatrical form of fantasy 'more expressive than reality'.[28] Appia's work, combined with expressionist subjectivity and Bakhtin's physicality, led to Barrault's stripped-down version of 'total theatre' where 'lived truth' is created by using the actor alone to project all aspects of the world through vocal and physical expression. Finally there is the most extreme form of 'total theatre': Artaud's total immersion of the spectator in the stage action, establishing 'direct communication' by a level of physical involvement that acts 'directly and profoundly upon the sensibility through the organs', and creates a receptive state in which 'all the senses interpenetrate'.[29]

Expressionist influences are still evident in the avant garde theatre of the 1960s. The Polish Theatre Laboratory repeats and extends their ecstatic acting style, with Grotowski's criterion of emotional sincerity, and his use of physical discipline to free 'elemental impulses' in his actors. When he defines his aim as enabling the performers to 'go beyond' themselves to spontaneous self-revelation under extreme physical stress, achieving a 'translumination', this is directly comparable to the expressionist 'transfiguration'; and his ideal of performance as 'communion' is equally expressionistic. Even Moreno's work finds definite echoes. Again in Richard Schechner's Performance Group the audience becomes the 'environment' for the actors. Indeed, it is a short step from Moreno's use of theatre to deal with the psychoses of an 'abnormal' group or his rejection of scripts and verbal communication, to Artaud's concept of using theatre as corrective therapy for a sick society, or his search for 'scenic rhythm' and 'concrete gestures' with 'an efficacy strong enough to make us forget the very necessity of speech'.[30] And the whole ideal of theatre as therapy is the basis for Robert Wilson's 'autistic' drama.

But the most striking parallel is between Artaud and the work of a leading expressionist painter, who also turned to the stage in a quest for ways of expressing his atavistic and apocalyptic vision: Oskar Kokoschka. Artaud's search for a visual language which is not a translation of words but a form of direct communication through using actions to form 'images that spring uniquely from themselves, which do not derive their meaning from the situation . . . but from a kind of internal necessity', is virtually a restatement of the position formulated by Kandinsky, Kokoschka and turn-of-the-century expressionist painters.[31] Reacting against the impressionists (the equivalent in visual art to reacting against naturalism in the theatre), their canvasses reflected autonomous interior images instead of the physical world, working with free associations which appealed directly to the senses. A key term for them too was 'internal necessity' and the characteristic elements in their pictures were the dynamic rhythms of curvilinear forms and the use of symbolic colours, both of which were designed to transfer emotional intensity directly to the spectator.

One of Kokoschka's plays, *Murderer the Women's Hope* (1909), transposes these principles from canvas to the stage, and the results prefigure Artaud's work so exactly that it could almost be called a paradigm of the Theatre of Cruelty. *Murderer* is an intensely personal vision which embodies Kokoschka's fear of what he called 'the female principle', whose erotic advance causes the breakdown of intellectual and social balance, so revealing 'dangerous and intriguing' depths in the psyche. The play's aim is to open the spectator's subconscious to these depths by presenting archetypal sexual patterns of domination and destruction. Its theme is 'the fatal confrontation' between what Kokoschka saw as the fundamental poles of existence that form the basis of our dreams, Eros and Thanatos[32] – a comparable dualism to Artaud's – which Kokoschka expressed in solar/ lunar symbols, just as Artaud was to do. The action is composed of mythic elements drawing strongly upon erotic violence. It is designed to evoke strong emotional responses on a subliminal level, as in a consistent use of inverted Christian images: a cock crowing three times to announce murder and massacre, a woman's body spread-eagled into the shape of a white cross. The whole play in fact presents the seven Stations of the Cross as an extended orgasm with the sexual climax being the crucifixion.

On one level the purpose is negative, to demoralize society by destroying unquestioned moral assumptions. But this also has its positive aspect, to open the spectators' minds by breaking down conventional responses through outrage – and these are precisely the tactics Artaud was to use in *The Cenci*. Even the weapon chosen, blasphemy, is the same. Kokoschka wanted 'the actors to offer the public a gesture of defiance', which would be an apt description of the Théâtre Alfred Jarry's intentions. But he was more consistent than Artaud. Instead of trying to attract society with gala openings, he took pains to insult public opinion in preparation for *Murderer*. He shaved his head like a condemned criminal to declare his rejection of social values in the most provocative way; and even the poster advertising the play was designed to shock. It was deliberately unaesthetic in execution and offensive in subject: a parody of the pietà in which a flayed male is being torn apart by a blue woman; and Kokoschka commented, with self-satisfied exaggeration, 'as I had intended, it sent the Viennese into paroxysms of rage'. Beneath this attack on society, again like Artaud, Kokoschka had a more idealistic aim: to reveal the religious nature of 'inner experience';[33] and a second poster was a variation on the expressionist *Ecce Homo*, a self-portrait with one hand pointing to a gaping wound in the breast.

The script of the play, which Kokoschka claimed was improvised in a single night of rehearsal – a claim clearly deriving from the value put on emotional immediacy and the direct externalization of subconscious states by the expressionists, since in fact the play had been written over a year earlier between 1907 and 1908 – is little more than a framework for gesture and visual effects. Choreography and patterns of visual images and colours are used to communicate instead of a fully articulated text; and for the first performance each actor was given no more than a bare outline of the action and the key phrases he was to speak, but drilled extensively in movement and vocal rhythms. The speeches still contained the sort of evocative and poetic verbal images that Artaud avoided, but they were chanted or intoned, broken down into sounds – a scream, cries in various pitches, arbitrarily stressed syllables – and obviously intended to have an effect comparable to Artaud's incantation. Colours recurred as motifs in the words and were repeated in the costumes, scenery and lighting. Primary colours were chosen for their emotional associations: blood for life, white for death, with red dominant – as it frequently was in Artaud's staging.

Kokoschka's paintings of this period give a fair indication of how the stage picture must have appeared under his direction. His illustrations for the play have strong but broken rhythms; the composition is geometric but the shadings escape through the boundaries of the forms; and the delicacy of fine, in conjunction with crude, shapes echoes the tension between flowing patterns and the brutal gestures they represent. As an artist Kokoschka initiated the practice of using moving people instead of still-life sitters for figure studies; and the action of the play is not so much a series of events as a sequence of rhythms. Wheeling and circling movements are used as a structural geometry in a similar way to the 'gravitation' used by Artaud in *The Cenci* (1935 – see pp. 67–8 in this volume). However the style of movement was almost certainly different. Where Artaud was influenced by what he thought of as the heraldic gestures of Balinese theatre, Kokoschka rejected the influence of African, Mayan and Inca art, or that of 'the Pacific islanders' as a retreat from 'original creativity' into exoticism. He stayed instead in the European tradition, and based his use of space on the tensions of gothic art. Rather than tending to tableaux, like Artaud's slow motion or his *trompe-l'œil* 'Marriage of Cana', Kokoschka used violent physical action, tribal dance steps and whirling fire-brands carried by the actors to create 'a wild atmosphere'. Both, however, shared the aim of creating a new model of theatre in which the stimulation of the audience by dynamic movement in space would replace the traditional draining of feeling through emotional transference. The similarity of approach, and the differences in execution, can be indicated by Kokoschka's comment: 'My performers . . . were not acrobats, but even so they could run, jump, stand and fall better than any of the Burgtheater actors, who often took a quarter of an hour to lie down and die.'[34]

The comparison between Artaud and Kokoschka can even be extended into details. Kokoschka's actors were directed to use stylized gestures becoming progressively more animalistic (for the women) or godlike (for the men) during the performance, which contrasted strongly with the highly structured impression of choral orchestration and geometrically patterned movement – effects directly paralleled in the *Cenci* production. The music for *Murderer*, like that composed for Artaud's *Burnt Breast* by Maxim Jacob (1927), was limited to percussion and woodwind: drums to intensify the rhythms of the performance, cymbals and pipes for an atmospheric tone of primitive wildness. But the most striking duplication was in the visual appearance given to the actors.

The costumes for *The Cenci* had the musculature of the body traced over the cloth, outlining the stomach, rib cage and limbs to give a skeletal effect. In exactly the same way Kokoschka painted 'face masks' for his actors, covering all their exposed skin (as primal beings they were scantily clad) with lines representing tendons and nerve structures. To some extent this was an extension of a familiar expressionist technique that can be seen in various pen and ink portraits, where abstract patterns of lines merge the face into the total design so that individual features dissolve. It also corresponds to the expressionist premise that external forms disintegrate under the intensity of extreme emotion, which paradoxically leads to the disappearance of the self in the movement down into subjectivity, and the transfer from ego to archetype. For Kokoschka it was particularly intended to represent the inner being of his figures, as if surface appearances had been flayed away, removing individuality and (in a typically Artaudian image) rooting deep emotional or spiritual states in the physical body:

> The Greeks put masks on their actors to fix characters – sad, passion-ate, angry, etc. I did the same thing in my own way by painting on faces, not as decoration, but to underline [essential] character. It was all meant to be effective at a distance, like fresco painting. All I was after was this enhancement of expression. I treated the members of the cast quite differently. Some of them I gave cross stripes, like a tiger or cat, but I painted the nerves on all of them. Where they were located I knew from my study of anatomy.[35]

How effective was *Murderer the Women's Hope*? Kokoschka, like Artaud, had a certain artistic reputation or rather notoriety. Already by 1908 he was labelled the '*Ueberwilding*' (super-savage) and had been dismissed from his teaching post at the art school because the Minister for Culture thought an exhibition of his work was a 'chamber of horrors'. As a gesture of defiance the performance was undoubtedly successful. It caused a riot, order had to be restored by force and the reviews were vicious, calling Kokoschka a 'criminal', a 'degenerate', a 'corrupter of youth'. [36]

The violence of the reactions seems to have been partly fortuitous, being due to an unusual and unexpected mixture of spectators. The play was put on outdoors; and the atmosphere of extemporization and the summer night might have had something to do with it. But, far more significant, the venue allowed a kind of spectator, who would never normally enter a theatre, to participate in the performance. Folding seats surrounded by a flimsy fence had been set up for the audience; and this enclosure was filled by reputable members of society (who had come to disapprove) and the intellectual élite (who were neutrally curious). On the other side of the fence common soldiers gathered. These were from a Bosnian regiment (renowned as the most primitive and backward part of a ramshackle empire) quartered nearby. The paying audience 'maintained a chorus of catcalls throughout the play' – and this alone would probably have been enough to arouse the soldiers. Yet perhaps the fact that they intervened

Figure 8a, b Kokoschka's sketches for *Murderer the Women's Hope*. Archetypes and the externalizing of spiritual being – nerves painted on the skin. Compare the skeletal musculature of the *Cenci* costumes, plate 10. Note too the shaved head indicating the author's identification with the protagonist.

at the point of climax in the symbolic orgasm might indicate that the pre-intellectual involvement intended by Kokoschka worked – at least on naive spectators. 'As the foot stamping, scuffling, and chair brandishing increased in pitch, the soldiers stormed in and a free-for-all followed between them and the audience. In the tumult the police had to be sent for.'[37] The play, however, was more than just a *succès de scandale*. The text, originally published in 1909, was reprinted five times between 1910 and 1920, and an operatic version was published in 1921. The dadaists – for whom another of Kokoschka's plays (*Sphinx & Straw Man*) had 'decided the role of our theatre, which will entrust the stage direction to the subtle invention of the explosive mind, scenario to the audience, visible direction, grotesque props: the DADAIST theatre'[38] – performed it in Zürich. Kokoschka produced it again in Dresden in 1917. And after the war it achieved a considerable reputation, being staged twice by Reinhardt in 1918 and 1919 as well as being performed in 1920 and 1921. Hindemith set it to music; and it was performed as an opera in 1921 and 1922.

The soldiers in Vienna, being infantry, had reacted with their feet rather than their souls. Industrial workers in France a generation and a war later were unlikely to be as unsophisticated or direct in their response as Balkan peasants. But the soldiers' enthusiastic involvment in Kokoschka's drama, however accidental on this occasion, indicates that Artaud's instinct to play to the masses rather than the cultural élite had possibilities despite the problems inherent in communicating with an uneducated audience. At the same time the spectacular stage history of *Murderer the Women's Hope*, taken up as it was by the whole theatrical spectrum from the iconoclastic dadaists to Reinhardt – the expressionist who became the representative *par excellence* of the grand tradition – suggests that Artaud's approach, which was so similar, could have been as applicable to the conventional stage as to experimental anti-theatre.

In fact, as we shall see, Artaud's productions failed, and as a result, his theatrical practice had relatively little influence (as against his essays). But the comparison with Kokoschka suggests that this lack of immediate influence cannot be put down to intrinsic flaws in Artaud's art. The reasons lay rather in his strategy; and his failure seems due as much as anything else to his habit of reaching beyond his grasp. First, the gap between his unrealistically idealistic theory, and what he actually achieved on the stage, raised expectations in his audience that his work was not even designed to meet. Second, Artaud's stage effects relied on complex technology and a high degree of control in the acting. Artaud's productions were conceived in terms of lighting which did not exist, scenery which was too costly for an *ad hoc* group to build effectively, and a precision in choreography that required long-term commitments by an expert troupe. By contrast Kokoschka issued no manifestos; and *Murderer*, although allowing for spectacular effects, was originally performed on the bare earth. It needs only one simple piece of scenery – steps with an open-work grille in the shape of a tower – while the savage atmosphere could be created by energy alone when there was no opportunity for discipline. Only in his later plays, when professional theatres were open to him, did Kokoschka introduce complicated or illusionistic effects. In a sense, then, Kokoschka's plays provide a corrective, as well as an introduction, to Artaud's work.

5

ANTONIN ARTAUD AND THE THEATRE OF CRUELTY

THEORY AND PRACTICE

When critics discuss the use of ritual in contemporary drama or avant garde directors describe their attempts to rediscover the primitive ritual function of theatre, Artaud's name is usually the first to be mentioned. Although he can hardly be said to have initiated the trend, with Artaud the focus on dreams and the primitive levels of the psyche becomes extended to include savage roots and primitive culture. Expressionist painters like Nolde had already turned to African sculpture for inspiration. However, Artaud was the first to search for theatrical forms that would not only be non-European, but also specifically 'uncivilized' (as distinct from Strindberg's thematic borrowing from Indian religion, or Yeats' imitation of the Japanese Nōh as a 'noble' and highly refined art). And what impressed him about the Balinese dance-drama was 'the instinctive survival of magic' in what he mistakenly believed were involuntary and visionary gestures. In his view these caused 'the movement of religious terror which seized the crowds at the Paris Colonial Exhibition'. This was the effect he aimed at; and he believed that both his Théâtre Alfred Jarry and the Balinese theatre 'fed off the true magical sources of the same primitive unconscious'.[1]

In an 'Open letter to the schools of Buddha' Artaud rejects logic and reason as 'the chains that bind us in a petrifying imbecility of the mind'. What he proposes as positive values in their place are irrational spontaneity and delirium, which would release repressed tendencies in an emotional purgation analogous to the classical/tragic effect of catharsis. Significantly, the model outlined in his theories follows the two syllogistic modes of reasoning that dominate mythological systems. Frazer defined these as the 'laws' of 'sympathetic' magic (like causes like), and 'holophrastic' magic (the part stands for the whole). 'Images of energy in the unconscious and gratuitous crime on the surface' of a stage presentation are assumed to evoke a mirror state in the spectator's mind, if these 'can be projected with the necessary violence'.[2] And this delirium will be contagious, exorcizing repressive behaviour patterns in society as a whole by its presence in the tiny percentage of the population who attend Artaud's theatre, an analogy to the plague that in Artaud's confused metaphor is 'spiritual freedom' causing 'all social forms to disintegrate' and spreads 'without rats, without microbes, without contact'.[3]

The linkage of physical and spiritual in this metaphor is typical of Artaud's approach. Metaphysics are to be imprinted in the mind through the skin. The dynamics of consciousness are embodied in scenic rhythms. The linear harmonies of a picture affect the brain directly. Theatre therefore had to develop a ritual language by rediscovering universal physical signs, or 'hieroglyphs', while verbal expression became incantation. These, in brief, are the elements that can be pinned down as the basics of Artaud's 'Theatre of Cruelty', to which must be added the thematic inversion of good and evil.

This moral reversal has been characteristic of the anarchistic avant garde ever since Strindberg; and as Artaud defines it in the letter appended to his 'Journey to the land of the Tarahumaras' or his 'Letters on cruelty', nature is antisocial by definition, while civilization – and particularly the moral demands of Christianity – are debilitating lies designed by effete elites to subjugate the strong. To exist at all, our supposedly artificial culture has had to label everything physical or natural as 'evil'. So, to be true to our proper nature and therefore free to reach our real potential as 'total' men, no longer split by the western body/soul dichotomy, we must do what we have been taught is 'evil', while to force ourselves into the mould that society considers 'good' is the ultimate perversion. Quite apart from the philosophical shakiness of this argument, Artaud is uncertain about the exact status of actual cruelty. At times violence is seen as a symptom of spiritual distortion, breaking out as the repressive behaviour patterns imposed by society become unbearable. Alternatively it is presented as proof of the intrinsic violence of European civilization compared with Rousseauesque noble savagery. At other times cruelty appears as the law of nature itself, sadistically Darwinian, creative through destruction. But whatever the case, the solution is to be a return to primitive existence, to pre-logical consciousness.

So Artaud's name elicits a formula: Primitivism – Ritual – Cruelty – Spectacle. But what is generally understood as his theory is contradicted in certain important ways by the theatre he actually created; and the closer one looks at what he wrote, the more ambiguous his influence seems. This is partly because his style is positively Delphic in its poetic obscurity. As a result it is the critics and interpreters of his ideas who have given definition to what is seen as 'Artaudian' in modern theatre – and their average approach is curiously uncritical, perhaps because Artaud is in many ways our *alter ego*. He mirrors the disillusion of the 1960s/1970s with conventional forms of society and religion, and pioneered the experiments with hallucinatory drugs. He anticipated the search for new modes of spirituality, which today range from the popular interest in eastern religious figures to the following gained by even an ex-conjurer such as Uri Geller, and from a widespread belief in the ancient superstition of astrology to the research into parapsychology and ESP at various university centres.

Artaud in fact is closely associated with fashionable existential uncertainties, which may be why almost everywhere he is accepted on his own valuation. 'Prophet', 'magician', 'visionary', 'shaman', 'tragic hero' – this is the common currency of description. Artaud has been attacked on various grounds: that his theatre was unrealizable, inaccessible or divorced from the social and political context of the audience; that it destroys the conventionally accepted principles of drama (which of course was precisely its intent); that it reveals basic misunderstandings of key fields (e.g. psychology and Balinese theatre).[4] Alternatively, Artaud is credited with a total 'reinvention' of theatre; creating a compelling harmony from the dialectics of the theatre by transcending his own schizophrenic psychosis; aligning art to the 'solar' and 'lunar' dualities of existence and thus tapping the essence of being.[5] In either case the evidence is drawn solely from his theories. Arguments revolve around abstract concepts which are oracular, and conclusions are derived largely from different attitudes towards Artaud's extraordinary personality. On this level Artaud is all things to all men, an inspiration, for example, to the communard students of Paris in 1968 (even though he dedicated one of his poems to Hitler), because his writings are sufficiently vague to allow for almost any radical or anti-traditional interpretation.

His basic position may be clear – 'our present social state is iniquitous and should be destroyed. If this fact is a preoccupation for the theatre, it is even more a matter for machine guns'[6] – but his programme is elusive and contradictory. As Adamov has noted, there is 'something effervescent about his dramatic ideas and when one . . . thought one had grasped them they vanished'.[7] By contrast the events of his life are known, his actions and ideas are fascinating in their irrationality and his character comes strongly through his writings.

Artaud is frequently hailed as the father of modern avant garde theatre, but in fact the relationship is one of immaculate conception. His theories have acted as a catalyst, but his work on the stage has been dismissed without even being explored. The typical reaction has been that 'it is difficult to speak of a theatre that did not take place'.[8] And a somewhat dated study of Artaud (1976) by Martin Esslin is a good example of where such a premise leads. Apart from one short chapter on 'Artaudian theatre – theory and practice', in which the practice is presented as the work of Barrault, Brook, Grotowski or the Living Theatre, the whole book is a biographical portrait. Since it is published in a 'Modern Masters' series, one is left with the irony that Artaud's 'masterpiece' is his life.

This is a curious blurring of the essential distinction between art and life, without which theatre cannot exist – a distinction that Artaud's followers deny in claiming that true art can only exist as 'process' (inseparable from the continually changing experience of life), and rejecting the notion of art as 'product' (an independent artifact). Yet Artaud's theories in fact do presuppose a dialectical relationship between the stage and the world. It is perhaps indicative that the passages most frequently quoted from Artaud's writings are those with least logical sense; and statements such as 'every real effigy has a shadow which is its double'[9] are made no less gnomic by familiarity. But Artaud was capable of being more lucid. Indeed his gloss on the title for his book in a letter to his publisher preserves a clear distinction between drama and daily existence, even if it reverses the normal relationship of the stage to society: 'If the [traditional] theatre is the double of life, life is the double of the true theatre.' Material existence is seen as an imperfect copy of what art – as a higher form of reality – symbolically expresses. Clearly, this 'true theatre' will consist of something which, though it may be potential, is not present in the experience of modern man: 'The reservoir of the energies made up of myths which man no longer incarnates is incarnated in the theatre.'[10]

The Theatre and its Double shows how Artaud, feeling incapable of expressing himself with words, tended to take refuge in arcane mythologies and confused metaphors, even before his travels in Mexico. But it is only then, after his mental breakdown, that he transfers his focus from the theatre to the cosmos. He still claimed to be seeking the means to stage 'true drama', but now this is divorced from the performing arts and 'may not have anything to do with theatre on the stage'.[11] After this point Artaud, suffering from his use of drugs and obsessed by a desperate search for himself in a series of asylums and institutions, has little relevance for the theatre, whatever value his interior drama may have as poetry. Some critics have claimed his last major poem *To Have Done With the Judgement of God* (which was divided between various voices to make a radio drama in 1948) as the only true example of his Theatre of Cruelty. But this ignores explicit comments in the poem itself:

> There is nothing I loathe
> And detest as much as this idea of a play,
> Of a performance,
> Because of the appearance, the unreality,
> Attached to all that is produced and that is
> Shown . . .
> This whole broadcast was only made in order to
> Protest against so called principle of appearance
> Of unreality,
> Of a play anyhow . . . [12]

Few contemporary directors have totally escaped Artaud's influence, but there has only been one consistent attempt to test Artaud's theories in practice. Unlike such self-styled disciples as Schechner, or Beck and Malina, who adapted what ideas they borrowed to hybrid forms of their own, Peter Brook and Charles Marowitz specifically took Artaud's writings as the basis for their work in 1964. Their 'Theatre of Cruelty' experiment was designed as a training for actors, and culminated in a series of demonstration performances that included the first staging of Artaud's surrealist playlet, *The Spurt of Blood*. The results were incorporated into a production of Genet's *The Screens* and Brook's striking interpretation of Weiss' *Marat/ Sade* (see pp. 127–30 in this volume). Interestingly, the conclusion that Brook came to was indeterminate: 'you should take Artaud unadulterated as a way of life, or say that there is something in Artaud that relates to a style of theatre'. This 'something' was defined as being 'certain limited, specific – almost technical – things, the use of yoga and breathing exercises, the expression of emotion by imaginatively locating specific feelings in different parts of the body'[13] (in other words those suggestions contained in Artaud's essays which have least to do with metaphysics or the state of western culture, 'An affective athleticism' and 'The seraphim theatre').

If Artaud's essays have eclipsed his practical achievements, it is as much as anything else because they promise something much grander than could ever be achieved in practice. Artaud had the habit of exaggerating to an extreme degree: indeed, in an illuminating postscript to a letter – asking Jean Paulhan not to publish one of his theatre reviews since what he had written bore little relation to what he had seen – he commented, 'I cannot write without enthusiasm and I always go too far.'[14] This, rather than any lack of financial backing, is the reason for the gulf between Artaud's theory and his practice; and a good example of this gulf is the emphasis on drama as 'process', not finished product, in what is commonly considered 'Artaudian' theatre.

His essays (and his disciples) claim 'direct staging' and improvisation as the basis of 'true' theatre. In his outlines for productions and his own actual stagings, however, Artaud stressed that a performance should only seem to be improvised and merely 'give us the impression of not only being unexpected but also unrepeatable'[15] – a normal indeed conventional standpoint. Even his attack on language in the theatre is not what it appears. With the possible exception of Yeats, who once expressed the frustrated desire that his actors rehearse their lines in barrels (in order to make it impossible for them to substitute gestures and movements for the rhythms and sense of his poetry), one can hardly imagine any director or playwright believing that the logical meaning of words is the sole means of theatrical communication. Yet it is this (non-existent) attitude that Artaud seems to be attacking. In fact his aim was to bring every element of a performance, including the script, under his rigid control; and his rejection of dramatic texts is really an argument for a more exclusive method of recording the totality of a production. Hence his wish for a system of notating gestures, facial expressions, attitudes, movements, tonal variations and breathing, and his search for ways of making these subtleties of expression exact, controllable and reproducible. What he wanted was 'a work written down, fixed in its least details' so that the 'final result' would be 'as strict and calculated as that of any written work' since 'the theatre, less than any other means of expression, will not suffer improvisation'.[16]

This did not mean that Artaud approached a script with a preconceived interpretation, or with moves already blocked out. According to actors who worked with him, he required that initially every line become a basis for 'free fantasizing', and that whatever emotional states might be evoked were translated directly into physical terms. Yet free expression was not encouraged. Rather he acted out all the roles himself, and imposed a uniform (if highly idiosyncratic) style by demonstration. The moves, gestures and intonations arrived at were then carefully noted and rehearsed so that there was nothing accidental about the final performance, however frenetic and arbitrary the effect might have seemed. As Raymond Rouleau, who acted the part of the Officer in Artaud's production of *A Dream Play*, noted:

> He did not prepare his productions in any precise way . . . His direction was a kind of introspection; he seemed to listen attentively to the promptings of his subconscious. At the first rehearsal, Artaud rolled around on the stage, assumed a falsetto voice, contorted himself, howled, and fought against logic, order, and the 'well-made' approach . . . When he felt that he had found the truth, which his interior voyage had disclosed to him, he fixed it very meticulously.[17]

From Artaud's early programmes of the Théâtre Alfred Jarry to Roger Blin's production notes in the prompt book of *The Cenci*,[18] what was stressed was disciplined precision and strictly organized performance. Even Balinese theatre was not just an ideal example of magical and mythological drama. It was equally valuable to Artaud for the 'reflective mathematics' of its precise gestures, regulated and impersonal, 'all producing methodically calculated effects which forbid any recourse to spontaneous improvisation'.[19] In the light of his stage work, it becomes clear that, even when he refers to theatre as 'not . . . an end but a means',[20] Artaud is simply transferring the emphasis from the play as such, to its effect on the audience's imagination. A performance still has to be a finished product: the 'process' takes place in the spectator's perception of it.

Not surprisingly, Artaud's theoretical writings overshadow his practical work in the theatre. But his primary intention was to create a new theatre through 'concrete examples', concrete (that is, what was physically representable) being one of his key adjectives. Other manifestos of the time, dadaist or surrealist, are mainly proclamations of principle. Set beside them his commitment to practice – expressed in the specific programme of works in his first manifesto, and the detailed scenario in his second – is striking. And it is in line with this that he announced that the public should look for the ideas of the Théâtre Alfred Jarry in its performances: 'better than any theories, our programme is there to make our intentions manifest'.[21]

Basing conclusions about Artaud's work on just the three full-length productions and four one-act plays that he managed to stage between 1927 and 1935 would be foolhardy, particularly when the text of one, *Burnt Breast* (*Ventre brûlé ou la mère folle*), is missing and the descriptions of sometimes highly prejudiced reviewers have to be relied on for many details. But if his scenarios both for screen and stage, the suggested production outlines that he submitted to Jouvet and Dullin, and his work in film are taken into account, then it is possible to reconstruct a fairly complete outline of his theatre.

Artaud's basic insight was that theatrical reality is different in kind from ordinary reality – that it is self-defeating for the stage to attempt to copy everyday life. As with the expressionists or surrealists, this reaction against naturalism implies a rejection of the philosophical assumptions of western civilization. Compare his earliest example of 'ideal theatre' in the original manifesto for the Théâtre Alfred Jarry – a police raid on a brothel – and his use of colonization as the theme for *The Conquest of Mexico* scenario in his last manifesto for the Theatre of Cruelty.

Both subjects have sexual overtones, and deal with basic human drives that arouse highly ambivalent responses. Both represent forms of exploitation that society disguises, but do so objectively as a 'spectacle' without a moral standpoint. Each shows a large number of people in conflict, which is one way of focusing on the event rather than the individual, and uses patterns of movement to suck the audience emotionally into the action. In Artaud's actual stage work the 'cruelty', which appears as a definition of existence in his metaphysical writings, is no more than an agent to heighten response by magnification: similar to Jarry's use of *grand guignol*. It is in fact the dynamics that are primary, not any intrinsic violence: 'the spectator . . . will be shaken and set on edge by the *internal dynamism* of the spectacle.'[22]

It is this dynamism that was Artaud's major concern in staging his only full-length play, *The Cenci* (1935). Although based on historical events – via Stendhal and Shelley – this is not just 'a tragedy' in Artaud's view. In his rather idiosyncratic terms it was a 'Myth', because it embodies his Sadean vision of 'cruelty'. Spirituality is a delusive ideal formulated by the weak to subjugate the strong. It inverts true values in condemning the universal 'laws' of instinct as evil, while elevating as 'good' a perversion of nature that prevents man from realizing his full potential. And this debilitating idealism is epitomized in Christianity, which 'consists of ascending into the sky as spirit instead of descending deeper and deeper as a body into hell, that is into sexuality, soul of all that lives'.[23] Hence Artaud's choice of a story that deals with the destruction of the heroine's soul, and is set in the context of the medieval age of faith. Hence, too, the characterization of the figures as 'incarnations of great forces' to be judged (à la Nietzsche) 'outside of good and evil'.[24]

Artaud reduced the traditional plot to an outline of brutal simplicity by cutting the self-justification and self-analysis, the tremors of motive or conscience out of which conventional dramatic psychology is built up. Count Cenci, who identifies himself with destiny, obeying his 'own law' as 'a force of nature', has the sole ambition of personifying absolute evil. He holds an orgiastic banquet for the rulers of Church and State where he symbolically drinks the blood of his sons, celebrating their destruction by God for which he has prayed, in a parody of the Mass. He rapes his own daughter Beatrice, who is driven to murder him, immediately arrested, tortured, then executed. The effect of Cenci's practice of evil is to liberate the demonic in all the people around him; and the nature of the crimes about which the play revolves, incest and parricide, break the deepest taboos and most fundamental social relationships – those of the family – being given their particularly horrifying character by Artaud's stress on Cenci's status as a father. But it is here that the logic of the play's statement falls apart, since Artaud also uses the image of fatherhood to represent social repression in the form of God the Father, and his regent on earth, the Pope, who refuses to intervene against Cenci:

> 'Am I to set myself up against the natural authority of a father? Am
> I to enfeeble in this manner the principle of my own authority?' Then
> he answered himself: 'No, never.'

Thus God is both 'the cruel necessity of creation' that Cenci embodies, and the Christian divinity he rebels against; the Pope is both as criminal as Cenci, and the epitome of right-thinking society; while even Cenci has a contradictory dual signification, not only 'a demon whose task is to avenge the whole world's sins' against nature, but also a figure symbolizing those 'sins' as the representative of the social structure that denies man's true being. Coherence of vision is obviously not as important to Artaud as the intensity, passion and extremity of the action, just as the script itself is only a framework to be filled with 'a whole language of gestures and signs in which the anxieties of the age will blend together in a sort of violent manifestation of feeling'.[25]

However, there is little sense of violence or cruelty in the 'scenic rhythms' that Artaud had defined as the most important aspect of the theatre's language. And the *Cenci* prompt book contains more notes on patterning and tempo (the controlling elements of a production) than on any other aspect. The banquet scene demonstrates the effect most clearly, since it employs the largest number of figures: not only all the characters but – echoing Jarry's *Ubu roi* – life-size dummies as well. The opening stage directions in the published text, with their reference to Veronese's painting of *The Marriage at Cana* (also underlining the sacrilegious theme), suggest a static tableau which erupts into chaotic movement. But the notes made by Roger Blin, who collaborated on the production and acted the part of one of the murderers, show that this movement was highly organized.

Starting from a hierarchic pattern of order in three ranks of three, the guests danced in circles of carefully gradated size and speed. The smaller the circle the slower it moved, with the dancers in the wider circles curving around and through the others. Superimposed on this was a repeated vocal pattern – a cry, followed by a laugh, then a sob – and the formalized effect was heightened by being contrasted with the erratic caperings of a dwarf. There was also an overt element of depersonalization, since certain of the guests were dancing with dummies. The impression aimed at is a dehumanized mechanization, which Artaud compared to the workings of a clock – the opposite to what one normally expects from 'a scene of orgy'. This openly inorganic structure was carried through even into small gestures. For example, when Count Cenci entered, the guests, now arranged in two parallel rows on each side of the set, threw glances at each other diagonally across the stage in an alternating and duplicating sequence. All the actors were required to move as a part of a whole, either in progressions – as when Andrea approaches with the goblet and Blin's note reads 'G, 3 paces; F, 2 paces; E, 1 big pace; J, 1 little pace . . .' – in opposition, or in unison – as when a guest calls for '. . . torches to light my way; I am leaving':

> Here Beatrice draws herself erect. Lucretia droops. Everyone rises. All throw themselves into the centre then draw apart when Cenci says to them: 'Wait.' They move in groups to the right, to the left . . . all rise, they take one pace . . . take 2 paces . . .

This calculated symmetry, which Artaud calls variously a 'dizzying' or 'inhuman rhythm', is undoubtedly how he would have staged even the most apparently chaotic scenes in *The Conquest of Mexico*. Take Montezuma's rebellion, where space is described as

> . . . gorged with a brawling mosaic where sometimes men, sometimes compact troops tightly pressed together, limb to limb, clash frenetically. Space is stuffed with whirling gestures, clenched fists, manes, breastplates, and from all levels of the scene fall limbs, breastplates, heads, stomachs like a hailstorm bombarding the earth with supernatural explosions.[26]

What sounds orgiastically wild on the page would have been organized into a similar dynamic of clearly defined patterns, as the inconspicuous 'mosaic' and 'whirling' indicate.

Artaud took considerable pride in the 'precision' and 'rigour' of the movements worked out for *The Cenci*; and when he referred to the 'mathematical comings and goings of the actors around others which traces in the air of the stage a true geometry',[27] he was being quite literal. Actions were broken down into mathematical sequences throughout the production. Mass movements were based on simple geometric forms, which would be instantly recognizable to the audience: parallels, circles or triangles. For instance, when the published stage directions state that the guests 'are huddled in one corner', Artaud's notes translate this into: 'Colonna places himself on the right, the others fan out into a triangle behind him . . . each, all together and very marked, one pace. . . .' These movements are even worked out to give the impression of familiar laws of gravity. For example, when the guests 'surge back from all sides in disorder. Panic stricken . . .', Artaud choreographed the actors into a pattern based on centrifugal forces:

> Colonna returns towards the guests who each describe a spiralling circle. Colonna moves in a large circle around them . . . as this whirlpool comes to an end the men find themselves flung outside the circle, the women in a heap in the centre.

The dynamics of these movements have a very precise and surprising (in view of Artaud's attacks on rationality) intellectual content. In a very real sense they carry the meaning of the play through symbolism; and in fact Artaud gave an explicit symbolic meaning to the dominant image of the circle, which forms the pattern for the majority of individual and group movements, and culminates in the torture wheel on which Beatrice swings. It directly represents both the 'circular and closed world' that Artaud associated with cruelty, and the force of necessity, the 'gravitational movement' of that world.[28]

Artaud, who named his theatre after Alfred Jarry, is after a similar effect to the hallucinatory distortions of the *Ubu* plays in the way he organizes his alternative stage world by substituting the laws of the mind for those of physics. Geometry is an abstract summing up of how we see our material environment. As such it determines our estimate of our positions *vis à vis* objects, our orientation to reality. By applying geometric shapes to a vision of anarchy and primitive excess, which would make the perspectives on life that they represent seem artificial and arbitrary, Artaud could hope to make his audience uncertain of their familiar assumptions about the physical universe. Simultaneously the dynamism is intended to draw the audience in, to involve them in this stage world, while the rigidly patterned movements give this imaginary creation a visually logical structure analogous to the way we customarily view reality. This was Artaud's way of creating an 'actuality of feeling and thoughts more than of facts' – discrediting our conventional concept of reality, while using its basic organizational principles as subliminal support for an alternative vision: 'reality seen simultaneously from recto and verso. Hallucination chosen as the principle dramatic means.'[29]

FORM AND THEME

It is a commonplace that Artaud's scripts and scenarios are mental dramas: the Mexican revolt against Cortez for instance, which takes place simultaneously on the historical plane and on 'every level of Montezuma's consciousness' with the struggle of white against red, repressive civilization against primitive instinct, is explicitly located as a 'battleground in the mind of Montezuma'. But it is incorrect to assume that his work is purely subjective, a realization of his own (increasingly precarious) psychological state. It is certainly true that Artaud was involved in his productions to such a degree that Barrault accused him of lacking 'sufficient distance' to stage a play successfully.[30] He also projected himself totally into a role like that of Count Cenci, and even claimed that there should be an identity between the psychology of the actor and his part, putting himself forward as the only person capable of doing justice to the figure of Usher in a film version of Poe's story on the grounds that his personal experience of mental illness fitted him for playing characters in torment.

Yet apart from one early film scenario, *Eighteen Seconds*, where the central figure has strong autobiographical features (being an actor suffering from a mental breakdown), Artaud's stage world was not intended to be a psychological reflection, but to achieve an objective existence. From the opening of the Théâtre Alfred Jarry with Roger Vitrac's *The Mysteries of Love* – when Artaud claimed that 'for the first time a real dream has been produced in the theatre'[31] – to his essays on cruelty, dreams are set beyond the personal by being consistently qualified with adjectives like 'true', 'concrete', 'the theatre's dreams'.

The expressionism of *The Road to Damascus*, then, was not Artaud's road. But there is a definite link between his aims and the way Strindberg was perceived in France, since his term 'cruelty' was first coined to describe *Miss Julie*.[32] In spite of Artaud's rejection of psychological subject matter and 'research into human personalities' as being 'what disgusts us most',[33] the surrealist ideal of staging dreams led him inevitably to Strindberg. And in his experimental production of *A Dream Play* (1928) he developed some of his most characteristic techniques.

When his earlier productions qualified as dreams, it seems to have been because of a certain thematic quality. *The Mysteries of Love* (1927) with its violent and unmotivated action, its illogicality and the suspension of cause and effect (as when a murdered man reappears laughing), as well as its direct assault on the audience (ending with a spectator 'killed' by a shot from the stage), is described as a 'real dream'. And its value for Artaud was that it 'realized on the stage the anxiety, the mutual isolation, the criminal ulterior motives and the eroticism of lovers'[34] – a parodistic synthesis of spiritual ideals and animality which also found expression in Vitrac's *Victor*. In this, the stage effect that Artaud seemed to have prized most was a Jarryesque offence to sensibility – the contrast between the beauty of the leading actress and requiring her to break wind every time she spoke. Although childishly scatological, the critics commented with disgust, while the first actress engaged for the part resigned loudly when she found out what was required.

Vitrac is one of the few successful playwrights produced by the surrealist movement. The dramatic output of Aragon, Breton or Ribemont-Dessaignes is hardly conceived in stage terms; and the surrealist principle of rejecting any connection between art and the material world is inconsistent with the physical nature of theatrical presentation. Artaud's expulsion from the surrealist movement (together with Vitrac), which forms the background to the surrealists' disruption of Artaud's *Dream Play* production, was inevitable. His concentration on staging was seen as a betrayal; and the aesthetic quarrel was further complicated by Breton's conversion to communism, which led Artaud to declare: 'In the theatre only what is theatrical interests me, to use the theatre to launch any revolutionary idea (except in the realm of the spirit) appears to me the most base and repulsive opportunism.'[35] Yet Artaud continued to follow the basic surrealist line. Thus his aim of creating 'profound transformations on the level of appearances, in the values of signification' by using the material of dreams and the subconscious to spark off 'that intense liberation' or 'metamorphosis of the inner condition of the soul' which can 'push back reality' ('À la grande nuit ou le bluff surrealiste', June 1927, a pamphlet rebutting Breton's attack on his work in 'Au grand jour') is a restatement of an early proposal, welcomed by the surrealists, that in his ideal theatre 'all that is dark, buried deep, unrevealed in the mind, should be manifested in a sort of physical projection, as real'.[36]

With such aims it was natural that the Théâtre Alfred Jarry should become the interpreter of Vitrac, who had described his work as subconscious images for a 'Theatre of Conflagration'. The most effective example of this is Vitrac's *Victor, or the Children Take Power* (1929). The title indicates the thematic inversion of conventional values; and the action is a Jarryesque mixture: simultaneously a parody of boulevard drama, and a dream. The total experience of life is telescoped into a bare three hours for the outsize Victor – 6 ft tall and visibly growing during the performance – on the evening of his ninth birthday. Brought face to face with the hypocrisy of his parents' bourgeois society, he changes from a model child to an anarchistic iconoclast. He smashes Sèvres china, disrupts his father's adulterous romances (the bourgeoisie epitomized in the clichés of Feydeau farce), and drives their cuckolded neighbour (patriotism in the shape of an ex-soldier from the 1870 Franco-Prussian war) to hang himself in uniform trousers and nightshirt from his flagstaff to the tinny sound of a military march on a gramophone. Finally Victor elects to die because experiencing every aspect of existence has shown him there is nothing worth living for. The distortions of time and scale, together with syntactical dislocations and nonsense language, reach a peak in the father's erotic daydream, where the figures from a soft-porn serialized romance (*Les Hommes de l'air*, 'a novel of sport and love') take on more reality than the 'real life' characters. The focal point in Artaud's production was Ida Mortemart, the ethereal *femme fatale* with a gross physical disability. Her entry signals a psychic liberation, even for Victor's socially repressed father, whose speech breaks through into stream of consciousness – 'Ida Mortemart, croupissant comme la mer Morte . . . Ida, dada, Ida, dada, Morte? Mortemart? J'en ai marre, marre, marre'[37] – and the power of dream to affect the real world was demonstrated by throwing stink bombs across the footlights every time she farted. This was also intended to bring home 'the poisonous effect of matter and moral grief' that 'spiritually crucified' the potential 'intelligence and superiority of the other world' that the dream woman represents.[38]

There are structural parallels between *The Mysteries of Love* and *A Dream Play*; and Vitrac still claimed to be following Strindberg in *Victor*, calling him 'one of the most admirable liberators of the mind'.[39] But here Strindberg's influence is only retained in a general emphasis on the falsity of external appearances, contrasted with the reality of dream states, and (following Artaud's defence against the surrealist disruption of his *Dream Play* production) in the negative aim of 'vomiting on his fatherland, on all nations, on society'. As the father's verbal associations on the name of Ida proclaim, it was dada that determined the way Vitrac developed Strindberg's concepts; and dadaist influence was already clear in *Poison* (1923), where the twelfth tableau which 'depicts a mouth that pretends to speak'[40] echoes Tristan Tzara's *Gas Heart* (1920).

The dada movement was not simply the artistic iconoclasm that it is still frequently seen as today. In Berlin, its attack on bourgeois principles had a positive political rationale. In Paris, dada shared the surrealist belief that the free flow of imagination and release of the subconscious could liberate the individual from repression. And beneath even the most negative statement of the dada attitude lie values of spontaneity, intuitive response, creative irrationalism and immediacy that the surrealist manifestoes also proclaimed:

Every product of disgust capable of becoming a negation of the family is Dada; a protest with the fists of its whole being engaged in

71

destructive action: Dada; knowledge of all the means rejected up until now by the shamefaced sex of comfortable compromise and good manners: Dada; abolition of logic, which is the dance of those impotent to create . . . Dada; abolition of memory . . . Dada; abolition of the future: Dada; absolute and unquestionable faith in every god that is the immediate product of spontaneity.[41]

The lines between the two movements in fact are almost indistinguishable when Tzara describes his artistic aim as embodying 'the forms, common to all men, of that poetic activity whose deep roots draw on the primitive structure of affective life'; and looking back on his activities after a quarter of a century, Tzara put the dadaist 'will to destroy' in its true perspective: 'much more of an aspiration toward purity and sincerity than the tendency toward a sort of vocal or plastic inanity, satisfied with stasis and absence.'[42]

Traces of dada can be seen too in an early work of Artaud's like *Burnt Breast*, when he was just beginning to formulate his theories of cruelty. Part of the same bill as *The Mysteries of Love*, this play can only be reconstructed from hints provided by reviews. It contained a typical dadaist parody of conventional authority symbols, such as a king and queen, and of the materialistic society that offers only surrogate experience, in bizarre figures like 'the Horn of Plenty' or 'the Hollywood Mystery'. But these were combined with surrealist elements that already show Artaud's attraction to the primitive and ritualistic. While Vitrac's play is fairly literary, although the protagonist demands that the author write plays without words and is told to spit out the words put into his mouth, *Burnt Breast* was almost pure mime, with dialogue limited to single words or isolated sentences that were apparently delivered with such overcharged emphasis as to be (deliberately?) incomprehensible. However, both plays shared the same disregard for cause-and-effect logic. Modern life was represented by a man suffering extremes of ennui despite the material plenty poured by a cornucopia in female shape. A violent storm announces the entry of another woman, embodying the celluloid fantasies of Hollywood, and gives the signal for wild dancing (variously described as a tango or a fox-trot) which culminates in the death of the king. His queen steps disdainfully over his body with a vulgar comment about cuckolds, and the performance ends in a long funeral procession that dances around the stage with flaring candles to what was obviously intended as primitive and atavistic music.

However little justice such a bare-bones description does to the play, it would need to have been acted with extraordinary skill to be effective. But with *A Dream Play*, new perspectives opened; and it was the work on this production which brought Artaud to formulate his idea of a stage reality quite separate from naturalistic illusion:

Nothing is less capable of deluding us than the illusion of fake properties, of cardboard and painted canvas which the modern scene gives us . . . There is in the simple exposition of real objects, in their combinations, in their order, in the relationships of the human voice with light, a reality which is self-sufficient and has no need of any other to live. It is this false reality which is theatre and it's that which it is necessary to cultivate . . . The false in the context of the true, that is the ideal definition of this *mise en scène*.[43]

The effect in this particular production was crude. The highly stylized acting was presented on a bare stage with a screen for projections as the only scenery, and an ordinary ladder for the ascent into heaven: an uncomfortable clash of fluid abstraction and overliteral concreteness. But working on Strindberg was seminal for Artaud's development. On one level it led to the parody of naturalistic conventions, as in the first act of Vitrac's *Victor* where Artaud suspended empty window, door and picture-frames from the proscenium in order literally to create a fourth wall and so make the spectators' role as 'voyeurs' explicit. More to the point, it resulted in his use of real objects for the decor instead of either the customary pretence of flats and backcloth, or the conventional way of representing dreams by impressionistic, atmospheric vagueness. These objects were not symbolic in the way the 'Horn of Plenty', coffin or crowns of *Burnt Breast* had been. They gained significance from being out of scale, or out of context; and where symbols were called for they were presented as deliberately artificial.

Artaud's production proposals for *The Ghost Sonata* provide a good example of this use of the stage. In Strindberg's play there is a surface level of 'crime and secrets and guilt', which corresponds to the adulterous or corrupting past revealed by the action of plays like Ibsen's *Ghosts*. But here the patterns of guilt are so complex and convoluted that they act as a parody of typically naturalistic concerns, exaggerated to a point where they become unreal. The play moves inward from the street to 'the hyacinth room', growing progressively more grotesque as the action becomes internalized. Fake social roles are peeled away, with a monstrous Old Man stripping a Colonel of his spurious family name, uniform, wig and false teeth – only to be unmasked himself as a murderer by the mummified corpse of a dead woman – until the physical world becomes transparent and we reach the dream level of subconscious reality. Here the embodiment of material existence appears – a vampire cook who drains the spirit of its vitality – and the saviour Student liberates the Hyacinth Girl from life by making her realize that 'she was withering away in this air charged with crime and deceit and falseness of every kind'.[44]

Corresponding to this, the settings Artaud envisaged were to be representational, though not naturalistic. The street for Act I was to have been composed of three-dimensional freestanding houses lining two streets receding up a hill, but with subtly conflicting perspectives, and details picked out in unnatural clarity. Various objects – the fountain, a cornice, perhaps a window or a pot of flowers – were to function as focal points, highlit with '. . . an intense halo of light. Most would be larger than life . . . the paving stones in the street climbing in the background in sharp relief as in a cinema set.' In some ways this corresponds to Otto Falckenberg's expressionist production of the play, in which physical details were exaggerated, with the cook carrying an oversized ladle and sauce bottle and with the clock dwarfing the characters. But Artaud's hallucinatory mix of actuality and distortion was a logical extension of the way he had staged *The Mysteries of Love*, where an early concern for the geometrical patterning that characterized *The Cenci* was also already evident:

> For the first time on the stage real objects could be seen: a bed, a cupboard, a stove, a coffin, all subject to a surrealist order, which is disorder in terms of ordinary reality, responding to the profound logic of the dream at the point where it abruptly materializes in life. Multicoloured lights responded to the same strange logic, to an identical preoccupation with equilibrium and musicality.

The same selective heightening of reality was carried over into Artaud's characterization. Strindberg's desiccated mummy was conceived as a perfectly ordinary, elderly, high-society widow, with the desired effect of horror being created by a subtle contrast between the visual impression of normality and her unnatural, poetic lines, delivered in a special voice. This would probably have repeated the effect Artaud had achieved with Genica Athanasiou's acting of Lea in *The Mysteries of Love* – not the artificial and dissonant vocalization of Jarry's *Ubu roi*, but rather: 'a gilded, quivering, mysterious voice . . . the true voice of archaic Greece, when in the depths of the labyrinth Minos sees the sudden crystalization of the Minotaur in the virgin's flesh.'[45]

The intention was to lift the action onto a visionary level. Together with the conventional appearance of the characters, being seen as independent of the inner personality, as an autonomous and objectified surface, this would make the audience question their assumptions about social reality. Similarly 'the acting should give at times the impression of slow motion in film', the effect being to make us aware of the musculature of motion while paradoxically divorcing this from its function. So the details we never normally see, broken down into separate elements, become real, while the overall movement seems illusory. By contrast an overt symbol such as the monstrous, life-sucking cook was deliberately artificial, being (literally) an object and one which could only be given movement, personality, purpose through the individual imagination of each spectator: 'The character of the cook will be represented by a mannequin and its speeches projected in an enormous and monotone voice through several loud speakers in such a way that it isn't possible to perceive the source exactly.'

The consistent principle is that the objects should be understood for what they actually are in an immediate sense. They are not transposed into intellectual signifiers. A movement is a series of motions. A street is built up of separate paving stones. A symbol is a symbol. Even where there is to be deliberate distortion, this is created by exaggerating a normal perception: say, the effect of reflections on glass or unexpected sound-proofing, setting totally silent movement in one area against the ordinary sounds of life on the rest of the stage, as in Act III where

> to the right and rear the little round salon will be set up, separated from the front of the stage by a large glass comparable to those of windows in department stores, of such a kind that everything which happens behind it will be flat and as if deformed in water; and above all no noise will come from this part of the stage.[46]

The mixture of magic realism and Daliesque distortion in this *mise en scène* is clearly intended to be hallucinatory. But it is worth noting that it is through a conviction of reality (in theatrical terms), rather than pretence (in terms of life), that this dislocation of perception and freeing of responses is to be achieved.

These techniques were extended in Artaud's subsequent stage work, scenarios and production outlines. *The Cenci*, for example, has distortions in scale (miniature men in armour 'like the figures on the face of the great

Figure 9 The Cenci. Evocative setting and the transposition of reality. Note also the stylized and choreographed movement.

clock of Strasbourg cathedral'), cinematic slow motion (characters 'moving extraordinarily slowly . . . walking at the same statue-like pace'), contrasts between mannequins and living actors, and juxtapositions of the everyday with the abnormal (as in the torture prison which 'sounds just like a busy factory').[47] In Artaud's production the acting was highly stylized, with the figures in the Banquet Scene presented as animals to symbolize the bestial nature of society beneath the fine robes. Similarly the setting isolated significant objects. It distorted perspectives through Escher-like staircases built on opposing diagonals, and was constructed of three-dimensional shapes which were evocative rather than naturalistic. As one impressed reviewer described it:

> a décor at once interior, symbolic and Italianate in which everything falls into place with extreme simplicity and force . . . The built-up scenery on which people walk is essentially architectonic and is reminiscent of a gigantic prison palace by Piranese . . . there is a scaffolding like a huge ladder and a round column against the sky which raises the Cenci palace to a frightening height.[48]

Sound effects in *The Cenci* were designed to have the same qualities as the visual elements of the production: unmistakable reality, heightened and transposed. The dialogue was neither conversational nor conventionally dramatic, but orchestrated for musical effect, and with the delivery formalized to create clear rhythms. Noises-off were as far as possible real sounds, rather than rolling a barrel in the wings for thunder, but, like the speeches, lifted out of their expected context. For example, although borrowing huge bells from a church proved impractical (to Artaud's disappointment), he still insisted on actual bells, making a recording of peals from a specific cathedral and then amplifying the reality of this sound by projecting it through loudspeakers at all four corners of the theatre. So the spectator was placed in 'a net of sonorous vibrations', set in an unusual and overwhelming relationship with the familiar. This effect was also used to transpose the characters directly into the audience's minds, with the performers' steps at times accompanied by recorded footsteps, amplified at full volume over the loudspeakers surrounding the auditorium and given symbolic resonance by the beat of a metronome oscillating at different speeds. The footfalls must have echoed like rhythmic stamping in the audience's skulls.

Similarly, the musical accompaniment by Roger Desormière came from an electronic keyboard capable of producing a far wider range of sounds than orchestral instruments. Being free of the 'art' connotations of conventional music it could only be called 'Musique Concrète' – sounds organized into patterns instead of notes composed into tunes – though in fact its structural principles were based on the seven-beat rhythms of Inca music and intended to give a primitive, exotic tone. Artaud summed up Desormière's achievement as managing 'to catch the noise of machines in an urban factory which would not be out of place in a torture chamber of the Middle Ages'; and indeed this impression came across. Reviewers found themselves unable to describe the music except by comparison to 'Negro fan-fares at the Exposition Coloniale' or 'the cry and the railway catastrophe'.[49]

This stress on actuality portrayed with hallucinatory precision, or perceived from unusual angles (and doubly unnatural in the theatrical context of pretence) is the keynote of Artaud's approach. Where figures are overt symbols, they are presented on a purely symbolic plane as 'concrete images' – like the 16 ft high mannequins proposed to Jouvet for the dream scene in a play by Alfred Savoir, which were to have recognizable faces of French politicians but carried such props as the Arc de Triomphe on their shoulders, or like the giant mask of the head of Montezuma in *The Conquest of Mexico*. With live actors, Artaud's aim was to create a new sense of man and his relationship to the universe through distortions of scale, movement, perspective – as with Cortez and his men larger than their ships, or the crowd forming patterns out of 'diverse and contradictory movements as an ant heap seen from very high up'.[50] Verbal expression and gesture were always heightened and unnatural, while real noises were used for sound effects, as in the *mise en scène* submitted to Jouvet for Vitrac's *Battle of Trafalgar*. Here, instead of attempting to reproduce the sound of a crowd of one hundred thousand with ten extras, an actual mob was to be recorded on disc then amplified through loudspeakers 'in all parts of the stage and auditorium'. The proposed set of this production was also typical. Houses and streets were to be constructed 'in relief . . . like a film set', or seen from a viewpoint foreign to the stage: 'The scene will appear through a cutout in a wall, not painted but showing on one of its sides its true thickness, as in certain film sets'.[51] It would have been along the lines of these examples that Artaud's lost play, *The Torture of Tantalus*, was intended to create 'a new reality' out of '*extreme* realism'.[52]

THE INFLUENCE OF FILM

The constant comparison to film is significant, and its relationship to Artaud's work was obvious enough for reviewers to apply the expectations and standards of cinema (usually unfavourably) to his stage productions – as for instance one comment on *A Dream Play*: 'This performance has confirmed me in the opinion that dreams or nightmares should go back to being the property of the cinema.'[53] Yet surprisingly little critical attention has been paid to the influence of Artaud's film experience on his theatre. His film career, where dealt with at all, is treated as completely separate to his theatrical experiments, and the only cross-references that have been made are tantalizing in their incompleteness.[54] But to see the one in terms of the other can be illuminating.

His early film scenarios and *The Shell and the Clergyman* (1927) pre-date the Théâtre Alfred Jarry, while his film acting and script writing continued throughout the period when he was formulating his 'Theatre of Cruelty'. In 1928 he was praising film as the new art form, through which alone his ideas could be realized; and it was only in 1933 with his essay on 'The premature old age of the cinema' that he rejected the screen – not as a medium in itself, but because it had become commercialized, turning art and artists into 'commodities', and because he saw the 'talking cinema' as 'an absurdity. The negation of cinema itself.'[55] The silent film was seminal for Artaud. Not only can its influence be traced in his stage work. It also explains the nature of some of his techniques, and accounts for why certain aspects of his productions were less than successful.

The relationship between the sort of reality that is accessible to the senses (the physical world of matter), and the 'mystical reality' of emotion and spirit (the instinctual world of the unconscious) is frequently referred to by Artaud in his discussions of cinema. His estimate of 'the present epoch' wavers from a belief that no time in history has been a better seeding ground for 'sorcerers and saints', because of the reaction against nineteenth-century materialism, to a conviction that the feeling for anything but the immediate and materialistic has been 'lost'. But film always lies in the interstices of this equation; and its development as an art form is seen as a direct response to what Artaud thought was the twentieth century's inability to communicate with words, or to represent life in conventional artistic forms. 'True cinema' for him was not representational, not story telling. Nor was it abstract or psychologically based. It was the camera's power to focus the attention on apparently insignificant objects that was important to Artaud. This could not only heighten details into images, but also make the inanimate seem alive, while cutting could create metamorphoses and rhythms through which the physical world became a subliminal image. As in the expressionistic film of *The Cabinet of Dr Caligari*, human figures could be stripped of their all too solid flesh and appear as phantoms in settings which were the shadows of the mind. For many critics of the time, this instant classic epitomized the nature of cinema as an art form, which led to the conclusion that 'film requires the ultimate in exaggerated and rhythmic gestures, in the expressive possibilities for transformation and variation inherent in the screen'.[56]

At one stage Artaud considered that this new art form, as a 'remarkable excitant', would relegate theatre to 'the wardrobe of memory', and it seems to have been only when commercial pressures turned it into a 'hybrid' art through substituting words for images that he began to work for 'total spectacle' on the stage – in conscious opposition to talking cinema.[57] But, not unnaturally perhaps, he attempted to transfer to the stage those unique cinematographic elements which gave film the 'magical' ability to transform the world into an alternate reality. Practically all his theatrical devices discussed so far correspond to film techniques, which Artaud believed acted directly on the brain. His description of *The Shell and the Clergyman* as 'the mechanism of a dream' is equally applicable to his structuring of theatrical performances. The spotlighting of objects in *The Ghost Sonata*, or the perspective through a hole in the wall in *The Battle of Trafalgar* is the equivalent of camera focus. The rhythms of movement in *The Cenci*, or the flying transformations of images in *The Conquest of Mexico* are intended to gain the same effect as cinematic cutting and montage. Even his plastic concept of sound (as in the stage directions to *There Are No Heavens Anymore*, where sound is described as falling 'from very high' and splashing 'widely out, forming arches, parasols'[58]) is related to his film experience.

The parallels between film and stage are perhaps most obvious in his use (or disuse) of dialogue: single words as the catalyst for extended movement, cries as an accompaniment for action – all of which corresponds very closely to the use of subtitles in early silent cinema. Being brief sentences or single words, these were limited to the key phrase of a whole conversation, the summing up of a complex emotional situation already acted out in a physical movement or a facial expression on the screen, or sometimes an editorial statement independent of the characters – and always, like small placards, they were presented in visual terms. Artaud was not so unrealistic as to think the theatre available to him was technically capable of achieving the fluid freedom of the cinema in moulding images; and much of the dialogue in his full-length play, *The Cenci*, functions conventionally in building character, expressing thought, explaining situation. Yet his film scenario, *The Butcher's Revolt*, indicates what Artaud was working toward in the theatre. This can be seen as an attempt to come to terms with talking cinema by using dialogue to extend the effect of subtitles. All the speeches are short; and some are separated from the scenario by being printed centre-page with a surrounding border. As Artaud announces in the introduction:

> The words pronounced have only been put there to make the images reverberate. The voices are there in space like objects . . . Voices and sounds [are organized] on the visual plane . . . in and for themselves and not as the physical consequence of a movement or an act.[59]

Some of the films Artaud acted in are as influential for his theatrical ideas as his own scenarios. He placed a great deal of importance on his major roles – Marat in Abel Gance's *Napoléon*, Massieu in Carl Dreyer's *Passion of Joan of Arc* and the Intellectual in Léon Poirier's *Verdun*. And some of the techniques, even the atmosphere of these films, can be paralleled in his stage projects. *Napoléon*, a landmark in the cinema's technical development, used simultaneous projection on three screens, the central action being flanked by rhythmically repeated images to give a subliminal impression of energy, transmitting emotion through movement. Gance also sought to involve the audience by giving the camera the viewpoint of the characters. He set the camera in motion on the saddle of a galloping horse, threw it from a cliff for Napoleon's dive into the sea and identified it with the emotional rhythms of the action – as when he attached the camera to the chest of a tenor while recording the Girondins singing the 'Marseillaise', so that the filmed scene pulsated with his breath. *The Passion of Joan of Arc* was originally intended to be a talking film. But, since there were no studios equipped for sound in Paris in 1927, Dreyer used close-ups and all the expressive possibilities of camera angles to compensate. The faces of the actors were without make-up to accentuate the interior play of thought or emotion, and to give the impression of reality – by contrast with the more usual film practice of the time where actors were made up as for the stage. Dreyer's comments on the film are remarkably like some of Artaud's statements about his stage intentions: 'I seek nothing but life itself . . . what is important is not the objective drama of images but the subjective drama of souls.'[60] And according to one observer, the cast became so emotionally involved in the production that there was a remarkable merging of fictional action and reality.

This account is worth quoting, because in many ways it represents Artaud's aim of creating a hallucinatory or alternate reality, which he was developing less than a year later in his work on *A Dream Play*. It also helps to explain his insistence on the director's control of every detail of a production, though here the effect was on the performers rather than on an audience. Apparently the atmosphere created on the set was so effective that the actors,

> caught up by the will-power and faith of the director remained unconsciously in their roles after the shooting had finished . . . living the drama as if it were actuality . . . Particularly impressive was the day when, in a silence as of an operating theatre, in a pale light as of the morning of an execution, Falconetti's [Joan's] hair was cut close-cropped to the scalp. Our sensibilities . . . were moved as if the mark of infamy had been carried out in reality. The electricians, the mechanics held their breath and their eyes were full of tears.[61]

Despite Artaud's emphasis on them, his roles in these films were relatively minor. Marat was a bit-part in an epic treatment of the revolution, which included the deaths of Robespierre and Saint-Juste as well as Marat, and covered Napoleon's career from infancy. Massieu, Joan's confessor, only appeared in scenes with Falconetti where the dramatic focus was on her. The Intellectual in *Verdun* was the centre of only one scene, in which he goes mad and has to be restrained from rushing over the parapet in the middle of a bombardment. But these characters echoed Artaud's concept of dramatic figures; and his portrayal of them explains what seems a very odd style of acting in plays like *The Cenci*.

Figure 10 Artaud as Count Cenci. Metaphysical characterization – 'incandescence' and visual cliché.

The characterization in *The Cenci*, deliberately unnaturalistic and allowing barely enough personalizing traits for psychological plausibility, was intended to work on a metaphysical rather than a social plane. The figures were conceived as superhuman 'beings' who incarnated the great forces of nature because they were in direct contact with the 'cruelty' at the root of existence. They were beyond moral judgement because (like such natural disasters as lightning or tidal waves) their acts were not the result of individual will. This, of course, is exactly what one would expect from reading *The Theatre and its Double*, where stage figures are seen as reflections of myth, so being objectified into 'nervous magnetisms', 'passionate manifestations'; and the actor is expected to depict 'total man' instead of an individualized personality.[62] But Artaud had already formulated this concept of dehumanized, moral rather than psychological characterization with reference to his film roles before he wrote the essays on 'Cruelty' or 'The Plague'.

Talking about his acting of Marat and Massieu in 1929 he described these characters as complementary opposites, absolutes of moral existence. Marat he called 'the first role . . . where it was given to me not only to try to be true, but to express the concept that I have of a figure, a character which appeared as the incarnation of a natural force'; and he contrasted this with the monk, Massieu, whom he saw as acting on the same universal level: 'This time I incarnated a saint, no longer in turmoil, full of paroxysm and perpetually torn away from himself, but calm instead. . . .'[63] Artaud saw these characters as 'decisive' for his development; and his portrayal of them was remarkable. There is a magnetism in the mobility of facial expression, and a stylized force in movement and gesture, which has considerable emotional impact. These portrayals in fact approach that degree of 'incandescence' which action, situation and images had to reach at least once in a performance, if a *mise en scène* was to qualify for Artaud as Theatre of Cruelty.

Looking at early silent film, today one is struck by an exaggerated style of acting in otherwise conventionally dramatic roles, which seems to falsify the emotion of the characters by raising it to an unnatural height. A comparatively minor thwarting of a character's purposes is enough for bulging eyeballs. Success of any sort brings out symptoms of ecstasy. Every situation is an occasion for large gestures and statuesque poses. This is partly due to the use of stage actors in film. The visual rhetoric they had learnt for the theatre, which has to be defined and broad to carry to the gallery, appears oversized in the intimate lens of the camera, which acts as a magnifying glass. It is also partly deliberate, a way of making silence speak, since subtle nuances are easily misread. Artaud took this film acting as a model – intensity being his criterion for effectiveness, and exaggeration, heightening, loudness apparently being mistaken for intensity. Artaud's theatre was also subject to some of the same limitations as the early cinema, since his downgrading of verbal communication to incantation in effect meant (as in silent film) replacing speech with a 'concrete language intended for the sense': in other words 'sign language'.[64]

His search for a physical, visual mode of communication follows logically from using the stage to appeal to the pre-rational and primitive level of the mind, and from the related attempt to create myths, which in surrealist terms were 'precipitates of the universal dream'.[65] This meant finding a symbolic vocabulary that had no allegorical connotations, and could not be translated into discursive terms. To evoke a purely subconscious response, it had to have the force of apparently involuntary expression; and Artaud's aims correspond to Jung's analysis in which 'the primitive mentality does not *invent* myths, it *experiences* them. Myths are original revelations of the pre-conscious psyche, involuntary statements about unconscious psychic happenings'. Similarly, Artaud's ideal of physical signs foreshadows Cassirer's later definition of mythopoeic thought in which 'the "image" does not represent the "thing"; it *is* the thing'.[66] Conventional symbolic forms being inextricably linked with the 'artificial' culture Artaud rejected, could only be presented as parody, as in *Burnt Breast*. Instead, he explored Egyptian hieroglyphics, Chinese ideograms, Mexican pictograms – but these were alien to his audience. Although their strangeness itself had a positive imaginative value, it prevented them from having the 'precise intellectual meaning' that he repeatedly stated his concept of 'physical thought' required.

Artaud realized the dangers of obscurity; and fearing (quite correctly) that his work would be misunderstood, he asked André Gide 'to prepare public opinion in advance' for *The Cenci* – just as he earlier suggested to Germain Dulac, the director of *The Shell and the Clergyman*, that because his film was composed of 'pure images . . . a few articles might be necessary to explain what you are trying to do'.[67] The uncertainty of physical communication made him search for 'concrete signs', which would be 'precise and immediately readable symbols'; and this led him to adopt a theory something similar to the 'correspondences' of French symbolist poets. Hence statements such as 'even light can have a precise intellectual meaning', which sound unrealistically hopeful at first sight, turn out to mean only that different intensities and colours of light could produce sensual

Figure 11 Iya Abdy in the torture scene of *The Cenci*. Heightened emotion and archetypal poses.

83

impressions of heat and cold, or emotional states of anger and fear.[68] A more exact vocabulary was needed. Visual symbols, like words, only communicate in so far as they have agreed and familiar definitions. In practice this meant that Artaud was driven back to conventional forms, and adapted his style from silent film and expressionism, as photos of the *Cenci* performance indicate. The actors' gestures are 'evocative' to the extent that they correspond with the typified expression of the screen, and to the degree that the 'emotive' attitudes compare with the archetypal schemata used in German expressionist theatre.

The danger is that using formalized symbols to express emotion formalizes the emotions expressed, particularly when the aim is to portray feeling with an intensity which depersonalizes it. This is one of the major flaws of early nineteenth-century melodrama – and the comparison is not coincidental. Quasi-religious, employing devils, ghosts and the machinery of the supernatural, and embodying a metaphysical vision of life in the conflict of absolute virtue and vice, while stressing events at the expense of characterization, and justifying itself solely by arousing emotional involvement in its audience, gothic melodrama shares many of the qualities of Artaud's Theatre of Cruelty. It mixed visions with realism of a spectacular kind. It subordinated words to action and replaced them with music; and it used stock formulas, which became ritualized by repetition. Not surprisingly, Artaud looked on 'the romantic melodramas' as the last 'valid' form of theatrical spectacle, praising them as being 'dramas of almost ritual situations'.[69] His output included adaptations of *The Fall of the House of Usher* and Lewis' *The Monk*. *Thirty Years* (*Trente ans, ou la vie d'un joueur*, 'a melodrama in three acts and in prose by Ducange and Dinaux') was at one point on the programme of his Theatre of Cruelty; and when Jouvet criticized the melodramatic basis of *The Cenci*, Artaud defended 'the simple elements which you despise: the good the evil and the traitor' on the grounds that what 'moves' an audience is very different from the type of play which aims at sophisticated understanding.[70]

The style of acting that would be appropriate in such a context is not hard to imagine; and, quite apart from the few photographs of *The Cenci*, practically every line in his film scenarios describes it. A brief glance through them gives us 'a gesture of cursing'; a man with 'his head in his hands, as if he held the terrestrial mass' being 'sunk in thought'; a man who opens a door by striking it with his fist 'like one exalted', and tears off a woman's dress 'as if he wished to lacerate her breasts', is shaken by 'a paroxysm', and gestures 'with intensity, frenzy, passion', his face in a 'hideous grimace'; a man who 'raises his eyes in the air' to indicate how engrossed he is in a book, while 'an unnameable fear' is 'marked by his fixed features, his trembling lips, his face pale as a corpse, the whites of his eyes'. These extreme physical manifestations of emotion also vary with extreme rapidity – 'he falls into a mad anger. He is sad. He sits down and wipes his brow'. Females are similarly afflicted: 'fixed', or in 'fresh convulsions', or 'trembling from top to toe'.[71]

By naturalistic standards, where psychological nuances are the key to plausibility, this passionate rhetoric would be (to say the least) unconvincing, and Esslin sums up critical opinion by dismissing Artaud as 'certainly an uneven, probably rather a bad actor'. Artaud, however, was trying to do something rather different, and ought to be judged by other standards. Undoubtedly, as Barrault commented, there were 'dissonances' – effects which failed. But he also acknowledged that Artaud reached 'sublime moments'; and even eyewitnesses of *The Cenci* who slated the performance, commented that his acting was 'so bad that it ended by interesting us'.[72] As might be expected, one of Artaud's greatest acting triumphs was in a melodrama, *Monsieur de Pygmalion*, where he played an incarnation of evil with the appropriate name of Urdemala. However, descriptions of Artaud's acting indicate an exaggeration that clearly goes beyond melodrama:

> Whenever Artaud had to move he tensed his muscles, he arched his body and his pale face turned hard with fiery eyes; like this he would advance using arms and hands as well as legs; he would zig-zag, stretching out his arms and legs and tracing wild arabesques in the air.[73]

Perhaps the nearest equivalent would be the rhetorical effect of theatrical acting in film; and it could be suggested that Artaud's aim was to create a similar 'unnatural' level of representation on the stage. The reviewer who commented that Iya Abdy who played Béatrice Cenci 'could have had a brilliant career in earlier days – in silent movies'[74] may have unwittingly touched on a key aspect of Artaud's approach. Yet it would not have been sufficient for Artaud simply to transpose the quality of acting in silent film back to the stage – in a theatrical context it would have lost its heightened effect.

Unlike some of his contemporaries (particularly Germans like Erwin Piscator) Artaud never seems to have considered using a cinema screen as part of a stage set in order to merge acted with filmed scenes, even though he had himself acted a variety of roles for a film sequence that was integrated with Ivan Goll's theatrical parody of materialistic life, *Methusalem*, in 1927. His one use of a screen, in *A Dream Play*, merely substituted background images for scene-painting. For Artaud the danger of transporting film onto the stage lay precisely in creating 'too familiar images'. What he wanted was a 'quasi-magical fabrication of life' as in surrealist films,[75] not the realism of the camera, but its ability to create images; and from the satiric attack on 'the Mystery of Hollywood' in *Burnt Breast* onwards, he experimented with gaining cinematographic effects by theatrical means.

The Spurt of Blood draws strongly on film techniques with its visible alterations in characters' physical shapes, the contrasts in scale from the macrocosmic of stars colliding to the minute of scorpions or a beetle and the cascade of objects, bodies and even abstractions, together with swift transitions and variations in speed from frantic acceleration to 'vomit-inducing slowness'. All these elements recur in *The Conquest of Mexico*. Like the perspective of crowds seen from above in *There Are No Heavens Anymore*, these effects require shifts of vision rather than changes in the object viewed; and in fact could only be accomplished convincingly by the camera, which was perhaps why Artaud never tried to stage these plays, even though *The Spurt of Blood* had been advertised in the programme of the Théâtre Alfred Jarry.

The Spurt of Blood, which anticipates *The Cenci* in its thematic use of incest and blasphemy, combines a childish level of Jarryesque insult ('*merde*', made more offensive in the mouth of that symbol of chivalrous nobility, a knight) with the hallucinatory shock effects of surrealistic film. All the main characters represent varieties of spiritualized ideal love as grotesque perversions of nature. The opening parodies a romantic duet on the trite themes of 'I love you and everything is beautiful . . . We are intense. Ah, how well ordered this world is!', rendering such clichés meaningless by artificial tonalities, and contrasting them with the spectacular collapse of cultural values symbolized by the fragments of classical architecture, religious temples and human limbs (a highly ironic echo of the Sophoclean man as the measure of all things). The last line of the playlet is the young girl's: 'The Virgin! Ah that's what he was looking for' as her lover flees with the whore.[76] All the figures standing for society – Priest, Shoemaker, Judge, Street Pedlar – are destroyed by strobe-like flashes of lightning intermittently illuminating images of earthquake and plague; and the death of God fertilizes the world of sexuality when the whore, literally 'signalling through the flames' as her hair bursts into fire in the grip of an enormous hand, bites God's wrist and 'an immense jet of blood spurts across the stage. The intention here is the same as the 'magical *mise en scène*' of *The Conquest of Mexico*, where 'Montezuma cuts the living space, rips it open like the sex of a woman in order to cause the invisible to spring forth', and the images that follow simultaneously illustrate the 'cruelty' of natural life and celebrate sexuality. The whore and the Young Man eat each other's eyes at the point of orgasm; an army of scorpions swarms out from between the Nurse's thighs and over the Knight's penis 'which swells up and bursts, becoming glassy and shining like the sun' – images which are comparable to the close-up slitting of the girl's eyeball with a razor blade in the Dali/Buñuel film *Un Chien Andalou*, using visceral shock to short-circuit rational response and release the subconscious.

One element of Artaud's staging worth noting is his inventive use of lighting, the most direct point of contact between film and theatre. His use of black light in *Burnt Breast* and the pulsating illumination of *The Mysteries of Love*, the aquarium effect called for in *The Ghost Sonata* scenario, and the strobe lights required for *The Spurt of Blood*, were all revolutionary for the time. In these experiments the lighting was clearly intended to disorient the spectator, or give emotional colouring to scenes. But in Artaud's view the true value of lighting was its ability to dematerialize stage action, transposing it into a primitive, subconscious key; and he referred to Lugné-Poe's production of *Pelléas and Mélisande* as his ideal: 'here was truly living light; it was aware, it emitted aroma, becoming a new sort of active force and giving to his settings and his actors a luminosity like that in the ultimate absence of consciousness of the "dervish".'[77]

'AN ABORTED THEATRE'

That these imaginative and vital elements of Artaud's work were not more widely appreciated at the time seems only partly due to lack of financial support, even though this did indeed cause great production difficulties. *The Mysteries of Love*, Claudel's *Break of Noon* and even *A Dream Play* had only one rehearsal on stage with costumes before the opening, while *Victor* didn't even have a complete run through. These were impossible conditions for achieving Artaud's ideal, in which images were to be given meaning through the dynamic relationship of parts to the whole in 'a grand harmony . . . in the gestures, in the interrelated movements . . . fixed and adjusted as in a well-wound mechanism'.[78] Yet *Victor* was looked back on as a valuable attempt – 'There was only a little lacking to have made it a brilliant success' – and he described *The Cenci*, which is generally considered a catastrophe, as 'total success' in 'a year of deceptions and failure'.[79] It is possible, of course, to see these comments as self-deceptions marking Artaud's inability to face the end of his theatrical career. But in Blin's view the *Cenci* production only had the limited aim of making the public aware of the concept of the Theatre of Cruelty. And much of the criticism it attracted was due to the publication of the Theatre of Cruelty manifestos shortly before the performance of *The Cenci*.

The reviewers had been led to expect an irresistible paroxysm of physical action that would have a direct effect on the central nervous system comparable to acupuncture performed by a street drill and inducing a collective delirium with a spiritual healing power that would make the theatre the equivalent of Lourdes. The effect, they believed, was to be 'a true therapy', which Artaud had imprecisely compared to snake charming, the 'medicinal music' of North American Indians, and the incantations of black sorcerers. In theory this would cure 'the patient' – the spectator, and through him society – by (confusingly) exteriorizing his latent cruelty, while at the same time forcing him to assume an external attitude corresponding to the state of psychological order which one wished to restore.[80] In fact no performance could realize these aims; indeed the abstraction of the manifestos, and the vagueness of Artaud's advertisement for *The Torture of Tantalus*, where the sentences are repeatedly qualified by '. . . *sort de* . . .', indicate that these generalizations are not conceived in practical theatre terms.

Yet Artaud seems to have been satisfied because, by and large, the critics did concede the effectiveness of the elements he considered significant, even if the way their approval was expressed showed they had been looking for something else, and their overall judgement was therefore unfavourable. They were receptive to the stylized presentation, and found 'the continual animation of the stage space' effective in creating a 'hallucinatory spectacle' which had 'the symbolism of nightmare'. Even highly critical reviewers had to concede that 'never the less, with his absurd violence, his staring eyes, his scarcely pretended fury, [Artaud] does carry us with him up above good and evil'. The tone is typified by the following review:

> Complex lighting, individual and mass-movement, sound, music revealed to the spectator that space and time form an *affective* reality . . . All the more then one can reproach the dramaturge, for . . . if Artaud had 'activated' certain fundamental acts of Cenci and Beatrice manifesting a total cruelty, he might perhaps have better avoided the excess of verbal material.[81]

Stylistically at least, then, Artaud achieved much of his theatre, although this was far from the total and revolutionary upheaval of traditional drama that his followers credit him with. But style is not autonomous. It is the choice of a mode of communication, a rhetoric determining what subject the material expresses by reference to its effect on an audience. Leaving aside Artaud's metaphysical abstractions (those notional theatres of ordeal or exorcism), what he actually tried to achieve was an intense emotional response, which would lead through a heightened awareness of inner potential, to the rejection of a rationalistic and materialistic society. In this context one of the most serious criticisms levelled at Artaud is that he ignored the question of the audience, and worked for psycho-social effects without considering exactly who would be affected.[82] For his style to be appropriate to his aims, Artaud would have had to take the established behaviour patterns of the spectators into account, since only in this way could he predict responses accurately and select sequences of images to gain precise reactions.

How far did he do this? He had a clear idea what social class the majority of his spectators would come from, and chose techniques which relied on certain cultural assumptions. His productions were not aimed at a 'committed public' who might be predisposed to applaud, but specifically at 'what one is accustomed to call the *public bien Français*' and their antagonistic response was calculated into the total effect of a performance: 'Their clownish reactions are an extra in the programme.' *Gigogne*, for example, was 'written and performed with the systematic aim of provocation'; and the juxtaposition of 'the most ridiculous infirmity' (flatulence) with beauty and love in the heroine of *Victor* is sufficient indication of his approach: an undermining of cherished – but from his viewpoint fake – ideals which the audience would find 'cruel' because gratuitous.

Nowhere is this clearer than in Artaud's staging of *Break of Noon* in 1928. This farcical treatment of a poetic celebration of Christian conversion, that Claudel had declared to be 'the first work in which I truly acquired the consciousness of myself', not only parodied the all too easy target of religion and automatically insulted the social establishment of which Claudel was a prominent member. Artaud's staging also implicitly rejected romantic assumptions about art as the expression of the unique self, and simultaneously attacked the traditional qualities of 'masterpieces', by turning *Break of Noon*'s rhetorical tirades, baroque imagery and Racinian psychological struggles into pretentious nonsense.[83]

Farce, always an element in Artaud's work (the scatological joke in *Victor*, and the operatic rendering of 'I love you' in *The Spurt of Blood*; the inanely grinning assassins in *The Cenci*, or 'the learned heads of the official spokesmen' in *The Conquest of Mexico*), is used for its corrosive effect, not for humour. Even the thematic 'cruelty' in his choice of material – for all his metaphysical justifications – is there to shock by reversing social assumptions. Civilization, organizing human relationships by legal curbs or religiously inspired spurs, is traditionally justified because it controls destructive urges, and limits violence. Artaud turns this upside down: civilization intensifies undesirable emotions by repressing them, so that society itself becomes an instrument of violence. The scenario for *The Butcher's Revolt*, for example, justifies the 'eroticism, cruelty, taste for blood, refinement of violence, obsession with the horrible, the dissolving of moral values, social hypocrisy lies, false-witness, sadism, perversion, etc., etc.' as a 'stocktaking'. These elements are not deployed 'with maximum plainness' for any ritual or psycho-spiritual reasons, but because they are seen as a true reflection of the reality commonly disguised by social appearances.[84]

The Conquest of Mexico is another formulation of the same theme. Both scenarios have political intentions: to destroy the justification of society's existence. One shows the repressive nihilism of civilization from the inside, in its metropolitan centre; the other from the outside, tearing away the 'civilizing' aspirations of colonialism by presenting the realities of conquest, and revealing its essential evil through the psychological effect of the conquistadores on a people whom Artaud believed to be 'natural'. In other productions Artaud attacked the principles on which society is structured. *Victor* was 'directed against the bourgeois family' as the basic social unit, while *The Cenci* was specifically an attack on 'the ideology of authority repented by the Father', seen as both the symbol and the root of 'the outdated ideas of Society, of Order, of Justice, of Religion, of Family, and of Fatherland'.[85]

There is a distinct absence of fine tuning here. Discredit the ideals held by the bourgeoisie who formed the body of any theatre audience; attack the basis of their society; and use the resulting expression of disapproval, disgust and rejection as a demonstration of the thesis that civilization is violent. Being crude this approach might have been expected to produce the broad effect Artaud anticipated, but he seems to have reckoned without the insensibility, self-assurance and cultural snobbism of his *'public bien Français'*.

Certainly his estimate of the composition of his audience was correct. The opening of *A Dream Play* was attended by the diplomatic community, an aristocracy of counts, viscounts, a duchess and royalty, eminent literati including Valéry, Mauriac and Gide, and members of the French Academy. The première of *The Cenci*, under the patronage of Prince George of Greece and the Princesse de Polignac, attracted all the fashionable society of Paris. Artaud's expectations remained much the same from the very first performance of the Théâtre Alfred Jarry ('howling, bawling reactions') to this last production, the full-length prototype for his Theatre of Cruelty ('they will howl, weep, whistle perhaps'). According to programme notes, *The Cenci* was officially intended 'to grip the audience by the entrails and the heart' with 'true tragic emotion'. But private letters showed that it was on account of the political provocation that Artaud expected 'the most violent reactions on the part of the spectators'.[86] Certain of Artaud's collaborators seem to have taken his wish for reality. According to Marc Darnault, who acted Victor, the production of Vitrac's play was 'terribly booed throughout the performance', while André Franck described a scene of chaos in *The Cenci*: 'the folding seats and chairs clattered; spectators rose crying in indignation or admiration . . . the public was still not ready'.[87] But in fact the audiences seem to have received Artaud with remarkable equanimity. Paul Block of the *Berliner Tageblatt* expressed his surprise that 'not a single protest' was raised against the social criticism in *Victor*, commenting that 'the audience by their amused reactions expressed a much more judicial judgement than the most experienced critics'. Similarly, according to Paul Arnold, who was in the audience of *The Cenci*, Parisian society was predisposed to approve, being eager for 'strong sensations'. Other descriptions of the audience's response by the critics range from boredom, to 'thirty people applauded wildly. The remainder of the room after a quarter of an hour took the tragedy with good humour.'[88]

Only two productions actually caused violent reactions – *Break of Noon* and *A Dream Play* – and in neither case was the staging responsible. It was Artaud himself who caused trouble after the end of the performance of *Break of Noon* – the play was put on in defiance of Claudel, who had publicly refused his permission, and (perhaps because the audience had sat quietly through the performance in spite of the way long speeches had been reduced to nonsense by being lifted out of context) Artaud added insult to injury by striding onto the stage and accusing Claudel of selling out to an infamous establishment. In *A Dream Play* too it seems probable that Artaud incited the violent riot which occurred. Having just publicly vilified the politics of his former companions, the surrealists, he knew them to be hostile. Yet no one else could have switched the place numbers of the central reserved block of seating to the balcony, which allowed the surrealists into the front rows; and the answers he shouted back at them from the stage could not have been better designed to anger the Swedes who had put up much of the money for the production.

None of this can be counted as successful theatrical agitation for the dismantling of society. But already, in plans for *The Torture of Tantalus*, he was transferring his attentions to a different audience, the uneducated working classes, and reading between the lines this move can be seen as a direct response to his inability to break through the intellectual defences of his Parisian public. *The Torture of Tantalus* was to be staged at Marseilles in a factory or public hall, and was aimed at 'the bulk of the masses' who, precisely because they had no time for 'subtle discourse' or 'intellectual gyrations', would 'not resist the effects of physical surprise, of the dynamism of cries and violent gestures, of visual explosions'.[89] One suspects that such spectators would have viewed Artaud's work with simple incomprehension, since his ability to communicate through symbols depended on prior cultural exposure. But at least when attacking society it is always more effective to appeal to the exploited, than to insult the privileged.

The failure of Artaud's techniques to produce any deep political effect, however, is due to more basic reasons than focusing on the wrong audience. As the dadaist experience demonstrated, it is contradictory to try to use artistic means to destroy culture; and Artaud's work in fact created new forms of expression in a very traditional way, by building on established conventions. It is also counterproductive to measure theatrical effectiveness by immediate and obvious audience reactions, since evidence suggests that the influence of art is subliminal; that it can only modify, not reverse cultural images; and that it may take a period of years to work through into social action.

Ironically, it is the view of Artaud as a unique innovator which has done most to undervalue his actual achievements. His work shows him to be firmly rooted in the culture of the 1920s and 1930s – even his flaws are symptomatic – and to reach a true evaluation he has to be seen in context.

Some of the theatrical forms mentioned by Artaud as if they were significant influences either seem to be imaginary ('Negro-American theatre', for example) or outside his experience (such as Soviet theatre, Artaud mistakenly looking on Russia as a country 'where theatre has become again a religion').[90] Others seem to have been misunderstood (for instance Balinese theatre, though this is hardly surprising, since Artaud was exposed to only one performance).[91] But even these references indicate how close Artaud was to his contemporaries. The only thing that Artaud could conceivably be describing in the mysterious category of 'Negro-American' at that time are plays like O'Neill's *Great God Brown* (1925) or *All God's Chillun* (1923), and the similarities to O'Neill's experiments with masks and rhythmic drumbeats simply underline the links between Artaud's work and expressionism. The only Russian theatre Artaud had seen was Meyerhold's, and some of the recommendations in his essay on 'An affective athleticism' parallel the practices of bio-mechanics, while there are certain correspondences between Artaud's stage sets and constructivist decor. As for the interest in Far Eastern theatre, that was a novelty that fascinated many of his contemporaries – including Brecht, who is commonly thought of as representing the opposite theatrical approach to Artaud.

Brecht of course developed along very different lines, but it is hardly a coincidence that his derogatory term for entertainment theatre, which he dismissed as 'culinary', is so similar to Artaud's description of it as 'digestive'. Both started from the same point, the rejection of naturalism. Artaud had a great admiration for the theatre that developed in the Weimar Republic, an enthusiasm to be expected since German theatre in the 1920s and 1930s was exceptionally rich in technical experimentation and the formulation of new dramaturgical approaches. Artaud indeed had fairly close connections with this theatrical powerhouse. He collaborated with Ivan Goll on the French production of *Methusalem* in 1927, being responsible for the film sequence that counterpointed the stage action. He also acted in the film of *The Threepenny Opera*, which he disapproved of for much the same reasons that led Brecht to disown it, and visited Berlin several times between 1923 and 1935. He was greatly impressed by the work of Brecht's collaborator, Erwin Piscator, from whom he probably took the initial idea of merging film and stage media; and it is when referring to his experience in Germany that he first mentions his intention to replace psychological drama with 'a theatre of action and the masses'[92] – an aim which is very similar to Piscator's. His use of different stage levels, streets receding up hills, or the balconies and staircases in *The Cenci*, is based on the same concept as Jessner's famous 'steps'; while the Bauhaus experiments with balletic sequences of forms and movement and their exploration of theatre as a spatial art also has similarities to some of Artaud's basic concerns. Even the stage space he envisaged for his Theatre of Cruelty – galleries around the perimeter of the auditorium, making it possible to transfer the action from the centre to the corners or play in the middle of the spectators, who were to be seated in revolving or mobile chairs – is an exact description of the theatre designed by Gropius, although Gropius allowed for film to be projected over ceiling and walls, as well as variable actor-audience relationships and the total immersion of the audience in a stage action.

Tracing influences is not particulary helpful for understanding Artaud's work – his selective use of film techniques, his updating of the melodramatic approach, even the replacement of verbal communication by the dynamic relationship of visual images, seem to have been developed largely independently. But the correspondences show him to be an integral part of the wider European theatrical movements between the wars. It is generally acknowledged that Artaud's work is comparable on some levels to that of Craig and Appia. But parallels with his contemporaries of the 1920s and 1930s are more precise than many realize. Indeed, as we have seen, Oskar Kokoschka can be seen as a direct forerunner of Artaud's ideal theatre some twenty years before the first manifesto of the Théâtre Alfred Jarry.

Artaud, then, was very much a man of his time, a seminal figure for modern drama, but not in fact an innovator. Rather he should be seen as a theatrical litmus, sensitive to the cultural physiology of the twentieth century which has been given comparable but independent expression by others as far apart as Kokoschka at the beginning of the era and Grotowski, who only came across Artaud's ideas after his style had already been fully developed with such productions as *Akropolis* and *Kordian* in the late 1960s. Judged by what he did rather than what he said, and evaluated in the context of his contemporaries, Artaud turns out to be less radical than his writings suggest, but more useful, giving us another model for anti-Aristotelian drama.

His theories (misunderstood or taken all too literally as in, say, the Living Theatre's *Paradise Now*) have produced only unrealizable strategies or self-indulgent, undramatic psychotherapy. However, the concepts that he picked up from the cultural currents of his time are among the most creative impetuses of modern theatre. His perception that the stage has a reality quite distinct from life, which can only achieve validity when presented with deliberate artifice, is mirrored in the overt theatricality of modern drama. His concept of extending the audience's imagination, by destroying conventional assumptions and simultaneously presenting alternate visions of the world, can be found in the work of dramatists as different as Genet or Robert Wilson, as can his methods of achieving this effect – hallucinatory distortions of scale and perspective, and overloading the brain with emotive images. On the level of technique his extension of stage language by emphasizing symbolic gesture, patterned movement, speech as sound, has been developed by Peter Brook and others. Above all his ritualization of theatre, with its accompanying aim to involve the spectator totally in the stage action, has become an ideal for much of the serious western drama.

Artaud's name has often been invoked – indeed too often, since whatever the value of his ideas as a catalyst, his practical work has had little influence. Outside of Barrault, it remained almost unknown until the mid-1960s. But he has made a decisive contribution to the major current in modern theatre, where archetypes from myth, or dream shapes from racial

93

memory, replace the classical hero figure; where the recognition affirms a comparable spiritual potential rooted in the blood, in the context of a pitiless world and against an evil civilization; and where what corresponds to catharsis is the total involvement of spectators in a dramatic action, with its therapeutic aim of liberating the natural man – instinctive, subconscious, cruel – from perverting social repressions.

6

RITUAL AND ACTS OF COMMUNION

JEAN-LOUIS BARRAULT

The direct link between Artaud and the modern avant garde is Jean-Louis Barrault. Taking only the more technical aspects of the Theatre of Cruelty, his work develops a 'total theatre' based on Artaud's concept of the actor as 'an athlete of the emotions'. Barrault's first production, a mime version of *As I Lay Dying* (*Autour d'une mère*), was performed barely a month after *The Cenci*; and Artaud's enthusiastic response led to plans for collaboration. They were to work together on staging Defoe's *Journal of the Plague Year* in a specific attempt to give tangible shape to the ideal image of drama that Artaud had outlined in 'The theatre and the plague' (the key essay in *The Theatre and its Double*). However, Artaud withdrew from the project because, as he wrote to Barrault, he was incapable of the compromise any collaborative work entailed and believed there were fundamental differences in approach: Barrault's mime being primarily descriptive, not symbolic, and relating to factual reality instead of presenting hieroglyphic expressions of the soul. But if any modern director can be counted a disciple of Artaud, it is Barrault.

Artaud introduced him to eastern mysticism, Indian mythology and yoga – all of which had a decisive influence on his work – and, above all, to the Cabbala with its division of breathing rhythms into six main 'arcana' (or combinations of masculine, feminine and androgynous principles), as exercises for inducing a trance state in which the body becomes the organ of the spirit. It is this ideal of psycho-physiological unity that forms the basis for Barrault's ideas and finds expression in his 'Little treatise on the alchemy of the theatre' or 'Alchemy of the human body'.[1] It has also been reflected structurally in his productions like *The Oresteia*, where each play in the trilogy was broken down into an 'organic' pattern of neuter, male and female phases.

In 1936 Artaud acknowledged Barrault as the only practitioner exploring his concept of a physical 'universal language that unites the total [theatrical] space ... to the hidden interior life',[2] while Barrault has repeatedly underlined Artaud's influence on his subsequent work. Artaudian phrasing recurs in his writing – particularly in statements of intention like 'the plague is rigged up on the stage, and we lance the tumour with all our dark forces. This purifies us and we go away clean and fortified' – and he claims to have identified with Artaud 'to the point of mimicry', both in style of acting and directorial approach:

> His view of the theatre was totally inner. He was a mystic and visionary who . . . reached right into the core of things, of people and of situations. He taught me to do likewise . . . He despised the cerebral actor, the didactic director. He felt his way into plays. My attitude is similar in that I don't 'intellectualise'; I act.[3]

Yet despite the way he assimilated Artaud's ideas, Barrault can hardly be said simply to have trodden in his footsteps. He formed a close association with philosophical playwrights like Sartre or Giraudoux, whose 'gratuitous gymnastics and intellectual capering' Artaud singled out as the antithesis of his ritual theatre. As director of the Théâtre de France, he was linked with the social establishment in a way that ran counter to Artaud's deepest principles; and considering Artaud's ridicule of all that Paul Claudel stood for, it is significant that Barrault's career has been so closely bound up with productions of *The Satin Slipper*, *Christopher Columbus* and even *Break of Noon*. Indeed Barrault effectively rescued Claudel's work from oblivion in using it as the basis for articulating his own spiritual theatre of 'total space'. Yet his focus always remained what Breton had called 'the latent content' of drama. For Barrault what made a play significant was its status as 'a precipitate of the universal dream', rather than 'the manifest content' of surface intrigue or social theme, since for him 'the art of theatre is specifically the art of dreams'.[4]

But in spite of his insistence on the revolutionary and subliminal nature of art, Barrault's aims are not comparable to those of the surrealists. Compared to Artaud, Barrault's concept of theatre as religion is conventional – hence the absence of contradiction in working with Claudel, the explicit advocate of Roman Catholicism – and he tends to associate 'sacred theatre' with 'ceremony' rather than primitive savagery. Where Artaud's image is of transfiguration through torture and the violence is that of rape, Barrault's is that of communion, or in his favourite metaphor 'the act of love' in which a stage presentation is a 'coupling' between actors and audience (no irony intended, since Barrault conveniently forgets that one party has paid the other): 'To perform is to make love – one gives, one gives oneself in an interchange, an act of holy communion.' The sense of duality remains, but in the quasi-sexual emotional identification supposedly 'each individual recognizes and shares with the rest a rediscovered Collective Soul'.[5]

Barrault's range has been eclectic, from the classics and Chekhov to

Ionesco and Beckett, from Feydeau to Genet and Sam Shepard. But in those productions that Barrault has picked out as defining his artistic credo – Claudel, and his own adaptations of *As I Lay Dying*, Kafka's *The Trial* (1946) and Rabelais' *Gargantua and Pantagruel* (1968) – there is a continuing attempt to generate myths in T.S. Eliot's sense of large controlling images, which give a meaningful structure to otherwise chaotic and fragmentary experience. The merely phenomenal is given spiritual significance by incorporating the whole natural world in the gestures and movements of the human body, an extension of mime into 'total' physical language where every aspect of stage presentation relates to a symbolic reality distinct from ordinary life. But the main thrust of his work picks up where Artaud left off; and his 'total theatre' is a logical extension of Artaud's ideas. Many of the people he worked with initially had been trained by Artaud. Génica Athanasiou, Lea in *The Mysteries of Love*, took a major part in *As I Lay Dying* (1935). Roger Blin, whose first appearance on stage was as one of the assassins in *The Cenci*, acted the role of a 'double' to Barrault's interpretation of the protagonist in *Hunger* (Knut Hamsun, 1939). Balthus, who had been doing only studio painting before *The Cenci*, designed the sets for several of Barrault's productions. And Artaud recognized *As I Lay Dying* to be an authentic example of many of the essential elements in his Theatre of Cruelty. Indeed, Artaud included his review of that performance in his 1938 edition of *The Theatre and its Double*.

Barrault's *mise en scène* emphasized the image of man and horse by extended episodes of running after the animal, leaping to seize its reins, leading it in a circle, jumping onto its back and breaking its bucking, rearing wildness into rhythmic dressage; while a letter of June 1935 describes the essential qualities of his mime as 'striving towards a purely animal state, for example the face becomes a natural mask, the concentration is on the breathing'. The elements of *As I Lay Dying* that Artaud singled out were: the creation of mythic symbols – like the 'centaur-horse' that Barrault created by simultaneously miming a stallion and its rider – and the transfer of emotional states to the spectators by tempos of breathing; the use of incantation and stylized gestures to create a 'sacred atmosphere'; and the replacement of psychology and plot by what he elsewhere calls 'the theatre's physics' or scenic rhythms. In fact Artaud describes Barrault's production in terms generally reserved for his own vision of theatre:

This spectacle is magical like those incantations of witch doctors when the clackings of their tongues against their palates bring rain to a countryside; when, before the exhausted sick man, the witch doctor gives his breath the form of a strange disease, and chases away the sickness with his breath . . . There is not one point in the stage perspective that does not take on emotional meaning.

In the animated gesticulations and discontinuous unfolding of images there is a kind of direct physical appeal . . .[6]

Significantly, these are also the qualities that Barrault has underlined as particularly fruitful for his future development.

Barrault described *As I Lay Dying* as 'pure theatre' – coining a phrase which has since been overused – because it only existed as performance, and its basis was actors, not a text. In the two hours of stage time there were only thirty minutes of dialogue; and much of this was in the form of choral songs or religious chants. There were no sets, and both costumes and props were minimal. The actors were practically naked, their only 'costumes' being belts, to which were attached symbolic objects, each representing the character's dominant passion. The performers created the environment for the different scenes by vocal sound effects and rhythmic gestures, producing unaided the rasp of a saw for building the coffin or bird calls for the forest. It was solely their movements as an ensemble that evoked the dominating context of the natural world: flowing and tumbling for the river in flood, a light and leaping dance for flames in the fire, or heavy mechanical bending movements for cotton-pickers in the fields. There were no atmospheric lighting effects and no external emotional tone from music, the only accompaniment being a tomtom. The single conventionally illusionistic element was the costume devised for 'the mother' when the actress playing the role fled (on discovering the degree of nudity required – shockingly revolutionary at that time) and Barrault took over her role in addition to acting the part of the illegitimate son, Jewel. Even then, although the impression of femininity was essential for the maternal image, his dress was hardly representational. Barrault's chest was bare; and his skirt of ribbons, the long black wig falling below his waist, and a stylized mask of black cheesecloth with reflective steel buttons for eyes, transformed the figure into a monstrous totem.

As I Lay Dying was chosen because Faulkner presents a way of life that has returned to the primordial, in which man is integrated with nature, and civilization is seen as an artificial accretion. The central image of dying gives a spiritual perspective to the picture of crude physical life, which Faulkner's extensive use of interior monologue has already transformed into a subjective state. The simplicity of the story, the tragic extremity of passion where innocence and guilt become obsessions, and Faulkner's use of external description to reveal his characters' souls are all easily translatable into mime.

Barrault's *mise en scène* focuses on the inner states of the characters and the emotional quality of landscape rather than events. The action opens with a mime of birth – anticipating a format that has become an archetype of ritual drama, one used both by Grotowski and the Living Theatre, and brought to its fullest expression in Schechner's *Dionysus in '69* – 'A birth.

The revelation of labour, the suggestion of suffering. Nothing individual-ized; a kind of annunciation . . . Relaxation. Each one turns back once more into a human animal; they dream of finding their true selves again.'[7] The family gathers around the dying mother, who signifies her desire to have her coffin made in her presence. Her body is taken by the father and her five children, including her illegitimate son (fathered by the village priest), to be buried with her parents in the town where she was born.

In one sequence where the family cortège comes to the river, for example, Barrault himself presented at one and the same time the figure of Jewel, the curvetting horse he rides, and birds of prey circling overhead. Other actors mimed the water, as well as a floating tree trunk that is swept into the cortège in mid-stream, overturning the imaginary wagon to throw everyone into the river. At this point the dead mother rises out of her imaginary coffin. Contrasting with the struggles of the living, her move-ments are 'aquatic and feline, forming rhythms of suffering', and having passed 'to the other side of life' she is freed from the limitations of mute existence and can speak. But, in a way that strikingly anticipates Ionesco, language is only a block to communication:

> The words signify nothing, the words never correspond to what they strive desperately to express . . . Sin, love, fear: the sounds for these are never sinning, nor loving, nor fearing, and those that are used for them have never been and could never be, at least until the words have been forgotten.

In the mother's death scene, the focal point of the performance, two further levels of ritualized and heightened reality were included. Onto a screen behind the death bed was projected a strongly rhythmic shadow-play of the priest administering the last rites and holding a mass for the dead woman's soul, accompanied by a chanted funeral incantation. These cere-monial rhythms were linked with organic rhythms established in the actual death sequence, particularly a stylized representation of the mother's breathing which was magnified into a pulse beat for the whole theatre.

> Her eldest son is making the coffin. The wheezings from her chest fit in with the raspings of the saw. All the rest of the family, like an enormous jellyfish, contracts and relaxes in unison with the mother and the carpenter. The whole theatre is in death throes – a pump rhythm, an octopus rhythm, and all of a sudden at the climax of a breath: total stoppage. The mother's hand, which had been raised as when someone wants to look out into the distance, falls slowly in the silence, like a water level going down. Life is emptying out. The movement is prolonged throughout the body until the rigidity of a corpse is reached.[8]

The aim was to regulate the spectators' heart beat by this driving pulsation which dominated every aspect of the stage image. It was a graphic example of Artaud's ideal that metaphysics should be made to re-enter the mind through the skin, and according to Barrault the effect

> took us into the real regions of the sacred, of prayer: a rite as strong and primitive as if we had been in the middle of a tropical forest among witch-doctors. Rhythm is the only thing that can take us out of ourselves – I am thinking of trances of the soul:
>
>
>
> *corps de Jésus*
> *corps de Jésus*
> *corps de Jésus* . . .[9]
>
>

It was also only a short step from this to the 'total theatre' that has become Barrault's theatrical trademark.

TOTAL THEATRE

The search for 'totality' in one form or another was one of the major motifs in French theatre between the wars. From Barrault the line runs back not only to Artaud with his concept of a theatre that could totally involve the audience, both physically and emotionally: it can also be traced through Charles Dullin, Barrault's first mentor whom he claimed to have 'absorbed to the point of looking like him', to the symbolists, and to Copeau's Vieux Colombier, where Dullin received his training. Copeau united a visual stylization derived from Gordon Craig with Adolphe Appia's concepts of rhythmic movement, sculptural lighting and 'musical space' in which actor and setting are united in a single plastic and express-ive image (a section from Appia's *Music and the Arts of the Theatre* was printed as a note in Vieux Colombier programmes). Dullin's aim was a 'total spectacle', creating a strictly theatrical stage world 'more expressive than reality' through a synthesis of stylized conventions, ranging from circus, and *commedia dell' arte*, to the Nōh.[10] All these elements recur in Barrault's characteristic productions, where they gain a quasi-religious significance.

Already in his early work Barrault was experimenting with combining different media, as in a film like *Les Enfants du Paradis*, where the highly stylized art of mime was dovetailed with the illusionism of talking cinema. He was also experimenting with new interrelationships between the differ-ent elements of theatre – in the play between light, setting and the geometry of movement in an actor climbing a staircase – or between sound and sense in sequences where meaningless words 'plastically [phonetically] reproduced' conversation, or spoken dialogue was answered by musical notes (Hamsun's *Hunger*). But it was primarily through his productions of Claudel in the 1940s and 1950s that Barrault developed his model of 'total theatre'; and their importance to him is indicated by the way he revived

The Satin Slipper (1943, 1953 and 1964), and the fourth section of the play, *Sous le vent des Iles Baléares* (in 1972), *Christopher Columbus* (1953, 1960, and several productions in Germany, 1961–3), *Break of Noon* (1948, 1961), and even an early play that Claudel had repeatedly refused permission to stage, *Head of Gold* (1959, 1967).

Claudel labelled his plays 'musical drama'. But although his approach has general points of resemblance to Wagner's *Gesamtkunstwerk*, and includes complex orchestral scores by composers like Honneger (*The Satin Slipper*) or Darius Milhaud (*Christopher Columbus*, which was originally conceived as an opera), music is more a structural analogy than a formal description. Claudel rejected Wagner's concept because it subordinated setting, dialogue and actor – and with the actor, drama itself and human emotion – to a monochrome symphonic form that was self-enclosed and tended to stasis. By contrast his idea was to use music to amplify character and dramatic situation. And in ideal terms this meant that, instead of being pre-composed and pre-set, the musical score would be orchestrated in direct response to the performance:

> giving impulse and pace to our emotions through a medium purely rhythmical and tonal, more direct and more brutal than the spoken word . . . music not only in the state of full realization, as a cryptic language portioned out among the pages of the score, but in the nascent state, rising and overflowing from some violent feeling.[11]

In this concept, music is not simply a resonator. It also has an active function: to unify the 'diverse voices' of a play into a harmonic 'enthusiasm', transforming the conflict of dramatic action into a 'final hymn'; and this is paralleled by a type of structural composition that weaves disconnected events into a single 'melodic' line.

Claudel's drama, which focuses on different varieties of religious conversion and sees human life in terms of the struggle of the flesh ('the Ordeal by Fire'), is yet another form of interior, mental drama. His plays are autobiographical and, as he openly acknowledged, both in *Exchange* (1914) and in *Break of Noon*, all the characters were projections of himself. His stage represents the soul; and the objects of the material world are veils for spiritual realities.

Nowhere is this clearer than in *Christopher Columbus*. The play opens with Columbus on the point of death, impoverished and rejected by the king, to whom he has come to beg for the means to finance another voyage; and the scenes are the past as he relives it in the continuous present of his mind. The hero splits into two figures: the actor in an epic of discovery, and the spectator who holds judgement on the temporal action from his standpoint on the threshold of eternity. A voyage into a spiritual geography, the materialistic preoccupations of social life in the form of greedy creditors, sceptical courtiers and mutinous sailors, are set against faith in the form of the luminous western horizon, or the revelations 'from beyond the tomb' that Columbus receives when he reaches the Azores. The world's ingratitude is balanced by one woman's saving love; and the play is bounded by the image of the dove. This is simultaneously the Holy Ghost, and stands for Columbus himself (through the double meaning of his French name, *Colombe*). It brings a message of hope from across the ocean to the child in Genoa at the beginning; and it carries the soul of man from a 'newly risen world' to the bosom of Christ Pantocrator at the end. In this world of symbols Columbus' life repeats the archetypal pattern of the Passion, with him crucified as his rebellious sailors lash him to the mast of his ship. The stage is a metaphoric altar; and the performance is a religious celebration, with a choir – adapted from the classical Greek chorus – representing the collective awareness of subsequent generations. This group mediates between the 'sacred mystery' being re-enacted and the audience, who are conceived as a church congregation.

In envisioning this religious drama Claudel was influenced by two traditional forms. He had been inspired by Ida Rubinstein's work, and by performances of the Medieval Studies Group to write a mystery play: *St Joan at the Stake* (1938). An oratorio, this had a structure based on Aeschylus' *The Suppliants*, and a chorus representing the French nation. But an earlier and even more significant model was the ritualistic traditional Japanese theatre.

Unlike Yeats or Ezra Pound, Claudel knew this at first hand – having served as French Ambassador in Tokyo during the 1920s – and he even had an exercise in the formal Nōh style, *The Woman and Her Shade*, performed at the Imperial Theatre with music by a Japanese composer in 1923. *The Satin Slipper* was structured according to the Kabuki model of a tetralogy spanning four 'days', each of the first three treating the same material in different tragic moods, while the last 'day' transposes it into an absurd light. And the whole dramatic conception of Claudel's other plays is consciously modelled on the Nōh, with its symbolic acting of legendary histories focusing on spiritual recognition, its emblematic world and its on-stage musicians integrated in the action, whose drums and flutes both evoke the characters, creating appropriate emotional states in the audience before the entry of divine being or demon, and respond to the characters' passions.

It was explicitly this strong Japanese influence in Claudel that determined the style of Barrault's acting company. It is also significant that, in Barrault's eyes, there were definite correspondences between Japanese Nōh drama and ancient Greek theatre. The masked *Shite* seemed the same type of figure as the masked Tragedian, whose image survives on Athenian pottery from the fifth century BC. The *kata* and the *mie* (a complex series of gestures and set choreographic patterns, accompanied by percussive rhythms and climaxing in a motionless, stylized expressive pose) could be compared to the Greek *cheironomia* (or code of symbolic hand and head

Figure 12 Rabelais, with Barrault in foreground. A bare stage and rhythmic gestures – the actor as simultaneously character and natural environment (here a ship at sea).

movements) and schemata (mimed action that crystallized into emblematic freezes at key dramatic moments). The centrality of the chorus and the use of dance in both types of theatre confirmed their essential similarity, which was taken as convincing evidence for the universality of 'original' theatre forms.[12] And Barrault's interest in tracing such parallels demonstrates that his 'total theatre' is another variant of the search for contemporary equivalents to an imagined archaic, primal theatre.

In the production of *Christopher Columbus* Barrault developed his idea of creating a purely theatrical and non-representational world from the gestures, voice and movement of the naked actor. *As I Lay Dying* had been a crude but powerful prototype. Now this was revealed as a polished and flexible style. He used the actors to represent nature and the elements, as well as the human condition. Thus in a scene where Columbus rescued an old sailor from drowning, the two actors expressed the impersonal surging force of the sea in which they struggled without going out of character, while other members of the cast hurled themselves across the stage like great waves or howled like the wind: a human universe. The same basic costume was used to suggest a court gown or peasant dress by simple alterations in shape; and, although Barrault tends to play down the role of music, film and lighting in order to underline that 'the theatre is man', in his most characteristic work all scenic devices do indeed appear subordinate to the human figures. Artaud had proposed that in his Theatre of Cruelty 'the set will consist of the characters themselves . . . and of landscapes of moving lights playing on objects and masks in perpetual interchange'; and in Barrault's theatre this has been refined to the point that, in his most frequently repeated statement, 'as soon as there is, on four raised planks, no matter where, a man, and nothing around him, expressing himself in the whole range of his means of expression, there will be . . . total theatre'.[13]

The path from *As I Lay Dying* to *Christopher Columbus* found its logical extension in *The Oresteia*, which Barrault staged in 1955. Ancient Greece provided the model for his ideal of the actor as an Artaudian 'emotional athlete'. Uniting the associated arts of sport and drama, 'dance was the common factor' between Aeschylean tragedy and his 'total theatre': 'Dances, chanting, choruses, trances. Drama reconstitutes these primitive ceremonies, which are theatrical play in its pure state.'[14] Indeed, it was his observation of magic ceremonies in Brazil, and of occult séances in which initiates were 'possessed' by spirits, that inspired his production of Aeschylus' trilogy. These formed the basis for his interpretation of Clytemnestra, whose invocation of the Furies became a black mass, and of Cassandra's prophetic frenzy.

Again his premise was the universality of primitive cultural forms. But for Barrault the fundamental link between Greek, Japanese and other forms of 'archaic' acting was a tempo that 'makes one think of universal gravitation' (echoing Artaud's description of movement in *The Cenci*). This 'organic rhythm', which in turn related to the cabbalistic 'ternary of creation', was read into the structure of *The Oresteia* – defined by Barrault as a neutral phase of mysterious preparation, a masculine phase of decisive action or fecundation, and a feminine phase of gestation (the gradual fruition of the act), 'fertilizing history' to form another neutral phase and repeat the pattern in the next play of the trilogy. And it is on this level that Barrault's theatricalized drama of the soul, magically conjured up out of nothing by the actor's expressive power, ties into Artaud's 'metaphysics of the theatre', in terms of which Barrault defines the inner focus of his work: 'the world of the fantastic, death, blood, famine, fury, frenzy . . . The river, fire, magic, my total theatre.'[15]

These contrasting sides of Barrault's 'total theatre' were brought together in the two productions that epitomize the final stage of his career, *Rabelais*

(1968) and *Jarry* (1970). The two works are closely connected. Both follow the trajectory of human experience through the imaginative universe of a writer's complete *oeuvres*: a natural extension of his stylistic presentation of the universe in purely human terms. Both also treat the same theme, with the two protagonists standing for 'free men' as satiric poets who confronted 'a world of total disorder', and reflected complementary aspects of 'truly contemporary experience' in their different epochs: Rabelais as 'Childhood grasping hold of life in both hands . . . An eternal student . . . fighting for new ideas', Jarry as 'identical to the conduct of certain contemporary youths who cannot adapt to the modern world, who turn their back on a bad world without working to mould an alternative world'.[16] The two pieces are also related by the incidental fact that Jarry himself had written a 'heroicomic' stage version of *Pantagruel* (produced posthumously in 1911, with music by Claude Terrasse, who had composed the original music for *Ubu roi*) in which 'King Pantagruel' was another embodiment of Ubu.

Initially the show had been conceived as a counterblast to the public outrage against Blin's production of Genet's *The Screens* (1966), which Barrault had not only sponsored but also acted in, taking the key role of Si Slimane. Inevitably, however, given the timing of the production, *Rabelais* appeared an act of self-defence in direct response to the youth revolution of May 1968, when the Théâtre de France was taken over and defaced by the students as the 'temple of bourgeois culture'.

Barrault, fired by the government for compromising with the revolutionaries, found himself rejected by both the regime and its left-wing opponents, and obviously saw Rabelais as an *alter ego*: 'Caught between Roman repressive orthodoxy and the progressive fanaticism of the Protestant "gladiators" he chose the most uncomfortable side: that of tolerance.'[17] Yet his actual play lacked any sense of this objectivity. The forces of repression were presented as cartoon caricatures. Picrochole's militaristic gestures were those of a Chaplinesque Great Dictator, while his henchmen were Marx Brothers' versions of Himmler, Goebbels and Goering. The Church was a grotesque aviary of preening, rapacious and bird-brained poultry. Against these grotesque forces was set beat music and jive dancing to express the joy of life. Formal education was dismissed as 'medieval' and deadeningly pedantic in being solely verbal and intellectual, while 'Humanist Education' was presented through mime illustrating the full development of the body as well as the mind, and developing into an outburst of jive marking a student holiday. In the Abbey of Thélema scene, figures representing moral deformities, physical ugliness and closed minds flung aside their cloaks to become the flower children of a 'hippy' commune, bare-breasted and mini-skirted in 'a blaze of light'. Their cry

Do as you will
Because people are free!

is echoed by an orgiastic celebration as 'the music and dancing rise to a frenzied pitch followed by a strange torpor';[18] while the magic herb that Pantagruel takes with him on his voyage is translated into cannabis.

Quite apart from such political and social themes, the essential action of both *Rabelais* and *Jarry* takes place on an interior plane. In *Rabelais* Barrault divided man into Gargantua, the sensual appetites, Pantagruel, the thirst for knowledge, and Panurge, the physical instincts – a simplistic separation of body, mind and emotion that he also applied to *Jarry*. There Père Ubu explicitly stood for the belly, Doctor Faustroll the head, and Sangle (from Jarry's *Jours et nuits*) the heart, all of whom had 'a double' in the figure of Jarry himself. Both plays also present the same pattern of experience to the audience. The first half of *Jarry* attacked formal education, militarism and social institutions, setting 'the trauma engendered by society' against 'the desire for a new man', while the second half (like the psychedelic cannabis voyage in *Rabelais*) moved into the subconscious as a 'surrealist dream, in the universe of drugs, which allows all hallucinations, all apparitions', and was designed 'to sweep us away' into an alternate reality.[19] The intention was liberty with a capital L, but unfortunately – symptomatic of Barrault's weakness as a thinker – each production reduced this to simple eroticism. At the same time, on a technical level these 'spectacles' were fascinating and imaginatively powerful.

Barrault brought together all the techniques developed in his earlier productions, mixing conventions from the circus, music hall and puppetry with rhythmic chants, elaborate masks, the formalized movements of Kabuki theatre and choreographed mime, to evoke the characters' environment and their unity with the natural world around them. *Rabelais* was presented as 'a dramatic game' by strolling players, with the actors in modern dress mingling with the audience as they entered, carrying their props or costumes. And this close relationship with the spectators was reinforced by direct address to the audience during the performance – for example discussing the way masks were being used by the actors to entertain rather than to deceive – as well as by the shape of the stage itself. In *Jarry* the action surrounded the audience on platforms constructed among the seats, in addition to being played out in a circular central 'circus ring'. In *Rabelais* the acting area was cruciform, set in the centre of the auditorium so that actors entered through the spectators up steps at each of the four ends. With ropes as the only scenery, everything was functional and evocative. Spreading from a circular canopy high above the edges of the stage, these ropes formed a circus tent image for the first half; and, simply by changing the place where they were tied down, they became the ship's rigging for the voyage. As in *As I Lay Dying*, Barrault mimed both Gargantua and his horse in the attack on Picrochole, while language was set against physical expression, as in a 'frozen words' fantasy where recorded voices were thrown by loudspeakers from different points in the auditorium and seemed to come out of the air. Rabelais' archaisms and obscure syntax were deliberately retained, sacrificing intellectual meaning to rich sound patterns; and in both plays the culmination was marked by strongly rhythmic music, amplified to an enormous volume of sound that enveloped the audience, as well as by a pulsing kinetic energy in dance and acrobatics, accelerated by strobe lights to a 'mesmeric climax'.

On the surface, all of this is directly equivalent to Bakhtin's ideal of 'carnevalesque' art, intrinsically anti-authoritarian in its 'dialogic' structure and mix of different genres/media, its use of the grotesque and affirmatiion of physicality, reviving the spirit of medieval festival. However, as in Artaud's theatre, although the actors are required to be 'completely pos-sessed' and the stage directions may specify that whoever plays Panurge 'goes into a positive ecstasy', the effect of spontaneity and anarchistic frenzy was always created from conscious and disciplined rehearsal. This became particularly clear in the 1971 British production of *Rabelais*, where Barrault's aim was 'to recreate as accurately as he could the sight and sound of his original production . . . the complex and precise ballet'.[20] A very high degree of precision indeed was required to integrate live dialogue with a multi-track, pre-recorded sound score of voices as well as musical effects; and a complete uniformity of mood and movement had to be achieved during the sea sequences to allow individual expression without destroying the image of a ship. To achieve it required the director as autocrat. Barrault's 'total theatre' then, is in various senses a theatre of total illusion.

7

BLACK MASSES AND CEREMONIES OF NEGATION

JEAN GENET

It is no accident that Barrault supported Genet; nor that Roger Blin, who had worked with both Artaud and Barrault, was the first director of Genet's plays. As Genet's English translator, Bernard Frechtman, was the first to point out, he 'is endeavouring to create a theatre which is ceremony. In *The Blacks* and *The Balcony*, ceremony is achieved through the behaviour of characters who enact a ritual.'[1] The concept of performance as a rite is similar to Barrault's approach, while the political radicalism of Genet's plays was also congenial.

However, Genet's politics are even more ambiguous. On the surface his dramatic subjects seem to be revolution and repression, class hatred and racial conflict, colonialism and Third World liberation. But any attempt to analyse his work in these terms inevitably leads to the conclusion that the plays are empty of significance – or, as Norman Mailer put it, 'White and Black in mortal confrontation are far more interesting than the play of shadows Genet brings to it' – although Lucien Goldmann contends that their 'mental structures' reflect the radical pessimism of the disillusioned European left.[2]

In fact Genet's rejectionism is far more extreme. His work, which has links with the expressionists and surrealists, presents social reality itself as illusory, and the human need for illusion as being so strong that no social order can be based on reality. Even revolutions are no more than 'someone dreaming'; and (as the final words of *The Balcony* make explicit) the audience's daily life is falser than the 'house of illusions' represented by Genet's brothel, or in wider terms by the theatre itself. If 'being' (in Sartre's terms) is defined as 'doing', but all action on the social level is self-deception, then only the achievement of a state of 'non-being', the negation of the self, can be authentic. Hence Genet's plots always centre on death, while his characters are roles, not personalities defined by a coherent set of internal qualities, but masks giving shape to a void or reflected images in a receding perspective of mirrors. Pirandello was the first to show the social personality as an unstable agglomeration of imposed and self-adopted roles, but the comparison that has frequently been drawn with Genet is misleading. Behind Pirandello's naked masks is the face – Genet's masks are empty, and the usual equation between appearance and essence has been reversed. The artificial appearance is the essence.

Nowhere is this clearer than in his first play to reach the stage, *The Maids* (1946). The apparent reality of mistress and maid in the opening tableau is revealed as false. Both are maids, one impersonating Madame, the other impersonating her own sister. But these roles are also undermined, since the two women are to be played by adolescent boys; and they are required to act incompetently, removing any reality from the performance as well. Although based on an actual case of two maids, the Papin sisters, these maids are capable only of acting out this revenge for their degradation by society in fantasy; and as male homosexuals their class hatred becomes transformed into a transvestite fantasy of sexual domination, which in turn is revealed as fake by showing it too as imaginary, a performance.

There are obvious problems in the way this reversal of reality and illusion is carried out, the main flaw being the breaking of the stage convention that the play itself sets up. If the maids are boys, what are we to make of the mental state of the third character, the 'real' mistress? If she too is played by a boy, what place has this intruder in the private world of a homosexual couple? Yet when the parts are played by women, as Jouvet got Genet's permission to do for the first production, then the essential complexity of self-cancelling reflections is lost.

But this negation of reality through role playing is the premise of all Genet's subsequent plays. In *The Balcony* (1957), the social roles of the 'clients' – bank clerk, plumber or fireman – have exactly the same status as their brothel fantasies of Bishop, General, Judge. When the rebels blow up the 'real' heads of the church, military and judiciary in the palace, they can take over since the 'reality' lies in the symbols – the ceremonial accoutrements of mitres and copes, robes and uniforms, crowns and decorations – not the men beneath. When these figures appear on the Grand Balcony as stiff gigantic effigies, the populace to whom they wave is represented by the Beggar, seen earlier as yet another role in the repertoire of the brothel. In this scenario, revolution represents the intrinsically puritanical reality principle; and as the rebel leader recognizes, success is self-defeating since it requires the emotional focus of an image – Liberty on the Barricades – thus becoming a 'combat of allegories'. As the Envoy remarks, after we have been given a demonstration of how the symbols of social order are perpetuated by press photographers, who ignore facts in favour of the 'definitive image', 'a true image' can only be 'born of a false spectacle'. And again, as in *The Maids*, the symbols ultimately reduce to

Figure 13 The Blacks. Masks, funeral rites and fake images in a multi-level action.

theatre, wearing 'garish make-up' and 'tragedians' cothurni about 20 inches high'.

Similarly in *The Blacks* (1959) the costumes 'suggest fake elegance', while the characters replaying the ritual murder of a white woman are not played simply by Negroes, but are transformed into artificial images of absolute blackness by 'beautiful shiny black make-up' – just as each of the court who judges them wears a stylized mask representing 'the face of a white person . . . in such a way that the audience sees a wide black band all around it'.[3] The re-enaction of the murder is a cover for revolt within the play against the (white) judges who condemn the Negroes, a deliberate adoption of the image of ritualistic savagery and evil imposed on them by their oppressors. But even the stage performance itself is fake, being intended (by the characters, who are identical with the actors) to distract the actual audience from the political struggle against the social order that is represented by the spectators. But the reported 'real-life' Black Power revolution (off-stage) has no more substance than the body of the murdered woman in the centre of the stage. Her catafalque covered with funeral flowers is revealed to be a sheet stretched over two empty chairs. And each of the other levels of the action recedes further into deception and illusion, so that the love story between Virtue and Village – who walk away from the audience hand in hand at the end in the clichéd stage image of romance – becomes a play within a play (Diouff's ascension into heaven) within a play (the massacre of images) within a play (the murder trial) within a play (the revolution); and on each level, as Archibald the Master of Ceremonies tells the court, the only reality is 'the theatre! We'll play at being reflected in it, and we'll see ourselves – big black narcissists – slowly disappearing into its waters.'[4] In Roger Blin's production, arbitrary change of vocal pitch and pace and stylized acting techniques were used in such a way that the presentation 'added to this willed multiplicity'. Indeed, according to Blin, even 'the author himself gets lost in this labyrinth' of 'reflections of reflections'.[5]

The immediate effect is one of radical nihilism, an absolute negation of reality, which denies any possibility of change since revolutions are subsumed in the images they challenge, and perpetuate the structure of reality they overthrow. In fact Genet's symbols of domination and submission are complementary, not conflicting. The slaves in his plays can only revolt by intensifying the image of evil and worthlessness imposed on them in self-justification by their masters. But this only serves to heighten the ascendancy and attraction of the images of authority, and indeed legitimizes them. Madame is transformed into a radiant symbol of beauty and spirituality precisely because the maids take on all the disgusting aspects of physicality, acting as 'our distorting mirrors, our loathsome vent, our shame, our dregs'. Similarly in *The Balcony* it is the sins of the penitent that make the Bishop holy, and this mutual dependence of moral opposites is emphasized by the Judge:

> You've got to be a model thief if I'm to be a model judge. If you're a fake thief I become a fake judge. Is that clear? . . . You won't refuse to be a thief? That would be wicked. It would be criminal. You'd deprive me of being![6]

Hence the only achievement of the revolution is to add two symbols to the nomenclature of the power structure, the Joan of Arc 'image of Chantal Victorious, our saint' and the black uniformed Chief of Police as an image of the brutal strong man in the modern dictatorial state – a pairing that embodies Genet's basic archetype, 'the eternal couple of the criminal and the Saint' aspired to by the maids.[7]

This nihilism is usually explained as the result of Genet's deprivation as an orphan, his criminal record, or the sterility of homosexuality. And this view, a simplification of Sartre's point in his influential *Saint Genet: Actor and Martyr* (1952), has been put succinctly by Blin, the director most closely associated with his work: 'Genet was a victim of this society, which he now seeks to destroy . . . But he does not try to correct the society he denounces. He does not try to substitute one order for another since he is against all order.' There is a certain obvious truth in this, and one of Genet's letters to Blin emphasizes that 'my books, like my plays, were written against myself . . . to expose myself'.[8]

However, Genet has given two very different versions of his initial crime, by virtue of which he claims his status as an outcast – alternatively stealing from his foster-mother's purse because he was hungry, or a murderous knife attack on another boy – one blaming the inherent evil in 'right thinking' society for his descent into criminality and perversion, the other claiming his nature itself to be intrinsically evil. Like his own characters, he 'embellishes' his guilt into an image of absolute evil, not only asserting himself to be condemned by all normal standards – violating religion as an apostate, patriotism as an army deserter, property as a thief, sexuality as a male prostitute – but also declaring himself to be an exploiter of other outcasts as a pimp, even a traitor to his own underworld as a police informer. And there is at least one well-documented instance of his accepting the punishment (and status – life imprisonment) for a crime he did not commit. As for the conclusion that Genet is against all order, this is contradicted by the obsession with hierarchy in his plays, from *Deathwatch* (1949) with its alternative title of *Rules of Precedence* to his final play, *The Screens* (1966). Here, because their discipline and patriotism makes them equivalent to the colonial troops, revolutionary fighters are inferior to arsonists and child murderers, while they in turn are inferior to Leila, who steals from them, and all rank beneath Saïd, who even betrays the revolution which his negative example has inspired.

This moral inversion echoes the theory of 'cruelty' Artaud derived from Sade, with its reversal of values based on the perception that 'in the manifested world, metaphysically speaking, evil is the permanent law, and what is good is an effort and already one more cruelty added to the other'.[9] So in Genet's 'rules of precedence' the more well-recognized the merit, the lower it is on the negative side of the scale, while the more infamous a deed is considered to be, the higher the status it confers. From *The Balcony* on, this takes the form of images that correspond closely to Sartre's concepts of 'being' and 'nonbeing'. The dominant classes in society identify 'good' with existing conditions, which are defined as 'being', while labelling 'nonbeing', which Sartre sees as active since it is the power of negation, as 'evil'. From this comes Genet's association of the active principle in existence with absence or death; and this is expressed in religious terms: 'The life which I lead demands the same unconditional renunciation of earthly things that is required by the Church of its Saints . . . Saintliness leads to Heaven by the road of sin.'[10]

This view of existence is not a personal aberration, nor can it be dismissed as simply a response to the unfortunate circumstances of Genet's life. It is characteristic of the avant garde, and can already be found in a short mystery play from Strindberg's inferno period, *Coram Populo! De Creatione et Sententia Vera Mundi*. In this, God is a usurper, who has deliberately created a 'world of madness' for his sadistic pleasure. He ordains sexual procreation, so that life will continue to exist 'for the mockery of the gods' even after Lucifer has persuaded man to taste the tree of knowledge, which for Strindberg represents salvation through extinction, because awareness of the true nature of existence makes suicide preferable: 'Eat of it and you will possess the gift of deliverance from sorrow, the joy of death'. Since this false God 'calls evil good, and good evil', the polarities of light and darkness are reversed, Satan being presented as Prometheus and Apollo, the true benefactor of mankind. Christ in this inverted Pantheon is Lucifer's son; and his crucifixion is designed to 'abolish the fear of death', which is the final masterstroke in Lucifer's campaign to liberate mankind from a humiliating existence. In the last scene God is dethroned, giving rise to a positive vision of destruction in which 'being' is transformed into 'nonbeing', since 'famine and plague ravage the nations: love is changed to hatred, filial love to parricide'.[11] The parallels to Genet (and indeed to other more recent Artaudian playwrights such as David Rudkin) are striking.

The Screens is Genet's most complete expression of such beliefs. As in *The Blacks*, the basic elements of human life are polarized and their values inverted. White, standing for civilization, is the colour of death-in-life. Black represents hatred and the void, the dark skin of slavery, savagery or the criminal in the night; and negation is the only creative force. Like the Negro Earth Mother's call to the Soul of Africa, the impetus for revolt therefore comes from an invocation to evil – 'miraculous evil . . . impregnate my people' – but where Africa symbolizes fertility in *The Blacks*, the evil evoked here is sterile. Its representatives are the unholy trinity of a mother, 'kicked out by the living and the dead', her son Saïd (whose 'rise' from total poverty into absolute criminality counterpoints the 'descent' of the liberation fighters from crime to recognized political status as an army), and his wife Leila, the ugliest of all Arab women, who makes herself even more hideous by adopting the gait of a cripple as well as becoming syphilitic and disfigured. Hatred is not just the only emotion available to outcasts, as in *The Blacks*, it is rigorously pursued in the relationships of this family as an apotheosis of evil. For Genet, 'the crimes of which a people is ashamed constitute its real history'; and it is Saïd's continued assertion of 'nonbeing' that sustains the Arab 'frenzy to the bitter end, or almost, heedless of the gazes that were judging us'.[12] Indeed, Saïd and Leila achieve so pure a state of nonbeing that at the end only her veil, the surface sign of her ugliness, remains, while he vanishes altogether. Consequently the illusions that define existence (and stage performance) disappear. Life ceases and 'the stage is empty. It is all over.'

This is the ultimate transcendence of reality, which lies behind the metamorphoses of his earlier plays. Despite the parallels to a study like Frantz Fanon's *The Wretched of the Earth: Black Skins, White Masks* (published in France the same year as *The Screens*), the oppression of colonized peoples is not depicted to promote political liberation. Their misery is exalted as a necessary step in a spiritual apotheosis, which (as the Missionary recognizes) is dependent on the 'cruelty and injustice' of the colonizers. As Genet explained to Blin, the play is 'the celebration of nothing', and its intention was to 'act upon thousands of Parisians without disturbing the world order, and yet bring about a poetic, fiery release so strong, so dense that it would illuminate the world of the dead . . . The feast of the dead must be beautiful . . . so that whatever separates us from the dead will be transcended.'[13]

As a homage to death, the play is designed to evoke a deep subconscious need in audiences who belong to a civilization that Genet sees as 'increasingly marked by death and turned towards it'. They are expected to follow the characters in leaping through the paper screens of illusion into the limbo of the dead. Hence Blin's presentation of the play as a subjective vision, picking up on the significance of dreams in *The Balcony*, and on the visionary approach in *Deathwatch*, which 'unfolds as in a dream'. Hence, too, his comparison of its effect to

> the street you see at night when you are drunk – you see it in a different way . . . This is true discovery. You are perceiving reality; for the first time all bonds and restrictions have been broken. Objective reality has been dislocated.[14]

The means Genet envisaged for achieving this transformation of reality echo many of Artaud's characteristic staging devices although, according to Blin, Genet had read little of Artaud's work. He required gestures to be unnatural, having no relationship to those used in everyday life, heightened and 'hieratic' or 'visible'. Vocal tones were to be distorted, and organized into a complex, quasi-musical score, 'which ranges from murmurs to shouts. Sentences; a tempest of sentences, must be delivered like so many howls, others will be warbles.' He expected the actors to turn themselves into animals, and called for emotional states to be presented in absolute terms, even mere apprehension being expressed as 'a painful vision of fear' in which the actors were to carry their trembling in every limb 'to trancelike lengths'. Exactly as in Artaud's design for *The Ghost Sonata* (the play that Roger Blin had also chosen to start his directing career in 1949), Genet called for larger-than-life props, encircled by a black line or with their shadows outlined on the screens by an actor 'to lend the moment a certain density'. The actors' make-up was not only mask-like and asymmetrical, but extended into a stylized tracery of tendons and veins comparable to the skeletal musculature of *The Cenci* costumes. The paintings on the screens were to be modelled on 'drawings done by madmen'; and Genet even recommended Blin to search for examples specifically at Rodez, the asylum to which Artaud had been committed.[15]

This was the first production of his work in which Genet had been extensively involved; and the stylized presentation of *The Screens* corresponded to the ideas that he had set out in a preface to *The Maids*. Already in that, twelve years earlier, there were clear parallels to Artaud in his references to 'Japanese, Chinese and Balinese revels', his ideal of dramatic art as 'a profound web of active symbols', and his description of the actor as 'a sign charged with signs'. But instead of concentrating on the inner significance of this symbolism, Genet emphasized its external form. The conventional 'masquerade' is not rejected for an Artaudian 'true vision', but for 'ceremony'; and the example chosen is the Mass, described as 'the loftiest modern drama' because 'the point of departure disappears beneath the profusion of ornaments and symbols'.[16]

It has become almost a commonplace to refer to Genet's theatre as a black mass.[17] This is not simply a figure of speech loosely based on Genet's constant allusions to the sacred, or on the presence of a priest as one of the major characters in each of his three full-length plays. In Genet's theatricalization of reality, where pretence is overt and every action is presented as performance, all activities take on liturgical significance. Separated from function, they become rites; and it is no accident that all Genet's plays except *Deathwatch* revolve around revolution, since, according to Frantz Fanon, 'revolution is the modern ritual' and its true aim is not an external change in the power structure, but the creation of a new identity for the oppressed by the violent exorcism of an alien presence that has dominated them through spiritual possession.[18] So in Genet's plays political revolution becomes a metaphor for spiritual transcendence, and 'funeral symbols' are substituted for the equally symbolic clenched fists or red flags.

Theatre itself becomes the ultimate image of this symbolic reality, since the illusory nature of performance is the opposite of 'being' and thus has intrinsic religious significance: 'The Devil makes believe. That's how one recognizes him. He's the great Actor. And that's why the Church has anathematized actors.' The theological aim of his plays thus becomes to abolish God; and as ceremonies, their structure is loosely based on church ritual.

Genet specified that *The Balcony* was to be 'performed with the solemnity of a Mass in a cathedral'. In *The Screens*, Saïd's apotheosis repeats Christ's Passion and Ascension in reverse, his family is ironically referred to as 'the Holy Family', the heart drawn on the screens in the orgy of destruction is 'the Sacred Heart of Jesus, with flames in place of the aorta'.[19] And in *The Maids*, partly because of its shortness, the pattern comes out clearly. The action, explicitly described as 'the Ceremony', is performed three times (a number with strong religious connotations), and its function is the direct opposite of the Mass. The emotion focused on the sacrificial saviour is a mixture of carnal lust and hatred, instead of spiritual love; and the celebrant achieves communion with the deity by destroying 'Her' image, not worshipping it. Madame's vanity table is referred to as 'the altar', the kitchen is 'the vestry', and in this symbolic context Solange's arrangement of the fall of Madame's dress on Claire is 'arranging [her] fall from grace'. Claire calls Madame 'a Lovelier Virgin', and the terms used to describe her, 'Your . . . ivory bosom! Your . . . golden thighs! Your amber feet!', are drawn from the 'tower of ivory' and 'gate of gold' in the litany of the Virgin Mary.

The first time the fragmentary ritual is performed it corresponds to the Elevation of the Host. The debasement of the symbolic maid is used to establish the distance between the worshipper and the divinity, while the symbolic mistress is deified:

> SOLANGE: (*in ecstacy*): Madame's being carried away!
> CLAIRE: By the devil! He's carrying me away in his fragrant arms. He's lifting me up, I leave the ground, I'm off . . .

The second time the ritual is repeated, in outline only, its focus is the real Madame and the act of worship is the act of murder, with the ultimate crime as a form of canonization modelled on 'the story of Sister Holy Cross of the Blessed Valley who poisoned twenty-seven Arabs'. The third repetition transfers the crime to a metaphysical level, not the murder of a God-surrogate but of God himself – 'It's God who's listening to us. We know that it's for Him that the last act is to be performed, but we musn't forewarn Him'[20] – and Claire's suicide, willing her sister to give her the poison she drinks, is a perverted reflection of Christ knowingly allowing himself to be crucified. The consecration is a desecration, self-annihilation is achieved by destroying God.

Genet's problem is that blasphemy is only possible for a believer, and today's society is secularized. As the wife of one of the colonists comments in *The Screens*:

> Betrayal's not what it used to be. In the old days, as my great-grandmother used to tell me, an engaged couple would marry on the eve of their wedding. The male would gash the female, and an invisible red spot under her white gown would prove that love was stronger than God. One had to believe in God, of course, and betray.[21]

Transformation, the 'unnameable operation' on reality, is one of the key words in Genet's drama. Yet, without belief, a communion wafer remains bread instead of the body of Christ. So Genet's false spectacle remains illusion, poetry without the force of a 'true image', although he tried to find an equivalent to religious belief in the force of hatred. This is one of the reasons why Genet consistently refused permission for *The Blacks* to be performed by white actors, and why he specifies that a black audience should wear white masks or be represented by 'a symbolic white', on whom a spotlight would be focused throughout the performance.[22] The opposition is designed to arouse extreme and irrational emotion by playing on racial fears and antagonisms. Another reason for insisting on a black cast was that, in acting out the fantasy of rape, massacre and revenge, Negro actors would be shocked into recognizing the truth of the 'gestures' the play required them to perform. The hatred they then projected would evoke a corresponding emotion in the white spectators.

Early productions of Genet's plays in Paris achieved this to some degree. Moral outrage and accusations of racism greeted *The Blacks*, while the cast – all 'assimilated Negroes who were shocked by Genet's language [and] did not want to be taken for savages', according to Blin – were indeed psychologically disturbed by their parts. The two actresses from Martinique playing the White and Black Queens were brought to a volcanic pitch of hatred for each other that liberated a primitivism quite in keeping with the play:

> I discovered that the White Queen was burning this incense to ward off the evil spell she accused the Black Queen of casting upon her . . . willing her to forget her lines. The Black Queen's witchcraft was present in her on-stage acting, in her secret, symbolic and ritualistic gestures.[23]

In terms of public response, *The Screens* was even more successful. The première provoked cries of 'traitor!' and mass riots during the performances, vehement protest in the newspapers and the very real threat of physical violence from the Ex-Servicemen's League outside on the streets. Yet political passions are by no means the same as spiritual transfiguration. Although these plays made the kind of mark on society that is all too rare in theatre history, and transformed the avant garde from a marginal activity to a central force, in Genet's own terms they have to count as failures, since for him 'a performance that does not act upon my soul is in vain'.[24]

FERNANDO ARRABAL – LINDSAY KEMP

This 'ceremonial' and spiritual – but anti-religious – line of avant garde drama was taken to its extreme by Fernando Arrabal. Writing in the strong Roman Catholic context of Franco's Spain, he was not faced with Genet's problem of addressing a secularized society, or audiences for whom religion was largely irrelevant, while the rigidity of right-wing dictatorship gave him a fixed and clearly visible social structure to oppose. Like many other avant garde dramatists, Arrabal took his starting point from Strindberg, whom he acknowledged as 'the master of us all' because of the central 'element of madness, of obsession' in his work.[25] The circular structure of Arrabal's *The Grand Ceremonial* (1965) was modelled on *To Damascus*; and other elements in his plays come from the surrealists through

Arthur Adamov – the French absurd dramatist who started off as a member of the group around Paul Eluard and knew Artaud well – and through the more flamboyant Spanish tradition of Salvador Dali and Luis Buñuel. He has also ranked his work alongside Grotowski, Brook and the Living Theatre, all of whom he classifies (with himself) as 'Seneca's descendants'.

Arrabal has described most of his plays as dramatized nightmares, 'direct manifestations of my inner world as revealed through my dreams . . . The visual – the dream – is my starting point.' But his emphasis on 'ceremony' (the external and formalized surface of his plays) together with the provocative extremism of his themes, his scatological obscenity, blasphemy and sado-masochistic eroticism, gives an impression of willed fantasy rather than true subconscious experience. This overt intention to shock, however, is more than simply *épater les bourgeois*. It is central to his aim of creating a 'panic theatre', which would arouse the same irrational and primitive terror in the presence of nature as the god Pan, though he also uses the term 'pan' in the sense of 'all-encompassing': 'For me the theatre remains a ceremony; it's a feast both sacrilegious and sacred, erotic and mystic, which would encompass all facets of life, including death. . . .'[26]

Arrabal associates excess with poetry. But in practice his extremism limits his vision to private caprice, rather than expanding it to the universal. The hunchbacks and cripples who inhabit his plays reflect the horrified fascination that he claims is his reaction to the physical side of existence – 'particularly during those moments when I feel myself assailed by a sterile lucidity'. Where he depicts lovers, they whip their women, who beg to be chained to beds or children's prams. These characters caress passionately, but always prove incapable of consummating their relationships. Instead they preserve their 'purity' by substituting murder for coitus, or by choosing life-size dolls and dead, or almost-dead, bodies as objects of their lust. Again this quite explicitly and consciously reflects neurotic obsessions: both 'the temptations inherent in purity', which according to Arrabal 'fascinate me even to the point of nausea', and his apparent belief that any erotic gratification except masturbation would defile his poetic inspiration.[27]

Most strikingly his strong Catholic upbringing is perverted into a deliberately blasphemous evocation of the sacred in plays like *The Solemn Communion* (1965), where a young girl, ceremoniously attired in an 'unbelievably baroque dress', is 'initiated' by killing a necrophiliac, who copulates in a coffin, or *The Automobile Graveyard* (1957), where the protagonist Emanou (Emmanuel) – who steals, lies, is hypocritical and promiscuous and admits to killing a Jew – repeats Christ's Passion in the parody setting of a vast scrapheap: born in a stable, betrayed to the police by a kiss from one of his group of musicians while the other denies knowing him, crucified on the handlebars of a bicycle.

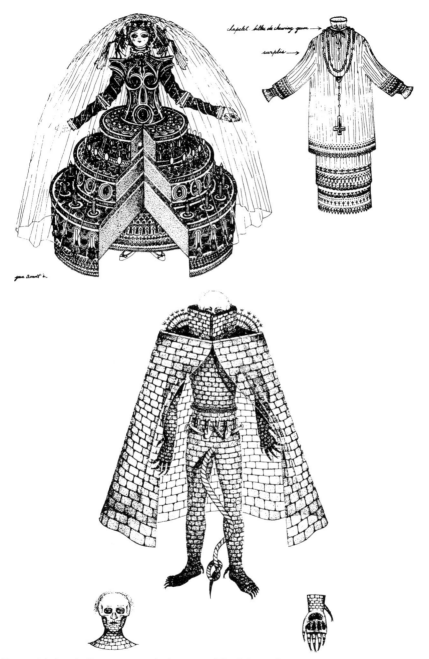

Figure 14 Arrabal's costume designs for *The Solemn Communion*: ceremonials, eroticism and perversion.

Perhaps the most interesting variant on this theme is *The Architect and the Emperor of Assyria* (1967), where the very vehemence of the denial of God becomes a paradoxical way of asserting His existence. The make-believe 'emperor' – the sole survivor of an air crash, who lands on a desert island inhabited by a single savage – has three interrelated obsessions. Having failed to prove the existence of God on a pin-ball machine by achieving the 'impossible' score of 1,000 with a single ball (a drunk tilted the table at 999), he attempts to provoke God to turn him into a pillar of salt by moving as he relieves himself so that his faeces trace the words 'God is a son of a bitch' on the beach. He also plays out a mock Passion:

How can I redeem humanity singlehanded?
He mimes the crucifixion . . .
The feet, yes. I can nail them better than the centurion but . . .
His gestures show that nailing the hands is a problem.

His second obsession, power, is linked to this through the figure of the emperor he dreams of being: Nebuchadnezzar, whom God punished for pride by making him believe himself an animal 'till thou know that the most High ruleth in the kingdom of men' (Daniel 4:25). And in the fantasies acted out during the play he not only pretends to be a horse, cow, dog and sacred elephant, but also at one point finds a pair of horns really growing on his forehead.

The action is solely composed of fragmentary and ritualized games of domination, strongly reminiscent of the ceremonies of the *cérébraux* in Genet's 'grand balcony'. The 'emperor' and the savage, whom he has dominated and drawn into his sexual fantasies, play out the roles of tyrant and slave, corpse and sexton, priest and penitent nun, woman-mother and lover-son (as in Arrabal's other plays, passion is represented by flagellation) and finally judge and accused. In the trial the 'emperor' acts not only as the criminal – himself – but also as all the witnesses, including his mother whom his evidence reveals as his victim. Here the game becomes reality, because it embodies the third obsession, which also incorporates the other two. He has murdered and eaten his mother (he claims to have fed her to his dog, linking her with the biblical Jezebel – however his games have already shown him in the role of his dog), and as expiation demands to be killed and eaten by his judge – the savage, who is dressed in his mother's clothes. His body is laid on an altar-like table; and this cannibalism is presented as a blasphemous Mass, but one in which God is finally manifested, though in a typically perverted form. Water miraculously turns into Jeyes' fluid, instead of the expected wine, proving that 'there is an afterlife . . . beyond'; and there is a real transubstantiation: 'the ARCHITECT assumes the voice, tone, features and expressions of the EMPEROR' as he digests his body, finally becoming him (the actors switch

roles) when he eats his brain. Typically too this is performed in a way
designed to arouse visceral revulsion:

> Thanks to your nucleic acid I shall be master of your memory, your
> dreams . . . and your thoughts. *He taps on the chisel placed behind the*
> EMPEROR'S *ear. He makes a hole: he sticks the straw in: he sucks out the*
> *brain, a substance like yoghourt trickles down his cheeks. He licks it.* Ooh![28]

Like most of Arrabal's work, the whole action is presented as a dream.
However, this is done in a rather self-conscious way that is perhaps
intended to make it possible for the audience to subliminate their probable
feelings of disgust, which might lead them simply to reject the play, by
interpreting the action on a metaphoric rather than actual level, as images
from the subconscious rather than representations of real events. Even the
scatological blasphemy of the 'emperor's' defecating habits is illusory, since
he is permanently constipated; and it is specifically stated that the characters are 'not in the real world'. To wake out of the dream they only have
to clap their hands, which the 'emperor' ostentatiously refuses to do,
while the visionary nature of the fantasy is underlined by comparing it to
Hieronymus Bosch's painting of the *Garden of Delights*.[29]

At the same time this is a monodrama. Both characters are opposing
facets of the same universalized personality, as the ending clearly demonstrates when the savage-transformed-to-emperor, once more alone on the
island, hears a plane crash; and the 'architect' enters as a sole survivor,
to repeat the opening of the play. The savage represents the primitive side
of man, with magical powers that enable him to speak to animals, move
mountains, turn day to night – all of which he loses as he takes on the
emperor's attributes. The dominating intruder represents the civilizing
intellect, flattering himself on a cultural heritage and proud of a philosophy
that has produced only death (war/murder) and sexual repression. The
action is endlessly repeated both because on the religious level ritual
sacrifice leads to resurrection, and because on the psychological level any
element of the personality that is repressed reappears in a new form.

In Arrabal's plays, which he claims are written 'spontaneously', the
avant garde exploration of dream states, primitivism and ritual becomes
an all too literal attempt to realize Artaud's call for 'a new idea of eroticism
and cruelty', anticipating a direction taken by avant garde groups in the
early 1970s (see pp. 223–4 in this volume). Even the so-called innocence
of Arrabal's retarded characters, whose incest and murder, sadism and
suicide are performed with child-like unconsciousness of the consequences,
appears as a further perversion. Significantly, he supports the accuracy of
a description of his work as 'midway between de Sade and St Theresa of
Avila'. As one of his characters says: 'Why am I presenting you with this
catalogue of horrors? . . . I want to dazzle you.'[30] Indeed it is only a
quality of crude simplicity in presentation that saves his fantasies from

pornography. At the same time similar shock effects are characteristic of contemporary drama – both avant garde and more mainstream political plays. For instance, the same image of cannibalism as simultaneously a religious mass and a quasi-sexual comm-union, reused by Arrabal in *The Young Barbarians of Today* (1975), recurs in plays like Heiner Müller's *The Battle* (1976) or Edward Bond's *Early Morning* (where it is given an additional rationale as a metaphor for capitalist competition).

Where Arrabal's 'panic theatre' parallels and extends key elements of Genet's plays, the direct influence of Genet can be illustrated in the striking dance-drama of Lindsay Kemp. His contribution has been to synthesize established experimental theatre forms with the most popular kinds of art – rock concerts (Kemp has choreographed David Bowie's shows), cabaret, circus, even strip-tease. Inhabiting the homosexual underground of the 1960s and 1970s, Kemp's work was largely ignored by serious criticism, although it attracted disproportionate attention from the police. His productions could be seen as an updating of the kind of avant garde atavism represented by Nijinski's *Rites of Spring*, and indeed his company included Anton Dolin, who had been one of Diaghilev's lead dancers in the *Ballets Russes*. But it was specifically from reading Artaud that Kemp developed his approach. His most characteristic production was *Flowers* (1966), an adaptation of Genet's autobiographical novel *Our Lady of the Flowers*; and it was Artaud's emphasis on myth, ritual and trance states that made him realize how Genet's vision could be actualized on the stage.

Opening with a scene of mass masturbation, orgasm and crucifixion, performed to pulsating lights and musical rhythms, *Flowers* assaulted the senses, sensibilities and preconceptions of the audience, overwhelming the spectator with audio-visual effects and images of perverse tenderness, sexual violence and spiritual cruelty. The opening was explicitly designed to induce a trance in the actors, in which 'the subconscious will take over the body' and liberate it 'to follow the subtle direction of the dance within us'. The performance, mimed and danced without words, was improvised around the fixed structure provided by a complex score of sound effects, taped and live music, out of a body of rehearsed material over three times the length. This meant that performances, which were in a continual state of development (*Flowers* remained in Kemp's repertoire for over fifteen years), could change every night to reflect the actors' personal emotions, or to relate directly to different responses in the audience; and the rhythms were deliberately kept 'very basic, organic. It's absolutely essential to adapt oneself to the breathing of the audience, the heartbeat of the audience for a performance to become a communion, a shared ritual.'[31]

The central image of this production was an inverted religious ceremony, a black mass celebrating sexuality – specifically homosexuality – and 'the idea was to create a mythological background to the particular images . . .

Figure 15 Flowers. Subliminal dances and erotic archetypes.

to bring in themes that resonated'. This was even more obvious in *Salome* (1974), where Oscar Wilde's text was preceded by a prologue of primitive dancing, lit by flames from incense bowls and culminating in orgiastic rape. This led to symbolic scenes of a snake destroying a dove, of John the Baptist as an angelic Dionysus – whose wings were torn apart and the feathers scattered through the theatre in a poetic analogy to the dismemberment of the Greek god's body – then to theatrical images from Hamlet reflecting the incest motif.

Kemp's work contained no characterization in a normal sense. The actors in theory expressed their own personality on a subconscious level; heavy make-up transformed their faces into masks accentuating their own features; emotions were exaggerated towards the simplicity of universal psychological states; and a highly formalized slowness and grace of movement successfully merged the individual and the archetype. But where specific characterization and dialogue was called for, as in Wilde's play, the effect verged on caricature. Indeed, the transvestite acting (Kemp's company was assertively male apart from one token girl) inevitably tended to high camp, which indicates the limitations of Kemp's approach. However, even this falsity could become a source of strength when the audiovisual rhythms were effective in drawing the audience into the action; and the theatricality was accentuated deliberately. Herodias is given a pair of huge rubber breasts; Dolin as Herod strips off his wig to reveal the old tired actor beneath; Salome's seduction is accompanied by a grandiose musical cliché like the *Liebestod* theme from *Tristan and Isolde*. Similarly, in *Flowers* the homosexual fantasy breaks into popular lyrics such as 'Somewhere Over the Rainbow' or 'Blackbird Bye Bye', with cathartic comic release. And in both productions the presence of a real girl served to underline the falsity of the men in drag – but this paradoxically transposed them to a higher level of imaginative reality. In Genet's terms, it became a true image precisely because the spectacle was fake. If it works, the challenge to the imagination involves the audience more deeply in the action than any conventionally illusionistic presentation could. But Kemp realized the dangers involved in relying so extensively on the subconscious, and in the overt incongruity of a 40-year-old man playing the 12-year-old Salome: 'Working with extreme images is grand guignol, melodramatic, which brings in an element of parody. You are on a tightrope of belief. We balance on a knife edge between the serious and the ridiculous.'[32]

Lindsay Kemp's aim was basically psychological; and his assault on the audience – simultaneously sensual, emotional, moral and perceptual – was intended to challenge the repressive norms of social behaviour, 'to liberate . . . who we are, releasing the bird, or the angel, or the natural dance which is in all of us, enabling us to fly'. And even if the explicit celebration of homosexuality was perhaps self-indulgent, or the fantasy dream world conjured up too special for many of the public to project their fears and desires into, with its *fin de siècle* images derived from Aubrey Beardsley and Gustav Moreau, as theatre it was spectacular. It also formed an international language, appealing equally to audiences in Poland, Holland and Spain, as well as in England and America. Kemp brought the avant garde to popular (sub-)culture; and his direct descendants can be seen in contemporary rock-videos.

8

MYTH AND THEATRE LABORATORIES

PETER BROOK

The search for a universal theatre language, one potential form of which Lindsay Kemp developed out of pop culture in the mid-1960s, has become a major and continuing theme in the work of Peter Brook. Unlike almost all the other representatives of the movement, Brook became a convert to the avant garde at a relatively late point in his career, having already made his name during the twenty years after the Second World War in brilliant, but conventional Shakespeare productions, and as a director of Covent Garden opera and light comedy (*Ring Around the Moon*, Jean Anouilh; *The Dark is Light Enough*, Christopher Fry; *Penny for a Song*, John Whiting). In the early 1950s Anouilh and Fry were being credited with reintroducing poetry into the naturalistic modern theatre; and it was through Anouilh and Cocteau that Brook came to a concept of non-verbal 'poetry of the theatre' (where 'the scenes are linked like the words of a poem'[1]). Despite the conventional nature of the plays, such a concept is analogous to Barrault's ideal of 'total theatre'. At the same time, despite a pragmatic box-office approach to the stage – not only reflected in Brook's repertoire during those decades, but also still evident in the way he has managed and publicized his later avant garde productions – this interest in poetic drama could be seen, at least in retrospect, as signalling his coming rejection of 'deadly theatre' – the standard fare of classical museum-pieces, social problem plays and commercial comedy.

Fired from the Covent Garden Opera House over a controversial updating of *Salome* in 1949 (another coincidental link with Lindsay Kemp), and breaking out of conventional limits in small ways during the 1950s – staging 'scandalous' American plays like Arthur Miller's *A View from the Bridge* (notorious for including a homosexual kiss) or Tennessee Williams' incestually provocative *Cat on a Hot Tin Roof* – by 1960 Brook was asking such questions as:

is there nothing in the revolution that took place in painting fifty years ago that applies to our own [theatrical] crisis today? Do we

125

know where we stand in relation to the real and the unreal, the face of life and its hidden streams, the abstract and the concrete, the story and the ritual?

And the answers he found were in *The Theatre and its Double*, which had only just become available in English translation (1958). Quoting Artaud, 'The theatre must give us everything that is in crime, war or madness, if it is to recover its necessity', Brook stressed 'the nothingness of our present position and the need for a search. A search for what? For something we will only recognize and be able to define when we have found it.'[2]

From then on, his connections with the French avant garde multiplied. It was Brook whom Genet asked to direct the Paris première of *The Balcony* (originally intended for 1957, but banned by the French government until 1960), while it was Genet's play *The Screens* which acted as the catalyst for Brook's exploration of Artaud in 1964. This attempt to translate Artaud's theories into practice, though brief, led not only to Brook's Artaudian staging of Peter Weiss' *Marat/Sade*, but also to his subsequent search for a ritual theatre. And his links with Jean-Louis Barrault were equally far-reaching. Barrault had started the Théâtre des Nations as a logical extension of his 'total theatre', envisioning a meeting-place where the traditions of the Far East – Bunraku, Kabuki, Nōh – could cross-fertilize with modern experiments by the Living Theatre, Grotowski (first exposed to the West through this festival) or Eugenio Barba. And when Barrault founded the Centre for International Theatre Research (CIRT) in 1968 as the corollary to the Théâtre des Nations – a 'laboratory' for exploring the potential and synthesizing the principles of the theatre styles showcased in the festival – it was Brook he invited to direct it.

In fact there are many similarities in their concepts of theatre. Like Barrault, Brook is a pragmatic director, who works empirically. Each pursued avant garde theatrical exploration at the same time as continuing to work with classical material (with Brook returning to Shakespeare, Chekhov and even opera – Bizet's *Carmen* – during his search for a mythic theatre that would restore drama to its primal 'roots'). Both have a catholic appreciation of different dramatic forms, while rejecting the theatrical *status quo* as a cultural garbage heap. Brook's concept of stage as 'an empty space' – the imaginative neutrality of which allows the actor to move freely through the entire physical world and into subjective experience, not only presenting 'man simultaneously in all his aspects', but also involving the audience collectively in 'a total experience'[3] – is remarkably similar to Barrault's 'total theatre'. He also rejects naturalism as a style identified with the Establishment: 'the official art of every regime'. And, like Barrault, the influence of Artaud was decisive for Brook too, marking a radical change in his directorial approach.

For Brook, the 1964 'Theatre of Cruelty' season has a significance out of all proportion to its actual substance or achievement, as his frequent references to it in his book *The Empty Space* indicate. Initially, Brook and his collaborator, Charles Marowitz, described their aims in a typically inflated way. These were: to create 'the poetic state, a transcendent experience of life' through shock effects, cries, incantation, masks, effigies and ritual costumes; to use changes of light to 'arouse sensations of heat and cold'; to present different actions in separated areas 'all flooding one's consciousness simultaneously'; and to create discontinuous physical rhythms 'whose crescendo will accord exactly with the pulsation of movements familiar to everyone', corresponding to 'the broken and fragmentary way in which most people experience contemporary reality'. And this eclectic mix of symbolist 'correspondences', dada and Artaud was labelled 'a rediscovery of the terror and awesomeness of the original semi-religious theatre'.[4]

On this metaphysical level the group's performances were a self-conscious and pretentious failure; but beneath it there was a pragmatic and limited purpose. As an exercise preparing the traditionally trained actors of the Royal Shakespeare Company for a performance of *The Screens*, the workshop was an exploration of theatre language designed to demolish their conventional dramatic values, particularly 'the Stanislavski ethic', and return to the roots of physical expression. It was a short-term prototype of Brook's subsequent laboratory work, and marked out his later theatrical territory.

The experiment began by each actor attempting to communicate an internal state by pure thought transfer, adding vocal sound and physical rhythms 'to discover what was the very least he needed before understanding could be reached', and developing a body language 'beyond psychological implication and beyond monkey-see-monkey-do facsimiles of social behaviourism'.[5] This return to basics in order to develop in a new direction echoed Grotowski's aims in a remarkable way, even though it took place almost a year before the first reports of Grotowski's acting methods were published in English, and two years before Brook's first opportunity to see Grotowski's work in Paris. And the parallel is not fortuitous. It comes from the fundamentalism that is an integral part of avant garde primitivism.

The material presented at the London Amateur Dramatic Association (LAMDA) – Artaud's *Spurt of Blood*, short abstract word collages by Paul Ableman, two surrealist sketches by Brook himself, a single scene from *The Screens* (replaced by Arden's *Ars Longa Vita Brevis* when the Lord Chamberlain demanded cuts in Genet's text), a montage of *Hamlet* by Marowitz, together with sequences of mime and improvisation – was little more than a series of acting exercises. The opening sketch, adapted from an incident recounted by Barrault, presented Artaud himself being auditioned by Charles Dullin who asks him to sit down, and watches with bewilderment as Artaud prances, staggers and finally creeps on all fours

Figure 16 Brook's experimental *Spurt of Blood*. Stylized simplicity and the exploration of basic theatre language.

towards a chair. Artaud exits, calling out 'Well, if it's realism you want, adieu!' – and this set the tone for the rendering of *The Spurt of Blood*. Artaud's mini-play was presented twice, the first time with the dialogue (delivered with extreme rapidity and variations of pitch) accompanied by a crude mixture of symbolic gesture and naturalism, all in three minutes. The same actions were then run through again in rehearsal clothes and faces covered by blank paper masks, with wordless sounds and action paintings. However, along with this abstraction, there was one visual effect that did follow the text: an enormous, three-dimensional 'Hand of God', suspended from the flies, which broke through a paper screen to appear above the actors and gushed out blood when bitten. According to Marowitz, this was the high point of the performance.

The audience, largely composed of other theatre professionals and reviewers, was not impressed. As Clive Barker commented:

> The narrator gives the line: 'Enter a knight in medieval armour followed by a wet-nurse, her breasts in her hands.' The physical effect of a man in one of the suits of the Black Prince – ornate to the point of sensuality – followed by a big girl cupping in her hands a pair of great steaming tits, milk dribbling from the nipples, must be almost overwhelming . . . I can [also] see it performed by a man

in a polished steel breastplate . . . [and] a girl decorated with a pair of crudely painted bladders, filled with water . . .

What we saw was a man in standard Old Vic imitation armour followed by a girl, inexplicably in pseudo 14th century costume, cupping her empty hands 18 inches in front of her. The contradiction between words and images depressed me beyond words.[6]

When *The Screens* came to be presented three months later, only the first twelve scenes were performed, the remaining two and a half hours being dismissed as repetitious elaboration by Brook. This performance was far better received. The frenzy of the acting, animalistic vocal effects, masks and ritualized rhythms were considered powerfully Artaudian, while the action painting on the screens, called for by Genet, was seen as revelatory:

Arab terrorists . . . come, swiftly drawing their murders, their rapes, their fear, until the screens are covered with scrawled images of evil. The result is electrifying: naked hatred is presented on the stage . . . an image apparently derived out of fantasy but which, like Picasso's *Guernica*, is a poetic distillation which contains a truth more bright than reality.[7]

However, Brook's shortened production of *The Screens*, too, was labelled as merely 'work in progress'; and the second half of the experimental season never appeared.

This was to have followed Artaud's first Theatre of Cruelty manifesto with classics of violence like Marlowe's *The Jew of Malta* and Büchner's *Wozzeck*, as well as Jarry's *Ubu roi* and Strindberg's *A Dream Play*. Out of this typically Artaudian selection, it is significant that the only one Brook actually came to stage was Jarry. Following Barrault, and taking his theatrical exploration back to Artaud's roots, as it were, in 1977 Brook staged a compilation of Jarry's work (entitled *Ubu dans les Bouffes*, after the Bouffes du Nord theatre into which Brook moved the CIRT in 1974). But, despite its highly provisional and incomplete nature, the LAMDA experiment established the principle of 'scientific research' into theatrical communication, on which all Brook's subsequent work has been based. And elements from it recurred in the key productions by which his search for a theatre of myth and ritual can be charted.

One of the improvisational exercises, expressing emotional states in fictional situations through Rorschach-like abstract action-paintings, which had been used in *The Spurt of Blood* and provided some of the most powerful moments in *The Screens*, was repeated in a more sophisticated form in *The Marat/Sade* (1964). Similarly, the powerful erotic image of Charlotte Corday whipping Sade with her hair had its prototype in Brook's playlet *The Public Bath*, where Glenda Jackson (who also acted Corday) as the scapegoat-saint – a double image of the notorious Christine Keeler and the bereaved

Jacqueline Kennedy – whipped a judge as he pronounced sentence on her. Marowitz saw this piece and *The Marat/Sade* as being 'mystically related', Artaud having not only cited de Sade in his definition of 'cruelty', but also played the role of Marat in Abel Gance's film of *Napoleon*. By contrast to German productions, which were faithful to Peter Weiss' intentions in bringing out the rational dialectic of social revolution in the play, Brook focused exclusively on the Artaudian side of the text.[8] As part of their preparation the cast were shown documentary film (by Jean Rouch) of a Nigerian native ritual, in which the participants reached extreme states of savage madness – an early indication of Brook's interest in primitivism – and the mental patients of the Charenton asylum were placed in the foreground of the performance. The acting consisted largely of pathological symptoms, graphically displaying the physical state of spastics, catatonics, paranoics, schizophrenics and syphilitics. And even though this was primarily a grotesque form of exoticism, it related to Artaud's madness, and echoed the positive value placed on insanity by various avant garde artists.

The image of a madhouse world dominated the action, which Sade was shown arranging for his own self-indulgent entertainment. Grotesquely comic mimes of disembowelling and guillotining accompanied descriptions of atrocities, to produce a visual and emotional shock treatment for the audience. This reached a climax when the obscene and convulsive hysteria, repeatedly inflamed and restrained by Sade, threatened to spill out into the auditorium. The forward surge of madmen was only halted by the stage manager's entry with a whistle – turning the whole performance into a monstrous version (for the audience) of the psychotherapy that the play-within-the-play is officially intended to be for the asylum inmates – and the actors ironically clapped the spectators, underlining the parallel.

This built on the LAMDA experiments with audience relationships, in which the spectators were surrounded by action or changed places with the actors, and the same technique was extended in *US* (1966). Representing the maimed of Vietnam, actors with their heads covered by paper bags (as in *The Spurt of Blood*) stumbled groaning in among the spectators, demanding physical assistance from the audience. This was an unfortunate confusion of symbolism with actuality, which was rapidly abandoned after the first few performances, even though it accurately expressed the focus of the production as an attack on the self-satisfied comfort of the 'uninvolved' British public ('us' rather than 'U.S.': hence the absence of any coherent statement about the war). Like the *Marat/Sade* production, which had distorted Weiss' intentions by stressing the Artaudian images of sadism, violence and insanity, *US* was preoccupied by cruelty and in particular the self-immolation of Buddhist monks and Quaker pacifists. This became a rather overliteral transliteration of Artaud's ideal actors 'signalling through the flames'. And together with the ending, in which a butterfly (in actuality only a piece of paper) was ceremonially burnt, followed by the full cast 'refusing' to leave the stage and thus forcing the audience into a 'decision' – to walk out, symbolizing their habitual avoidance of moral responsibility or involvement – it illustrates two intrinsic flaws in Brook's approach: his tendency to simplification and aestheticism.

However, the attempt to go beyond language, and to find more direct ways of relating the audience to the action, has yielded some of the most exciting interpretations of conventional drama, like Brook's 1970 production of *A Midsummer Night's Dream*. It also provided the springboard for his search for a ritual theatre, which had indeed been the rationale for his *Screens* project: 'The direction I want to explore is . . . a field in which ritual and what one calls outside reality completely overlap: and this is the world of Genet'.[9]

For the *Dream* Brook rehearsed his actors intensively in improvisational exercises, 'attempting to alter or strengthen the initial impulse that lay in the centre of the physical movement', and to form a 'vocabulary' out of acrobatics. This was extrapolated into the circus metaphor of the production, circus conventions being physical and presentational, as opposed to the imaginative evocation of verbal poetry. And in poetic passages that Brook felt had become clichéd by familiarity, the words were reduced to sounds and merged into patterns of physical movement. The premise that the opposite worlds of the play were identical, with Theseus doubling as Oberon and Hippolyta as Titania, was extended to encompass the separate worlds of stage and audience. Puck 'girdled' the auditorium; Hermia was almost forced off the stage into the spectators' laps; the cast exited through the audience at the end, literally enacting 'give me your hands, if we be friends' by shaking hands with the spectators. The formal parallels between Athens and the magic wood, together with the omnipresent fairies – who acted as stagehands, bringing in props, or created the lovers' environment by forming themselves into trees, and even literally transported characters from place to place on the stage – all corresponded to the submerging of rational verbal communication beneath acrobatic activity. Beneath Shakespeare's poetry Brook revealed a 'secret play' of total 'anarchy' and 'wild joy', where the world of the spirit in 'the wood and its inhabitants pour forth a primitive wildness which infected all who came into contact with it'.[10]

This interpretation, like the rehearsal methods and the 'empty space' of the square white gymnasium set, or the direct physical contact with the audience, clearly related the *Dream* to his experiments with Seneca's *Oedipus*, and with *The Tempest* (both in 1968). As in Brook's *Lear* immediately preceding the LAMDA season, where the perspective was explicitly Beckettian and the world was reduced to corroding 'facades and emblems' so that 'ironically, as characters acquire sight, it enables them only to see into a void',[11] the focus of both these productions was drawn from Jan Kott's existential interpretation of Shakespeare and Greek tragedy.

131

In the *Tempest* exercise Prospero and Caliban were presented as complementary aspects of a single personality, with 'This thing of darkness I acknowledge mine' as the central motif, and the intellectual, spiritual aspect of the mind losing control of the atavistic, instinctual Caliban. So the performance became an exploration of the anarchic and primitive side of human nature. The choice of Seneca's *Oedipus* (rather than Sophocles' humanistic version) also emphasized the violent and irrational side of life. Like Brook's *Lear*, where conventionally humanizing elements – such as the servant's protest against Gloucester's blinding – were cut, the thematic point of both productions was to explore how much suffering a human being could sustain without splitting under the pressure. Brook's aim was to oppose a rigorous objectivity to the 'romantic' view, 'where we leave an experience of horror finally strangely comforted' because of the author's 'complicity'.[12] Yet neither production was intended to be nihilistic.

Not only was existential honesty itself seen as 'the most positive' attitude available in the twentieth-century context of genocide, political torture and total warfare, the destructive anarchy of sexual urges expressed in these productions was itself considered liberating. The phallic golden spike, on which Jocasta impales herself at the end of Ted Hughes' adaptation of *Oedipus*, was paralleled by the farcically overliteral 7 ft golden phallus that the chorus danced around in a bacchanalian epilogue to the tune of 'Yes, we have no bananas', an incongruity that highlights Brook's problems in updating archaic ritual to the modern day. The same theme was even more explicit in Brook's version of *The Tempest*, where Caliban led a mass revolution, raping Miranda and then sexually assaulting Prospero, but this 'dark' side of sexuality was balanced against an innocent paradise of pre-civilized responses to nature, in which the final marriage ceremony was performed as a tribal mating ritual.

Given the way Brook was moving away from text, his choice of Seneca's *Oedipus* may seem odd since, having been written for declamation, not performance, the drama lies solely in the words. However, in this Brook was following Barrault and Roger Blin, who had recently staged Seneca's *Medea* and *Thyestes*; and by any definition Brook's *Oedipus* clearly counts as Theatre of Cruelty. Making thematic use of Artaud's metaphor, the production was based on the idea of a city devastated by plague. The David Turner/Ted Hughes text drew parallels between the bloodshed in Thebes and Vietnam, modern agnosticism and Seneca's Rome where 'official religion . . . had lost any hold on private thought', being replaced by 'a mixture of mysticism and quasi-scientific humanism'. The closing Bacchic dance was modelled on the Maori *haka*: a ritual of aggression symbolizing the destruction of an enemy. The speeches were patterned on tribal chants including African shamans, Tibetan monks and South American Indians,[13] delivered in a 'depersonalized' monotone, with stylized emotional effects achieved by strong and irregular rhythms of breathing derived from recordings of a witch doctor in a trance. The moves of the principle actors were abstract, devoid of feeling or contact, as in the slave's long description of Oedipus' blinding, which was accompanied by cold and formalized gestures:

> 1. Slowly lifts arms. 2. Hooks fingers in front of eyes. 3. Raises arms, palms out, hands hooked. 4. Drops arms, X over Box to U/R – stands. TIRESIAS rises, X to OEDIPUS. 5. Slave sits as TIRESIAS puts hands on OEDIPUS's eyes.[14]

The same dichotomy between images of extreme violence and stoically dispassionate expression – an avoidance of conventional rhetoric, which paradoxically gives an impact of almost unbearable intensity by restraint – characterized the whole presentation. The visual picture was one of extreme plainness, with the actors in dark suits and black roll-neck sweaters standing in an opened-up, empty golden cube in the centre of a bare stage, off which blinding light was reflected at high points in the action. And this impression of bareness was reinforced by the static immobility of the protagonists, with Gielgud in the whole of Oedipus' opening four-page impassioned speech being restricted to one emblematic movement, raising his arms to heaven. This abstraction was offset by emotive vocal effects from the chorus placed around the perimeter of the auditorium. They repeated the protagonists' words to create echoing chants, accompanying the description of the plague with rapid rhythmic panting, punctuating the speeches with ululations, ritually beating their chests at Oedipus' self-accusation. In the LAMDA experiment Brook and Marowitz had found that 'facial expressions, under the pressure of extended sounds, began to resemble Japanese masks';[15] and the same effect was used here, depersonalizing the actors at emotional peaks to give them mythic status.

In the preface to the published version of *US*, written during the rehearsals for *Oedipus*, Brook commented that the potential power of myth is insulated in direct proportion to its distance from contemporary issues. This points to the basic problem facing all the inheritors of Artaud who seek to affect spectators directly by using rituals in the modern secular context – where these have no religious significance, and therefore no subjective value for the public. The *Oedipus* production was an effective attempt to gain immediacy by throwing the subject of human 'cruelty' into stark relief through impersonal presentation and ritualized response. On one level the performance was a sacrificial rite; and reviewers found the primitive rhythmic orchestration hypnotic or compared it to *The Rite of Spring*. On another level it was a visceral assault on the audience, and so effective that some of the actors had moral doubts about presenting it at all:

> The play is such a violent vehicle [but] to play it down would be

dishonest . . . Blood, torn eyeballs, torn insides and torn gizzards are mentioned about every five seconds for two hours. Death, disaster, plague, sickness, horror are the main ingredients of the play . . . In fact I wondered whether it was right to perform this in front of people. In one of the speeches – the one in which the slave describes Oedipus tearing his eyes out – people in the audience became physically ill, and the St John's Ambulance Brigade was always on hand ready to carry people out. It happened quite often.[16]

In rehearsals for *Oedipus*, exercises were developed from Tai Chi, using gravity as the only source of energy to achieve economy of movement: a reduction of expression to essentials that characterizes all Brook's experiments at the CIRT.

The initial impetus for this research into theatre language came from the response to the RSC tour of *Lear*, by Eastern European audiences, who understood practically no English. Noting that cultural or linguistic contexts in fact act as 'barriers' to communication on a deeper, universal level, Brook

> set out to explore what the conditions were through which the theatre could speak directly. In what conditions is it possible for what happens in a theatrical experience to originate from a group of actors and be received and shared by spectators without the help and hindrance of shared cultural signs and tokens . . . ?[17]

This determined the international composition of his company, which has included actors from Japan, Africa, Persia and Spain as well as France, Britain and the USA. It also led to their African tour in search of audiences who lacked even the concepts of story line and pretence, the assumptions about linear narrative or acting out make-believe, on which theatre is based.

In practice it has meant reversing the traditional priorities of communication: elevating the secondary elements of gesture, pitch, tone and the dynamics of sound or movement that give expressive values, over the primary element of intellectual meaning. The difficulty is that all forms of language – verbal, vocal, emblematic or physical – communicate with any precision only to the extent that their symbols are known and shared. And to counter the danger that, in rejecting all shared signs, expression would be reduced to the purely private, Brook's emphasis has been on integrating the individual actor in the group on the dubious premise that expressive forms created by a collective, however small, will have the force and universality of archetypes. This exploration of non-semantic body language implies that (extending Barrault's concept) theatre should not imitate life, but directly create experience. And behind it lies a quasi-mystical belief in the metaphysical significance of the body as an 'organic root' uniting all men:

> Our work is based on the fact that some of the deepest aspects of human experience can reveal themselves through the sounds and movements of the human body in a way that strikes an identical chord in any observer, whatever his cultural and racial conditioning. And therefore one can work without roots, because the body, as such, becomes a working source.[18]

In terms of *The Tempest*, which was presented as 'work in progress', this meant cutting all the surface play of plot, characterization and 'pretty writing' that Brook found 'uninteresting' and 'hardly worth reviving'. Instead, he concentrated on the 'buried themes' of social exploitation, violence, incest, sexuality and revolution, to turn it into a universal statement on 'the whole condition of man'.[19] The bare stage was set in the middle of the audience, some of whom were seated on multi-level mobile scaffolds that were pushed on and around the acting area, and over which the actors climbed, swung and performed complex gymnastics. Spectators were also encouraged to mingle with the actors for close-ups on the action – techniques that anticipated Schechner's 'environmental theatre'. In addition, the opening 'mirror' exercise, with pairs of actors each facing the other and imitating each other's movements, provided an image of the ideal feedback between performer and observer, where every action arouses a corresponding reaction that in turn modifies the next action. Brook's primary concern was the creation of physical images by articulating space through the movement of the group as a whole, as in the storm sequence where the ensemble huddled, trembled and swam trance-like through waves of sound from the Japanese Ariel, giving vocal expression to a dream of tempest and terror. The climax was a mass copulation mime, an inverted pyramid being formed on the scaffolds with the violated body of Prospero as the apex at the bottom, and Caliban triumphant on the top. And this stress on the collective was carried over into a thematic focus on power and isolation: how one actor could impose his will on the group as a whole, or in the way detached figures became reduced to machines or animals, when contact with the ensemble was lost.

The text was treated in a similar way to the 'collage *Hamlet*' of the LAMDA experiment, where Marowitz had attempted 'to open up the play from the inside' as a montage of dialogue fragments and discontinuous scenes, comparable to the film structures of Truffaut or Resnais with their cross-cuts, close-ups and slow dissolves, or to the dissonances in the music of Schönberg. It was also intended to correspond in a dadaist way 'to the tempo of our time'. But Marowitz's aim in the earlier production had been to create an expressionistic image of the subconscious mind, presenting the play in the form of 'subliminal flashes out of Hamlet's life'. This was intended to mirror the distorted perception of reality by a 'boy in . . . a stress situation'; and it presupposed 'that there was a smear of Hamlet in everyone's collective unconscious'.[20]

However, Brook's superficially similar juxtaposing of speeches reduced to single lines, merging of characters and rearranging of sequences in *The Tempest*, was designed to transform Shakespeare's play into a mythic image of the primitive nature of man beneath the veneer of civilization. And the dialogue was either transformed into hieratic chanting – like the final marriage sequence which was accompanied by elaborations on 'And my ending is despair' / 'Unless it be relieved by prayer' – or showed language as an instrument of oppression – as in Prospero's attempt to control Caliban by teaching him single words related to identity, beginning with 'you/me' and ending with 'slave/master' in a remarkable anticipation of Peter Handke's theme in *Kaspar* (also first staged in 1968, and produced by Brook in 1972).

For *Oedipus*, Brook had introduced the cast to recordings of primitive native rites. He required them to model their delivery on 'certain peculiar breathing methods' used 'for ceremonial purposes', and on

> the pattern of [native] sounds and the pattern created by the use of hands and feet, and the extraordinary things the witchdoctor did with his voice. Brook talked a lot about what was the common root of *Oedipus* and the primitives. It was rhythms and the use of the voice to engender excitement . . . All this fitted in perfectly with Brook's idea of Theatre as Ritual [but] we didn't want to copy a native ritual; so we made up our own rituals. Breathing was our beginning.[21]

The CIRT work was based on the same principle, but extended it from borrowing primitive speech patterns, to using archaic ceremonial languages, and to integrating ritual with the dramatic material, instead of merely applying it to a text. In order to compensate for the 'vocal poverty' of contemporary speech and what Brook saw as the limitation on autonomous physical expression imposed by intellectual meaning, he trained his actors in the use of African chants, Latin and Avesti 'the ancient Persian language of Zoroastrian incantation'. The common factor was that these were 'dead' or incomprehensible languages associated with religious ceremonies. Thus expressive qualities of tone, pitch and rhythm could be exploited, without the interference of conceptual meaning, in his attempt to find a pre-logical, universal form of communication. The effect obviously relied heavily on exoticism and mystery – in that texts like Aeschylus or Seneca in the original contained specific content for the actor-initiates, which the audience could sense but not understand – as well as gaining an abstract impression of spirituality from the pre-existing religious connotations.

TOWARDS A THEATRE OF MYTH

These linguistic experiments culminated in the production of *Orghast* at the 1971 festival in Persepolis. Working with the group, Ted Hughes created a special speech, also labelled 'Orghast', to underline the organic unity of content and form in his play. This language was not only designed to reflect 'the sensation of a half barbaric world'. It was also intended to affect 'magically' the mental state of a listener on an instinctive level, in the same way that sound can affect the growth of plants or the patterning of iron filings. Vocal sounds were given specific emotive values; and words were invented intuitively, to avoid what Hughes called the 'gabbled gibberish of static interference' in conventional speech. The analogy to music struck many of the critics who attended the Persepolis performance, and in Hughes' terms:

> If you imagine music buried in the earth for a few thousand years, decayed back to its sources, not the perfectly structured thing we know as music, then that is what we tried to unearth. A language belonging below the levels where differences appear, close to the inner life of what we've chosen as our material, but expressive to all people, powerfully, truly, precisely.[22]

The intention was to compose blocks of sound that would have the status of physical action, and be indecipherable by intellectual analysis. However, in practice the 2,000-odd 'words' created all had semantic meanings, and could be translated into other languages. Many of the roots were an onomatopoeic rendering of physiological states – GR . . . for 'eat', KR . . . for 'devour', ULL . . . for 'swallow' – while more abstract objects were expressed by compounds such as BULLORGA (from ULL, 'absorb', plus ORG, 'life') meaning 'darkness', and KROGON meaning the destructive principle. Alternatively the sounds for representing specific things became fixed when it was discovered that arbitrary formulations corresponded to words in languages outside the occidental framework, these coincidences being naively taken as evidence that, in returning to the roots of language, they were rediscovering the universal and organic sources of meaning. Thus Hughes' term for 'light' (HOAN) was confirmed when it turned out to mean 'a ray of light' in Farsi, while USSA 'was just a provisional name [for his "Woman of Light"] until we discovered it meant "dawn" in Sanskrit'.[23]

Perhaps not surprisingly, apart from its word-for-word translatability, 'Orghast' has strong similarities to the early dada experiments with 'plastic' sound that arose out of the surrealist interest in automatic writing as direct subconscious expression. The structuring principle parallels Zdanévitch's 'zaoum' language, which used onomatopoeic roots as 'the sense support' for other similar-sounding words. The intention is much the same as Kurt

137

Schwitters' 'Sonata in Primeval Sounds'. And the general effect (with allowances made for the author's base in French rather than English) corresponds closely to Tristan Tzara's use of free association and African rhythms, as a brief comparison will show.

M. CRICRI: **DSCHILOLI MGABATI BAÏLUNDA**
LA FEMME ENCEINTE: **TOUNDI-A-VOUA**
SOCO BGAI AFFAHOU
M. BLEUBLEU: **FARAFANGAMA SOCO BGAÏ AFFAHOU**
(*La Première aventure céleste de Monsieur Antipyrine*, 1920)

GOD-KROGON: BULLORGA   SHARSAYA
OMBOLOM FROR   NULBULDA BRARG
darkness opens its womb   I hear chaos roar

IN OMBOLOM
BULLORGA
in the womb of darkness

FREEASTAV   NILD US
OMBOLOM   GLITTALUGH
freeze her womb   rivets like stars

ASTA BEORBITTA   CLID OSTA
BULLORGA
icy chains   lock up the mouth of
darkness

IN OMBOLOM KHERN FIGYA GRUORD
in her womb I make my words iron
(*Orghast*, 1971)

'Orghast' itself was the name Hughes invented for the fire of being – in metaphoric terms the sun (from ORG for 'life/being', and GHAST for 'spirit/flame') – and the material for the play was a myth of creation compiled from the legends of Prometheus, Chronos devouring his children, and the sun-worshipping cults of Helios and Zoroaster. It included passages from Aeschylus' *Prometheus Bound* and *The Persians*, and Seneca's *Thyestes* and *Hercules Furens* in the original Greek and Latin as well as sections in Avesti; and in the same way that Hughes sought to return to the source of language, this collage of mythical material was an attempt to rediscover the universal root myth buried under a wide range of archetypes. As a note in the programme stated:

> *Orghast* stems from certain basic myths – the gift of fire, the massacre of the innocents, the imprisonment of the son by the father, the search for liberation through revenge, the tyrant's destruction of his children, and the search for liberation through knowledge – as reflected in the hymns of Zoroaster, the stories of Prometheus and

138

Figure 17 Ted Hughes' physiology of *Orghast*. Key: Orghast – creative force (the sun + conception). Krogon – the destructive principle (usurping God-King + vulture). Moa – creation, chaos (womb + earth). Moasha/Ussa – descendants of Moa (imprisoned light). Sogis – Krogon's liberating son. Sheergra – strength. Furorg – enslaved life. Bullorg – darkness.

Hercules, Calderón's *Life's A Dream*, Persian legends, and other parallel sources.[24]

Brook's interest in the Prometheus myth extended back to 1965, when he had commissioned a new translation of Aeschylus' play from Robert Lowell. The action of *Orghast* not only revolves around the figure of Prometheus, it also takes place on a symbolic level within his being, as Hughes showed in an explanatory drawing of the 'physiology' of his play. This concept of mythology literally embodied in man – which has more than a coincidental family likeness to the human 'chart' of the Living Theatre's *Paradise Now* (1968; see p. 188 in this volume) – carried over into the historical level of the play, where decisive battles like Salamis were presented as extensions of the primal conflict that take seed in the mind of future generations, an analogy to Lévi-Strauss' view of the way in which 'myths operate in men's minds without their being aware of the fact'.[25]

Despite vocal delivery stressing the 'animal music' of Hughes' text, and choruses structured 'like a requiem, a solo voice rising in lament or rage above chanting' accompanied by percussive rhythms on drums and metal pipes, the whole was paradoxically bloodless and abstract. This was an inevitable side-effect of a production in which the anecdotal details and narrative side of the myths were stripped away, so that 'the abstract, the hieratic spectacle, barbaric sound structures, would grip like music'.[26] The result was that few of the characters were well enough defined by the action for the audience to comprehend the mythology; and not unnaturally some reviewers reacted with considerable intellectual frustration.

In fact, despite the Artaudian emphasis on 'total man', like most of the ritualistic and anti-rational trend in avant garde theatre, *Orghast* was one-sided in its appeal. And ironically its emphasis on the primitive night-side of nature seems only to have worked with the overeducated, intellectually sophisticated spectators at the Persepolis festival, perhaps because of the highly literary sources for the collage of creation myths. When *Orghast* was performed to a supposedly primitive (and therefore in theory more susceptible) audience of villagers at a site some twenty miles from Isfahan, they found those dark primordial cries hilariously funny. Even when restaged in Paris it fell far short of the desired liberation of the unconscious; and one can only conclude that it was the unique integration between theme, style and place which made the first performance effective.

Part I, which takes place in the spirit world, was performed in Ataxerxes' tomb and on the bare terrace in front of it looking out over the ruins of Persepolis; and the use of Avesti, the ceremonial language of the long-dead king and of the religion that constructed his tomb, the entry of Irene Worth as Moa, the female principle of creation, from the mouth of the burial chamber, and the ball of fire suspended above a carving of a fire-worship ceremony, all gave the ritual enaction of the myth intense imaginative force. The links between Part II, in the world of the dead, and its setting on the cliff-face of Naqsh-e-Rustam (the City of the Dead) in which four emperors' tombs are carved, was equally striking, with Aeschylus' lament for the deaths of the defeated Persians, and the fall of Xerxes in which Persepolis was destroyed, resounding before the graves of Darius and Xerxes themselves. The use of fire as a natural form of lighting in the ball of flame suspended in front of Prometheus, chained high on the rock-face, and the flambeaux carried by the actors, also had immediate symbolic power. So did the correspondence between the timing of the performances and Hughes' Manichaean vision of existence, with its eternal conflict of light against dark. Part I, with Krogon's perversion of the original creative fire that represented divine harmony, took place at sunset, with the violation and enslavement of nature paralleled by the growing darkness. Part II ended the cycle at dawn, with the rising sun striking a Zoroastrian temple at the base of the cliff where Hercules' descent into the underworld had been enacted. This unity with nature, the reverberations of almost legendary history, and the association of the artificially constructed myth with archaic religion, gave *Orghast* a level of reality and intensity that could hardly otherwise have been achieved.

As such it must be counted a vindication of Brook's Theatre of Ritual. But the European critics who attended the Persepolis performances (a total of five for Part I, and a single performance for Part II) pointed to serious internal contradictions: the collage of western and Asiatic myth, intended to be pre-rational, had been painstakingly constructed and was highly intellectualized; the supposedly universal language of the script turned out to be incomprehensible, and in fact became a barrier to communication; or, most damagingly, the effectiveness of the piece was solely due to the unique physical surroundings and special circumstances of the occasion. The production could therefore not serve as a model for 'mythic theatre', although Brook has frequently attempted to revive the same ambience. Over a decade later, for instance, in mounting *The Mahabharata* inside a stone-quarry he was clearly seeking a comparable unity with natural grandeur; and when the production was transferred to a standard stage, as at the Bouffes or in Glasgow and New York, he re-created as much of the physical surroundings as possible, covering the floor with sand, modelling the back wall of the theatre to look like a cliff (which in Zürich was lowered at the end to bring in the sunrise), and even building-in a 'river' below it, as well as a pool at the front of the stage.

However, even before the public unveiling of *Orghast*, Brook had already set off in a new direction by taking theatre to 'authentic' villages where an audience might be found who (in theory) had no preconceptions about dramatic performance. In addition to *Orghast*, the troupe had performed a farcical sketch by Ted Hughes, unrolling a carpet in the middle of a mud courtyard for their stage. This became Brook's motif on an African tour in 1972–3, out of which came *The Conference of the Birds*.

Leading a small multinational group of actors from Algeria, through Nigeria to Dalhomey and Mali, Brook was searching for audiences without even a word for 'theatre' in their language, in order to develop a fundamental – and thus truly universal – stage vocabulary. Attempting, with only very partial success, to discard all culture-specific conventions and symbolism, their return to basics is illustrated by the titles of the shows that developed as frameworks for improvisation: 'The Box Show' (comprising images from Ted Hughes' poems), 'The Ogre Show', 'The Shoe Show' (scripted by John Heilpern, the group's official chronicler), 'The Bread Show', and 'The Noise Show' (initiated by Brook acting as Pied Piper with a flute). In each of these, the action was extemporized around the simplest of physical objects; and the phrases that recur in Brook's comments on the tour were 'the right sort of simplicity', 'organic', 'natural state of childhood innocence', 'human contact . . . without a shared language', 'an exercise in heightening perception'.[27] However, the record shows that even footwear or bread had very different significance to people who walked barefoot, lived on a subsistence level and ate yams, while the actors continually fell back on routines from their conventional theatre background, or from the CIRT training, in their improvisations. A performance of *Orghast* in Kano aroused little more than ridicule, and the early versions of *The Conference of the Birds* that they were working on failed to hold the attention of any African audiences. The American founder of the National Black Theatre in Harlem accused the group of patronizing neo-colonialism, a charge substantiated by Brook's inclusion of a French film crew in his safari.

Yet the important factor was not what Brook brought to native audiences, but what he took from the experience. It sharpened his rejection of western culture *in toto*, while at the same time causing him to modify his definition of primitivism. In a subsequent interview about the trip, he declared: 'It is quite obvious that, in the total sickness of the society that we're living in, the possibility of affirmation through the [official] theatre is virtually excluded . . . [It] can . . . never affirm more than husks of values.' He outlined three alternatives: anarchic and disturbing productions within the establishment theatre, reflecting the insanity of society (as with *Marat/Sade* or *US*); 'ethnic' performances, redefining the elements of theatre in purely local terms (anticipating Barba's ISTA project – see p. 168 in this volume); or 'returning to roots . . . in a different way. And that is to say that within the human body there is another root, because the human body in all its aspects, organically, is common ground for all mankind.' Going beyond the colonially oriented idealization of the 'native', Brook's search was now to be for a sort of primitive fundamentalism:

> Our work is based on the fact that some of the deepest aspects of human experience can reveal themselves through the sounds and movements of the human body in a way that strikes a chord in any observer, whatever his cultural and racial conditioning. And therefore one can work without roots, because the body, as such, becomes a working source.[28]

Such a statement has clear echoes of Grotowski, whose book *Towards a Poor Theatre* had been published in French just two years earlier. But in fact Brook can hardly be said to have adhered to this fundamentalism over the next two decades. At most it dictated his rehearsal practices, while his productions have come to rely increasingly on both written scripts, and the type of intercultural borrowing denied by his concept of 'ethnic theatre'.

The anthropological gaze, which led to a shared workshop with El Theatro Campesino and with the Native American Theatre Ensemble when Brook's group travelled across the United States following their African tour, was still very much in evidence in *The Ik* (1975, based on

Colin Turnbull's case-history of a dying Ugandan tribe). *The Conference of the Birds* was built on a twelfth-century Persian poem, and developed from an improvised piece in which even the story-line varied from one performance to another – as in a week-long performance workshop in New York at the end of their American trip – until being fixed in a text by Brook's playwright-collaborator, Jean-Claude Carrière, for the Avignon Festival in 1979. And the final outcome of this search for a theatre of roots was a far more conventional analogue of *Orghast* in the 1985 *Mahabharata*, which was distilled from an ancient Indian epic, borrowed eclectically from Kathakali and Nōh techniques, had scripted dialogue and was originally performed overnight in a stone-quarry.

If *The Birds* was anthropomorphic, with the actors miming falcons, peacocks, sparrows and mythical beings, while the pure white costumes and luxurious colours of the carpet that formed their acting space contained imaginative richness, *The Ik* carried theatrical minimalism to its extreme. Its subject was the ultimate edge of human existence: a displaced and marginalized people, reduced by famine to such exigency that even the most fundamental of human relationships had broken down. Apart from the anthropological paraphernalia of camera and tape recorder carried by the Turnbull character, the only stage properties were the most basic and real of objects: earth scattered over the acting area at the beginning of the performance, stones, sticks, a few empty tin cans, a small bonfire. The cast wore ordinary clothes, without make-up, and made no attempt to look like Africans. As tribesmen they spoke a meaningless variant of the *Orghast* language, but with voice-overs from the actor playing Turnbull, or with an actor stepping out of role to read passages from Turnbull's book. And there was no story in a conventional sense, the action being a sequence of vignettes from the daily life of the tribe. However, in developing Turnbull's material through improvisation, the group not only imitated the precise physical postures of the Iks from photographs, but also built an exact replica of the Ik stockade, in which they lived during the rehearsals. Through this, the cast were intended to experience the inner state of the tribe whose social structures had disintegrated under the pressure of starvation; and the insights achieved were to be expressed in bodily terms alone. So, instead of 'acting' the appearance of Iks, they would share the essential 'being' of a people on the verge of extinction.

At the same time, their everyday clothing made a clear connection with western society. Faced with the Ik, Turnbull had initially found himself saying 'how inhuman', then questioning the presupposition 'that there are certain standards common to all humanity', and finally coming to see the potential parallels in the industrialized welfare state, which leads to an appeal for his European readers to work for a change in social direction: 'It is difficult to say how long the choice will be open to us before we are irrevocably committed' to a similar moral deterioration.[29] Through this documentary material Brook was able to combine an attack on the (social-ist!) value system of western civilization with a presentation of primitivism. This provided a natural basis for purely physical communication, in which stripping theatre to its bare essentials became a precise correlative for the reduction of human nature to its irreducible minimum. Even so, there was still an element of romanticism behind his approach that contradicted the negative (indeed horrific) view of the Iks' primitive state, on which his condemnation of modern society was based. Brook saw the subject as one where objective facts coalesced with a 'poetic, mythic' reality; and more than one reviewer commented on 'a Rousseauesque lament for our own lost innocence' in the style of presentation.[30]

This romantic vision was undisguised in *The Mahabharata*, which formed an explicit return to theatre of myth. In the 1979 restaging of *The Birds* for the Avignon Festival, Brook had used authentic Balinese masks, and Balinese puppets for the human figures when seen from a bird's-eye per-spective, together with scenes played in the style of Oriental shadow theatre. These elements were combined with highly symbolic, abstract gesture and movement: for instance, the pain and ecstasy of love was represented by a ball being knocked across the carpet by a huge croquet mallet, while a whirling musician played the violin. All this was designed to make the performance a manifestation of universal and timeless archetypes, appealing directly to the spectator's imagination. *The Mahabharata* was also initially a Festival production, and used similar techniques.

As the longest and, with its earliest versions going back to at least the fifth century BC, one of the earliest epic poems reflecting historical wars in the second millennium (several hundred years before the fall of Troy), the Hindu classic of 'the Mahabharata' could be considered to have an intrinsic universality. It contains a complete non-western mythology; and Brook saw his production as celebrating 'a work . . . which carries echoes for all mankind'. Indian art also offered an alternative model for the type of theatre he had been pursuing since *Orghast*. Its approach was not only comprehensive – linking together 'all aspects' of human experience, 'practi-cal, artistic and spiritual', extracting the essence from even the movement of a finger and revealing it as 'a meaningful part of an inseparable whole' – but also made 'the line between performance and ceremony . . . hard to draw'.[31]

In order to capture the all-embracing unity of the original, Brook and Carrière covered the whole poem, compressing the families, who though closely related, destroy each other in fighting over their kingdom, to two Kauravas (from the original 100) and five Pandavas. Many secondary digressions were omitted; and the main story-line was reduced to its bare bones. Even so, the final production was a nine-hour marathon, requiring twenty-two actors and six musicians (who also took part in the action), beginning at sunset and, like *Orghast*, ending with dawn. When Brook first saw part of 'the Mahabharata' on stage, it was in a traditional Kathakali presentation, played by a dancer in

> red and gold. His face was red and green, his nose was like a white billiard ball . . . two white crescent moons thrust forward from his lips, his eyebrows shot up and down like drumsticks and his fingers spelled out strange coded messages. Through the magnificent ferocity of the movements I could see that a story was unfolding. But what story? I could only guess at something mythical and remote . . . [32]

What he worked for was the same mythic status, but without the barrier of an alien culture. And although Brook kept certain Kathakali-like elements – such as a scarlet-faced figure of divine retribution, who dances round a mighty warrior about to die – his staging was marked by a striking economy of visual effect and gesture. Instead of a drowning king writhing on the stage, one corner of a scarlet cloth was dipped into a river. The image of a luxurious court at its ease was created by unrolling a carpet, cushions piled on the sand, and a few candles in silver saucers floating on a pool. For the dust and smoke of battle, the actors threw a handful of powder into the air. When one of the key heroes died, an arrow was carried, twisting *'through the air with infinite slowness'* across the acting area.

Such symbolic simplicity was required by the scale and extravagance of the story, which not only includes supernatural beings – the sun-god in blinding radiance, or a 'vast bellied' demon in a chariot 'drawn by monster horses' who swallows a 'cloud of arrows', multiplies into an army, and 'rains down a torrent of blood, streaked with lightning and meteors, a hurricane of axes and uprooted trees' – but also deals with 'a universal struggle without pity' between heroic combatants with magical 'sacred weapons, those that bring all existence to its end'. Any attempt to represent this naturalistically would be ridiculous. Yet by relying on the figures of the actors alone to inspire the audience's imagination, Brook deliberately brought myth down to the human level. This is also emphasized in the script: Krishna, the god who plays the dominant role in this apocalyptic struggle, appears 'in the form of a man, because he is a man'; and the elephant-headed god Ganesha, who tells a boy (and the audience) 'he's you, he's fire, he's the heart of all that's invisible', lifts off his mask to become the human Krishna. The significance is that men and gods are interchangeable, divinity is within each of us; and the link between archaic myth and the present is underlined by a narrative frame imposed on the action. 'The poetical history of mankind' is presented by the mythical, quasi-divine poet Vyasa (who is also the father of both sets of warring cousins).[33] But, written down by Ganesha as the poet envisions each scene, the story is also being told to an anonymous boy: the distant descendant of the Pandavas.

As listener, this boy literally represents the audience, who see the action through his eyes; and when he is told 'If you listen carefully, at the end you'll be someone else', Brook clearly intended that too as representative. The performance is to be therapeutic, producing a spiritual change in each spectator by revealing that (as the boy discovers) 'I have the same blood. I come from the gods', to which indeed Vyasa replies: 'That's what the story tells.' It is no coincidence that one of the key actors was Ryszard Cieślak, Grotowski's lead actor from the 1960s who was known for achieving an effect of 'translumination', in which the spirit shone through the flesh, that being exactly what the production was designed to demonstrate. But 'the Mahabharata' was seen as having contemporary relevance on quite a different level as well.

In Brook's view, the poem has the status not only of archetype, but also of prophecy. It is a forecast of the disasters caused by western commercialism, such as the Bhopal chemical catastrophe, and of the ultimate end for its aggressive civilization – the nuclear holocaust, primed by Hiroshima, that still seemed very much a possibility in the mid–1980s. And when one of the characters foretells 'the age of destruction', the words express Brook's rejection of modern society and its coming ruin:

> 'I see . . . a vicious ruined world, where puny, fearful, hard men live tiny lives . . . no more flowers, no more purity; ambition, corruption, commerce; it's the age of Kali, the black time. The countryside's a desert, crime stalks the cities . . . The fire rises borne by the wind, fire pierces the earth, cracks open the underground world, wind and fire calcinate the world . . .'

However, this is no warning intended to produce a change of heart in the public, and so save civilization from its fate.

In *The Mahabharata* mankind has to destroy itself in order for the characters to reach Paradise, which is the final vision greeted by the dawn. Following the same Hindu philosophy picked up by Strindberg in *A Dream Play*, its revelation is the illusory nature of all material existence; and even the 'hell' of death is only 'the last illusion'.[34] There is a strong sense in the play that Brook would welcome global destruction as the price of liberating the spirit. Implicit already in *The Ik*, this takes the anarchistic – and politically reactionary – aspect of avant garde primitivism to its extreme, where even nuclear war is romanticized.

The theme of illusory existence is exemplified in the make-believe of theatre itself, which makes the vision of Paradise no less of an illusion, even when symbolically reinforced by a real sunrise (as it was, particularly in the Zürich production, where the back wall of the stage was lowered at the climatic moment to reveal the morning sun over the lake in precisely the same way as Dalcroze and Appia had used the vista of Lake Geneva in 1914). And the problematic quality of such mythic drama was unintentionally brought out by one scene that Brook regards as the key to *The Mahabharata*.

In the final war Krishna offers the two sides a choice – one can have him 'alone, unarmed, taking no part in the battle', the other will have the aid of all his armies – and Arjuna, who chooses Krishna for the Pandavas, is given a lesson on the meaning of existence at the moment of giving the signal for battle. Although this apparently relates to 'universal being', which 'is where you live, where we all live', and answers the question of 'How can one reach the truth if one is born in illusion', nothing beyond these vague generalities is given. Instead we are given third-person narration by Krishna:

> He began to teach [Arjuna] the ancient yoga of wisdom and the mysterious path of action. He spoke for a long time, a very long time, between the two armies preparing to destroy themselves . . .
>
> He showed him the deepest movements of his being . . . It's the most secret knowledge. He showed him the whole of truth; he taught him how the world unfolds.

Krishna also '*murmurs in his ear*'. Beforehand, Arjuna has decided to let himself be killed, rather than be responsible for the massacre of his family who are opposing him: 'If this is the price, who can wish for victory?' Krishna's unstated words lead him to declare 'My illusion is dissolved, my error destroyed. Thanks to you my understanding has returned. Now am I firm . . . *Arjuna blows on his conch*' for the battle to begin. Yet whatever the mysteries that may have been revealed, they are obviously too secret to be divulged to an uninitiated contemporary audience. Everything Brook rejects in modern society is made sufficiently clear, but the spiritual alternative to be affirmed turns out to be indefinable. The myth is hollow at the centre.

In fact the play's form itself implies as much. In addition to the narrative frame, the poet's control over his characters is strongly asserted – as with a flashback, when Vyasa declares 'I stop all motion' and '*everyone remains motionless, heads bowed*'[35] – and a significant proportion of the dialogue within the play is either reported speech or, especially at climactic points, third-person description. Although there may have been no other solution to presenting such a mammoth epic, the effect is to distance the action. It became a pageant of highly theatrical images, a display of acting skill, instead of being an embodiment of mythological truth. And the impression of unreality was reinforced by the international nature of Brook's acting group. This may be the justification of a laboratory like CIRT, which is designed to develop a universal theatre language, but in the case of such a text-based play it caused considerable problems with conflicting accents (Cieslak's delivery sounding particularly 'foreign', at least in the English version).

The significance of *The Mahabharata* for Brook is indicated by the fact that he and Carrière worked on the adaptation for almost ten years before it reached the stage. As such, the production becomes a valid test case for a 'theatre of myth' and reveals some of the intrinsic flaws – practical, as well as philosophical – in the more grandiose aspects of avant garde primitivism. At the same time, the return to 'roots' in the sense of exploring the basis of theatrical communication – the continuing focus of Brook's laboratory work – has produced an extraordinarily flexible acting style that creates truly striking stage images. In this case, for instance, sticks turned into beds, shelters, forests, complex war machines. Ladders measuring 20 ft were whirled like the spokes of a wheel to become a magic defence weapon, its deadly nature convincingly shown by the breathtaking acrobatics of a single actor slipping between them. The energy of the archers' pose persuades us we see flights of arrows, when their bows are ordinary sticks and have no strings, a tangible demonstration of the principle that, on the stage, less is more. But, conversely, as the problematic qualities of Brook's wider aims indicate, on the mythological level too much striving for significance may add up to very little.

9

SECULAR RELIGIONS AND PHYSICAL SPIRITUALITY

JERZY GROTOWSKI

In many ways, the work of Jerzy Grotowski parallels Peter Brook's search for a theatre of myth through a return to 'roots', exploring the fundamentals of stage performance. Grotowski had already developed his ideas and distinctive style, cut off behind the Iron Curtain, before there was any direct contact between them. However, Brook realized the potential of Grotowski's work for his own research as soon as the Polish Laboratory Theatre reached the West, and invited Grotowski to conduct a three-week workshop for his acting group as early as *US* in 1966. Even if never direct collaborators, they appeared at several of the same theatrical forums over the next decade; and their approach was similar enough for Ryszard Cieślak, the star example of Grotowski's training methods in the 1960s and early 1970s, to fit in with Brook's troupe when he produced *The Mahabharata* in 1985.

At the same time, their careers have been widely different. Beginning in small-scale counter-theatre, Grotowski's stage work was effectively limited to a bare handful of productions over a single decade from 1959 to 1968, although his final production of *Apocalypsis cum Figuris* continued to evolve in a series of transformations until 1980. Where Brook only turned to Indian sources at a late point in his development, one of Grotowski's earliest experiments was *Shakuntala* (based on Kalidasa's *Siakuntala* from the fifth century AD); and in contrast to Brook's eclecticism, the distinguishing mark of Grotowski's approach has been rigorous internal consistency. So, while each used almost exactly the same terms to describe what they were doing, the directions they pursued were widely different. Brook wrote of an 'Empty Stage' and a 'Theatre of Roots', Grotowski of a 'Poor Theatre' and a 'Theatre of Sources'. Yet where Brook's interest was in discovering mythological archetypes, and led towards spectacle, Grotowski's quest was spiritual therapy. His emphasis was on ritual forms (instead of mythical material) that became an exclusive focus on drama as 'process' (in place of 'product') and resulted in his complete withdrawal from public performance, a divergence that mirrors the characteristic split in the avant garde movement, which was already obvious both in the German expressionists and in the disputes between Artaud and the French surrealists.

In a sense it is logical that any theatre rejecting twentieth-century society for its materialism and rationalism should turn to the alternative value scale of religious faith, while continuing to reject organized religion as being associated with the *status quo*. It is an attitude as evident in Strindberg's later drama or Claudel's plays, as in Kokoschka and Genet, or in the work of Barrault, Brook and the American avant garde groups of the 1970s. But the most striking achievements in this line are those of Grotowski, whose simplest description of his aim is 'to cross the frontiers between you and me . . . To find a place where a communion becomes possible.'[1]

The terms he uses to describe his work are, like Genet, characteristically religious: transgression, profanation, passion, incarnation, transfiguration, atonement, confession and, above all, communion. But although his productions specifically attacked what is sacred in the form of organized Christianity, his choice of texts has always been within the 'great tradition'. The visual images created by his actors were derived from popular hagiography too, so that he avoided the communication problems inherent in a return to the past (like Brook's *Orghast*) or a search for oriental alternatives (like Artaud) which, however comprehensible as reactions against contemporary western society, are self-defeating to the extent that they cut the theatre off from the cultural context of its audience. This religious emphasis and the specifically Christian context of Grotowski's stage-work can be traced to his roots in Polish culture, with its strong Roman Catholic tradition, while growing up under Marxist dictatorship gave him a more rigid and philosophically consistent form of materialism to react against than the liberal capitalism experienced by his western counterparts. Of them all, the closest in background was Genet – not only Catholic in upbringing, but also a conscious outcast from the social system – yet Genet's stress on criminality, and his use of hatred as an emotional focus, is alien to Grotowski.

Like Brook's Centre for International Theatre Research, Grotowski's Polish Laboratory Theatre (founded in 1960, and given official research status in 1962) concentrated on exploring the essentials of theatrical communication. And still more radically than Barrault or Brook, Grotowski's search led him to discard music, representative scenery and illusionistic lighting, make-up or any but the simplest costumes, eliminating all the external paraphernalia to expand the one element that distinguishes theatre from film or television, and without which it would not exist: 'the actor–spectator relationship of perceptual, direct, "live" communion'.[2]

Such a communion requires the total integration of spectators in the performance. Initially he concentrated on finding methods of turning a dramatic action into an emotional environment for the spectators by simple changes in physical placing. In the group's first significant production, Byron's *Cain* (1960), this was limited to reducing the physical distance from the actors by using the forestage and the centre aisle between the rows of spectators, a surprisingly tentative move towards breaking out of the frame of the proscenium already anticipated by Copeau, who removed the footlights and linked the auditorium to the stage by steps at the Vieux Colombier in the early 1920s. Grotowski's following productions abandoned any formal delineation of the stage; and in *Ancestors* (1961) and Wyspianski's *Akropolis* (1962) the spectators were seated separately and apparently randomly throughout the hall, the whole of which was used as an acting area, 'removing all frontiers' to create a single 'living organism'.

In the former this was fairly conventional, with the audience being sucked into the action by the patterns of movement woven among them, and with those willing to participate physically in the climax being led by an actor as the 'chorus' in a harvest ritual. But in *Akropolis*, transferred by Grotowski to Auschwitz from its original setting in Cracow Cathedral on the basis of a description of it as 'the cemetery of the tribes' in one of Wyspianski's letters, the fragmentation of the audience was used to isolate the spectators. The actors ignored them while moving through them, so that the physical proximity paradoxically emphasized distance. The actors were the dead, a community without individual characteristics 'initiated in the ultimate experience'; the individualized audience, the living. And this simultaneous effect of separateness and immediacy was intended to give the impression of a dream, setting the action on an interior subconscious plane. As Grotowski commented, physically mingling actors and spectators under the banner of 'direct participation' frequently only aroused psychological barriers, while 'experience proves that by putting a distance between the actors and the spectators in space, one often rediscovers a [psychic] proximity'.[3]

This dualism of participation and distancing was used in a progressively subtler way in Grotowski's next two productions. For Marlowe's *Dr Faustus* (1963) the audience were seated on benches around three refectory tables, which functioned as both stage, settings and props. As they entered, Faustus, already seated in the centre of the head table, invited them to take their places as guests at what was specifically a Last Supper. The 'food' served up to them by Faustus was a montage of the scenes of his life, acted in front of them on the tables. And at one point these were even up-ended and demolished by a courtier trying to kill Faustus, with a violence that was physically frightening because of its proximity. However, at the same time as being participants in a metaphoric communion, where they were receiving the sacramental offering of Faustus' sacrificial damnation, the audience also found themselves representing the banality of everyday existence. The servants' dialogue in the comic scenes, deflating

151

and mocking Faustus' pretensions, was spoken by two actors seated among them, who had entered with them in modern clothes, bringing home the point that 'our daily platitudes are themselves arguments against God'.[4]

The same overlap between the reality of the audience as spectators and their role imposed by the performance, between the modern world and the mythic archetype, was even stronger in *The Constant Prince* (1968). Here the framing metaphor also embraced the basis of drama as a spectacle of conflict, as well as reflecting the experimental nature of the Polish Laboratory Theatre. So the context of the performance duplicated the premises of the play in a way that made it hard to distinguish real life from imagination. The associations evoked as the audience peered down from the rectangular wooden barricades were simultaneously those of voyeurs (the conventional image of an audience in naturalistic theatre), of spectators at the barbaric ritual of a bullfight (one of the images presented in the play), and of 'witnesses' in a religious sense to Christ's apotheosis in the martyrdom of the title figure. In addition (since the stage arrangement was also modelled on Rembrandt's *Anatomy of Dr Tulp*), the spectators were placed in the role of professionals observing the scientific dissection of a human being; and, exploiting the usual behaviour of audiences at a play, they were clearly identified with the inhuman society of the torturers by their passive fascination for the torture enacted beneath.

The second of the constant factors in Grotowski's experimentation is the search for authenticity in performance. The actor as 'priest', the other pole of this 'communion', must present a revelation that evokes belief if the circle is to be complete. Only thus can a play have the intrinsic significance for each spectator that justifies his/her structural integration in the action. In terms of a secular religion, spirituality can only exist within man, so that for Grotowski 'body and blood . . . that's where "God" is'; and his training methods were designed to remove psychological blocks in the actors, to allow them to strip away the 'daily mask of lies' that form their external personae, leading to 'a liberation from complexes in much the same way as psychoanalytic theory'.[5] In theory, this enables the actors to reveal their essential being in performance so that, as Grotowski's theatre developed, every production became not only a celebration of the 'holiness' of man, but also simultaneously an existential challenge to the audience in reversing normal behaviour patterns, which are designed to cover and protect this private centre of personality – a 'self-penetration' which is even more provocative in that most public of forums, the theatre, where traditionally the actor dissembles and disguises his true face with masks.

Grotowski's aim was to achieve an extreme intimacy, where 'this act of the total unveiling of one's being becomes a gift of the self which borders on the transgression of barriers and love'. Indeed, this can be seen as one reason for the increasing restriction on the number of spectators in each successive production, from approximately sixty-five for *Kordian* (1962), to under fifty for *Dr Faustus*, between thirty and forty for *The Constant Prince*, and only twenty-five for *Apocalypsis cum Figuris* (in the original 1968 version). This breaking down of the barriers between individuals goes together with breaking down barriers within the individual. Performances were structured so that at the most intense moments of self-revelation the actor would transcend his 'self' in an apotheosis of human spirituality. This created an effect of 'translumination', in which the soul would literally shine through the flesh by 'the integration of all the actor's psychic and bodily powers which emerge from the most intimate layers of his being and his instinct'.[6]

Grotowski's approach assumes that personality is superficial, artificial, while at its 'roots' humanity is generic. Hence any true manifestation of unconscious psycho-physical reactions will automatically correspond to Jungian archetypes, in particular to those postures and groupings embodied in archaic or religious sculpture. So the achievement of such stereotypes comes to be taken as a guarantee that the true expression of the subconscious has been reached, that the actor has indeed become 'the living incarnation of myth'.[7] In fact, however, as Eugenio Barba, one of Grotowski's collaborators, has implicitly confirmed, these symbolic physical attitudes taken up by the group, like the medieval procession of flagellants and pilgrims that recurred in *Akropolis* and *Apocalypsis cum Figuris*, or by the individual in the moment of 'translumination', like the classic poses of *pietà* and crucifixion repeated more explicitly in each production from *Kordian* to *The Constant Prince*, were consciously adopted. Gesture and intonation were developed through extensive rehearsal to echo

a definite image. For example, the actor stops in the middle of a race and takes the stance of a cavalry soldier charging, as in the old popular drawings. This method of acting evokes by association images deeply rooted in the collective imagination.[8]

The result was closely related to the expressionist acting style (see p. 45 in this volume) – an exaggerated definition in movements, together with the elimination of those that were merely functional or mimetic, rather than expressive; the cutting of gestures defining individuality, as well as the transposition of conventional attitudes into expressions of 'pure' emotional states; and the stiffening of facial muscles to transform individual features into a rigid mask.

There are also obvious similarities to Artaud's concepts, although Grotowski only read *The Theatre and its Double* in 1964 after the basic elements of his style were already set. He also subsequently distanced himself from Artaud, pointing out that the 'transcendental point of reference' for his own work was 'man', not the 'cosmic trance' that Artaud speaks of. Yet, since Artaud was an integral part of the wider avant garde movement – Grotowski cites similar ideas in Vakhtangov and Meyerhold or his native

Polish tradition – it is in a sense immaterial from what sources Grotowski developed his approach. Still, the archetypal ideograms which he created to awaken latent emotions in the spectator through subconscious associations are the equivalent of Artaud's 'hieroglyphs', while his use of 'masking' is precisely that which Artaud admired in the Balinese dancers: 'in this systematic depersonalization, in these purely muscular facial expressions, applied to the features like masks, everything produces a significance, everything affords the maximum effect'.[9] Grotowski also parallels Artaud's vision in his continual references to primitive religious drama, as well as in his double use of mythology. He focuses on the archetype of the saviour-martyr, while dismissing the conventional images of harmony, aspiration and spiritual nobility associated with such an archetype (the deceptive values of a false civilization), in order to create a 'dialectic of mockery and apotheosis'. There is a consistent emphasis on 'cruelty', too. In Grotowski's productions this took the form of torture and suffering, where spiritual ecstasy was to be achieved through the mortification of the body. Although this is rather different from Artaud's proposed sublimation of cruelty and violence in the spectators by liberating such instincts, reviewers were quick to note that productions like *Dr Faustus* and *The Constant Prince* epitomized the Theatre of Cruelty that Artaud himself had been unable to realize.[10]

All Grotowski's productions can be seen as variations on the single theme of self-transcendence. He described the basic principles of the '*exercises plastiques*', which he developed for training his actors, as relating the psychic to the physical in a way that encouraged the exploration and liberation of the subconscious. And he commented: 'When I say "go beyond yourself" I am asking for an insupportable effort . . . there are certain points of fatigue which break the control of the mind, a control that blocks us.' Rehearsal was designed to produce a state of exhaustion through which the actors could transcend 'the limits we impose upon ourselves that block the creative process'.[11] And this was carried over into performance. The actor playing the Christ figure in *Ancestors* reached a point of physical exertion where his physiological state overlapped with the archetype he represented; and the blood Christ 'sweated' from his crown of thorns appeared as the sweat running down his brow. Ryszard Cieślak literally drove himself to the limits of physical endurance in *The Constant Prince*, with the result that the spirit seemed to shine through the flesh.

The same self-transcendence was echoed in the way Grotowski handled the dramatic situation of each play. Physical action was translated into subconscious terms, external intrigue stripped away, to leave a structure of physical suffering leading to spiritual apotheosis. In *Kordian*, *Akropolis* and *Dr Faustus*, the original plots or real-life events were internalized, and projected as hallucination, dream or memory, while the conventional values of good and evil were reversed. Grotowski's interpretation of *Dr Faustus* turned God into a demonic deity, whose 'laws . . . are traps contradicting morality and truth'. Mephistopheles became an *agent provocateur* of God, who donned papal robes to carry Faustus to hell, while Faustus was presented as the archetype of a saint, saintliness being defined in quasi-Artaudian terms as 'an absolute desire for pure truth', which can only be realized by rebellion against an evil God.

The actor playing Faustus was selected because of his physical resemblance to the archetypal picture of St Sebastian; and the scenes were organized around a structure of symbolic images. There was an annunciation with Mephistopheles stretching diagonally over Faustus as a 'soaring angel' whose words were accompanied by the chanting of 'an angelic choir', a baptism, and a *pièta* with a female double of Mephistopheles as the Virgin. There were images from the life of Christ – the absolution of Mary Magdalene (in the shape of the Seven Deadly Sins, each represented by Mephistopheles); the cleansing of the temple (the assault on the Pope); the Garden of Gethsemane; and the female Mephistopheles as 'the Mother of Sorrows following her son to Calvary', when Mephistopheles drags Faustus off upside-down to his inverted crucifixion.

As in *The Constant Prince*, the moment of ecstasy comes at the point where conscious control over the body is lost. The spirit is exalted to the degree that a man is reduced to his animal 'roots'. Faustus 'is in a rapture, his body is shaken by spasms. The ecstatic failure of his voice becomes at the moment of his Passion a series of inarticulate cries . . . no longer a man but a panting animal.'[12] In the dialectic of saintliness and damnation, where spiritual potential is liberated by the mortification of the flesh, Faustus becomes a Saviour in human, as opposed to religious terms. And the actor's 'total unveiling of being', in divesting himself of all the defensive shells and props of personality, was intended as a challenge and model for the audience:

> Through excess, profanation and outrageous sacrilege [revealing] himself by casting off his everyday mask, he makes it possible for the spectator to undertake a similar process of self-penetration. If he does not exhibit his body, but annihilates it, burns it, frees it from every resistance to any psychic impulse . . . he repeats the atonement; he is close to holiness.[13]

The attempt to create 'a secular *sacrum* in the theatre', and this transposition of spirit into body, were particularly clear in *Apocalypsis cum Figuris*, which also serves as a good illustration of how texts were treated in the Theatre Laboratory. The title refers to the prophetic Revelation of St John of the Cross that foretells Christ's Second Coming; and the action is set in a contemporary religious festival, among the touts and beggars camping out around the shrine, who play out the Second Coming as a brutal drunken game. The central figure is a simpleton, in Polish *ciemny*, literally 'the dark one', a term with satanic overtones meaning a man possessed and deformed as a mark of his contact with the supernatural, but also an idiot incapable of comprehending the world, who traditionally represents childlike holiness and thus a different value scale. One of the drunkards, whose name happens to be Simon Peter, persuades this simpleton that he is in fact Christ, telling him he was born in Nazareth and died on the cross for men who fail to recognize him as God. He then nominates others as Mary Magdalene, John, and Judas, after which this cast of degraded social outcasts perform archetypal scenes of Christ's Passion and Cruci-fixion, expressing their sadistic instincts, subconscious needs and resent-ments through parody. This ridicule of the sacred, together with the use of the grotesque and the background of gothic carnival, is all reminiscent of Bakhtin's vision of 'carnevalesque' art; and for the audience the effect was a testing of the Christian myth, challenging its validity through blas-phemy. Simon Peter, the Simpleton-Christ's antagonist, rejects the super-human demands of spirituality in the words of Dostoevsky's Grand Inquisi-tor, and is only answered by lines from T.S. Eliot's 'The Waste Land', expressing despair of ever attaining spiritual grace. Yet even though the atheist has the last word, the torment of the simpleton still produces a moment of 'translumination', a physical demonstration of the soul's existence.

At the end Simon Peter extinguishes the candles which have served to light the barbaric 'entertainment', and commands the Simpleton, who chants the liturgy from the darkness, to 'Go and come no more!' But the production contradicted the text by asserting the reality of the spirit in human terms. It also implicitly affirmed the possibility of a sacrificial saviour, even in the abused idiot, who served as a catalyst to strip his everyman tormentors of social masks, facing them with a challenge that undermined all their preconceptions. The spectators were expected to go through a comparable psychological process, from the rejection of official religion to the rediscovery of spirituality in the despised and rejected. But, as a whole, *Apocalypsis cum Figuris* can be seen as embodying a ritual vision of theatre outlined three years earlier, which in fact could only be com-pletely effective for the closed community of the actors themselves:

> Primitive rituals are the first form of drama . . . through their total participation, primitive men were liberated from accumulated uncon-scious material. The rituals were repetitions of archetypal acts, a collective confession which sealed the solidarity of the tribe. Often ritual was the only way to break a taboo.[14]

In previous productions Grotowski's focus on the actor's self-exploration, self-revelation and self-transcendence had automatically conflicted with the characterization required by conventional dramatic scripts. In *Dr Faustus* Marlowe's characters were used 'as a trampoline, an instrument with

156

Figure 18 Poster for the Theatre Laboratory. Religious imagery and archetypal experience.

which to study what is hidden behind our everyday mask – the innermost core of our personality – in order to sacrifice it, expose it'. The actors played against their roles; and the dialogue was limited to what each found personally relevant. As Grotowski admitted, 'We eliminate those parts of the text which have no importance for us.'[15] Consequently the textual montages and even the themes changed as the actors developed new insights into their own personalities; and a play like *Akropolis* went through five distinct versions from 1962 to 1967, while *The Constant Prince* went through three.

Apocalypsis cum Figuris was different in that it evolved out of acting exercises and improvisations, which were specifically designed to facilitate the actors' self-exploration. The structure of images that were finally pieced together and expanded directly reflected the preoccupations that had moulded the previous productions. So there was an organic relationship between the 'score' (the objective actions and relationships presented during the performance) and the inner process that this was designed to communicate to the spectator. The characterization was built on archetypes that the actors had come to identify with through their earlier work, with individual traits based on their own personalities. The dialogue was limited to quotations which were not only non-dramatic, but also so widely known that the words were no longer associated with their author, and thus could be taken to represent the consciousness of mankind itself. As might be expected from the theme of the Second Coming, this montage was derived primarily from the personal, religious poetry of T.S. Eliot and Simone Weil, the existential questioning of *The Brothers Karamazov*, and above all the Bible. But speech was limited to what was essential for bringing out the symbolic significance of the mimed action, while words were increasingly reduced to pure sound during the preparation 'to bring spontaneous associations to the spectator's mind', an expressionist technique that led to the use of incantation and liturgical chanting (including even the Kyrie eleison).

Thus *Apocalypsis cum Figuris* came closest to Grotowski's ideal of 'autonomous theatre', where 'the "peripetia" of the plays (as we do them) do not correspond to the text. They are expressed through purely theatrical means.'[16] Even so, it was Grotowski's version of *The Constant Prince* that had the most direct influence, although the significance of this production for the avant garde was partly fortuitous, political circumstances having kept Grotowski's work unknown to the West until it was already fully developed. The performance of *The Constant Prince* at Barrault's Théâtre des Nations festival in 1966 therefore came as a revelation.

At first glance Calderón's *El principe constante*, with its highly mannered and rhetorical verse, its extended plays on words and convoluted dialectics, its melodramatic action culminating in the ghost of the dead prince leading the Portuguese army to victory, and its complicated equation of heroic values in the conventional form of love versus duty, seems an unsuitable text for Grotowski's treatment. But beneath the surface plot glorifying Prince Fernando's historical invasion of Algiers and his refusal to be ransomed in exchange for the city of Ceuta, the play is an *auto sacramentale*, a study of how man achieves sainthood that symbolizes the conflict between eternal and mundane values, the spiritual versus the physical, in the battle between Christian and pagan worlds. Its inner focus is on the protagonist's fortitude (defined by Aquinas as the cardinal virtue), which is shown through his ordeal of degradation and starvation. And this realization of spiritual potential through the mortification of the flesh directly parallels the self-transcendence aimed at in Grotowski's acting techniques. In the Slowacki translation used for this production, the play is also linked to the Polish romantic tradition of baroque revival that Grotowski had built on in his earlier work.

The text was altered even more radically than in *Dr Faustus*, with the number of lines cut by almost two-thirds and switched between characters, or out of sequence, and with fragments from the Polish liturgy interpolated at key points. The fourteen major roles plus slaves and courtiers were reduced to seven and played by six actors. The centre of the action became an erotic relationship between Fénix, the Algerian princess, and Fernando, which was barely hinted at in the original, while almost all reference to Ceuta was cut, together with the battle scenes. At the same time the Moorish and Christian characters were united into a single group, freeing the action from its historical context, and turning it into an archetypal conflict of an individual versus a sadistic, spiritually castrating society. Instead of the conventional exposition, complication and resolution of the original three-act form, with each act divided into three scenes, Calderón's geometrical sequence of nine 'days' was collapsed into a single action focused on three monologues. In each of these, Ciéslak (as Prince Fernando) reached an ascending level of 'translumination', structured into seven musical 'movements'.

The 'Overture' was the First Prisoner's assimilation into the society of his persecutors, which is possible because his opposition to them is a form of collaboration, being on their own level. This sets the 'normal' pattern, and establishes the negative pole of the conflict in its extreme form of perverse sexual domination:

THE KING MOUNTS HIS SLAVE . . .

KING: *Climbs over the body of Don Enrique. He gestures to the prisoner between his legs . . . grabs his left hand and holds it to his heart . . .*

> I chose myself a horse with an empty saddle . . .
> It suffered from this internal wound.
> From the consciousness of the conquered
> That the conqueror sits in his saddle . . .

Don Enrique's face is distorted with pain and his body twitches violently . . . The body of the King bows to one side and tenses. The rhythm of his speech carries over into Don Enrique's body, which jerks in ever shorter intervals . . . The King's voice rings ever shriller. He stares fixedly up. Both bodies are rigid – climax.[17]

After this spiritual 'death' in physical orgasm, the prisoner is symbolically castrated by Fénix, and dressed in the quasi-military black cloak and boots of his torturers. When the same sequence is repeated with the Prince, the castration cannot be carried through because, in a myopically wishful distortion of political realities, he responds with 'only passivity and kindness, referring to a higher spiritual order. He seems to offer no opposition.'[18]

This section was presented as a divertimento – including a *corrida*, with the courtiers as bulls – and its thematic significance is given by the subtitle to one of its sections: 'Don Fernando is called to Christ'. It was followed by a 'Solo', the Prince's first monologue 'To die for the faith', in which he achieves a state of 'translumination and ecstasy' on the repeated lines

> So that all may see
> How constant my belief makes me.

Then came a 'Rondo' made up of minuet and polka, simultaneously presented as a litany and the Agnus Dei, in which the court expresses its anger:

> *Fénix lashes Don Fernando with the red cloth, rolled into a whip. At each* 'Pray for us' *she strikes the Prince's reddening back. The court watches on its knees . . .*
> MINUET-CRY I: *After the whipping Don Fernando turns around, throws himself on the floor and cries like a small child in the marked rhythm of a polka . . . all except the Prince and Fénix dance a minuet to the Prince's 'polka' with different variations . . . with closed eyes he hits himself in the stomach with his bunched up shirt. He rubs his head on the floor, one hand tearing at his hair . . . He beats himself violently in the genitals and face . . . He lies flat on the floor and licks it at each sobbing cry . . . his sobbing cries change without a break into clear, vibrant, echoing voice* [ringing like that of a preacher in a cathedral]. *Fénix kneels and confesses softly to the Prince, who . . . answers in a melodic crystalline tone. The court stiffen into schemata. Fénix kneels weeping beside the seated Prince* [whose position is that of a popular image of Christ in Polish folklore].

After this comes the second monologue or 'Solo' on the theme of physical suffering and humiliation; an 'Allegro' which includes a communion where each courtier approaches in turn and bites into the Prince's flesh while the others chant in prayer, and the 'Golgotha' of 'the Prince-Job'; then the final 'Solo'. A short coda follows over his body, glorifying his death, and transforming his sacrifice into a cult that will allow others to be killed in his name.

The third and final monologue on the spiritual rewards and joy of martyrdom was punctuated by paroxysms of laughter from Cieślak at those points where the original prince would have been most sincere. This was designed to undercut the 'official' religious theme, and to internalize the dialectic of derision and apotheosis in a way that clearly distinguished the actor's personality from the dramatic character. The climax of 'translumination, ecstasy' was thus divorced from the divine stereotype, while retaining the parallels to Christ. It presented the triumph of the spirit over physical existence as reality for Cieślak himself by undercutting the fictional situation and the ideological propaganda, a significant thematic shift that defines the focus of Grotowski's theatrical experimentation.

Calderón's hero allows himself to be sacrificed for the spiritual welfare of his fellow men; and his suffering – which is merely one of Calderón's various interlocking levels of constancy and honour, though the only one to be emphasized by Grotowski's production – is treated with detachment in the original play. Grotowski's Prince, having no objective beyond himself, became a self-willed martyr, controlling his own torture and using his persecutors to destroy his body in order to purify his spirit. This exclusive

Figure 19 Via negativa: The Constant Prince. Minuet-Cry I. The stage as bull-ring, schemata and the triumph of the spirit through mortifying the flesh.

focus on the protagonist was reinforced by his extreme emotion, his rage against the flesh that made much of the violence self-inflicted, and by the level of realism in which actual rather than pretended suffering was presented. Following Grotowski's principle that 'the actor must not illustrate but accomplish an "act of the soul" by means of his own organism',[19] Cieslak's body expressed his psychological state in physical reactions that are usually considered involuntary – sweating profusely while remaining still, a red flush spreading over his skin, tears flooding from closed eyes – giving an effect of absolute authenticity to the experience presented. As a result, however, the self-transcendence became an act of voluptuous masochism. Indeed, this element of wilful perversion was actually emphasized by expanding the King's accusation in the original, and making it more explicit:

> Who forces him to suffer?
> . . . has he not sealed his own fate? . . .
> For his faith he will suffer he says
> For that will open the doors of paradise to him.
> He seeks death . . .
> It is not we who maltreat him
> It is only he who makes himself suffer.

161

The intention may have been to bring out the dubious aspects of Christ's sacrifice, in line with the concept of 'religion expressed through blasphemy'.[20] This also provided a rationale for the Prince's self-absorption, turning him into an anti-Christ whose own salvation is achieved through provoking the evil instincts in his fellow men, an apotheosis damning those who made it possible. But the effect was intellectually confusing, because of the emotional power in the truth and intimacy of the actor's self-revelation, which was heightened by the mesmeric ritualistic elements of the performance and by the actors' symbolic poses that carried mythical associations. Its validity was also confirmed by the audience's functional role as voyeurs watching something prohibited, as well as by the sense that deeply rooted taboos relating to personal exposure as well as religious reverence were being outrageously violated.

The production of *The Constant Prince*, and particularly Ciéslak's inspired performance, was generally acknowledged as a complete realization of Grotowski's approach, the most extreme example possible of an actor overcoming psychological blocks to achieve self-transcendence. It was seen as justifying such terms as 'purification', 'act of humility', 'secular holiness', which until then had been received with scepticism.[21] But this culmination of his technical search had brought Grotowski into a totally different territory, where the requirements of theatre no longer applied.

PARATHEATRICAL THERAPY

By 1970 Grotowski was declaring that 'We are living in a post-theatrical epoch. It is not a new wave of theatre which follows but something that will take its place.'[22] But already in the Polish Laboratory Theatre's stagings, the '*via negativa*' – Grotowski's reduction of the theatrical performance to its essence by a process of 'distillation' and 'contradiction' – had led to the virtual elimination of plot and character. Instead of an imaginary action, *The Constant Prince* had become an experiment in laying bare the essential spiritual nature of man by sacrificing the body. It was a psychological dissection that, in a very real sense, could only proceed if the actors had generated sufficient spiritual intensity on each preceding level. Instead of conventional characterization, roles were developed from improvisations. In these the performers searched for their basic impulses as individuals in reaction to the demands of the group situation, creating a personal 'score' rather than projecting themselves as actors into a fictional 'other'. And the principle of self-cancelling contradictions set dialogue, physical action, vocal expression, and gesture each against the other, as when the King's accusation was sung as a litany with the court echoing the ending of each sentence in a sing-song chant, or when the agony of the Prince was expressed in a dance rhythm while the court performed a minuet, played a grotesque masquerade, or stiffened into animalistic shapes. What remained was the actor as an example of spiritual potential, and the cathartic 'communion' with the spectator.

At the stage of development represented by *The Constant Prince*, as Grotowski pointed out: 'The Theatre Laboratory seeks a spectator-witness, but the spectator's testimony is only possible if the actor achieves an authentic act. If there is no authentic act, what is there to testify to?'[23] But the new authenticity in performance revealed, indeed intensified the inherent artificiality of the actor/audience relationship, even when the public were functionally involved in the performance and given a role that overlapped reality. It imposed passivity on the spectator; and in doing so, effectively created a division between thinking and acting, which reflected the split between mind and body that Grotowski (as with so many of the avant garde) sees as the prime destructive characteristic of western civilization. It was thus incompatible with all the techniques specifically designed to overcome this split that Grotowski had evolved to liberate the individual actor spiritually through physical stress, an aim corresponding to Artaud's dictum about reintroducing metaphysics through the skin.

Perhaps in reaction to this problem with actor/audience relationships, Grotowski's subsequent development led to the gradual elimination of any distinction between actor and spectator: 'The very word "spectator" . . . is theatrical, dead. It excludes meeting, it excludes the relation: man–man.' But eliminating the audience meant, ultimately, the abandonment of performance itself. This led to a withdrawal from the stage in the mid–1970s. Grotowski's evolution from the frontiers of drama to a type of work that has little in common with theatre was also motivated by the perception that those rituals and myths, which he once believed were inherited through 'the collective subconscious' and therefore made the basis of his productions, in fact had little validity in a fragmented society:

> After so many explorations, experiences and reflections, I still doubt the possibility of direct participation in today's theatre in an age when neither a communal faith exists, nor any liturgy rooted in the collective psyche as an axis for ritual.[24]

In its place, Grotowski gathered together a fluid 'transcultural group' to find keys to personal being that preceded cultural, or even individual differentiation, and thus formed the 'sources' of human experience. Through physical techniques associated with different, specifically non-Christian, and non-western religions, such as yoga (India), dervishes (Islam), shamanism (North American Indian) and the martial arts of Zen Buddhism, he arrived at a 'Theatre of Sources', which had nothing to do with stage performance or productions in any sense. Instead it was 'devoted to those activities which lead us back to the sources of life, to direct, primary perception, to an organic, spring-like experiencing of life, of existence, of presence'. At the same time, his search for 'authentic' participation continued with self-selected and very limited groups of the public in a series of 'Special Projects' from 1973 on, the more extensive of which were given titles such as *Mountain Project* or *Earth Project*. Through these Grotowski arrived at a concept of 'Active Culture', which he described in mystical terms of 'cleansing' as 'a certain kind of individual creative experience . . . to be oneself . . . one individual in relation to another, in the tangible world'.[25] Words such as 'primary' or 'organic' are typical of this ultimate stage in his development, where primitivism becomes a search for elemental simplicity.

The initial steps in this process came during performances of *Apocalypsis cum Figuris:*

> In the first version of *Apocalypsis* the spectators sat on benches placed in a certain space so that each person was to feel alone . . . Then we looked for different bridges between us and the people – a kind of answer to their presence, an answer that is almost invisible – totally open to their reactions . . . Then we asked at certain points for people who want to come within us and improvise with us during the performance.[26]

From this position, which is superficially similar to the approach of the Living Theatre, Grotowski developed a total concentration on the internal process of self-discovery in groups of the public. In effect, they were subjected to an extended session of psychotherapy based on the acting exercises developed by the Theatre Laboratory. These now had the sole aim of rediscovering primitive roots, and in fact corresponded to 'rites of passage' described by anthropologists such as Van Gennep.

The concept of a 'meeting', lasting anything from forty-eight hours to several months, superseded the idea of performance. Even in his early work Grotowski had defined theatre as an 'elite' art, an 'elect moment' demanding a spectator 'who really wishes, through confrontation with the performance, to analyse himself', and limited to those aware of 'genuine spiritual needs'.[27] During the early 1970s, performances of *Apocalypsis* were used to find self-selecting groups of participants for these 'paratheatrical projects', as Grotowski came to call his therapeutic workshops. And in 1975 the Theatre Laboratory formed 'research universities' in Pittsburgh and at Wroclaw. There all the different forms of 'meeting', developed in the Theatre Laboratory since Grotowski's 1970 decision not to create any new stage productions, were brought together. These ranged from physical exercises and 'acting therapy', to workshops labelled 'meditations aloud' and 'song of myself', which were used as preparation for two 'special projects'.

In one, a large group of between seventy-five and two hundred people were gathered in a dark confined space, lit only by a charcoal brazier and flambeaux carried by the actors. Here they participated in group improvisations, or exposed themselves to basic tactile experiences, while an extempore musical accompaniment on guitar and primitive reed flute responded to the moods of the moment and unified them – a direct extrapolation of the search for 'how to disarm ourselves step by step from our daily acts, how to free ourselves from this fear that divides human beings, how to find the simplest and most elementary relationships' that Grotowski had outlined two years earlier.[28]

The other, a 'narrow special project', was designed to strip away individuality and the accretions of culture, to return participants to their physical roots, and to build a primal grouping based on the individual's awareness of a primitive relationship between man and the natural world. This took place with a small group at night in open country. The first part of the experience corresponded to an initiation by ordeal, isolating individuals, depriving them of light and requiring them to run barefoot through the woods. This direct contact with the environment, emphasizing the senses of touch and smell atrophied in modern civilization (which participants felt liberated them from 'mental habits' and returned them to the state of 'a wild animal'),[29] led to a 'baptism' in a stream. After that the sound of tom-toms guided individuals to a fire, around which they danced as a group for the rest of the night to the beat of the drums. The experience ended with a 'monastic' breakfast and relaxed games improvised by the group in sunlight.

Such 'special projects' have lasted a week (with symbolic connotations of the creation of the world) in Poland, or for ten days at Penn State University in 1978; and the details have varied. In one session, each participant was required to lie in a hole in the ground, while the group threw dirt on his body in a symbolic burial of the previous socialized self. In another, bread for the final breakfast was communally baked at sunrise. But the overall pattern, with its strongly ritualistic overtones, remained basically the same; and participants have commented on the hallucinatory effects of the initial sensory deprivation, or the disorientation of physical exhaustion. And it is hardly coincidental that both the pattern of the experience and the effect closely parallel African and Melanesian initiation rites, or the mysteries at Eleusis. Indeed, it is a measure of the degree to which Grotowski adopted primitivism that this phase of his work attracted the attention of anthropologists.[30]

This progress from theatre to psychotherapy, from presenting ritualistic images of self-transcendence to creating rites in which participants are 'reborn', and the consequent rejection of stage performance as inseparable from 'concealment and shame', are logical extensions of Grotowski's 'via negativa'. They are the end product of his stress on authenticity and unity. In fact the method of what he describes as the 'Theatre of Sources' corresponds to a psychological theory of 'positive disintegration' developed by Dabrowski, one of the lecturers at the 1975 'research university'. The aim of this is to create a scale of alternative values based on 'openness' and the 'elemental roots' of human nature in opposition to the 'shame and fear, the need to hide oneself and, also, the need for continually playing a part which is not us' supposedly imposed by society. This is to be achieved through

> an experience that has no spectators. There is no separation between the creative process and the creative result. This is the experience of Active Culture. It comes from all the participants and is shared by all of them, and not the results of [previously worked out and artificially recreated] experience . . . Shared activity and not shared expression.'[31]

Although Grotowski has continued throughout to refer to his work in theatrical terms from 'Poor Theatre', to 'Theatre of Sources' or most recently 'Objective Drama', the process of elimination that was his basic principle from the beginning led inherently to a rejection of everything associated with stage performance. It also quite logically resulted in the disbanding of his Polish Laboratory Theatre in 1984, since the group came to recognize that they had 'ceased to act as a creative ensemble' and 'become a co-operative of individuals conducting a variety of multidirectional work and independent research'. Behind Grotowski's search for archaic pre-theatrical forms, and the primal identification with nature, lies a retreat into mysticism illustrated by the titles given to the three workshop levels of *Mountain Project*, 'Night Vigil', 'The Way' and 'Mountain of Flame', and his attempts to reach the fundamental sources of existence can only be seen as a regression that could never reach any practical conclusion. This is represented even in the way Grotowski defined his work, always prefacing such concepts as poor theatre, or theatre of sources, with conditional terms like 'Towards . . .', or 'Wandering Towards . . .'; and is summed up in one of Cieślak's comments on the special projects: 'By the end, I felt . . . that I had *begun* to search in a very physical way for roots and sources.'[32]

166

10

ANTHROPOLOGY, ENVIRONMENTAL THEATRE AND SEXUAL REVOLUTION

EUGENIO BARBA – RICHARD SCHECHNER – JOE CHAIKIN

Grotowski's approach aroused considerable interest among the major avant garde directors in the late 1960s and early 1970s. Among those he has worked with are Barrault and Brook, as well as Joe Chaikin and Luca Ronconi, all of whom also participated in his 1975 'research university' in Wrocław, together with his leading disciple, Eugenio Barba. Brook, who arrived at a parallel concept of theatre as 'the terrain of self-discovery' during his African tour, has held joint workshops with him; and Grotowski's influence is directly responsible for the various 'theatre laboratories' that sprang up in the early 1970s. Typical of these are the Théâtre Laboratoire Vicinal in Brussels, where discursive speech was rejected for 'poor' language limited to 'the cry, the shout, the litany or the chant', and the plays produced were textless, structured solely by 'certain fundamental rhythms that [supposedly] every man may feel', and appealing 'to the unconscious of the spectator';[1] or the Atelier de Recherche Théâtrale Georges Baal in Paris, where a bare stage, and the absence of costumes or pretence, was united with themes from Artaud, and an attempt to liberate audiences by breaking taboos; or Terayama's Tenjo Sajiki Laboratory in Tokyo, where extreme means were used to destroy the 'artificial frontiers' between drama and reality, with performers being subjected to real physical violence and spectators being overcome with claustrophobia, assaulted, or even burnt (at the 1973 Shiraz festival, Terayama's actors exploited the audience's fears by continuing without a break, and jabbing flaming torches toward their faces after people in the front rows had been badly singed by a fireblowing circus act, although Terayama later tried to fend off criticism by claiming the 'incident' was accidental).

Grotowski himself rejected such direct attempts to create audience participation as 'a new myth', pointing out that true intimacy is more likely to be achieved through physical distance. He also attacked many of those (particularly in America) who claimed to be following him, for lack of

167

discipline, emphasizing 'the presence of a consciousness . . . structure, clarity, the precise line' that balanced the spontaneity in his work.[2] In a sense, Grotowski's only true followers were his own acting group, although the Polish Laboratory Theatre only achieved one independent production before their dissolution, *Thanatos Polski* (*Polish Lament*, 1981), a highly abstract and musically structured participatory piece, directed by Ryszard Cieslak, with an all too accurate poster depicting two coiled serpents swallowing each other's tails. Yet if Grotowski's theatre eventually became so inward-looking that it consumed itself, his work was continued by Eugenio Barba, Grotowski's assistant during the early, more conventional years of the Polish Laboratory, and Barba was the only avant garde director to be acknowledged by Grotowski as his disciple.

Barba's Odin Teatret (full title: Nordisk Theater-Laboratorium för Skuespillerkunst), founded in 1964 and transferred from Oslo to Denmark in 1966, has remained within the circle of the stage while rhetorically announcing 'the death of the theatre', and condemning even experimental theatres as 'the blasphemous caricatures of a ghost'. Barba's continuation of Grotowski's research into the psycho-physiological basis of acting led to the formulation of a 'new theatrical language', or so he claimed. In practice, it strongly resembled the iconographic style of early expressionist silent films in using archetypal gestures, postures and facial masking to transform 'spontaneous' emotions into 'pure' states of Fear, Pain or Desire. In more theoretical terms articulated during the 1980s, this search for the basics of emotional communication produced another sort of theatrical laboratory: ISTA (International School of Theatre Anthropology).

Specializing in the 'transcultural analysis of performance', ISTA applies the techniques and artistic approach of Oriental traditions – Nōh, Kyogen, Kabuki and Kathakali, Balinese and Indian Odissi dance – to developing a western form of physical stylization. In conscious opposition to the standard European focus on psychology in acting (from the conventional focus on characterization, to Grotowski's psychotherapy), the work of the school has focused on neurophysiological analysis of the actor's 'presence', and vocal studies of the differences between speech in everyday and 'performance' situations. It commissioned a psychologist to conduct an 'intercultural study of corporal-emotional expression' (formalizing Barba's earlier experiments), and explored improvisational techniques in a wide variety of countries. Using the same terminology as Grotowski, in describing ISTA's aims as the development of 'pre-expressivity' through focusing on a 'biological' level, Barba defined 'Theatre Anthropology' as 'the study of the behaviour of the human being when it uses its physical and mental presence in an organized performance situation'.[3]

However, just as this remained a technique for actor-training, rather than becoming a therapeutic process with little theatrical relevance, so Barba's work has retained the dimension of stage performance, while

moving from a drama rooted in myth towards something akin to international circus. Barba's theatre in its first appearance was more directly
political than Grotowski's could ever have been in the Polish context under
Communism; and in productions like *Feraï* (1969) or *Kaspariana* (1967)
myths were used as images of 'the worn-out stereotypes that make up our
habitual social conduct' to reveal these as inherently primitive, repressive
and violent. Against these false myths were set 'ritual' behaviour patterns,
'biological reactions that spring up in extreme situations', where the socially conditioned gestures of everyday life are transformed into a 'natural
physical language', which paradoxically was also a 'sacerdotal sign language' of hieratic attitudes.[4]

Feraï attempted to present a universal paradigm of social structures by
combining the legend of King Fredegod – whose rule was so Draconian
that valuables could be left on the open street, and whose death was
concealed for three years in order to preserve social discipline – with the
myth of Alcestis, Pherai (the Thessalian town ruled by Admetus) with
The Faeroes (in Latin, Ferai). The body of the dead king formed a rather
crude symbol for the death of the spirit under dictatorship; and Fredegod's
kingdom was emblematically represented by a blanket spread out on the
stage and weighted down with stones at the edges. Admetus, who succeeds
to this kingdom by winning Fredegod's daughter (Alcestis) in a duel, is
unable to introduce freedom by political reform. To the proto-fascist
people, liberty means only the destructive licence of a drunken orgy; and
they disinter the corpse of the dead dictator in a parody of Christ's
resurrection. But the play ends with Alcestis' suicide and apotheosis, which
creates a 'mystical' transformation in the state. On another level the play
is a conflict between male and female principles, symbolized in the three
props that formed the only material or scenic aids in the production: the
masculine symbol of a knife with leather thongs, which was used as a
whip representing political repression, as a sabre for the duel, as a royal
sceptre, as a flute; the feminine and passive symbol of a blanket, used to
represent the subjugated kingdom, swaddling clothes, Alcestis' corpse; and
an ivory egg, symbolizing life and death, a skull and the fertile womb. As
even such a brief summary indicates, reliance on mystical reverberations
and archetypal dualities can be both confusing and simplistic. But the
intention was to present a complex of expressionistic images with multiple
meanings, which each spectator could decipher in terms of his own experience, though this was more effective in *Kaspariana* because the metaphors
were more familiar.

The figure of Kaspar Hauser has almost become a hallmark indicating
Grotowski's influence, being used as an image of 'natural man' versus
society not only by Barba, but also by Joseph Chaikin (in *The Mutation
Show*, 1971) and by Brook (1973). When the 16-year-old boy, who had
been kept totally isolated from all human contact since birth, appeared in

Nuremberg in 1828, he immediately struck the public imagination as the epitome of ideal innocence. His murder shortly afterwards came to symbolize the death of the spirit under the pressures of social conditioning; and his story has since become a familiar literary archetype. The progressive deformation of this 'beautiful soul' by education had been the subject of a novel (Jacob Wasserman's *Kaspar Hauser, oder die Trägheit des Herzens*, 1908). His image as the holy fool, whose murder is a metaphor for the breaking of man's natural relation to the universe, was a familiar theme in expressionist poetry (Georg Trakl's 'Kaspar Hauser Lied', 1913, or Hans Arp's 'Kaspar ist tot', 1910), and Peter Handke used the story to demonstrate the breakdown of personality under the impact of language – language being seen as the basic tool of social integration – in his play *Kaspar* (1968).

Barba's version exactly parallels Handke's play in scenes where Kaspar learns to walk, or where 'the community as educator' makes its appearance. But Handke's social criticism is transposed into a religious perspective. Knowledge inherited from the most distant cultures (a choir which mingles Hebrew, Sanskrit and Greek) must be passed to its new member. Kaspar is violated with words – a prayer, a false syllogism ('Jews are bad, Christians are good; we are Christians, we are good')[5] – and his 'social birth' is marked by a hymn: 'Behold in awe, my child, the true God.' His life is prefigured in a 'saga' of a king who sends his son out among his subjects, only to have him killed by them. And in the final scene Kaspar allows himself to be 'consecrated' to arms like a medieval knight on the Darwinian/capitalist grounds that struggle is the basis of existence, having sought an alternative in the Bible but found only the words 'I have not come to bring peace but the sword. I have come to divide a son from his father, to set brother against brother.' The final image of *Kaspariana* is that of willing sacrifice as he is left to face his executioner. As the sacrificial knife is raised the lights go out, and the play ends with the heavy irony of a psalm: 'Beautiful is the earth, Beautiful is God's Heaven, Beautiful is the pilgrimage of the soul towards its celestial home.'

As in so much avant garde work, the main problem with a production like Barba's *Kaspariana*, which was also referred to as an atheist mass, is that any challenge to religion presupposes a climate of belief, which has become increasingly marginalized in western society. At the same time, although Barba's intention may have been 'to force the audience to drop its social mask and face a world in which old values are destroyed, without offering in their place any metaphysical solutions', the spiritual pole of existence that is opposed to socially conditioned and destructive behaviour patterns can only be communicated in images derived from the very religion that has been rejected as dead. But the value of Barba's work lies in its synthesis of Grotowski's ritualistic transcendence with an uncompromising existentialism akin to Samuel Beckett, which leads Barba to compare the function of his actors to Hindu *Alvars*:

> *Alvars* profess that divinity does not exist, that hope does not exist, that all is illusion. In the search for a truth beyond all this, they perform acts disapproved by all society, which make a scandal of them and isolate them. But they are the *fools of God* and their conflicting passions in search of a unity fall into a realm which society respects: religion.[6]

The eclectic mix of archaic languages in *Kaspariana*, and the choice of an Oriental comparison to define the aims of his group, point to the direction taken by Barba in the 1970s. Following the line marked out by Peter Brook, but devoting five years to the process instead of a few months, the Odin Teatret travelled to southern Italy, the Far East and South America in search of 'regions without theatre', where they established a system of 'barter', exchanging demonstrations of their art for 'any form of performance organized by the local people'. Taking the avant garde cult of primitivism a step further, instead of receiving foreign images through the filter of anthropological studies or (as with Artaud's experience of Balinese drama) in a western context, the actors became anthropologists. However, like Brook, they were accompanied by film crews, both in Italy and in South America, and their method of gathering material was hardly objective. Their performances and even presence in the various locales was specifically designed to have a political effect, and when subsumed into productions for European or American audiences, the bartered vignettes or acting styles were reduced to exoticism.

Using Danish as a working language in Italy or Venezuela automatically restricted communication to a physical level (which led to the later ISTA focus on physiological modes of expressiveness common to all cultures), so that the Odin Teatret offerings in the early stages of their global tour were dances. These developed into processional performances incorporating pieces garnered in previous locations, such as Balinese death figures. The purpose of this street-theatre in gathering spectators from the whole community, who would then perform something in their turn, was to foster indigenous, non-professional theatre groups that would act as 'the cells of a new social body'. These Barba labelled the Third Theatre (in distinction to both the establishment, and the experimental avant garde drama), cultural 'islands' serving as a refuge from the official values of exploitive modern societies. 'Barter' is a two-way process, analogous to the theatrical dynamic between actor and audience in performance, both being conceived as having a 'function [that] means relationship, something dialectical that changes, not something static'.[7] Thus for Barba's group to act as a catalyst, it was essential for their art to change, while conversely, if somewhat solipsistically, changes in their performance could be seen as guaranteeing an equivalent effect on the global 'cells' of the Third Theatre, and two of the various Odin Teatret's productions from this period are representative.

Come! And the day will be ours (1976) was based on historical incidents and images from the conquest of the American West, the title coming from the last letter sent by Custer before he and his soldiers were all massacred at Little Bighorn in 1876. The six actors, each identified only by the colour of their clothes or the musical instrument they played and divided into three 'civilized' (white soldiers or settlers) and three 'not civilized' (Indian) figures, presented a sequence of stylized vignettes: the murder of Crazy Horse, betrayed by his chief warrior; a shaman's dance, and pioneers at prayer meetings or staking out their farms; Sitting Bull's performance in Buffalo Bill's circus; the poverty and degradation of the reservations, and the massacre of Indian women and children at Wounded Knee. The performance space was arranged as simultaneously a sun dance circle and circus ring, with benches for the audience in a circle around a central post carrying a ring of lights. The spectators were thus an integral part of the action, representing the tribespeople around a campfire or city crowds at the circus. The only other parts of the set were two small platforms with arched door-frames, also bearing light-bulbs, at opposite sides of the perimeter, suggesting medieval Mystery play 'mansions', one for the 'civilized', the other for the 'not civilized'.

The abstraction of these terms reflected the generalization of the theme, in which the genocidal process of American colonization was intended to be merely a paradigm for 'the way one man destroys another in the name of values which he believes to be universal . . . the violence hidden behind words such as Altruism, Progress and Truth'. The simplicity and participatory nature of the performance, which meant it could be presented anywhere on their travels, was characteristic of the style already arrived at by the Odin Teatret. But the material was 'a reflection on what the Odin has seen while travelling: the destruction of cultures, the elimination of that which is different and the final blow to those already destroyed by the use of their culture as folklore'.[8] And indeed, one performance was given for a dying tribe of Amazonian Indians along the Upper Orinoco river.

The Million (1979), prepared after the group's return from global travel, offers a fuller example of such reciprocity and its implications. Part circus-display of performing styles and genres from around the world, part carnival, this was intended to form a universal synthesis of popular cultures. Japanese Nōh meets Amazonian Indian war dances. Balinese ritual drama was performed to the syncopation of New Orleans Jazz, while Kabuki mixed with Brecht/Weill cabaret, culminating in a funeral procession that turns into an orgiastic dance, which ends with the ritual decapitation of two monstrous death figures on stilts. Taken from the witch-like Balinese Rangda and previously used in the travelling street-theatre processions, these stilt-figures wore Balinese masks and costumes above the waist, carnival dancers' skirts below, and pranced on to 'Oh Susanna'. Associating birth and death, joyful affirmation and dismemberment, the carnival tone exactly echoed Bakhtin's concept of peoples' culture. Yet the Bakhtinian element of parody that came from mixing western and Oriental styles reduced the material 'bartered' by Odin Teatret to precisely the kind of folklore that Barba had condemned as 'the final blow to those already destroyed'. Primitivism and ritualistic drama became a striking display of physical virtuosity.

Another director to have labelled himself explicitly as Grotowski's disciple is Richard Schechner, whose Performance Group in New York achieved overnight notoriety with *Dionysus in 69* (1968). Some years earlier Schechner had analysed *The Bacchae* as an absurd drama in which the petty and all too human qualities of egoistic vanity and capriciousness, revealed in Dionysus' vengeance, represent a cosmic scheme impossible to comprehend or propitiate. He argued that Dionysus incites Pentheus to blasphemy, that his rationale for destroying Thebes is unconvincing since those he kills are his worshippers, and that the image of Dionysus as an irrational, ungovernable ecstatic life force, asserted by the chorus, is contradicted by Euripides' characterization of the god as ironic, self-controlled and intellectualizing – a death force.[9] This interpretation formed the basis of *Dionysus in 69*, where the ambivalence of the god was intended to represent the tendency to fascism inherent in the retreat of the 'new left' from political revolution, to the introverted sexual liberation of the drug culture. But this theme was almost totally overlaid by the ritualistic structure of the action, and the orgiastic emphasis on nudity and dancing. It was also contradicted by the automatic association of the central conflict between the formally dressed Pentheus and the nude Dionysus (played at one point in the production by a woman), with the contemporary clash of the authoritarian social establishment versus 'hippy' freedom, sexual fulfilment and the student revolution.

This was Schechner's most overt attempt to recreate ritual drama, an aim which led *The Drama Review* under his editorship to explore modes of non-verbal communication, the connections between human and animal behaviour patterns in play and ritualized activity, and the types of religious performance surviving in primitive cultures.[10] In his view, the intrinsic structure of avant garde theatre corresponds to that of primitive ceremony (ignoring the fundamental differences between the avant garde tendency to improvisations, the value it places on spontaneity, or its opposition to contemporary society, versus the rigidly fixed lines and delivery, or the integration of the actors in their cultural context that characterizes archaic drama from the simple performances of New Guinea or Australian Aborigines to the highly developed Balinese theatres). Both are seen to share the same principles of 'wholeness', 'concreteness', 'transcendental experience' and the stress on performance as 'process' not product. However, the real link would seem to be in the notional ideal of 'community', which leads Schechner to describe archaic tribal culture as 'communal' rather than 'primitive', and explains his emphasis on audience involvement.

As opposed to a conventional play (an action presented by professionals to a separated and passive collection of individuals), ritual is defined as an action in which all the members of a community actively participate, one which symbolically or even actually transforms the status and identity of the group, depending on the degree of participation. Not only ritual, but also the existence of a community are assumed to be incompatible with modern society so that, in a syllogism typical of the avant garde, persuading spectators to participate gives a performance the status of ritual by transforming them into a community. Participation is thus seen as a political act in itself representing, and so indeed automatically achieving, radical changes in the social order. Nakedness is also seen as 'a rejection of the system', as much in affirming 'the body' as in discarding the social conventions/uniform of clothing.[11] So the meaning of *Dionysus* (as with the Living Theatre's *Paradise Now*, also 1968) lay not so much in what was performed, as in simply getting spectators to strip.

Euripides' play was restructured into an initiation rite. 'Opening ceremonies' were designed to create contact between actors and the audience, who were carried individually from the entrance to the performing area in explicit imitation of ceremonial practices described by Van Gennep.[12] The

Figure 20 The birth ritual in *Dionysus in 69*. Initiation, nudity and communal acting.

whole cast formed the chorus, which became the dominant element of the play, with scenes and characters emerging from choral activity and dissolving back into it as 'initiation by example'. The rhythmic writhing and groaning of the group, naked and in unison, the men stretched out flank to flank on the floor with the women standing above, legs straddling them from shoulder to buttock to form an arched tunnel of flesh, created the dominant image of a birth-canal, adapted from a New Guinea rite of passage. This was repeated twice, at the beginning, when the actor playing Dionysus was 'reborn' as a god, being literally pushed through the 'passage' by pelvic thrusts, and again, reversed, at the death of Pentheus. Instead of being torn to pieces, the actor was symbolically reingested into the community that he had tried to dominate as an individual.

Within this framing image Euripides' plot was reduced to its basic elements with the intention of making it easier for the audience to join in the story by keeping it simple. (For the same reason there was a deliberate avoidance of professional acting techniques that might set the performers apart from the man in the street, although Schechner later came to admit that the majority of the performers were just poor actors, a common factor in many of the groups that sprang up in the 1960s, where the emphasis was on the community as an alternative lifestyle and on self-expression rather than skill or talent.)[13] A bacchanal, broken up by the puritanical Pentheus, was followed by a confrontation between Dionysus and Pentheus, based on encounter-group psychotherapy. Then came Pentheus' search for a willing female sexual partner from the audience, his homosexual seduction by Dionysus and a 'total caress', during which tender embraces by the whole cast were gradually intensified into animal violence that led to an 'erotic love-death'.

The spectators were invited to join the bacchanal:

DIONYSUS: . . . Together we can make one community. We can celebrate together. Be joyous together. So join us in what we do next. It's a circle dance around the sacred spot of my birth . . .[14]

Indeed certain sections of the performance could not be completed without a predetermined response from a specific number of spectators, while at the same time simple rules were laid down to increase the degree of participation. Only those who had taken off all their clothes were allowed into the 8 by 12 ft central acting area that was designated as 'the holy space'. The audiences were subjected to the same erotic embrace and attack as Pentheus in 'the caress', and almost every night some participated in the second birth sequence. This was taken as a tangible measure of success. But at the same time the nature of this involvement was both made overexplicit, and left curiously unfocused. As Dionysus repeatedly announced, 'It's a celebration, a ritual, an ordeal, an ecstasy', and the

audience were encouraged to join 'the community' by stripping and dancing with the performers as a positive act, even though by the time this
level of participation was reached the group had a negative significance in
terms of the play, mindlessly following a megalomaniac quasi-fascist leader
in acts of violence.

Indeed, when Schechner gave his audience a more specific function –
as in *Commune* (1971), where fifteen randomly selected spectators were
required to act as villagers in the My Lai massacre, or find others from
the audience to take their places – the actors' relationship to them was
clearly one of intimidation. Here the discomforting effect was intensified,
because there was no way of signalling what their responses ought to be.
In short, what the Performance Group approach demonstrates is that
meaningful participation requires an established ritual familiar to all, not
an alien rite where, however authentic the imitation, the performance is
bound to be fake. This is not only impossible in a society where cohesive
religious belief has gone and its ritual forms have lost their validity, but
doubly so, given a political radicalism that rejects the social context, since
whatever communal forms do exist are there.

In addition, participation only becomes more than an illusionistic device
when it can change the outcome of the performance. This possibility was
built into *Dionysus*, though in a way which effectively precluded its realization. If Pentheus can persuade any girl in the audience to allow him to
copulate with her, that liberates him from the power of Dionysus. In
theory, the rest of the performance would then take a different course, but
clearly it was never anticipated that any spectator would actually cross
the line between pretence and real sexual activity. However on one occasion
the actor was successful, leaving Dionysus to announce: 'Tonight for the
first time since the play has been running, Pentheus, a man, has won over
Dionysus, the god. The play is over.' Similarly in one performance of
Commune some of the spectators selected refused to act as 'victims', and
the play was broken off for over three hours while the cast and other
spectators argued with them. At the very least then, participation disrupted
the 'prepared rhythms' of the action, that is, diminished both the dramatic
effectiveness of the structure and those qualities that made the performance
ritualistic. Taken to its extreme it made performance of any kind impossible.

Schechner derived his term 'Environmental Theatre' from Kaprow's
concept of the Happening, and tried to incorporate such disruptions by
interspersing organized action with 'open' sections:

> not improvised moments – where performers work freely from a set
> of objectives or rules – but truly open [unprepared] moments when
> all the people in the room, acting either individually, in small groups,
> or in concert move the action forward. This 'action' is not necessarily

known beforehand, and may have nothing to do with the dramatic action of the play.[15]

But in his later work participation was limited to physically following the action, with scenes being played throughout the available area, forcing spectators to change their position in order to see, or as a simultaneous montage so that spectators had to be selective, each making their own logical connections. In a sense this becomes subjective theatre, with the spectators perceiving a different play from changing perspectives that they themselves determine, and that this is a logical extension of avant garde trends is indicated by Peter Stein's independent development of the same approach in Germany with productions like *Shakespeare's Memory* (1977).[16]

This movement through a complex arrangement of multi-level and sub-divided acting areas, literally made the audience the environment of the play in Schechner's *Makbeth* (1969), where the performance was given focus by the way groupings of spectators gathered and dispersed. They became the soldiers, guests or crowds, powerless to intervene but compliant, watching a brutal power struggle with the same vicarious titillation as the modern man in the street crowding round an accident or the scene of a crime. At the same time spectators were set inside the environment of the play, as in a 1975 production of Brecht's *Mother Courage*, where the whole of the Performance Garage was conceived as the wagon, with ropes and pulleys strung from walls and ceiling to represent harness or the tents of a military camp, and with the Performance Group itself presented as Mother Courage's 'small business'. There were also rather fake attempts to move the theatre out into the real environment with Dionysus leading bacchantes and audience through the opened garage doors in a triumphal procession up the street, or with Mother Courage's haggling played out on the pavement. Such blurring of performance and reality reached its peak in Schechner's version of *The Balcony* (1979–80), which also brought an end to Schechner's association with the Performance Group he had founded, and its dissolution.[17]

Genet's play, once a revolutionary text for the avant garde, had now become a 'modern classic' for Schechner; and just as Marowitz had done with *Hamlet*, he 'deconstructed' it, eliding scenes and altering sequences. He also used extensive doubling (both of actors and roles), as well as cross-gender casting. Intended to bring the play's disguised 'homoerotic basis . . . into the open', this became an expression of the 'secret desires' of the individual actors, which corresponded with Genet's theme but contradicted the actions required by the script. As personal fantasies, they also contradicted each other. For instance, the revolution on which the plot turns was reduced to yet another fantasy of Genet's brothel, reflecting the failed revolution of the 1960s, which had been the catalyst for Schechner and the whole American avant garde movement. 'A very nostalgic myth, that of revolution', as Schechner put it, expressed by making the street battles no more than a recording on a phonograph controlled by one of the whores and interchangeable with Musak. But for the actress playing Chantal – the whore-singer, elevated to the archetype of Liberty on the Barricades – who composed the score, it represented a feminist revolution of consciousness, which thus also became parodied and (literally) prostituted.

Instead of sexual/political revolution, the mainspring of the performance became theatre itself, both experimental theatre and brothels being seen as in the business of selling fantasy. Thus instead of different prostitutes serving the General and the Bishop as horse and penitent, the scenes were intercut and both customers were serviced by the same girl, highlighting not only the cheap tawdriness of the brothel as she rushed from one to the other with quick costume changes, but also the role-playing, while the girl's own dream was to be a 'real' actress. The spectators, walking around among the movable platforms of the brothel studios or in 'expensive' seats on platforms right in the middle of the action, were in the position of 'clients'. Indeed, the actors playing Madame Irma's customers rose from among them to take up their parts. For Schechner, these were all ways of showing that 'theatre is a "house of illusion", sister to the whorehouse. After all, one of the root meanings of prostitute is substitute: someone who stands for someone else (in the mind/body of the client).'[18]

But the metaphor works both ways. Here the Performance Group ideal of audience participation was explicitly voyeurism, a perhaps unintentional acknowledgement of what had always been essentially the effect of their attempts to create direct physical involvement. Schechner's production of *The Balcony*, which indicates the continuing connections in the avant garde movement, must also be seen as an epitaph for the experimental theatre of the 1970s. Other radical American groups followed much the same trajectory in their careers, such as Joe Chaikin's Open Theatre, which developed from a closed acting workshop to ritualistic performances of archteypal material with *The Serpent* in the same year as Schechner's *Dionysus*.

Chaikin, who had started out with the Living Theatre and worked with Peter Brook on *US*, began developing *The Serpent* following sessions with Grotowski and Cieślak at a Grotowski workshop laboratory in 1967. A collaborative piece, based on the Biblical myths of Genesis, Eden and the Fall, this combined all the major avant garde modes of the time. The serpent, created by the intertwined bodies of five actors, was presented as a positive life force, while God (made in man's image, a typical inversion of religion) was the voice of psychological repressions within the actors, and God's curse was expressed through grotesquely distorted physical postures. These emblematic 'locked actions' recurred throughout the production, as when Cain kills Abel, or with the assassinations of Kennedy and Martin Luther King that were acted out as analogues to the 'primal' murder. In opposition to such negative sections were liberating sequences: the awakening of consciousness, where actors moved out into the audience and embraced spectators, or the discovery of sex (the 'Begatting', which led into a birth sequence comparable to that in *Dionysus*). Apart from apples and primitive musical instruments, there were no props or scenery, all images being created by the bodies of the actors; and the performance began with the contemporary material, moving into the Biblical scenes through an autopsy. The premise was that surgery on the brain could stimulate racial memory, so the action traced modern events back to mythic roots.[19]

The Open Theatre's subsequent productions included one of Jarry's *Ubu* plays, along with three pieces developed out of ensemble improvisations: *Terminal* (1969), *The Mutation Show* (1971) which was partly based on the histories of Kaspar Hauser and the wolf-girl Kamala, and *Nightwalk* (1973). These explored taboos, social rituals and dreams, in a search for states of being where spiritual reality broke through into everyday life. In the process of dying, the theme of *Terminal*, spirits of the deceased (a dead creole mystic, a murdered political activist) were imagined possessing the bodies and tongues of the terminally ill to address the living. *Nightwalk* presented a symbolic journey through sleeping minds, from semi-conscious fantasies to the depths of the psyche. But in performance the trances and spiritual possession were acted, not actual; and although the physical images (corresponding to Brook's search for a primal 'root' in the human body) might be seen as having quasi-mythic resonance in the degree to which they conveyed subliminal meaning, the action resolved into a display of Open Theatre techniques. Even more than the Performance Group (since Chaikin's productions garnered Obie and Drama Desk awards, first prize at the Belgrade International Theatre Festival and a Rockefeller Fellowship), critical success tended to institutionalize their work, and in 1974 they disbanded.

In both the Open Theatre and even more in the Performance Group, the merging of illusion and reality and the stress on total commitment, together with the subjective nature of the dramatic event, turned productions into a form of psychotherapy. The characteristic direct address and physical involvement of the spectators could only break down superficial barriers, since the focus of performances was not so much the audience's experience, as catharsis for the performers themselves. In *The Serpent* and *The Mutation Show*, even though writers like Claude Van Itallie were involved, the dramatic material came from the actors' exploration of their inner selves; and this was taken to an extreme in the work of Schechner's group. Each actor wrote his own dialogue for *Dionysus* and *Commune*, incorporating

179

inflated personal experiences and trite life histories, so that as one actor playing Dionysus only too revealingly commented, 'I am acting out my disease, the disease that plagues my inner being, that stops the flow . . . *Dionysus* is not a play to me. I do not act in *Dionysus. Dionysus* is my ritual.'

Personal tensions constantly plagued the Open Theatre, fostered by the incompatibility between ensemble creation and productions that expressed Chaikin's vision as a director. But the situation was still more intense in the Performance Group, where communal living was a political ideal. When *Dionysus* opened, almost half of the cast were under psychoanalysis, and group therapy sessions were held once a week, through which personal neuroses and resentments were brought to the surface. These fed into the theatrical work to such an extent that the tensions and conflicts within the 'community' became the real focus of *Makbeth*, leading to the breakup of the original Performance Group, while the subject of *Commune* became the analysis of different kinds of group – Manson and his 'family', soldiers and their Vietnamese victims, the actors and their audience – and the play itself was conceived as 'a collective dream'.

The model for all Grotowski's disciples was that of the Asian performer, whose training was seen as 'holistic' and 'the primary means of personal growth' (as opposed to western training, defined as an 'instrumental' and acquired skill). Their ideal was to recreate a shamanistic performance exorcizing the 'disease' of the community in the form of taboos, hostilities, fears. But the effect (as Grotowski himself noted, criticizing the absence of discipline in American groups) was frequently self-indulgent, and self-expression tended to cliché. Possibly the desired states of shamanistic 'trance and possession' could be achieved only by the total identification of performers with their roles. But the result was both naive and, as Schechner himself realized, narcissistic.[20] As with Grotowski, characterization – the projection of the self into an 'other' – was discarded, while texts became hypnotic structures of sound, and the separation between spectator and actor was dissolved. The aim was to transform theatre into psychotherapy. But here any demonstrable effect seems to have been limited to the acting group themselves, and could hardly be called therapeutic. As in Barba's work, the potential flaws in Grotowski's approach become clear. Indeed, some of the negative implications in this theatrical development are summed up by Schechner's description of the avant garde as 'more iconographic than iconoclastic . . . radical not in a political sense, but in the manner in which it attempts to go to the roots'. In fact his claim that 'the locus of the essential theatre shifted from the page to somewhere between the navel and genitals of each performer'[21] – from his point of view a positive and progressive state of affairs – was unfortunately all too accurate.

THE LIVING THEATRE

Many of the same criticisms apply to the work of the Living Theatre, which – with an eclecticism that is itself typical of the avant garde – drew together almost all of the different trends so far discussed. When they founded their first (abortive) theatre in 1948, Julian Beck and Judith Malina concentrated on Nōh drama and medieval mystery plays. Their early Living Theatre productions included an adaptation of the *Oresteia* with masks and dances derived from Japanese theatre, *Ubu roi*, Strindberg's *Ghost Sonata* and the surrealism of Picasso and Gertrude Stein, while images from early expressionist films were used for their version of *Frankenstein* (1965). Artaud's theories inspired their production of *The Brig* (Kenneth Brown, 1963), and provided the dominant image of *Mysteries* (1964), which ended with a staging of Artaud's description of 'the Plague' as 'the very embodiment of his theatrical philosophy'.[22] Their development led naturally to the ritual of Genet's *The Maids*, which they performed with an all-male cast and which was almost the only production (apart from Lindsay Kemp's) that was faithful to this aspect of Genet's vision.

But it was Grotowski who set the tone of their major stage work. Their notes for *Paradise Now* (1968) repeatedly refer to Grotowski's acting exercises and Cieslak's 'transluminations', which they saw as a model for removing psychological resistances. Translated into 'flashouts' – 'a transcendent moment in which [the actor] is released from all hangups of the present situation' – these marked the end of each section in *Paradise Now*, while Grotowski's term *apokatastasis* ('the transformation of the demonic forces into the celestial')[23] was used as its central structuring principle. They repeatedly labelled their political aim 'prophesying', described their theatre as 'performing a ceremony' and its intended effect as 'an absolute communion', referred to the actor as a 'priest' or 'shaman', and pointed out their 'concern with primitive and mystic rituals'.[24] In their performances plot, characterization and (in *Mysteries*, *Paradise Now* or their 1967 version of Brecht's *Antigone*) scenery were replaced by sequences of physical images, or 'hieroglyphs' formed solely from the posture and grouping of the actors. Comparable to Grotowski's 'schemata', these drew on archetypes from Greek mythology (Icarus, Europa, the Minotaur), on Egyptian bas-reliefs, Amerindian totem-poles, the legend of Buddha and eschatological clichés (the *pietà*, or the horsemen of the Apocalypse). Similarly, the overall structures of action were derived impartially from the Cabbala, from Tantric and Hassidic rituals, and from initiation rites such as the mysteries at Eleusis. From an ideal of theatre 'as a place of intense experience, half dream, half ritual, in which the spectator approaches something of a vision of self-understanding, going past the conscious to the unconscious', they developed an extreme form of audience participation where performance 'would no longer be enactment but would be the act itself'.

Even their European exile was justified in exactly the same terms as Brook's African journey – 'to find ways of communicating with each other beyond those which involve speech. To find a way of communicating our feelings and our ideas through signs and being'[25] – while their later development took them, like Grotowski, outside the theatre altogether. In short the Living Theatre recapitulates the sources, aims and successive stages of the whole avant garde movement in microcosm.

The base root of all avant garde theatre is an uncompromising rejection of contemporary civilization and existing social structures. Even if it has also led to the rejection of conventional modes of political action and accepted ideologies, it is this ultimately political position which has determined the almost universal appeal to irrationalism with its exploration of dream states and search for archetypal expression, as well as the return to primitive dramatic forms in ritual with its emphasis on religious experience and Eastern mysticism. And nowhere is the link between politics and the apparently apolitical emphasis on the subconscious or mythology clearer than in the Living Theatre, with its overt commitment to anarchism.

However, where this commitment was explicit it produced little but empty wish-fulfilment and simplistic equations – such as the Becks' assertion that 'the hippies' are 'reincarnations of the American Indian, aspiring to be the natural Man as represented by . . . the great suppressed cultures'. Perhaps reflecting the naivety of American radicals in the 1960s, their slogans were at best sophomoric statements of conviction, with little relevance to the actual situation, such as 'Fuck the Jews. Fuck the Arabs. Fuck means peace', where 'universal intercourse' was proposed (without any sense of irony) as a solution to the problems of the Middle East. The simplicity of their approach is illustrated by the way the word 'Anarchism', spelt out by the bodies of the actors across the stage, was transformed into the word 'Paradise' with a shout of 'now!'[26] Yet to dismiss the Living Theatre's work as unpolitical, as many critics did, is beside the point. Their assumption was that individual spiritual change is the pre-condition for meaningful exterior political change; and that dealing with a social issue on its own terms will only perpetuate the established cycle of violence and oppression, of which it is a symptom. So their aim was to create images that would act as an emotional inspiration, to challenge taboos and socially conditioned patterns of thought.

Perhaps unsurprisingly, the most powerful and convincing images were negative: representations of a dehumanizing system of repression and exploitation, developed or reproduced from production to production, which were designed to cause an instinctive revulsion in the audience. One such image was derived from *The Brig*, where the dramatic action is contained solely in the 'regulations' of the US Marines prison:

No prisoner may speak at any time except to his guards. A prisoner must request permission to do any and everything in the following way: 'Sir. prisoner number – requests permission to speak, sir' . . .

At each exit and entrance there is a white line. No prisoner may cross any white line without requesting to do so . . .

Under no circumstances will a prisoner be permitted to walk from place to place. He must run . . . [27]

Humiliation, physical punishment, isolation and depersonalization are intrinsic parts of this particular play's logic, not to be confused with the similar expressionistic technique used for generalization in a play like Elmer Rice's *The Adding Machine* (1923). It has the explicit function of 'rehabilitation', instilling an automatic response to orders in prisoners whose 'crimes' have been infringements of discipline.

This image of social conditioning as dehumanizing brainwashing, with the military framework implying that the end result of deadening normal human emotions is killing, was reused in *Mysteries*. However, it lost much of its significance out of its original context, and had to be given additional associations by a 'poem' composed of all the numbers and words on a dollar bill that was recited as an accompaniment. It was reused again in *Frankenstein*, where 'world action' was represented as a multi-storey prison structure through which the actors moved in a perpetual cycle: whistle, blackout, each prisoner moves to the next cell . . . lights, each freezes in a position expressing mental agony, becoming more mechanical and zombie-like as they progress through the structure . . . and at each whistle one leaves from the last cell (death) while another actor is dragged out of the audience to the first cell for fingerprinting and mug shot.

A comparable image was 'the plague' – the groans, cries and distorted bodies of the dying, acting out repressed sexual desires in their death throes; survivors lining up the rigid bodies, then laying them one on top of the other in a 'wood pile' with its connotations of cremation and the gas ovens. This was used unchanged in *Mysteries* and *Antigone*. What made such images effective was not their accuracy, certainly not any philosophical depth, but solely their simplicity and specificity, a point clearly demonstrated by the development from *Frankenstein* to *Paradise Now*. In the first, Artaudian 'cruelty' was presented in the whole spectrum of execution from beheading and crucifixion, to the firing squad and electric chair. In the second, all across the stage paired-off actors took up the positions of the Saigon Police Chief and Vietcong prisoner in Edward Adams' award-winning photo of 1968 – a graphic and immediately evocative image that was made unendurable for many spectators by its multiplication and reiteration: 'In unison . . . the victims rise, the executioners fire, the victims fall. This is repeated twenty times.'[28] A complex system had been reduced to a single, concrete and instantly comprehensive essential that, however superficial, carried conviction because the picture was already loaded with connotations.

By contrast positive images in the Living Theatre's work, intended as inspirational, were all too often generalized to the point of abstraction, or totally obscure, as in the static physical representation of Greek mythological situations, or the use of incantation, yoga breathing exercises, or Hindu mantras and ragas to symbolize hope, aspiration and 'revolutionary' action. In *Mysteries*, for example, scenes presenting the 'problem' of the present state of the world were set against 'solutions' in the form of an alternative life style suggested by 'ceremonies' celebrating the senses. *Tableaux vivants*, supposedly communicating 'that whatever posture our bodies assume it will always be beautiful',[29] were intended to exercise the eye. Incense carried in procession through the auditorium in darkness stimulated the sense of smell. A 'chord', built up from the actors in a circle tuning in to the notes made by their neighbours, indulged the ear in a deliberate but ultimately meaningless confusion of categories: politics against aesthetics.

Similarly, the structure of *Paradise Now* was based on the principle of transformation, with the 'demonic' qualities of 'rigidity' or the 'hostility resulting from an unsatisfactory life' being 'exorcized' by the influence of 'movement' or the 'love force'. In the 'Vision of Apokatastasis', for instance, the executioners repeated the phrases shouted at the audience by the company in the opening rite to represent the frustrations and repression of the social system – 'I am not allowed to travel without a passport . . . I'm not allowed to smoke marijuana . . . I'm not allowed to take my clothes off' – while the victims replied with words from the 'rite of prayer' that had been used to 'sanctify' the spectators – 'Holy eyes . . . Holy legs . . . Holy mouth'. And this chanting continued 'until the executioners are moved to respond, not with violence, but with love, and gently address the victims with the words of the Rite of Prayer. The "Vision" ends with the embrace of victim and executioner. (Flashout)'.[30] Again there is a confusion of categories, though here it is even more basic, stylized pretence being taken as a real event; vicarious emotion assumed to be objective actuality, and not just subjective experience; theatre confused with life.

This attempt to merge theatrical performance and reality is characteristic of the avant garde approach. But the Living Theatre took it to extremes. Comparable to Brook's preparations for *The Ik*, in *The Brig* the actors voluntarily submitted themselves to 'Rehearsal Discipline Rules' paralleling the Marine regulations of the play. They not only wore their costumes all the time, but also continued the prescribed attitudes of sadism (on the part of those playing guards) or absolute obedience (the prisoners) off-stage to create a real atmosphere of hostility, persecution and isolation. The production of *The Connection* (Jack Gelber, 1959) was a natural extension of this. The dialogue is largely devoted to establishing that the actors are in fact drug addicts, paid to come to the theatre to provide a sociological 'experience' for the audience. The actors were required to stay in character and mingle with the audience during the intermission; and the theme asserted not only that 'straight' society was morally inferior to the counterculture, but also that the two were identical (pushers being 'business men' while business men were 'addicted' to money, sleeping pills, nicotine, etc.).

Judith Malina described this as 'a very important advance for us . . . from then on, the actors began *to play themselves'*. Costumes, make-up and characterization were avoided, even in a fairly conventional play like *Antigone*, where she commented 'I don't want to be Antigone, I am and want to be Judith Malina'.[31] Naturally, with this value put on 'playing oneself', dramatic action was increasingly improvised; and this led to a confusing lack of observable form, even in such a highly structured play as *Paradise Now*. This was conceived as 'a spiritual voyage and a political voyage' charted in an ascending series of eight gradated 'Rungs'. Each 'Rung' was sub-divided into a 'Rite' establishing contact between actors and spectators; a cerebral 'Vision' performed solely by the actors; and an 'Action' to be accomplished by the audience. Yet improvisation resulted in the poor execution of what was often brilliantly conceived physical imagery. It also limited dialogue to a simplicity of the 'You Jane. Me Tarzan' variety, and reduced the action to a repetitive expression of extreme emotional states (hatred or passion being easier to communicate than nuances of sentiment). All this led critics to condemn the Living Theatre (not unfairly) as converts rather than actors, self-indulgent and unskilled.

But in a sense crude acting, unsustained characterization and imperfect physical imagery was a logical, even obligatory expression of the group's anarchist ideology, with its emphasis on essence or process, and its total opposition to form or product. This was intentionally 'State of Being Acting as opposed to Enactment Acting . . . something between chance and free theatre'.[32] On another level the actors really did experience something of the emotions they presented, even the 'state of transcendent energy and transformation' defined as a 'flashout', through a form of self-hypnosis. Normal feelings could be heightened to a state of emotional intensity by using physical tension, by provoking hostility against themselves in the audience, and by using communal rhythms or repeated movements. Drugs were also openly used 'to attain a state of inspiration, what we sometimes call a "trance" '[33] – even though this can only have impaired communication, substituting the performers' gratification for emotional impact on the audience.

In the last analysis, however, a performance could only be turned into a real event by the total involvement of the audience. Initially this was limited to an attempt to disorient spectators: for instance, submerging them in a 'dream' by painting the auditorium black, with 'narrower and narrower stripes converging towards the stage, concentrating the focus, as if one were inside an old-fashioned Kodak, looking out through the lens, the eye of the dreamer in a dark room'.[34] But the subliminal soon gave way to the physical. In *Frankenstein*, the barrier of the footlights was broken, though vicariously, 'victims' of the system fleeing to the auditorium for refuge, with teams of 'police' pursuing and dragging them (plus other actors seated among the audience) back to torture and imprisonment on the stage. Then in *Antigone*, the audience were involved thematically in the action. They stood for Argos, all the actors on stage represented Thebans, and the battles were mimed assaults on the auditorium, with the actor playing Megaros as a supposed spectator who was butchered in the aisle. Already in *Mysteries*, the Living Theatre had experimented with creating feelings of unease in their audience by opening with a silent and motionless actor literally staring them down; and here the aim was to evoke fear and hostility, like Genet in *The Blacks*. As the audience took their seats, the actors entered one by one, a counter force, antagonistic and contemptuous, forming different groupings and moving slowly down stage 'to spot each

Figure 21 'Authenticity' instead of costume or character in *Antigone*, and symbols from physical grouping. Aggression as a substitute for audience involvement.

one and decide who you don't like' (according to Beck's directive),[35] then charging straight down into the audience in the attack on 'Argos' once sufficient hostility was thought to have been established. At the end, after the defeat of Thebes, the pattern was reversed, the actors lining up along the edge of the stage to receive the judgement of their 'conquerors' (the audience), then retreating and collapsing, trembling and whimpering with terror at the applause.

This pattern of antagonism, with the same inherent confusion from arbitrarily ignoring actual responses, and treating even expressions of approval or solidarity as hostility, characterized the opening of *Paradise Now*, where the audience were approached as if they represented the repressive forces of society. 'I'm not allowed to travel without a passport . . . smoke marijuana . . . take my clothes off' was shouted in spectators' faces with increasing urgency and hate, and each actor used any response, however sympathetic, 'to increase his expression of the frustration at the taboos and inhibitions imposed on him by the structure of the world around him', with the dubious aim of evoking in the audience a 'growing frustration at the sense of a lack of communication' with the actors.[36]

The whole play that followed was designed to transform this alienation into its opposite, physical unity, in the 'Rite of Universal Intercourse'. Here naked spectators and actors embraced indiscriminately, even copulating – the ultimate extension of the involvement and liberation of man's instinctive nature, which Barrault had aimed at metaphorically, and Schechner counterfeited in *Dionysus* – leading finally to the transformation of society outside the theatre, with love and nudity supposedly spreading contagiously as the naked actors led the unclothed spectators in a pied-piper procession through the streets. The 'Rite' on each 'Rung' of the ladder leading to 'Permanent Revolution' was explicitly conceived as a 'rite of passage'; and the overall structure corresponded to the primitive pattern described by Van Gennep: separation of the initiates from the social environment they were identified with through (in this case verbal) flagellation, purification and integration in a new group, which was frequently marked by sexual licence 'as a complete expression of that same idea of incorporation. It is the precise equivalent of a communal meal.'[37]

In terms of this ritual form, spectators had to achieve particular states of consciousness at each step, before the performance could proceed. Awareness of 'the structures which make these prohibitions', as well as the alternative of 'Natural Man', was to be followed by the formation of groups of five – an analogy with 'the elemental structure of the cell [biology being merged with Bakunin's revolutionary theories] as a pattern for social structure' – and by 'PRACTICAL WORK . . . to rally those who are ready and to ready those who are open'. After (sexual/comm-)union came 'a projection into time future', the visionary 'expansion of human potential. This

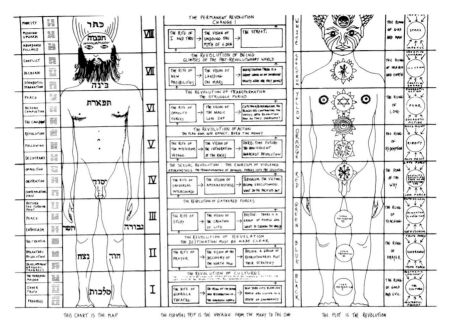

Figure 22 Programme chart for the 'spiritual voyage' of *Paradise Now*. Symbolic structures and eclectic imagery. Compare the physiology of *Orghast*, plate 17.

could lead to flying' since 'freed from the constraint and injury brought down on us by the errors of past civilization, we will be free to expand and to alter the nature of our being'. Finally the production attempted to actualize this image of the future: 'The theatre is in the street. The street belongs to the people. Free the theatre. Free the street. Begin.'[38]

The idea of walking out naked into the sub-zero temperatures of a Midwest American street in December or January was itself ludicrous, although occasionally a few spectators were sufficiently carried away to do so. Equally unconvincing was the syllogistic confusion of the biological with the political, the physical with the spiritual, the ideal with the possible, and the image with actuality, although this epitomized the radicalism of the 1960s. Significantly, the most effective part of this programme was a symbolic act, not a real action: the flying. One person at a time, members of the audience as well as actors launched themselves, as if diving upwards, off a high platform to be caught in the interlaced arms of the others standing in a double line below. And this corresponded so closely to shamanistic folklore and shamanistic performances that it can hardly be a coincidence:

Shamans are able, here on earth and as often as they wish, to accomplish 'coming out of the body', that is, the death that alone has power to transform the rest of mankind into 'birds' . . .

Magical flight is the expression both of the soul's autonomy and of ecstasy . . . The breaking of the plane effected by the 'flight' signifies an act of transcendence . . .

Strictly speaking, what is in question is not a 'flight' but a dizzy trajectory, mostly in a horizontal direction [representing] the desperate effort to be rid of a monstrous presence, to free oneself . . . [39]

'Flying' became the trade mark for the Living Theatre, and was taken up by others like Schechner's Performance Group.

But aside from this, physical involvement only occurred on the most basic level. Grotowski had cast his audiences in well-defined roles that corresponded to their function as spectators, and reinforced their passive receptivity. By contrast the Living Theatre demanded a degree of participation that transformed the spectator into the protagonist, but without giving anything more than an abstract 'map' or generalized slogans to indicate exactly what action was required. The resulting response was only too often cheap humour (animal noises, shouts of 'louder!' or 'begin!', directed at the silent actor in the prologue to *Mysteries*), self-indulgence (sexual gratification), or the provocation of precisely those instincts the performance was intended to eradicate (as in 'the Plague' scene of *Mysteries*, where although normally one or two spectators did 'die' with the actors or comforted the 'dying', the actors were frequently tickled, kicked or abused to try to get the 'corpses' to move, and once Malina's hair was even set on fire).

There were comparable problems even when preaching to the converted, as the Living Theatre increasingly did once their work became associated with the student revolution that culminated in the events of May 1968 in Paris (where, ironically, it was Malina and Beck who led the takeover of Barrault's Théâtre de France). From Brooklyn all the way to Berkeley in their 1968–9 American tour, whenever the actors announced they were not allowed to smoke marijuana, the audience lit up joints and filled the house with the pungent smell of hashish. As the cast were claiming they were not allowed to strip, clothes were being flung off all over the auditorium. And in at least one performance the injunction to 'free the theatre' swamped the stage with naked spectators and the play was brought to an abrupt end by a public discussion on the political relevance of the Living Theatre itself.

In an attempt to cope with this, explicit stage directions were included in the dialogue of *Paradise Now*, though these tended to the abstract, like

- Stop the fear.
- Stop the punishment.
- Make it real.

– Do it Now.

or the inflated, like

– Be the heart. Act. Find the pain. Feel it. Make the sound of it.
– The heart of Africa.
– The sacred heart.
– Enact the impulses of the collective unconscious.[40]

The actors also provided examples for the audience, and tried to guide whatever actions they initiated, while the performance was left as open as possible so that only about one-third of the time was scripted. And the Becks asserted that the revolutionary paradise could be achieved

> at any point . . . If the audience became so incensed at these prohibitions that it – without our saying another word consummated a revolution, whatever we mean by that – that's perfect, just as in the levitation at the start of *Frankenstein*, we say: 'If she levitates, the play is consummated.'[41]

However, in claiming this, the Living Theatre implicitly acknowledged the impossibility of controlling the level of participation they required. Beck tended to put this down to the unregenerate nature of society, so that failure became an additional justification for their work. But their use of the term 'consummate', as well as the admission that they have no definition of revolutionary achievement in such a statement, is telling; and *Paradise Now* highlights the incompatibility of improvisation and art, direct physical audience involvement and the aesthetic imaginary basis of theatrical performance. At every 'Rung' on the 'vertical ascent' the audience were exhorted to 'free' the theatre as a paradigm of revolutionary action:

> – Free theatre. Because in the society we envisage, everyone is free.
> – Free theatre. Free being. Free life. Do anything. Do nothing. Be.
> – Breathe.
> – Expand consciousness.[42]

Yet Malina's conclusion, after a whole year of discussions among the company, was 'I don't think . . . that it is possible to obtain a satisfactory response from a whole audience under actual conditions'. Calling for 'spontaneous' actions from the public effectively abdicated their control: 'Some of [the audience] performed "choices" that were really beautiful and absorbing, although some were sort of extravagant, more foolish and horrible. But when you do "free theatre", you cannot say that this is bad and this is good.' At best, the ordinary person will resort to repetitive clichés when required to express his 'consciousness' or 'being'; and, as Beck himself realized, 'there's something wrong with a play that keeps reducing an audience to that low level'.[43] When an extended co-operative action of any subtlety or coherence did occur during *Paradise Now*, this was because the performance had been infiltrated by professional agitprop (agitation and propaganda) groups who staged their own pre-rehearsed, alternative play.

With *Paradise Now* the limits of this line in the Living Theatre's development were reached; and in 1970 the group split up. After that the Becks' rhetoric became more ideological. At the same time, the Becks' concept of 'Guerilla Theatre', elaborated into 150 miniature playlets to be performed in procession in front of appropriate buildings in any city, was still based on myth, and contained many scenes lifted from their earlier work. Where the subtitle of *Paradise Now* was 'Undoing the myth of Eden', the overall title of this mammoth street spectacle was *The Legacy of Cain* and its intention was the 'exorcism' of slavery by presenting images of enslavement in everyday activities. The different sections that were performed at various times include 'the Plague' (Artaudian liberation through the destruction of society) and a 'Prison dream play' (staged in gaol after the group were arrested in Brazil). 'The money tower', performed outside a steelworks in Pittsburgh, presented the economic system as a multi-storey structure comparable to the 'prison' of *Frankenstein*, in which men live an existence of 'visions' and 'nightmares', 'the visions of the poor' being 'the nightmares of the rich'. More directly, there were 'Seven meditations on political sado-masochism', and 'Six public acts', in which the actors 'go to the sources of institutionalized murder', supposedly by creating simple images to 'reverse public consciousness': for example, the actors pricked their fingers and encouraged spectators to do the same, mingling their blood in a ritual of brotherhood, and smearing it on a flagpole (designated 'the House of State' at Ann Arbor) as a symbol of the deaths caused by wars, the police, the national guard, etc., with the repeated chant of 'this is the blood of us all'. Finally there was 'Turning the earth: a ceremony for spring planting in five ritual acts'.[44]

The Living Theatre Action Declaration of January 1970 had announced the breakup of the original group with the call to 'Abandon the theatres . . . Create circumstances that will lead to Action . . . Smash the art barrier', aims which were reflected in their move to Brazil (as a country in the initial stages of revolution), then to the US rust belt centre of Pittsburgh (as the dying endpoint of industrial capitalism). This rejection of the theatre for direct intervention in reality is a logical development of avant garde aims, one already inherent in the expressionist attempt to create an immediate and therapeutic transference of emotion to the audience, or in Jarry's and Artaud's equally self-destructive acting out of their dramatic principles in their lives.

But the Living Theatre's continuing definition of action as provoking a shift in consciousness – an interior change in the nature of the spectator – also epitomizes the avant garde. The logical means to achieve this end are subliminal or spiritual, leading to a return to the idealized conditions of archaic drama. This explains the Living Theatre's continuing emphasis on performance as a religious and ritual event, on ceremonies of exorcism, initiation and communion, and on the projection of dream states, even 'meditations', all designed 'to transmute violence into concord' (the rationale appended to the title of 'Six public acts'). It produces the adaptation of primitive rites and the concept of a 'holy' actor as shaman, as well as the formalized audio-visual structures of archetypal images and hypnotically repetitive incantation. All these elements distinguish this dominant line of avant garde theatrical exploration from the various experiments in straight political theatre on the one hand, and from the Happening or Russian formalism on the other.

However, as in much of the Living Theatre's work, such primitivism has an inherent tendency towards arcane or facile exoticism, and 'Turning the earth' is a good example. As scenery, a large mandala of the birth of the earth was reproduced from Jung's *Mandala Symbolism* (quite incomprehensible to anyone who had not read the book) and set up in an uncultivated city lot. The action consisted of a series of rites, 'Retching the Past' – suggested by an obscure ceremony from the Omaha Indians, in which the actors put pebbles symbolizing 'dead earth', the crippling effect of 'the heritage of violence', etc., in their mouths and spat them out – followed by celebrations of 'Rebirth' and 'Community':

> When all the people in the circle have completed their ritual [giving each other symbolic names to indicate that they have been 'reborn'] they rise and form a circle, arms around each other, and create a chordal sound together, beginning with a low hum. The low hum rises rapidly and gives birth to choral musical notes of throats opened in unity and ecstasy.

This culminates in a token planting of trees and flowers, and although 'the intention of the play is to stimulate a fresh relationship in the community towards the earth, towards land, towards the question of property', the only discernible effect of the ritual is to make a simple activity unnecessarily pretentious.

11

INTERCULTURALISM AND EXPROPRIATING THE CLASSICS

SHAKESPEAREAN ADAPTATIONS

As Ruby Cohn has pointed out, the most obvious reason for adapting Shakespeare's plays is to modernize them.[1] In the past this usually meant rewriting scenes and altering endings to correspond to the ethos of the age, the classic example being Nahum Tate's notorious eighteenth-century version of *King Lear*. This is still generally the case. Brecht's version of *Coriolanus* (1952) or Edward Bond's *Lear* (1972) reflected current political issues – class warfare and the triumph of a people's democracy over the military aristocracy, or the self-defeating necessities of power and the self-sacrificing activism that may eventually succeed in dismantling the structures of fear and repression – while Stoppard's *Rosencrantz and Guildenstern Are Dead* (1966) expresses the existential philosophy fashionable in the early 1960s. It should also be noted that these three examples all use a Shakespeare play, or their audiences' awareness of it, as alien imaginative material. They either present an action so different that it only bears a paradigmatic relation to the original, or decisively alter the perspective, to create a dialectical opposition between their themes and Shakespeare's vision. And this is partly because adapters from Bernard Shaw to Bond have been motivated by a reaction against the general romanticization of Shakespeare:

> As a society we use the play [*King Lear*] in a wrong way. And it's for that reason I would like to rewrite it so that we now have to use the play for ourselves, for our society, for our time, for our problems.[2]

However, from the end of the 1960s on, there has been a whole series of adaptations that these general observations do not apply to. Instead of modernizing their Shakespearean material, these emphasize primitive or mythic elements. Instead of attacking the popular images of Shakespeare, they use these as subliminal echoes to evoke pre-intellectual responses. In a sense the whole avant garde movement began by adapting Shakespeare in the parody of *Ubu roi*. But these new adaptations are serious (sometimes to the point of pretentiousness), and must be seen as an attempt to align the avant garde approach with the cultural mainstream, although until the last decade they were still treated by critics as experimental theatre. The major exponent has been Peter Brook – in particular his primitivist and Artaudian interpretations of *The Tempest* (see pp.132 and 133–5 in this volume). But the play that has almost become an avant garde trademark is *Macbeth*, which Jan Kott had picked out as the archetypal modern tragedy in *Shakespeare Our Contemporary* (1961).

Two 'collages' that reached the stage in 1969, Marowitz's *A Macbeth* and Schechner's *Makbeth*, are representative. Even the earliest adaptation of the play (William Davenant, 1974) had enlarged the role of the witches. But in these avant garde versions the supernatural became totally predominant. For Marowitz, who had worked with Brook, the killing of Duncan represented 'the murder of God' and Macbeth kills 'not for kingship but to experience the ecstasy of such an action'. Similarly in Schechner's interpretation, Duncan is 'the Primal Father', with Cawdor, Malcolm, Macduff and Banquo as his sons, all of whom share the impulse to kill him, so that Macbeth's murder of Duncan becomes a form of titanic rebellion embodying an archetypal psychological conflict. In both, the witches are omnipresent and omnipotent. As 'Dark Powers' in *Makbeth* they played the roles of all the common people – soldiers, messengers, servants – as well as representing 'female energy', which according to Schechner was repressed in 'this patriarchal world'. So they were forced to operate 'behind the scenes, from underneath, in the guise of Lady Macbeth and . . . the energy and anger of the masses, the workers, the exploited'. As voodoo spirits in *A Macbeth* they 'infiltrate' Lady Macbeth's body 'as the spirit of the dead occupies the frame of a human being designated as a medium'; and they not only initiate the action, but also determine every detail by homeopathic magic. Taking Macbeth's line 'To crown my thoughts with acts / Be it thought and done' literally, they

> don the costumes of Lady Macduff and child, and act out the murder Macbeth has envisaged. In the world of black magic it is possible to destroy an enemy by simulating his death . . . it follows 'naturally' that Macduff learns his wife and children have been slain.[3]

Although this focus was clearly derived from Orson Welles' 'Voodoo *Macbeth*' of 1936, there is an essential difference which marks the atavistic avant garde influence. Welles set the play in nineteenth-century Haiti, where primitive superstition might be more credible. Although voodoo drumming and chants formed an insistent background to the murders of Duncan, Banquo and Macduff's family, Hecate was a flesh-and-blood priest (the leader of the voodoo chorus), Banquo's ghost was a death mask, and the supernatural was only present as a belief of the uneducated characters, which the premise of the production demonstrated to be unreal.

By contrast, Marowitz's version presupposed that 'diabolical intention, devoutly held and fastidiously practised, unquestionably produces tangible results'. Thus he claimed that by 'tackling the play in terms of pre-Christian belief, in terms of spells and hexes, I have found a diabolical centre . . . in restoring the play to its proper "religious" setting, it begins to operate more organically'. At the same time, this supernatural 'reality' was located in the subconscious as a hallucination imposed on Macbeth by the witchcraft of his 'possessed' wife: 'What we see on stage is only a reflection of what Macbeth sees, and so all questions of reality have to be referred back to the psychotic protagonist through whose distorted vision we view the play.' Actions are doubled and characters multiplied, as in the Strindbergian dream play convention. The murders of Duncan and Banquo are performed twice, at one point there are three identically dressed Macbeths on stage, and as in Marowitz's earlier *Collage Hamlet*, the simultaneous and discontinuous scenes were intended to mirror 'the broken and fragmentary way in which most people experience contemporary reality'. The aim was to involve the spectators subliminally through structure, as well as by using 'a stream of images' (Shakespeare's original play) that were assumed to be dormant in their minds.[4]

Similarly, in Schechner's *Makbeth* the major image was 'totemistic cannibal feasting'; and the final script was arrived at by threading together 'association exercises' (in which random fragments of Shakespeare's text were used to evoke the personal fantasies of the performers), while all the formal elements of the production were designed to liberate a corresponding level of subconscious activity in the spectators. The performance area, which encompassed the audience, was divided into distinct 'territories' for each group of 'archetypal characters' ('Doers': Macbeth and Lady Macbeth, 'Victims/Founders': Duncan and Banquo, 'Avengers': Malcolm and Macduff, and 'Dark Powers'), while a central 'table' was the 'no-man's-land' each group struggled to control. A vocal score was composed by Paul Epstein 'to replace dramatic (linear) text with choral (simultaneous) textures', distorting the form of words to create tonal patterns, and 'layering' speeches by dividing them between different voices or having them spoken as 'rounds' in which themes were repeated and varied as descants.

In many ways the production was unsuccessful. But the intention was well illustrated by the 'maze' that the audience had to find their way through before entering the performance area. Life-size photographs from previous (traditional) *Macbeths*, placards bearing well-known lines from the play, and mirrors formed the irregular walls of a twisting passage. Its dim lighting was imitated from Madame Tussaud's Chamber of Horrors, where such illumination makes spectators seem to merge with exhibits and tableaux apparently come to life. As the designer commented, the result was

frankly disorienting. Walls turn into mirrors and mirrors into walls.

Spectators bump into each other and excuse themselves for having jostled what turn out to be only reflections, and the audience begins to be joined with the distorted and reorganized fragments of the *Macbeth* legend.[5]

Ionesco's *Macbett* (1972) shares the same dream quality of doubling action and multiplying characters. In this version, every figure carries the personalities of others as potentials within them. The same actress plays Lady Macbett and a (beautiful and naked) witch, who transforms herself into Lady Duncan, a character unmentioned by Shakespeare. Since this pair assassinated the previous ruler to gain his position, murder becomes simply the established means of transferring power. Macbett and Banco are indistinguishable, wearing identical costumes and beards, speaking the same long monologue on bloodshed with the same gestures, and repeating the rebellious speeches of Candor and Glamiss word for word, while the witches' call to Macbett is '*alter ego surge!*' Again the witches represent not only subconscious urges in the characters, but also supernatural forces who control every detail of the action.

As a result, there is no question of guilt; and what is presented (in Macbett's words) is a 'senseless world, where the best of men are far worse than the wicked'; and the play, with its circular structure, is an image of existence as surrealistic cruelty. The vision of future kings, conjured up for Macbett by the witches, is a line-up of historical and mythical monsters from Genghis Khan to man-eating giants and Jarry's King Ubu (while Macbett's dying word, '*Merde*', is a deliberate echo of Ubu's opening statement). The keynote is struck by the twice-repeated description of life in death:

> MACBETT/BANCO: . . . Millions died of terror or committed suicide. Tens of millions of others died of anger, apoplexy or grief. Not enough land left to bury them all. The bloated bodies of the drowned have soaked up all the water of the lakes . . . Not enough vultures to rid us of all this carrion flesh. And to think there are some left who go on fighting . . .[6]

The opening picture of unrelieved tyranny is even bleaker at the end, with serried ranks of guillotines filling the rear of the stage as a paranoid megalomaniac Macol (Malcolm) takes power.

The exaggeration of this '*jeu de massacre*' may be intended as farcical – for Ionesco '*Macbett* is a comedy nonetheless. I hope that people will laugh'[7] – but Heiner Müller uses much the same extremism to form an unambiguous image of Artaudian cruelty in his version of *Macbeth* (also 1972). At the time, Müller claimed to be working within Brecht's 'epic' form of theatre; and one of his subsequent works is a rewriting of Brecht's 'teaching play', *The Measures Taken*. But his aim here was 'to swamp' his audience, instead of imposing a distanced, objective attitude. He interpreted Brecht's scientific theatre as a 'laboratory for social fantasy', and saw it as 'only effective when the audience are swept into the action from the start'. The result is an openly irrational and mythic drama, intended to create an image that the spectator will both identify with subliminally, and find unendurable: 'The time for intervening to alter something is always less. Consequently there is really no more time for discursive dramaturgy, for a calm presentation of factual content.'[8]

Müller cuts Shakespeare's verse to the bone, and transforms every incident into a perspective of horror illustrating the theme that

> The world has no exit but the knacker
> With knives to the knife is life's course.

Macduff's sword nails the porter to the door he was slow to open. Banquo's murderers castrate him, and take his genitals to Macbeth to prove that he is dead. A lord is skinned alive on stage, while the irrationality of human nature is stressed in the witches. They end the play by hailing Malcolm with their opening greeting to Macbeth; and their dominant role is epitomized by their degrading power over Macbeth, 'tearing his hair out and his clothes to shreds, farting in his face, etc. Finally they leave him lying half naked, screeching they throw the crown to one another until one of them puts it on.'

This accentuation of violence may indeed be a response to the urgent need for political action; and the undertones are full of repressed class conflict, as when the peasant soldiers, ordered to execute a landowner, flay him alive to learn 'how a lord looks underneath his skin'. One perceives his flesh to be the same as a peasant's; and Macbeth orders the other soldiers to kill him too, to prevent the formation of any revolutionary solidarity. Macbeth quotes Ovid while watching the lord being skinned, echoing the classical string quartets outside the gas chambers in Nazi concentration camps. And this is made a keynote for the play, challenging the audience's conventional aesthetic response to theatre by contrasting the brutality on stage with a frame of pictures – Michelangelo, Botticelli, Rubens – which line the proscenium. But the visceral impact of Müller's presentation overpowers any political interpretation.

Despite references to fascism, the Artaudian 'cruelty' transforms history into a nightmare; and the verbal compression, together with the completeness of Müller's condemnation of the world he presents (which effectively denies any possibility of an evil political system reforming itself), gives an impression of determinism. Thus a peasant, threatened with execution by both his Scots oppressors and his English 'deliverers', hangs himself as the only release from fear. Macbeth's death 'makes the world no better'; and Malcolm's first act as king is to show what he has 'learnt from his example' by having Macduff murdered.[9] Müller's image of society has mythic dimensions, being both feudal and futuristic as well as fascist; and the negative parable is so forceful that the final impression is of cruelty as a universal, unchanging human condition. Indeed the violence is so extreme as to be surreal. So the sadism becomes a seductive fantasy of fear, which led East German critics of the time to attack the play as pornographic. Such an accusation could be levelled with justice at certain attempts to exploit the avant garde approach in other Shakespearean adaptations – for instance, Marowitz's *An Othello* (1972), where Othello's epileptic fit was turned into a paranoiac vision of an adulterous Desdemona indulging in an orgy, with blocking and movements lifted directly from *Oh Calcutta!* – but the bleakness of Müller's vision preserves it from any pornographic effect.

HEINER MÜLLER AND ROBERT WILSON

More recently, Müller has joined forces with another avant garde artist, the American Robert Wilson, a development that has brought a significant advance to the work of both. On the surface such an alliance seems unlikely. As not only a dramatist, but also a poet, Müller's work is highly verbal, while Wilson conceives his theatrical work almost exclusively in pictorial, visual terms, and indeed coined the term 'autistic' drama to describe it. In addition, Müller's compressed, elliptical style is almost untranslatable, yet Wilson speaks practically no German. However, their highly productive collaboration throughout the 1980s is still further evidence of the homogeneity of the avant garde movement.

Even though their work appears to be at opposite ends of the theatrical spectrum, Müller's emotionally charged violence and politicized views presenting an extreme contrast to the pictorial stasis, slow pacing and rigid formalization that characterizes Wilson's productions, they were independently developing similar principles. As early as 1975 Müller was calling for the stage to adopt the 'new technologies' of visual art, specifically 'the collage method' that would correspond to his treatment of dramatic material. To some degree this had already happened in America in the 'Artist's Theatre' of the 1960s, which combined the 'action painting' of abstract expressionists such as Jackson Pollock, with the dadaist collages of Kurt Schwitters. These theatrical experiments were influenced by John Cage, whose musical principles of indeterminacy, chance and the simultaneous presentation of unrelated events also derived from Dadaism, and led directly to the 'assemblages' of such painters as Robert Rauschenberg or Claes Oldenburg, as well as to Allan Kaprow's 'happenings'. Wilson's productions with his Byrd Hoffman School of Byrds (founded in 1970, and named after a dance therapist whose approach had influenced Wilson's work with autistic patients) was a continuation of this 'Artist's Theatre', just as the compositions of his main musical collaborator, Philip Glass, also derived from Cage.

It was precisely such a theatrical approach that Müller was demanding when he declared that 'a script is given life by the contradiction between intention and material, author and reality', and by extension between script and staging. Rejecting logical continuity, Müller asserted the necessity for contemporary drama 'to show as many points as possible simultaneously, so that the audience are driven to make choices', and linked this with 'fragmentation of the action' (which both reflected the collapse of coherence in contemporary life, and had a typical avant garde rationale: to 'emphasize its nature as process, preventing the disappearance of the production into product'). These were indeed the qualities that Wilson was exploring, though in a far more instinctive fashion; and when he came to speak of his work – which significantly he only began to do after his collaboration with Müller – it was in remarkably similar terms. For Wilson, 'contradiction is the basis for theatre'; and this is linked with deconstruction, meaning being defined as 'like molecules that are breaking apart . . . It's many things or nothing. But to fix it is, perhaps, a lie.' So, from *Deafman Glance* in 1969, Wilson's aim has been to avoid closure or imposing any specific interpretation, in order to leave audiences the 'space' to 'draw their own conclusions'.[10]

The characteristics of Müller's drama before his meeting with Robert Wilson can be illustrated by his treatment of German history in *Germania Death in Berlin* (1972) or *The Battle* (1975). In the first play the rise of Hitler is shown, not as an aberration, but as the inevitable end product of a mentality developed over two thousand years of brutalization. Fact and mythology are interwoven – from the Niebelungs, through the suppression of the medieval Peasants' Revolt, the Thirty Years' War and Napoleonic invasion, to the glorification of Prussian militarism – in a visionary montage of images that are simultaneously parodistic and horrifying. Frederick the Great is represented by an insane circus clown who has the delusion of being the martinet founder of modern Germany; the Third Reich (a bestial monster) is literally born of sexual coupling between Hitler and Goering, a grotesque Caligari mating with a transvestite Valkyrie. The psychological dimension of this expressionistic replay of the national past is laid bare in the five short scenes of *The Battle*, covering the Nazi decade from the Night of the Long Knives in 1934 to the defeat of 1945. Factual representation is progressively transformed into phantasmagoria. The murderous power struggle, and the slaughter on the Russian front (where three starving German soldiers shoot and eat a comrade in a cannibal parody of the Last Supper) culminate in a merging of fantasy with reality.

Müller exemplifies the self-destructive psychology of violence in two images depicting the last moments of the war. In the fevered mind of a man whose life has been dedicated to his Führer, Hitler steps out of a portrait on the wall to order his suicide, which he prepares for by first shooting his wife and small daughter. When a butcher, having killed a downed American airman, is persuaded to drown himself for fear of reprisal by his wife (who has sold the American's body as pork to her customers and pushes her husband's head under the water to provide a scapegoat), the exterior cruelty is transposed into grotesque hallucination.

> The inside of an animal/man. Forest of guts. Rain of blood. An overlifesize doll hangs from a parachute, clothed in the stars and stripes. Boar masks in SS uniforms shoot at the doll . . . sawdust runs out of the bullet-holes. The shots make no noise . . . when the doll is empty it is torn down from the parachute and ripped up. Dance of the boar masks.[11]

In these nightmares of seductive fear the SS appear as angels of death, moving with black wings to the music of Wagner, while Müller's intentionally defective verse presents German as the language of sick dreams.

Rejecting the conventional bases of drama – plot, character, dialogue – Müller creates a collage of contrasting styles and fragmentary images to mirror the contemporary mindscape. In this (from his view, psychopathic) mentality, the detritus of culture coexists with history as a motivating factor. So one of his standard techniques is interleaving literary classics with his own version/response to the archetypes. Some of his pieces are ironic amalgams of shards from the European canon, dismantling the concept of a stable and unified self, as well as challenging the possibility of coherent experience. Even in an early play from his quasi-social realist phase, a dramatization of Gladkov's *Cement* (1972), Müller inserted counter-texts of 'the Revenge of Achilles' and 'the Freeing of Prometheus'. He performed a similar operation on Shakespeare with *Hamlet Machine* (1977, first performed in France in 1982), which was given its New York staging in 1986 by Robert Wilson; and the linkage of this kind of literary montage to his evocations of racial pyschology is summed up in the title of a later play: *Günding's Life Frederick of Prussia Lessing's Sleep Dream Scream*.

In *Hamlet Machine* the original play and modern text are juxtaposed to demonstrate the extent to which the human condition has deteriorated over the centuries.

> LOOK, THE MORN IN RUSSET MANTLE CLAD/WALKS O'ER THE DEW OF YON HIGH EASTWARD HILL. Almost four hundred years later, a different reading: IN A RED CLOAK MORNING WADES THROUGH/THE DEW THAT ITS STEPS TURN INTO BLOOD. In between, for my generation, lies the long march through the hell of the Enlightenment, through the bloody morass of ideologies.

From this perspective, the Renaissance was a false dawn. Hamlet becomes a symbol for the impotence of intellectuals, who think to reform society from the top, while Ophelia's tortured voice turns into a call for revolution from all the oppressed. Shakespeare represents the cultural system of the West, the mental frame within which even would-be revolutionaries operate; and since no one can escape the categories of his own thought, the system is incapable of being reformed from within. So the same nightmares are continually replayed, with the contemporary version referring to the mass murders of Charles Manson and the terrorists of the Baader-Meinhof Gang. For Müller, 'the penetration of time into the play constitutes the mythos. Mythos is an aggregate, a machine, onto which ever new and other machines can be attached.'[12]

In Müller's own staging of *Hamlet Machine* (at a 1990 festival of his work in Frankfurt, which included over forty productions of his plays and ballets or operas based on his texts), tragedy alternated with despairing farce, corresponding to his *Projection 1975*: 'In the century of *Orestes* and *Electra*, which is upon us, *Oedipus* will be a comedy.' And it is hardly surprising that he has continually turned to classical myths for his dramatic material, starting with variations on the herculean archetype – *Hercules 5* (1966), *Hercules 2, or the Hydra* (1974) – and moving on to Euripides' *Medea* in *Desolate Bank Medea Material with Argonauts* (1982). But, unlike Peter Brook, for Müller myth is not a positive spiritual alternative to contemporary materialism. It represents dark patterns in the psyche that still condition our behaviour.

Robert Wilson's early work, which has acknowledged affinities with Gertrude Stein and led Louis Aragon to proclaim him 'heir to the surrealists', took its approach from two of his first collaborators: a deaf mute and a man with severe brain damage. Working with them in a form of drama therapy, Wilson discovered that their disabilities had given them a radically different form of perception. This allowed them to understand things that escaped normal people who were primarily concerned with words (corresponding to the self-promulgated myth that up to the age of 17 severe stuttering had kept him virtually speechless). He noted that the deaf mute picked up sounds in the form of vibrations or 'interior impressions', and seemed to think in terms of pictorial images. Similarly, the other created a 'graphic' logic from the aural shape of words independent of conventional sense:

> the word Katmhandu [sic]. Later it would be Cat; then Cat-man-ru. Later it would be Fat-man-ru, and then it would be Fat man ... The words were really alive. They were always growing and changing ... like molecules bursting apart into all directions all the time – three dimensional.[13]

Wilson's plays, like *Deafman Glance* (which formed part of the basis for *KA MOUNTAIN AND GUARDenia Terrace*), are created to express this more sensitive and physical perception of the world, as opposed to the conventional intellectualizing approach. Their structure is musical in the sense that the action is an architectural arrangement of sounds, words and movement, in which images are restated or varied to form thematic motifs. On one level, the pacing and choice of images is a direct reflection of autistic thought patterns. On another level, the presentation is designed to sensitize the spectator to the same subliminal range of nuances as a brain-damaged deaf mute. The stage becomes a projection of 'abnormal' inner states, which gain imaginative power to the extent that they evoke the unconscious fantasies of the spectator, and Wilson sees autism as an increasingly common psychological response to the pressures of contemporary life:

> More and more people are turning into themselves . . . You can see it in the subways, where everyone is bunched together, and nobody is looking at anybody. What they are doing is signing off. They have to because there's so much overload . . . It's actually a means of survival.

Twelve years later, repeating the subway example, Wilson gave this state a more positive value: 'They're dreaming and there is this interior image. We are functioning on this level all the time. So in the theatre that I have done maybe there is more time for the interior reflection.'[14]

The aim is therapeutic, to open the audience to 'interior impressions'; and the result is an audio-visual collage of dream-like and seemingly disconnected images, in which words and events are deliberately presented with obsessive repetitiveness and painful slowness. Even his first work, *Deafman Glance*, which was completely wordless, took seven hours to perform, and has been continually expanded: it became the fourth act of *Joseph Stalin*, which was a mammoth conflation of Wilson's earlier pieces; and by 1985 just the prologue to *Deafman Glance* had become a complete performance. This kind of temporal fourth dimension reached its fullest extension with *KA MOUNTAIN AND GUARDenia Terrace* at the 1972 Shiraz festival, which took 268 hours spread over seven days. The action moved out from a small picture-frame stage, open at the rear to show a mountain through the proscenium, to cover the whole of the mountain face. Actions were performed in extreme slow motion, both to gain a dream quality and to intensify the audience's awareness, to focus their attention. At one point the only movement was that of a live turtle crossing the empty stage, which took almost an hour, while the mountain behind was dotted with unrelated visual images in the form of two-dimensional cardboard cut-outs: Noah's ark, a dinosaur, flamingoes, the Acropolis surrounded by a ring of ICBM rockets, Jonah's whale, a graveyard, and the Manhattan skyline on the summit. This last cut-out was burnt to the ground on the final day of the performance, and replaced by a Chinese pagoda with the

Lamb of God inside (the original plan, vetoed by the Iranian festival authorities, had been to blow up the mountain top or paint it entirely white).

There was no intellectual sense to be made out of this apocalyptic collage, despite readings from the Book of Jonah and *Moby Dick* in one section of the performance. Actions stood in an oblique relationship to the dialogue, as when the words of Melville and the Bible were 'answered' arbitrarily by an enthroned Wilson, either with falsetto whimpers and cries, or with a deep bass echo of what had just been read. Even where the dialogue was in character it resembled automatic writing, or dadaist free association:

> The journey. The old man. The body. The old man. The stories. The old man leaves. Birth. Ocean. Birth. Ocean. The beginning of movement. The beginning of sound. Branch. Bench. Horizontal zone. Spring . . . Winter Burial. White mountain. Green garden. The old man returns. The body. The old man. Thatit cotet quantet yeatet. As you, an earthfather geetly childed gatet, greetet, growtet, gaitet, because that is how it is. Take this basket to the riverbank and fill it follet, fotet, fountet, fatet. As you, an old man, mother mourning, morning, morn, for it can be no other way. Whalet whartet woetet wantet waitet upon the bank of yonder river and thy basket shall be there abundant filled. Birth. Broken earth. Black. Day. A whale in the cube room . . . There are are seven days. There are seven levels. Seven fires light the day dies dancing six times unto the last a seventh day, a SUNDAY, a SUN CITY . . .[15]

The mythical connotations may all be obvious: Moses in the basket, Jonah, the creation of the world corresponding to the seven-day performance of the play, 'ka' representing the soul, the seasonal birth/death/resurrection pattern. But unlike Grotowski or Artaud, these fit into no coherent concept. Each spectator has to make his own 'sense' out of this stream of consciousness; and this can only be achieved on the level of subliminal association since the random form, the repetitions and even the inertia make intellectual, 'exterior' connections impossible.

KA MOUNTAIN was on an epic scale, with more than fifty actors plus a small zoo of live animals. But Wilson's 'chamber' pieces, like *A Letter for Queen Victoria* (presented at the Spoleto festival in 1974 and on Broadway in 1975), have exactly the same qualities, except that here the dream images are drawn from social rather than religious archetypes. Queen Victoria appears, in full regalia, to be read a long and totally incomprehensible letter. Couples in white sit at café tables gesticulating frenetically and all speaking the same lines – 'chitter-chatter, chitter-chatter' – simultaneously. But the effect is disorienting rather than satiric, with two ballet dancers slowly spinning either side of the stage throughout the performance, complex choreography in slow motion, and somnambulistic characters talking in endless *non sequiturs*. Again there are apocalyptic overtones. A sniper shoots the couples who collapse one by one across their tables, and the performance ends with a long-drawn-out scream. But such inconsequential violence is designed to be psychologically disturbing, not melodramatic. And rather more obviously than in *KA MOUNTAIN*, the images focus on perception itself, instead of on what is perceived: four aviators/Lindberghs stand with their backs to the audience looking at a changing land/cloudscape through a huge window; a Chinaman stands behind another enormous window-frame staring out at the audience through a continually opening and closing Venetian blind.

Wilson's principles and production methods remain much the same since joining forces with Heiner Müller: for instance his 1982 *Golden Windows* presented a series of almost static tableaux, in which the *non sequitur* dialogue was completely unconnected to the gestural action. Yet their collaboration has produced a significant gain in complexity. For both it is precisely the difference between their cultural backgrounds and theatrical approaches – in Müller's words, the 'collision . . . between a German subconscious and an American one' – that makes their work complementary. Indeed the active factor is the disjunction between words and staging that has always characterized Wilson's own drama. This also parallels Müller's technique of juxtaposing contrasted texts and fragmenting dialogue, which is something that Wilson has borrowed, as in his 1986 production of *Alcestis*, where a disillation of Euripides' tragedy was framed by Müller's prose poem 'Description of a Picture' and by a seventeenth-century Kyogen farce (*The Birdcatcher in Hell*) from Japan. To Wilson, the 'very compressed' nature of Müller's writing allows 'enormous freedom, a space' for his productions, while Müller, rejecting the search for inner meanings in the standard directorial interpretation, has commented that his 'text can speak for itself . . . Wilson never interprets. He just gets the text and tries to find room for it.'[16] Coexisting independently, Müller's verbal poetry and Wilson's visual imagery, like the separated halves of metaphor, form overlapping layers of sign versus signifier, content versus form, where the multiple possible meanings are more than the sum of the statements, while making comprehension on an intellectual level almost impossible.

Such oppositions extend into every level of production. For instance, Wilson's 1986 Stuttgart staging of Müller's *Quartet* – which itself contrasts Laclos' voluptuous *Liaisons Dangereuses* with pared down monologues by the two aristocratic seducers, now elderly and reminiscing about long-past conquests while awaiting extinction in an air-raid shelter after the global holocaust of atomic war – set a bleak post-modernist minimalism against the ornate decor of the Baroque theatre in which it was performed. This tension between time-frames, external context and presentation, was carried over into casting against concept, as well as shaping a visual action that had no illustrative relation to the speeches. In Müller's text Valmont takes on the role of the virtuous wife he has driven to suicide, while the Marquise switches gender to become Valmont himself in celebrating her (male) power over him. Wilson added a trio of other figures to this (double) duo, turning the 'Quartet' into a quintet (septet). The compression and emotional intensity of the words was set against a rigid precision and extreme slowness in the movements; and in different tableaux a fish tank appeared on the stage apron (twice) – or in the background a male figure hung head-down, a young girl having strung him up by one foot, with no obvious connection to the words.

This surrealistic unrelatedness and conflict of opposites has become the hallmark of Wilson's drama, reaching its fullest expression in *the CIVIL warS: a tree is best measured when it is down*, the most representative example of his collaboration with Müller. Only segments of this 12-to–20-hour multi-lingual, multi-media epic, originally intended for performance at the 1984 Olympics, have reached the stage: Act I, scene B in Rotterdam (1983), Acts I, A; III, E; IV, A and Epilogue in Cologne (repeated without Act I at ART in 1985), plus Act V in Rome; and the thirteen short entr'actes, *The Knee Plays*, in Minneapolis (1984), although two further sections were rehearsed in Marseilles and Tokyo. For Wilson, the whole was uniquely dependent on the international context of the Olympics, having the same aim – to 'bring the people of the world together in civil competition. That's why I called it the "CIVIL", capitalized, and lower case "warS".' As Müller described Wilson's concept:

> His theatre is a resurrection: the dead are set free in slow motion . . .
> *the CIVIL warS* defines the theme of our era: war between classes and races, species and sexes, civil war in every sense of the term. . . .
> When eagles in their soaring flight tear to pieces the flags that separate us, the theatre of resurrection will have found its stage.[17]

The German section was compiled of texts by both Wilson and Müller, plus excerpts from letters by Frederick the Great and Kafka, and fragmented passages from Empedocles, Goethe and Hölderlin, *Hamlet*, *Timon of Athens* and Racine's *Phèdre*. These accompanied an action based on a sequence of pictures drawn by Wilson (the initial step in any of his productions from which movements and tableaux are developed); and the flow of images turned history into a multinational stream-of-consciousness. The starting point of Act III scene E was Mathew Brady's photographs of the American Civil War, with the presence of Frederick accompanied by an extended family in an anachronistic vintage car that inches across the stage during the whole scene, and references to Fredericksberg linking with Act IV scene A, in which Frederick the Great was used as a focus for other types of conflict: Frederick's own version of war between the

States, in which the invasion of neighbouring territories to unify Germany spread to North America, becoming a prototype for the world wars of the twentieth century; Frederick's battles with his father representing familial conflict; Frederick's schizoid combination of Enlightenment liberalism and militaristic brutality as the emblem of a single person at war with himself. The final section of the Act started off with an apocalypse in documentary film of New York high-rise buildings being demolished, while twenty from the cast of twenty-six take up position in a group, smile in unison at the audience, with their grins held to become grimaces, then leave one by one until the stage is empty.

Although this kind of linear structure might be inferred from the material, while at times the production verged on simplistic allegory, the overall effect was very different. Fantastical figures – elongated Black Scribes bearing huge black quills like swords, a White Scribe dressed in ornate folds of paper and transfixed by a massive pencil, a half-human dog – share the stage with historical characters – Frederick the Great (disconcertingly played by a female) and Abraham Lincoln. A conical spaceship descends, to deposit polar bears that waltz in slow motion. Visual patterns are created out of long white wands (reminiscent of Bauhaus ballet). Time frames merge: a vaguely turn-of-the-century family, Frederick in eighteenth-century uniform and (long dead) as an equestrian statue on a sculptured steed that is also a rocking-horse, astronauts. A line of 'submariners' in grotesque death-mask make-up, whose heads rise out of traps/hatches along the front of the stage, chant as a disembodied chorus. One actor speaks while another mouths the words, or voices are carried over loudspeakers distributed through the audience. In the epilogue, Lincoln (a stick-like 20-ft top-hatted puppet, which topples like a felled tree) is juxtaposed with mythical beings – Snow Owl, and Earth Mother – and with King Lear mourning the dead Cordelia (actually a pile of crumpled newspaper), while their intercut monologues are a medley of Brothers Grimm, the Song of Solomon, Shakespeare and Müller, plus Hopi Indian prophecies in their original language.

The result is an extremely static kaleidoscope of disconnected symbols. Wilson has compared his approach with watching television, with the sound off, while listening to something completely different on the radio, and although 'you can adjust them so that sometimes what we're seeing actually *does* relate to what we're hearing', each individual spectator is left to 'put them together'.[18] Only a percentage of the symbols are meant to be identifiable intellectually, a Cologne audience being unlikely to have much familiarity with Brady's Civil War photos, while Frederick the Great would have had little resonance for the Americans at the ART performance. The overall impression was of dreamlike fluidity. Terms like 'dream', 'somnambulist', 'hypnotic trance' recurred in the reviews; indeed Wilson's work is sometimes compared to an expression of the collective

Figure 23a, b Robert Wilson, scene sketch and staging for *the CIVIL warS*. Multimedia and multiple stages: Frederick the Great with polar bears, Submariner chorus and Black Scribe, film of waterfall. ART production.

unconscious.[19] It serves to intensify the hallucinatory quality that is basic to Wilson's work (as well as Müller's), and carries over into the kind of dramatic structure he creates. Indeed *CIVIL warS* has been described in terms that exactly echo Strindberg's note to *A Dream Play* – 'the action of a Wilson "play" takes shape, dissolves, overlaps, fragments and reforms. Two or three "stories' may be told simultaneously' – and its essential quality has been labelled a 'myth sponge'.[20]

History as hallucination. Time-scales that distort conventional ways of perceiving, and thus undercut rational modes of thought. Deconstructed reality as myth, with the unfamiliarity, as well as surreal juxtapositions of the images appealing to the subliminal, and signalling Wilson's Jungian belief that in the deepest levels of the mind all archetypes are the same. Indeed, there is a large amount of repetition in his work. In pieces produced several times, even after more than a decade (as with *Einstein on the Beach*, 1976–88), the interweaving of images and choreography, down to micromovements, are rigidly reproduced. Act I scene A of *CIVIL warS* begins with the infinitesimal progress of a large plastic tortoise across the whole width of the stage, just as in *KA MOUNTAIN AND GUARDenia Terrace*, while the apocalyptic filmed ending of Act IV scene A is a variation on the burning model of Manhattan. Similarly the conjunction of ICBMs/factory chimneys and an acropolis recurred in *Alcestis*. Asked whether any knowledge of the other sections of *CIVIL warS* was required to appreciate the two scenes in the ART performance, Wilson replied that 'it's all a part of the same thought'.[21] Even *The Knee Plays* contain the whole theme of *CIVIL warS* in miniature. In the first playlet, a figure sits in a tree reading a book, with a lion prowling below. The tree is cut down and made into a boat that successively becomes Noah's Ark, the Merrimack battling the Monitor and Commodore Perry's frigate sailing to Japan, in a bird's-eye survey of the cyclical history of civilization. The boat is finally transformed into a book, out of which a tree grows; and the lion reappears as Hercules in his lionskin costume.

This sort of conceptual simplification makes Wilson's images curiously abstract, despite their concreteness, laying the ideas incorporated in his work open to the charge of vagueness or vacuousness, which is compounded by the extreme slowness of pace in his productions and their repetitiveness. However, the reductionism is effective to the degree that his symbolism achieves the universality claimed for them. Another sign of the drive towards universalization is his stylistic borrowing, in which classical Greek or American junk culture images are combined with oriental theatre techniques, particularly those drawn from Japan.

In addition to the Kyogen play attached to *Alcestis*, during the latter part of the 1980s Wilson worked increasingly with a Japanese dancer trained in Nōh and Kabuki which, together with a Japanese costume designer and a musical score including oriental percussion, gave a strongly

Asian tone to his 1990 German production of *King Lear*. Though the most conventionally verbal text taken on by Wilson, his interest in Shakespeare had already been signalled by *CIVIL warS*, and exactly the same approach was used as in his previous work. The 'stage pictures' were designed independently of the dialogue (which was intercut with fragments of a William Carlos Williams poem about old age and death, used as a prologue), and were conceived to 'project' the words, not to 'illustrate' them.[22]

By any standards, Wilson's work has moved – like so many of the avant garde during the 1980s – from counter-theatre to the mainstream. It not only requires increasingly complex and expensive stage resources, the reason for the cancellation of *CIVIL warS* at the 1984 Olympic Arts Festival being the $2.5 million required to stage the whole cycle. It has garnered establishment accolades, with Obie Awards, Guggenheim Fellowships and Rockefeller Foundation grants. It is also intended to be popular: he referred to *CIVIL warS* in terms of rock concerts and mass entertainment; and in 1987, following Peter Brook in searching out an audience with no theatrical preconceptions, for a performance with communal (and given the venue, even religious) significance, Wilson mounted a piece for a crowd of 4,500, over half of whom were Greek villagers, at Delphi. He also parallels Brook in his collaboration with a Japanese actor, though the avant garde director who has taken the combination of Shakespeare and Asian performance style furthest is Ariane Mnouchkine.

ARIANE MNOUCHKINE

The influences on Mnouchkine's development have been diverse. Her early work with the Théâtre du Soleil in the 1960s and early 1970s was 'peoples' theatre' in the sense of Jean Vilar's Théâtre National Populaire, expressing radical socialist themes and designed for working class and trades union audiences, with a hyper-realistic production of Arnold Wesker's *The Kitchen* being performed at striking factories in 1968. Coupled with Jacques Copeau's emphasis on improvisation, *commedia dell' arte* and the performance qualities of the circus, this led to such major collaborative works as *1789: The Revolution must stop at the perfection of happiness* (1970) and *1793: The City of the revolution is of this world* (1972). These were revisionist interpretations of French history, seen from below through the prism of the short-lived student uprising of 1968 and showing 'that bourgeois power was born in 1789, and that the people were robbed of their revolution'.[23] The framing device of an eighteenth-century troupe of fairground performers gave the events presented in the first a carnevalesque quality that Bakhtin would have recognized. The second represented the later phase of the French Revolution through reproducing one of the *sans-culottes* assemblies as a model of people-power and participatory democracy; and in both the audience were directly involved, sharing the same space as the performers and implicitly cast as the revolutionary masses – a stripped down, more politically relevant variant of Richard Schechner's 'environmental theatre'.

However, in the early 1980s the approach of the Théâtre du Soleil underwent a radical change, influenced partly by Peter Brook, with whose work Mnouchkine's displays clear affinities, going back to her 1968 production of *Midsummer Night's Dream*, which explored the same elements of primitivism and the liberation of primal instincts as Brook's *Tempest* production of the same year. Mnouchkine's most recent productions have followed the avant garde line from Jean-Louis Barrault to Heiner Müller and Robert Wilson, in turning to the Greek classics. One of the links between Mnouchkine and Brook is Artaud, whose theories she only took on towards the end of the 1970s. Since then, Artaud's statement that 'the theatre is oriental' has become a repeated motto of Mnouchkine's, although her fascination with Asian styles and themes was already anticipated in her first production some years before the founding of her company, *Genghis Khan* (1961). There the orientalism was limited to spectacle: exotic costumes, flaming torches, colourful banners. However, in preparing material for *The Age of Gold* (1975) Mnouchkine began to experiment with the non-representational symbolism of Chinese theatre, and with the use of masks, the aim being to create a contemporary equivalent that would challenge standard modes of perception through its alien (and therefore alienating) roots. As the programme stated:

> We are not resuscitating ancient theatrical forms, *commedia dell' arte* or traditional Chinese theatre. We want to reinvent the rules of the game by which everyday reality is portrayed, revealing it not to be familiar and unchangeable, but astonishing and capable of transformation.[24]

These concerns – historical reappraisal, and oriental perspectives – came together in Mnouchkine's projected ten-play Shakespeare cycle, of which only the first three reached the stage (*Richard II*, 1981; *Twelfth Night*, 1982; and the first part of *Henry IV*, 1984). The initial impetus for this was to use Shakespeare's history plays as a model for dramatizing political events, which Mnouchkine was finding problematic in trying to write a script about the genocide in Cambodia, a country she was deeply concerned with, having toured it in the early 1960s. That visit had also taken her to Japan, where she discovered Nōh theatre, and even then her response had been 'It's like Shakespeare', because an Asian actor was 'a creator of metaphors' whose aim was 'disclosing the interior of a human being', in contrast to the external naturalism of western acting.[25] So applying a Japanese performance style to Shakespeare's texts was a logical step.

Richard II – evoking a medieval world that even for the Elizabethan audience was long vanished and a state of divinely appointed order to

210

contrast with the ever-widening circle of anarchy and moral corruption traced in the subsequent history plays – is the most hieratic and formalized of Shakespeare's works. The poetic language, particularly in the opening scenes, is highly stylized, the structure deliberately artificial. Mnouchkine's aim was to accentuate these unnaturalistic qualities. In her view, 'Richard has no psychology. *A fortiori*, there is no pyschological depth in the nobles. A figure like Northumberland, for example, has no characteristics apart from those that the actor playing the role gives him.'[26] Instead of attempting to make the play approximate to modern ideas of realism, as in most standard Shakespearean productions, the company developed a theatre form corresponding to its heightened, ceremonial quality. The costumes, based on full-skirted Japanese Samurai clothing but combined with Renaissance cloaks and Elizabethan ruffs, characterized the approach. The impression was alien, without actually copying any specific Japanese technique.

The set, corresponding to Brook's 'Empty Space', was an open, tented performance area, edged with layers of red, gold and silver silk hangings over the gold-painted masonry walls. These cloths, suggesting among other things sun and moon in the abstract, were successively pulled down during the performance to reveal the next colour. Two *hanamichi*-style ramps were used for entrances; and on-stage musicians provided percussion accompaniment throughout, punctuating verbal climaxes with gong strokes. Although the pace of the production was ritualistically slow, the continual drumming gave a sense of urgency along with acrobatic movements and the rhythmic declamation of the speeches, most of which were delivered directly to the audience by actors with slightly bent knees and lifted heads, a pose echoing Samurai warriors in combat. Masks reminiscent of Nōh theatre were used for older characters, stylized make-up on a white base for the younger protagonists. At the same time, the emotion expressed was always extreme and intense. The effect – highly stylized and arcane – was carried over into *Henry IV* and even *Twelfth Night*, although there the imagery was more Indian and Persian, corresponding to Mnouchkine's concept of a world of polychrome folklore deities, rather than heroic demi-gods.[27]

It also carried over into the Théâtre du Soleil productions of Hélène Cixous' *The Awesome but Unfinished History of Norodom Sihanouk, King of Cambodia* (1985) and *The Indiad, or the India of their Dreams* (1987), which dealt directly with the issue of orientalism. The script of *Sihanouk* contained echoes, even direct quotations from *Richard II*, and represented the protagonist as a Shakespearean king who embodies his country, with his character determining its fate. The acting was equally heightened, with extroverted emotions; and the stylization was at one point strikingly reminiscent of Barrault's performance in *As I Lay Dying*, indicating the extent to which Mnouchkine is continuing the line of Barrault's 'Total Theatre'. In response to the news of Vietnamese support, the exiled Sihanouk imagines riding back triumphant into Phnom Penh on the 'Communist elephant', and the actor created the physical image of a trumpeting elephant through mime, becoming both animal and rider in an exuberant release of energy.

In a sense, given France's colonial connection with Cambodia and the large Cambodian community of refugees from the Pol Pot regime, the subject had immediate relevance for French audiences. Indeed Sihanouk himself saw the production, and spoke with the cast about his role in the history they were presenting. Yet the stage environment stressed the difference in cultural context.

The performance space, painted in scarlet lacquer and paved with small bricks, evoked the image of a Buddhist temple, and was permeated by the smell of Asian food on sale in the foyer. Around the walls on a high shelf stood over 700 individualized statuettes, effigies of the Cambodian population forming a silently accusing audience both of the French public's response to the performance, and of the events (in which they had been accomplices) leading up to the atrocious Khmer Rouge regime. Victims of the genocide, these were copied from a photograph of tomb figures ranged on a cliff-face by a South East Asian village. A yellow silk curtain at the back of the acting area, shaken by attendants to signal important entrances from behind it, specifically echoed a traditional Kathakali technique; and the role of Sihanouk's father was played in a Balinese mask. However, this hieratic character also rode a bicycle, and was juxtaposed with actors in modern European dress, an overt incongruity that epitomizes Mnouchkine's brand of orientalism.

Traditional European views of the Orient portray Asia in terms of exoticism and femininity, simultaneously savage, seductive and vulnerable, as both the Outsider, and the Other – the negative opposite of western civilization, which by contrast thus becomes defined as rational and masculine, situated at the geographical power centre of the world. This justifies colonialism, giving it a sexual subtext of empowering phallocentricity.[28] Although this metaphoric alignment is picked up in a play like Peter Shaffer's *The Royal Hunt of the Sun* (see p. 227 in this volume), in English literature it is mainly expressed through the clichés of popular entertainment, as for instance in some nineteenth-century Drury Lane melodramas or the novels of Rider Haggard. But it is central to the French dramatic tradition, with Racine's tragedies revolving around colonized women – Bérénice, Phèdre – whose emotional passion and uncontrollable sexuality threaten the neo-classical order embodied by male imperial rulers. So in mounting Asian productions such as *Sihanouk* or *The Indiad*, Mnouchkine was overtly challenging a recognizable mind-set that could be taken to characterize the Establishment; and this becomes explicit in a subtitle like *The India of their Dreams*. The Orient is represented not only as strange, but also as an extension of the West, imperialist influences having submerged both its customs and traditional costumes.

In *Sihanouk* the eight-hour performance time was not only designed to assert the importance of recent Cambodian history (a subject both marginalized by colonialism and treated as politically irrelevant by America in its conduct of the Vietnam war). It also served to accustom the audience to the unfamiliar attitudes, ceremonies and style of presentation, so that the Asia of the play lost its initial exoticism to become normal, while a map of the world in the foyer placed Cambodia in the centre with red lines radiating outward to indicate its impact on the 'developed' countries. This reversal carried through into the perspective of both productions, where it was the European characters who appeared alien and bizarre in the Asian contexts. Kissinger, hunched over a map table and lit from below, became the gargoyle of a medieval demon. In *The Indiad* it was the British soldiers in their scarlet uniforms who seemed exotic, while the one major European character, Mountbatten, was played by the only male Indian actor in the cast.

At the same time, Nehru was represented by a white actor as both a feminized man (reflecting the conventional western image of the Orient), and as dominating by the moral force of his personality: a power-figure dissociated from the phallus. This feminist alternative to standard constructs of power was taken a step further by the play itself. According to Cixous,

> instead of having one king, a chief, I have decapitalized [the action], and instead of having a Shakespearean, pyramidal system . . . there are 20, 30, 40 characters who are equal. There are none who are stronger than the others. . . . It is not called *Ghandi*, it is not called *Nehru*, it is called *L'Indiade*. For the actors it was terrible, because they too are structured in a way which is, as one says, phallocentric, even if they are totally capable of femininity. But they were accustomed to having a leader, and all of a sudden each one had to be his own leader.

For Mnouchkine, even the stylization derived from oriental theatre has the same kind of significance as this polycentric dramatic structure: 'In Asia every act is perpetually formalized. The everyday aggressiveness in the West, especially in France . . . is due to the total loss of any formalization of relationships.'[29]

The superficial impression of these Théâtre du Soleil productions may be similar to the primitivism that characterizes so much other avant garde art, and the essential quality of the East is also seen as a corrective to standard western/capitalist/masculine constructs of power. Yet where the earlier forms of primitivism unconsciously adopted the colonial attitude that was basic to the society they rejected, Mnouchkine makes it the focus of her attack. As such, her work stands in opposition to the approach of Eugenio Barba or Peter Brook, and marks a decisive new step in the primitivist movement.

12

FROM THE MARGINS TO MAINSTREAM

POPULARIZATION AND PUBLIC ACCEPTANCE

Initially, of course, 'avant garde' was synonymous for 'esoteric' or 'incomprehensible'. Despite the (scandalized) public attention attracted by their work, Alfred Jarry and Antonin Artaud remained on the theatrical fringes of their time. Indeed, like Oscar Kokoschka or the dadaists, they consciously chose the role of social outcast as ratifying their counter-culture status, an attitude shared by almost all the members of the movement. But, as we have seen, Jean-Louis Barrault mounted an avant garde takeover of the epitome of establishment theatre; and in some ways his career typifies the avant garde as a whole.

By the 1950s the productions of leading avant garde directors were already being classed as major cultural events. The Shiraz Festival in Persia under the Shah became an avant garde showcase, giving wide publicity to Peter Brook and Eugenio Barba's Odin Teatret despite the reactionary politics and distant location. Jerzy Grotowski moved rapidly from a tiny back-street stage to world-wide tours in the mid–1960s, and performances at the Edinburgh and Parisian Théâtre des Nations Festivals, as well as at the Cultural Olympics in Mexico. A work like Brook's *Mahabharata* was not only produced at the Avignon Festival and on Broadway as well as in Glasgow, but has also been shown around the world on television. In the following generation, the leading avant garde directors gained this sort of public position almost immediately. Robert Wilson's work – which was also first given international exposure at the Shiraz Festival, always demanded the resources of main-stage theatre, and has been mounted in Paris, Berlin and New York. Ariane Mnouchkine's stagings of Hélène Cixous' scripts and of Shakespeare have not only attracted large audiences from all levels of Parisian society, but have also been presented at Festivals in Avignon, Venice, Brussels, Madrid, and at the Los Angeles Olympics. With the exception of those who withdrew from the theatre altogether like Grotowski or the Becks, the whole avant garde has made this transition. It is noticeable that even though there may be

214

an appearance of scenic minimalism (as with the Avignon *Mahabharata* performance in a stone quarry), today's avant garde productions tend to be expensive, and require the full resources of the illusionistic stage (as when Brook reproduced the exact conditions of the Avignon quarry in a New York theatre). By any standards, they have become part of the cultural mainstream.

However, even at some far earlier points, where a nation's official culture had been destabilized by political events, the alternative values of primitivism moved over into centre-stage – as with expressionism in Germany, following the chaotic and violent aftermath of the First World War. In America, where nineteenth-century theatrical traditions lingered on (or became extended into a materialistic orthodoxy, like Belasco's hyperrealism) until the establishment stage was almost completely discredited, the very roots of modern drama – which in the US is dated from Eugene O'Neill's early plays – came from the avant garde.

EUGENE O'NEILL – EUGÈNE IONESCO – SAM SHEPARD

O'Neill's first major success, *The Emperor Jones* (1920), is practically a text-book illustration of the links between expressionist techniques and primitivism with its use of drum beats regulating the pulse rate of the audience to create direct emotional excitation, its presentation of dream visions as true reality beyond everyday appearances, and its atavistic theme. The black protagonist's regression to naked savage in the jungle is also a reversion to racial memory and universal Jungian archetype; and this is portrayed as positive even though it destroys Brutus Jones who (corrupted by white civilization) cannot divest himself of the self-obsession, which O'Neill continually referred to as the self-deceiving 'lie' of individual personality. The same theme is extended in *The Hairy Ape* (1921), where industrial, urban civilization is presented as a hell, a cage in which those imprisoned by destructive rationality are reduced to mechanical marionettes, while the brutalized epitome of working-class subjection – symbolically named Yank – finally achieves unity with nature by being crushed to death in a gorilla's embrace. Although O'Neill retreated from expressionism in his later work, the communication of subconscious states, distorted perspectives, masks and symbolic characterization that he experimented with were picked up by Elmer Rice in *The Adding Machine* (1923) and Thornton Wilder in *Our Town* (1938), and carry over as one of the elements in the work of such mainstream American dramatists as Tennessee Williams and Arthur Miller (for instance in the memory frame of *The Glass Menagerie*, 1945, or the dream context of *Death of a Salesman*, 1949, and the subjective exploration of *After the Fall*, 1964).

Even Jarry's iconoclastic work became fashionable almost immediately after his early death. Similarly, Genet's plays – a central part of avant garde development in the 1950s – progressed rapidly from *causes célèbres* to modern classics. Indeed, many of the writers associated with the 'Theatre of the Absurd' – Martin Esslin's influential, but misleading philosophical label for non-naturalistic European drama of the 1950s and early 1960s – had avant garde associations. A case in point is Eugène Ionesco, one of the founding dramatists of the 'Absurd', whose approach is derived from Jarry through the surrealists.

Ionesco's appreciation of *grand guignol* puppet theatre, and his position as a 'Grand Satrap' of the Collège de Pataphysique (an anarchistic parody of academia) link him to Jarry, while surrealists like Phillipe Soupault and André Breton have hailed his work as a natural extension of their own. A play like *Hunger and Thirst* (1966), originally titled *Life in the Dream*, is on one level a reworking of Strindbergian themes, with not only a structure derived from *To Damascus* and disgust at existence symbolized (as in *A Dream Play*) by dirt covering the walls of a family home, but also a Christ-figure protagonist who is in addition a projection of the author. His pilgrimage in search of an elusive ideal in female form ends in a 'monastery-barracks-prison', where inmates are brainwashed into believing themselves to be poisoned by thoughts of freedom. Ionesco acknowledges his work to be following Artaud in his aim of creating a 'metaphysical' theatre – 'to change the metaphysical condition of man, to change life, but from within out and not the reverse, from the personal towards the collective' – as well as in his attack on '*petit bourgeois*' attitudes as a 'false culture' that 'separates us from everything and from ourselves'. For Ionesco 'it is precisely the process of this devitalized culture, imprisoning us in an inauthentic reality which Artaud perceived' that defines one pole of his work, and his solution also parallels Artaud in the consequent 'necessity of breaking language in order to reconstitute it, in order to "touch life", to put man back in contact with the absolute'.[1]

Although there are other, more conventional thematic levels in Ionesco's work, the rejection of social conditioning, which forms one of its major motifs, parallels a recurrent avant garde message. For Ionesco the conceptual structure of reality is on the point of collapse; and his plays are 'helping to accelerate this process of disintegration' by reproducing in the spectator those states of awareness 'that could set the world ablaze, that could transfigure it'. As he describes this vision in his autobiography:

> every notion, every reality was emptied of its content. After this emptiness, . . . it was as if I found myself at the centre of pure, ineffable existence . . . I became one with the essential reality.
>
> . . . to feel the absurdity or improbability of everyday life and language is already to have transcended it; in order to transcend it, you must first saturate yourself in it.[2]

In his early work the emphasis is on creating the pre-condition for this 'transcendence', and it is this that explains the breakdown of language and the reduction of those logical concepts, like time, by which we structure our lives, to farcical absurdity (as in *The Bald Primadonna*, where a clock strikes the hours out of sequence and irrelevantly). In the same way the menacing magnification and proliferation of objects in a human vacuum where characters lack inner being or consistency, as well as the rhythm of his plays with their mad mathematics of geometrical progression and acceleration, are designed to drain all social and material existence of meaning. As he noted with reference to Kafka, it is 'when man is cut off from . . . his religious or metaphysical roots' that activity becomes senseless; and it is here that his apparently 'Absurd' work links up with the preoccupations of Brook or Grotowski. Indeed, the motive force behind this transcendence – what makes it possible for man to escape from the 'stereotype' to which he has been reduced by society – is 'God', defined as 'the universal energy that we partake of and participate in . . . a universal consciousness'.[3]

Ionesco's later work follows the psychological line of avant garde drama even more directly; and in his own production of *Victims of Duty* in 1968 in Zürich, it was this level of the play (rather than the detective-story parody) that he emphasized. Outlining his motive for writing as 'spontaneous research' into 'the unconscious', he stated that the scenes were transcriptions of his own dreams, in particular the central sequence where the protagonist, entangled in a wood, sinks down into a bottomless pit of mud, reappears as a child and climbs up a ladder to fly in a strong blue light. He noted that these were dreams which Jung had classified, and explained to the actors that

> the main theme . . . is the revolt against the Super-ego and the defeat of this Super-ego. The policeman – that is censorship, the conscience of society, which is also the father, that is the incarnation of society – is killed by the anarchist.[4]

On this surrealistic, Jungian level Ionesco sees his work as a universal and 'primitive . . . drama of myth' springing 'from the soul of the people'. He has drawn a parallel between the different kinds of archetype – 'truth lies in our dreams . . . there is nothing truer than myth' – and almost all of his later plays are interpretable as dreams. In *Exit the King* (1962) the stage is literally the consciousness of Bérenger, Ionesco's self-projection, whose castle is the inside of his head, disintegrating in death as he and the figures representing the different elements of his psyche dissolve into the neutral grey light of nothingness; and the image of flying to express transcendence recurs in *Amédée* (1954) and *A Stroll in the Air* (1963). As he has said:

For me, the theatre is the projection onto the stage of the world within . . . as each one of us, in the depths of his being, is at the same time everyone else, my dreams and desires, my anguish and my obsessions do not belong to myself alone; they are part of the heritage of my ancestors, a very ancient deposit to which all mankind may lay claim.[5]

This points to a very basic divergence between directors and dramatists in the avant garde movement. Since directors like Brook or Grotowski are primarily concerned with the physical performance, they tend to see a return to 'primitive roots' as being located in the body. By contrast, Ionesco is typical of the dramatists in turning to the subconscious; and this is equally the case with Sam Shepard, whose work has largely defined the themes and techniques of contemporary American drama.

Like O'Neill almost half a century earlier, Shepard's early plays are characteristic of the avant garde, although he has won more Obie awards than any other living playwright and a Pulitzer Prize, while as a film actor he became an idol of Middle America (for instance in *The Right Stuff*). One of his first major plays, *The Tooth of Crime* (1972), was produced by Charles Marowitz, who founded the Open Space theatre – a name clearly echoing Chaikin's company – in London after working with Brook on the Theatre of Cruelty season, and whose own plays included *Artaud at Rodez* (1975). Other direct links with the avant garde include Joe Chaikin, with whom Shepard collaborated on the Open Theatre's *Nightwalk*, as well as several short pieces (*Tongues, Savage/Love*, 1979; *War in Heaven*, 1984).

But where the search for mythic sources led others to Biblical material (Grotowski, Chaikin), Indian, Persian or South American legend (Brook, Barba) and literary classics from ancient Greece to the Elizabethan (Brook, Marowitz, Mnouchkine, Müller, Wilson), Shepard has focused almost exclusively on the contemporary American scene. In his plays, the mythological dimension comes from rock music and the drug culture associated with it, which provides hallucinatory alternative realities, pop art and the indigenous rituals of the American Indians. At one time a drummer for the Holy Modal Rounders rock group, rhythm dominates the action of *The Tooth of Crime*, a duel to the death between competing rock stars, which offers the most overt statement of Shepard's counter-culture ethos.

Shepard was not the first to draw on the potential of rock music. This had already been attempted two decades previously in *The Sport of My Mad Mother* (1958) – the earliest example of Artaud's influence in Britain, predating even Brook's Theatre of Cruelty season – by Ann Jellicoe, who defined her play as 'anti-intellect . . . not only because it is about irrational forces and urges but because one hopes it will reach the audience directly through rhythm, noise and music, and their reaction to basic stimuli'. There are many similarities with *The Tooth of Crime*. On-stage musicians accompany the action (although their involvement is relatively limited), and teen-gang street warfare is presented as an apocalyptic struggle between allegorical figures, which becomes a basis for 'symbols, myths and rituals'. As in Shepard, these are drawn from contemporary patterns of everyday behaviour, which reveal archetypal analogues, here seen from a feminist perspective in the figure of a man who castrates himself after being sexually rejected by the mother figure of the title, the Hindu death goddess whose destructive nature incarnates the anarchic life-principle ('All creation is the sport of my mad mother Kali'). Jellicoe emphasized the psychological function of rites as a significant mode of expression that gains a 'magical' efficacy through hypnotic effects, quite independent of religion or belief:

> A ritual generally takes the form of repeating a pattern of words and gestures which tend to excite us above a normal state of mind. Once this state of mind is induced we are receptive and suggestible and ready for the climax of the rite. At the climax the essential nature of something is changed.[6]

However, applying this sort of heightened patterning to deliberately banal material reduces the examples of rituals within the play to parody, while conflicting levels of illusion are confused, leading to a farcical theatricality when one of the musicians threatens the audience with his banjo, as if it were a machine-gun, and urges them (in lieu of an ending for the play) to break up the theatre-building for a bonfire.

By contrast Shepard achieved a remarkable fusion of ritual technique and dramatic action through making the musicians/rock singers the protagonists. The way he describes Bob Dylan's 'true magic' – 'this transformation of energy which he carries ... a high feeling of life-giving excitement ... the kind of energy that brings courage and hope and above all brings life pounding into the foreground'[7] – also defines Shepard's own use of rock music both as a vehicle for channelling audience emotion and as a symbol. It is also simultaneously the music of mainstream American youth culture, and the expression of an alienated or oppressed counter-culture, having developed out of Negro spirituals to become the voice of the drug scene. In addition, linked to jazz, its improvisational form offers a model for a spontaneous and dynamic dramatic structure. All this is directly reflected in *The Tooth of Crime*, which forms a basis for much of Shepard's later work.

Here, the competition for top place in the pop charts becomes a musical duel to the death between archetypal forces – Hoss (the Rip Torn era) versus Crow (the younger Keith Richards generation) – drawing on a whole range of junk culture images. On one level it is presented as a sci-fi star wars, set in a post-Jagger and Townsend future, with electric guitars as 'Killer Machines', a publicity agent as an updated Star Trek figure and a disc jockey named Galactic Jack. Equally, it is seen in terms of cowboy westerns and gangland mafia. Hoss describes his rise to the number one spot as 'like John Wayne, Robert Mitchum and Kirk Douglas all in one movie', while his drug pusher compares himself to another 'Doc' who rode with Buffalo Bill, slaughtering the Indians. The battle is over 'turf' (specifically Las Vegas) ruled by biker gangs under the control of shadowy 'syndicates', with the guitarists as 'trigger' men. Another collection of metaphors relates to sport – boxing, wrestling and particularly speed car racing – the whole rock music competition being a game with penalties, points and a referee. There are also references to class war and political revolution. Unlike Ann Jellicoe's play, in which the single defining image leads to self-parody, all these metaphors coexist as detritus from the public subconscious, which is thematically appropriate since the battle is over which image can dominate the musical market. But beneath the kaleidoscopic symbolic surface, the action resolves into the 'root' myth (as defined by Frazer's *Golden Bough*) of the vegetation king, ritually slaughtered each year to be resurrected in the younger challenger, a myth reused by Shepard in *Buried Child* (1978). Thus in defeat Hoss is finally able to transcend his personality cult in suicide, 'a true gesture' that marks him out as 'an original' and gains him a form of immortality by becoming one with 'the power'.[8]

Rock star figures recur in *Melodrama Play* (1967), and in *Mad Dog Blues* (1971) where celluloid fantasies of Mae West and Marlene Dietrich take on a tangible reality in the hallucinatory world of a singer, Kosmo. The symbolic implications of his name are picked up on in *Cowboy Mouth* (also 1971), where 'CAVALE *has kidnapped* SLIM *off the streets with an old .45. (She wants to make him into a rock-and-roll star, but they fall in love . . .)*'. On the surface such a situation is crude and cartoon-like – 'disposable drama' (as several critics termed Shepard's early plays) for a disposable civilization – but it takes on a religious dimension in which the rock star is 'a sort of god in our image'. The girl's aim is to find a replacement for a singer who, like Hoss, achieved a sacrificial apotheosis by shooting himself in the mouth during a performance. Although Slim (a stock cowboy name) refuses the role of 'rock-and-roll Jesus with a cowboy mouth', the play ends with a 6 ft lobster cracking out of its shell to reveal '*the rock-and-roll saviour*' who '*raises the pistol to his head and squeezes the trigger*'. The title of *The Tooth of Crime* was taken from a poem by Mallarmé; and the hallucinatory figure of the lobster is an explicit tribute to the symbolist Gérard de Nerval, who is said to have confided his visions to one. In addition, this 'saviour' is referred to in lines quoted from W.B. Yeats' poem 'The Second Coming', linking him to the 'Savage God' that Yeats labelled Jarry's future followers. In this play Shepard consciously presents himself as a neo-surrealist, whose characters aspire to an inverted hierarchy. As Cavale puts it, 'the highest form of anything is sainthood. A marvellous thief like Villon or Genet . . . they were saints 'cause they raised thievery to its highest state of grace.'[9]

In other early plays Shepard turns to indigenous American equivalents, for instance Hopi Indian myths and psychedelic drugs, which are linked with the Vietnam anti-war movement in *Operation Sidewinder* (1970). In this surrealistic scenario, the gigantic snake in question – a computer designed to 'transcend the barriers of human thought and penetrate an extra-terrestrial consciousness' through 'rhythmic movements' – turns against its creators, a Dr Strangelove-like scientist, the CIA and the military establishment, all portrayed in grotesque comic-strip terms. The young revolutionary plans to drop LSD in the army water supply, but his Indian allies are inspired by the snake to reject violence for a very different form of liberation. As their shaman puts it:

> Tonight the spirit snake shall become one again [having earlier been decapitated to save a woman from its erotic embrace] and with it shall join all its people . . . You are free, Pahana [whites]. You have brought us to our emergence. It will take us to a place we will never come back from.

Indeed, this happens at the culmination of a long scene of ritual dance and chanting, in which '*Everything . . . is spiritual and sincere*' in contrast to the parodistic treatment of the social scene. The strong, unified rhythmic patterns of sound and movement are clearly intended to draw the audience – like their two white representatives on stage – into the ceremony, with the climax designed as an overwhelming revelation of spiritual/hallucino-genic vision as a '*tremendous bolt of blue light issues from the sidewinder, matched by one in the sky. Thunder booms . . . The combination of voices chanting reaches an incredible shrieking, like lightning. The whole scene crackles like high voltage wires.*'[10] As with so much avant garde drama, the desired effect could hardly be achieved, unless perhaps the audience themselves were on drugs during the performance, but the play is a good example of the way the quasi-religious, anarchistic and psychological primitivism of the movement merged with the Flower Power counter-culture of the late 1960s.

This modern myth making, and the affirmation of crime or violence that characterizes almost all of Shepard's work, goes along with the typical avant garde rejection of western civilization. Typically too, Shepard's rad-icalism is not expressed in terms of any political ideology; rather his attack is on the psychology of the *status quo*, and his target (like that of more conventional playwrights, such as Arthur Miller or Edward Albee) is the American Dream, encapsulated in Hollywood. This remains a continuing reference point in his later plays, but again is given its fullest expression in an early work, *Angel City* (1976). Here too Indian shamanism is the redemptive force – in the shape of stolen medicine bundles carried by a 'script doctor' (who is thus also shaman and quack doctor, the same merging of metaphors that was used in *The Tooth of Crime*), the only 'authentic' one being a bundle 'for looking inside yourself' – and what it reveals is the monstrous nature of the film industry, with the green slime that covers the faces of the movie moguls (plus '*fangs, long black fingernails*', etc.) spreading out to engulf the cinema audience, symbolic of their narcoticized minds. Again there is an on-stage musician, 'experimenting with various rhythm structures . . . to produce certain trance states in masses of people', though here he has been corrupted into working for the commercialized and megalomaniac establishment. The play not only exposes but also embodies the mechanics of image making, as a demonstration of how movies both feed off and determine the fantasies of the population, substituting for, and eventually shaping, reality. Images gain an autonomous existence, the city itself being 'the concrete reality of the dreaming machine'.[11] But here, co-opted by society, the creative potential – which in other circumstances might be spiritually liberating – leads to apocalyptic disaster. In this dystopia, the American Dream industry destroys both the environment and inner life.

The surface action of Shepard's later plays may be less overtly surrealistic, but they still incorporate the same themes and similar principles. Hollywood and the cowboy archetype reappear in *True West* (1980). A film star's imagined photo is as real as the actual woman in *Fool for Love* (1983), where the material world becomes a projection of the subconscious, as it explicitly is in *A Lie of the Mind* (1985). All these plays include dreamlike, unmotivated acts of violence, while the Pulitzer prize-winning *Buried Child* strips away Norman Rockwell stereotypes of the American family in a search for true roots that leads to ritual sacrifice and symbolic resurrection, an amalgam of avant garde motifs. Social ideals, particularly the normative values of the family, are continually portrayed through the prism of American gothic – rotting guilt, dynastic curses, incest and bad seed – in a wasteland of junk culture, against which are set the possibility of redemption through the liberation of primitive instincts and the power of the psyche.

SPREADING THE AVANT GARDE

With Shepard, as in different ways with Mnouchkine or Robert Wilson, the avant garde has mounted a successful take-over of the traditional/establishment stage, making its principles the driving force of contemporary mainstream theatre. But during the 1970s and 1980s primitivism also became an exceptionally widespread aspect of theatrical culture in general, with the experiments of innovators being recapitulated by a multiplicity of different groups.

The main variants of the avant garde line among the smaller, more transitory theatre groups can be illustrated by three examples, whose approach and focus is (with variation) interchangeable with any number of other groups over the last two decades. What distinguishes the three groups selected is their extremism, which highlights the different qualities.

A group like John Juliani's Savage God theatre, which claimed to represent 'that direction of the theatre that extols participation and process . . . above observation and product',[12] is an example of the first tendency. The second can be seen in the neo-Artaudian work of Ralph Ortiz; and the exoticism of a group like the Floating Lotus Magic Opera Company is representative of the third variant.

The name of Juliani's theatre, taken from Yeats' comment on *Ubu roi*, refers (like Shepard in *Cowboy Mouth*) back to Jarry, but his work built on a large number of avant garde strands. A 1971 'laboratory' season of fifty-one mini-productions in Vancouver (under the inflated acronym of PACET – Pilot investigation in an Alternative Complement to the Existing Theatre) ranged from 'consciousness-raising exercises', to 'explorations in sensory deprivation'. At one extreme there were unannounced performances in public places, Strindberg's *The Stronger*, for instance, being presented just once in a crowded downtown café by actors pretending to be ordinary members of the public and making no attempt to draw attention to the piece. At the other extreme, audiences were guided through a series of darkened rooms to the accompaniment of disorienting sounds and lights. Aiming to obliterate what was seen as a false distinction between theatrical performance and life, PACET abandoned technical expertise and even rehearsal, together with the concept of a stage. The artificiality of such an exercise was clearly revealed by *An Evening of Arrabal*, when Juliani in the role of the author answered questions put by three of the actors in a semi-improvised 'interview', with excerpts from Arrabal's plays presented to illustrate his points. This led to an enactment of *Erotic Bestiality*, where balloons and confetti were distributed to the public at the point of orgasm in the performance, while 'Arrabal' stripped to reveal a bra and garterbelt beneath his everyday clothes, announcing: 'I think, as a playwright, I am greatly overrated.' A later 'production'/happening discarded all the elements of pretence that had made PACET meretricious, carrying the fusion of art and actuality to a perhaps unique and generally unrepeatable point, which also challenged the whole notion of what was theatrically acceptable, by having Juliani's wife give birth to their child live on stage before a Vancouver audience.

A similar combination of extreme realism and shock effect, which again only reached a single performance, characterized Ralph Ortiz's *The Sky is Falling* (Temple University, 1970), although here the key factor was physical violence. Following Artaud, from whose essays the title of the piece was taken, this 'cruelty' was both deliberately tasteless (taste being a legitimate object of avant garde attack), and gratuitous. But Ortiz clearly took the view that, the symbolic images of violence Artaud advocated having become a form of aesthetic titillation through familiarity, now the desired emotional purgation could only be achieved through actual atrocities. Thus the scenario called for 'one hundred live mice in a wire screen and two gallons of blood in plastic bags' to be placed inside a piano, which was then ceremonially smashed, spraying the audience with blood and mangled or half-dead rodents.[13] The actors stripped and burnt their clothes, dismembered live chickens on stage, and systematically brutalized one of their members, who acted the part of an epileptic so convincingly that some spectators called for a doctor. At the opening, the audience were 'interrogated'; they were subjected to verbal abuse if they refused to participate at any point; and at the end, insults were screamed at them as 'a bunch of fucking voyeurs'. In the event, treating Artaud's concept of 'cruelty' all too literally, any sense of a metaphysical plane was lost. Purely visceral reactions replaced subliminal responses (at least one member of the audience vomited). In such a context, designating two of the actors as 'shamans' and the spectators plus the rest of the cast as 'initiates', or describing the actions as 'destruction rites' (as Ortiz did) became irrelevant. Conversely, the attempt to give this orgiastic sadism a political extension – in referring to the chickens as Vietnamese babies, smashing eggs with cries of 'enemy foetuses' – was undercut by the purely rhetorical symbolic level, on which Lieutenant Calley of the My Lai massacre was identified with Kali, the Hindu goddess of destruction.

A comparable, but still more extensive confusion of symbols marked the exoticism epitomized by the Floating Lotus Magic Opera Company's performance of *Bliss Apocalypse* (1970). Again one of the major figures was Kali, though here the action transformed the death goddess into simple naked Woman, clean as primal earth, and Mother. Other characters included the Cretan Minotaur, the Phoenix, a 'Sun-Dancer Prophet', a 'Shaman' and 'Vairocana', a figure combining Tibetan Buddhist iconography with an American Indian totem. This eclectic universality in the conflation of mythological archetypes was also mirrored in the conceptual level aimed at, which was so vast as to be undefinable: 'The whole vision was designed', according to its author, 'to be performed outside in the raw air of IT, on a hillside after civilizations all blow their plugs'. A magnification of the visionary romanticism in the Living Theatre's final phase, as well as an expression of the counter-culture vision drawn on by Shepard in *Operation Sidewinder*, this performance piece was 'conceived as an initiation ceremony opening areas of sound and image, guiding them with the chanted sound of vocal AUM'.[14] Prefiguring the cross-cultural work of Barba's Odin Teatret, it was presented in a wild mixture of contradictory styles, the only common factor seemingly being that all were highly conventionalized and alien to western culture. 'Gagaku No-drama' and 'Kabuki sounds' (defined as 'wheezing . . . high-pitched microtonal sound' and 'high-pitched singing notes') accompanied 'battles of forces . . . as in Javanese dance battles, angular'. This combined with a 'ritual hieroglyph dance' and movements supposedly 'as in Tai Chi', while what little dialogue there was substituted rhetorical inflation for sense:

O Face to Face with the Spirit of Enlightenment
AWAKE! AWAKE! LIGHT FLOWS UP THROUGH OUR SPINES!

Paradoxically, it is precisely the evident flaws in these examples – a lack of imaginative integrity in the recapitulation of earlier avant garde achievements, the self-indulgent quality of the violence or the exoticism – that indicates the degree to which the movement had gained wide acceptance, because of the amount of attention paid to them. *The Sky is Falling* was sponsored by a university, Juliani's 'laboratory' season even received governmental funding, and all three were extensively reported in journals like *Theatre Quarterly* and *The Drama Review* as imaginatively exciting and potentially productive new directions.

These variants of the avant garde have continued to be a factor in the last decade, extended in America through the work of Schumann's Bread and Puppet Theatre, the Wooster Group (with productions like *LSD*), or the Roy Hart Theatre (*Hymn to Pan*). Even in England, where primitivism has had comparatively little influence, there is one significant representative among contemporary playwrights. David Rudkin's first play was considered as possible material for Brook's Theatre of Cruelty season, and Artaud's influence is explicit in his subsequent dramas of demonic possession, mythic sacrifice and spiritual redemption.

Rudkin declared from the first that 'Theatre is a ritual';[15] and *Afore Night Come* (1962) centres on ritualistic murder in an atmosphere of primitive rustic menace. Located in the naturalistically drawn contemporary countryside, the action implies the continuance of ancient, atavistic urges beneath the surface of modern society. The ritual decapitation of an old tramp is juxtaposed with an apocalyptic rain of pesticide from a helicopter, spraying down on the labourers as their knives slash the sacrificial corpse. It symbolizes that this superstitious violence is not only an expression of deep subconscious needs denied by society, but also the end-product of a dehumanizing technocratic civilization. The absolute rejection of modern materialistic values (capitalism along with Christianity) in favour of religious primitivism – an inversion also expressed in anal sexuality, and male/female transpositions – is given still more violent expression in *The Sons of Light* (1976) and *The Triumph of Death* (1981).

Children of the isolated, evangelically obsessed islanders in the earlier play have been abducted by a Caligari-like psychologist, whose experiments have turned them into 'demented and deformed' grotesques: boy-woman and girl-man. The convicts of his subterranean/subconscious concentration-camp (non-conformist or rebellious citizens sent for 'treatment' by the mainland establishment) and the primitive islanders above-ground are equally victims of the insane scientist's brainwashing techniques; and the new pastor denounces his congregation's belief in an evil god of 'Wrath. Only His chastisement can transfigure you? God? Ungod!' This vision of evil is even more graphic in the later play, set in a generalized medieval period. Opening and closing with the excremental images of defecating religious figures (the 'Feminine' boy whose faith led to the massacre of the Children's Crusade, and a transsexual Luther), the symbolic 'Dark Ages' are ruled by a monstrous female Pope, whose face is '*a farded skull of cancerous death. Crown a Triple Tower, from which diminished human figures imprisoned scream and reach*'. His/her principle agent is a nun, who changes sex to seduce the homosexual spiritual opponent of this demonic-Papatrix, finally being transformed into a repugnant parody of modern femininity as a medical doctor (following Rudkin's consistent rejection of science). Against these forces of morality/evil stands a Christ figure, who is revealed as '*Satan, Cernunnos, Pan, call Him what you will. Night*'.[16] Devil and God have exchanged places; moral and sexual norms are reversed. So here, extending the pattern of Rudkin's earlier plays, homosexuality is glorified in Pan's coupling with a worshipper, sanctifying the body that 'Crosstianity' debases; and out of this inversion comes a spiritual affirmation.

The visceral and extreme violence, repellant and unremitting, is intended to be purgatorial, as well as representing the brutalizing effect of civilization, produced by the false values of repressive Christianity and materialism. These baleful influences can only be countered by shattering the audience's social conditioning, in itself an agonizing process, which Rudkin's plays are designed to achieve in performance and demonstrate in their action. For instance, the 'pure . . . primal essence' of a murdered slave-soldier rises from the incinerated embers of his dismembered body in *The Sons of Light*, where a saviour – the pastor's son – decends into 'The Pit' and brings 'the tower of death to dust'. Taking on the role of a 'King of Love' (as the antithesis of the God of Death), he urges the entombed prisoners 'Up! Into your proper Kingdom . . . Your light has come', during an apocalyptic earthquake. This 'Surrection' (the title of the play's final section, a word that merges political insurrection with spiritual resurrection) miraculously frees a schizophrenic idiot from her demonic 'possession' by inherited behaviour patterns, symbolized in a '*mother-persona, barren, destructive*' and '*father-persona, repugnant, devouring*'.[17]

Rudkin has described his drama as aspiring to 'the quality of an archetypal myth'; and his plots are based on Biblical fable and fragmentary Shakespearean or historical images, all of which combine suffering with salvation. The martyrdom of Joan of Arc (as the daughter of the lone survivors from the Children's Crusade) is replayed in *The Triumph of Death*, the Harrowing of Hell in *The Sons of Light*, and both plays revolve around the Massacre of the Innocents. These archetypes chart a geography of the mind. Rudkin's dramatic settings are purely psychological landscapes, inhabited by symbols. Their subterranean geology is the strata of the subconscious. As self-admitted reflections of the author's own 'psychic turmoil', the visionary horrors enacted on stage lay claim to an unusual degree of authenticity, which is designed to transmit their hysteria to audiences. Following Antonin Artaud, who appears as a character in *The Triumph of Death* in the demonic role of Joan's confessor from Dreyer's 1927 film *The Passion of Joan of Arc*, Rudkin's theatre is intended as 'the truthful precipitate of dreams'; and these 'images of energy in the unconscious and gratuitous crime on the surface' are intended to exercise a therapeutic Artaudian 'Cruelty' against the spectators.[18]

Rudkin's is a drama of exorcism. However, the traumatic degree of human suffering and assault on audience sensibilities necessary to achieve this spiritual purgation has been counterproductive; and none of Rudkin's later plays have reached a wide public. By contrast Peter Shaffer is an example of a popular playwright, whose work is basically conventional, but borrows widely from avant garde techniques.

COMMERCIAL ADAPTATION AND CULTURAL FESTIVALS

Peter Shaffer's first major success was *The Royal Hunt of the Sun* (1964). Specifically intended as 'total' theatre, involving not only words but also rites, mimes, masks and magic, it translated Barrault's concept of 'total theatre' into exoticism with striking visual and aural images. These range from ritualized mime to symbolic schemata. On the one hand, the great massacre in which a wave of Indians with barbaric feather head-dresses rise to be cut down by the conquistadores again and again to 'savage music' and violent drumming – a geometric dance of slaughter ending with a vast bloodstained cloth, dragged out from the centre piece of a gigantic golden sun representing the Inca empire and bellying out over the stage to the sound of screams. On the other hand, the final tableau as Pizarro kneels by the strangled Inca, believing desperately in his resurrection and waiting through the night for the sunlight to strike his body, surrounded by Indians in huge funeral masks intoning 'a strange chant . . . punctuated by hollow beats on the drums and by long, long silences in which they turn their immense triangular eyes enquiringly up to the sky'.[19] But these vivid theatrical moments remain mere spectacle, separate from the theme of the play, which is carried by the dialogue.

The characters seem to raise important philosophical issues – the loss of faith and the search for meaning in life, or individualistic capitalism (Spain) versus Communism with its regimentation and material rewards (the Incas) – yet there is no true dialectic, because the answers given are the easy ones that confirm popular preconceptions. The good qualities of both civilizations are one-sided, so materialism and individualism are equally destructive. Spiritual needs can never be met by institutions, and so on. In the National Theatre production the visual imagery of the Inca's garrotting was specifically that of crucifixion and pietà, which turned his death into an agonized rejection of Christianity. Shaffer's theme is the

Figure 24 Pop myth in *Equus*. Nudity, stylized theatricality and bare stage.

search for God; but the action substitutes a humanistic 'joy' for religious experience, effectively making questions of God irrelevant.

The same problem recurs in *Equus* (1973), which combines the psychological thriller and self-discovery on a psychiatrist's couch with the exploration of myth, atavistic religious belief and magic. Technically it borrows eclectically from the avant garde. A bare stage echoes the call for 'poor theatre'. All the devices for spectator involvement are deployed, with part of the audience seated behind the acting area to intensify the response by allowing spectators to observe the reactions of others, an actor seated among the audience, and sound effects from speakers placed throughout the auditorium. There are dream sequences, and a scenic structure that cuts across the logic of time as well as cause and effect following the irrational associations of the subconscious, plus ritual chanting, stylized masks and mythic archetypes: Apollo versus Dionysus. In addition, the terms describing the audience/stage relationship exactly echo the details of Grotowski's setting for *The Constant Prince*, with the spectators as 'voyeurs' and 'witnesses' on 'tiers of seats in the fashion of a dissecting theatre' surrounding a square inner stage that 'resembles a railed boxing ring'.[20]

As in *The Royal Hunt of the Sun*, it is this avant garde stylistic level that generates theatrical excitement. The visual imagery is totally compelling, the stylized centaur-horses, formed from sombrely clad actors wearing skeletal silver horses' heads and hooves, creating an effect of magical transformation, while the boy's nightride on a revolve, whirled around by 'horses' standing at the perimeter, indeed suggests an ancient and uncompromising force come to life. The images are more closely integrated with the theme than in Shaffer's previous play. But the weight of the overall statement discredits their imaginative reality, partly as a result of the play's genesis.

The starting point was a true story of a stable-boy who blinded twenty-six horses, the dramatic value of which was that it 'set up all sorts of reverberations';[21] and the first draft focused on the boy. In the final version the interest shifted to the effect of the boy's experience on his analyst, and although the programme notes contained excerpts from Frazer's *Golden Bough*, the dialogue presented an explanation in Freudian clichés. Sexual experience is the test of normality. But a repressive upbringing leads to perversion, and this results in impotence and guilt feelings, which can only be resolved by an act of violent sacrilege. The myth that the boy creates, and his orgiastic ceremonies with his private god – incarnate in the horses, which both satisfies the fundamental need for worship and liberates natural instincts (symbolized in the, by this point, cliché image of nakedness) – become a mere flight from repressive reality that can be dismissed as personal fantasy. At the same time the analyst is brought to recognize that the 'normal' is sterile and passionless, that his own detachment disguises sexual frustration, and that 'curing' the boy of his obsession means destroying the spiritual intensity and individuality which alone give life value. Again significant issues have been raised, but only as a form of intellectual titillation. The audience's desire for archetypal significance – itself perhaps an indication of avant garde interests filtering through into public consciousness, or expressing the same reaction against contemporary materialism that has motivated the avant garde exploration of the primitive – has been satisfied without disturbing them on any fundamental level.

Equus was a worldwide success. The avant garde approach had, as it were, arrived, but in a watered-down and conventional form. It had also spread beyond the theatre, in particular defining one of the directions taken by contemporary dance. The subconscious focus together with environmental performance techniques characterized the 'dance-music-theatre pieces' of Meredith Monk in the 1970s (indeed several of her earlier pieces were presented in Schechner's Performing Garage), while mythic primitivism and the ritualistic use of body rhythms were explored by other American dancers like Ann Halprin, both lines being extended into the 1980s internationally through the work of Jan Farbre, Jozef Nadj or Maguy Marin.[22] The type of popular spectacle promoted by Peter Shaffer, combined with an exotic symbolism reminiscent of the Floating Lotus Magic Opera Company, an extension of Peter Brook's experiments with primal language and natural settings, as well as an audio visual approach comparable to that of Robert Wilson, has also given rise to what can only be called avant garde monumentalism in the musical performance pieces of Murray Shafer.

Citing Lévi-Strauss and Margaret Mead, Murray Shafer's epic seven-section *Patria* Cycle is an attempt to recreate a primitive art predating the development of reflective consciousness, and gain an equivalent effect to

> spectacles in which beating hearts were plucked from victims, in which dead men were brought back to life, in which gods boxed with thunderbolts, or the dead sun was kindled to life again and restored to the sky, or ghostly spirits were released from their wanderings . . .

As environmental theatre in a rather different sense to Schechner's, the function of Shafer's work is to foster awareness of a transcendental unity, destroyed by the anthropocentric humanism of western civilization, thus creating 'a new relationship between ourselves and the wide cosmos'.[23] This religious tone has led him to adopt Artaud's term 'holy theatre'; and the *Patria* Cycle borrows eclectically from dead religions, native myth and popular culture. *Patria Six: Ra*, for instance, draws on the animal-headed gods of Ancient Eygpt, while the fourth part carries the subtitle of *The Black Theatre of Hermes Trismegistos*. By contrast, Part One centres on the figure of Kaspar Hauser, here a mute Displaced Person who struggles to keep his identity against the overwhelming ubiquity of the mass media in his adopted country, and *Patria Three: The Greatest Show* recreates a 1930s circus fairground. A form of community theatre involving the townspeople (about 75 per cent of the cast when first produced in Peterborough, Ontario, in 1987), and forcing the audience to participate by restricting some segments of the show to those who performed a required act or game, *The Greatest Show* has strong overtones of Bakhtin's carnival. On the other hand, the as yet unperformed *Hermes Trismegistos*, 'a very mystical work about alchemy', was specifically 'designed to be produced in a deserted mine at midnight to a fairly exclusive group'.[24]

Conceived as a labyrinth with the myth of Theseus and Ariadne as Part Five and the minotaur also appearing as one of the circus animals in Part Three, the overall theme of the Cycle is set in a prologue, *The Princess of the Stars* (1981, and Banff festival, 1985), based on a North American Indian legend. Unintentionally injured by the Wolf when she falls from heaven, the Daughter of the Sun-God is imprisoned at the bottom of a lake by a demon, the Three-Horned Enemy; and the Wolf is sent on a pilgrimage through the ages, taking on different human shapes (Theseus, a dead Pharoah calling on the sun to raise him to heaven, a clown) in search of the princess, and of the redemptive spiritual power that will release her and transfigure him. A piece for soprano, two mixed choruses, four actors (or 'sound poets'), six dancers and an orchestra restricted to wind, brass and percussion – plus twenty canoeists – it is designed for pre-dawn performance on a lake surrounded by mountains, off which the singers' voices can be 'bounced'. The musicians are hidden in the trees around the lake, with the action taking place on the surface of the water. The performance ends, like *Ra*, with the sunrise; and this emphasis on the unity between the story, its presentation and the 'living environment' of the natural setting, carries over to the spectators, who are also in the trees at the water's edge. At the beginning of the piece a 'thaumaturgical incantation' by a shaman (the Presenter) 'turns us into trees in order that we may observe the events without interfering'.

Apart from *Patria One: The Characteristics Man* (produced by a standard opera company in 1987), this is one of the more passive roles assigned to spectators in the Cycle, who in other sections are cast as 'initiates' (carrying the sarcophagus, or processing blindfolded through the streets in *Ra* at the 1983 Holland festival), while the actors take on the role of 'hierophants' or 'priests'. In *The Princess of the Stars*, however, the mythic figures were

Figure 25 Mythological pageants and the grandeur of nature.

231

represented by huge three-dimensional shapes mounted on canoes, and the only human part was the shaman, who served as an interpreter for the singers and 'sound poets'. Like Ted Hughes' *Orghast* language, Shafer's text was in an invented speech, the Sun Disk's vocal patterns suggesting Latin cognates that contrasted with 'monosyllabic abruptness' in the Enemy's 'compact vowels and waspish consonants', while the Dawn Bird's chorus was partly derived from ornithologists' notebooks. The choruses were composed of Amerindian words from various tribal languages, or from an international selection of different cultures, used for 'colour' rather than syntactically, the invocation for the Sun Disk, for instance, beginning with the ancient Japanese word for sun followed by equivalents 'in a geographic curve around the world through the languages of Asia, Africa, and Europe'.

If this paralleled Peter Brook's search for a universal 'root' language, the slow performance tempo – exploiting the conditions imposed by distance, with sound (travelling at 330 m a second) taking three seconds to reach the audience, and a further three seconds for the echo to return to the singer before the next word – duplicated the effect of Robert Wilson's early 'autistic' drama. Shafer's rationale was quite different in relating this to ritual, however: 'Something strange happens when nothing happens. The senses are sharpened with alertness, ready to print the decisive action when it occurs. There can be little doubt that primitive rituals are deliberately structured in this way.'[25]

Ritual is a recurrent term in Shafer's commentary on his 'Theatre of Confluences' (a title with similar implications to Grotowski's 'Theatre of Sources'), being seen as a tool for generating spiritual renewal in a modern audience cut off from the natural world. While eclecticism is mistaken for universality, his use of ancient or arcane rites, exotic historical contexts and tribal legend, consciously relies on strangeness – forms alien to the isolated and materialistic existence of contemporary urban man – as a way of recovering 'the sacred'. At the same time, like Peter Shaffer's plays, the spectacular nature of Shafer's productions is extremely expensive (despite its emphasis on 'nature'), and requires the resources of major cultural festivals or government funding. His call for a return to the primitive is misleading, since the scope of the *Patria* Cycle is Wagnerian (Shafer's own label) and depends for its existence on the society it rejects.

As such, Shafer's work is typical of the present position of the avant garde. It is also representative in merging so many of the earlier approaches, building on the 'laboratory' experiments of Brook and Grotowski; on Bakhtin's theories and the studies of anthropologists; on Robert Wilson's brand of neo-surrealist perception; on the integration of theatre with the natural world, which is standard for so many avant garde productions, and the emphasis on therapeutic audience-participation that runs from the expressionists to the Becks or Richard Schechner; as well as on

Artaud's concept of a 'holy theatre'. Shafer's resuscitation of vanished rituals and the recovery of myths, both ancient and from popular culture, together with his attempt to extend the range of communication onto an instinctual and subconscious level through tempo and images, all lead us back to the original avant garde appeal to the pre-social, spiritual and communal 'roots' of man. But, as with Wilson and Müller or Mnouchkine, the anarchism that also initially defined the movement has been transformed into 'high' art.

NOTES

1 INTRODUCTION

1 Renato Poggioli, *The Theory of the Avant-Garde*, Cambridge, Mass. 1968, p. 224.
2 The previous version of this study included a discussion of the avant garde line in modern dance, using Mary Wigman, Meredith Monk and Anne Halprin as representative examples (see *Holy Theatre*, Cambridge 1984, pp. 53–4 and 247–51) as well as consideration of some figures only tangentially related to the movement, such as Samuel Beckett or Peter Weiss.
3 See Mircea Eliade, *Myths, Rites, Symbols*, New York 1967, vol. 1, p. 88.
4 Peter Brook (following Grotowski), programme note to the *Tempest*, Centre for International Theatre Research, 1968.
5 Sigmund Freud, *Standard Edition*, vol. 20, p. 72. For a discussion of Freud and Lévi-Strauss in relation to primitivism – and of the way modern attitudes have been conditioned by Edgar Rice Burroughs, Conrad, D. H. Lawrence, or art exhibitions such as Roger Fry's Post-Impressionist exhibition of 1910 and the 1984 MOMA 'Primitivism in 20th-Century Art: Affinity of the Tribal and the Modern' exhibition – see Marianna Torgovnick, *Gone Primitive*, Chicago 1990.
6 Mikhail Bakhtin, *Rabelais and his World* (trans. Helene Iswolsky), Cambridge, Mass. 1968, p. 224.
7 *W. B. Yeats and T. Sturge Moore: Their Correspondence, 1910–1937*, New York 1953, p. 156; Yeats, *Essays and Introductions*, London 1961, pp. 333 and 224ff; and Yeats, note to *A Vision*, cit. in Richard Ellman, *The Identity of Yeats*, New York 1964, p. 166.

2 THE POLITICS OF PRIMITIVISM

1 Cf. Mikhail Bakhtin, *Problems of Dostoevsky's Poetics* (trans. Caryl Emerson), Minneapolis 1984, p. 126, and *Rabelais and his World* (trans. Helene Iswolsky), Cambridge, Mass. 1968, p. 3.
2 *Rabelais and his World*, pp. 92 and 255.
3 *Ibid.*, pp. 39 and 48.
4 *Ibid.*, pp. 7 and 10; and Matei Calinescu, *Five Faces of Modernity*, Durham, NC 1987, p. 275: although Calinescu refers only to painting and poetry, the combination is equally characteristic of avant garde theatre – see the epigraph to Alfred Jarry's *Ubu Enchained*, discussed on p. 27 in this volume.
5 Leopold Jessner, cit. in D. Calandra, *Theatre Quarterly*, vol. 6, no. 2 (1976). p. 52.
6 Charles Marowitz, in *Mobiler Spielraum – Theater der Zukunft*, ed. Karlheinz Braun, Frankfurt 1970, p. 127. Ionesco made exactly the same point in his

argument against Tynan's criticisms: see *Notes and Counter Notes*, New York 1964, pp. 101ff.

7 Eugenio Barba, *TDR (The Drama Review/Tulane Drama Review)*, vol. 19, no. 4, p. 53, and Richard Schechner, *Theatre Quarterly*, vol. 1, no. 2 (1971), p. 62. See also Judith Malina and Julian Beck, *Paradise Now*, New York 1971, p. 7. The dubious premise that ritual is efficacious is derived from anthropologists like Eliade: 'Rituals are symbols acted in reality; they function to make concrete and experiential the mythic values of a society.... Hence rituals *act*, they perform, modulate, transform' (*Myths, Rites, Symbols*, vol. 1, p. 164).

8 Eliade, *Myths, Rites, Symbols*, vol. 1, p. 164.

9 The programme is reported by Leonard Pronko, *Theatre East and West*, Berkeley 1967, p. 24.

10 The suggestion has been made, based on Artaud's vague descriptions in *The Theatre and its Double*, that this Barong performance might have been an episode from the *Mahabharata*: see Kathy Foley, 'Trading arts: Artaud, spies and current Indonesian/American artistic exchange', *Modern Drama*, March 1992.

11 Antonin Artaud, *The Theatre and its Double* (trans. Mary Richards), New York 1958, pp. 57–8.

12 *Ibid.*, pp. 53–4.

13 See Beryl de Zoete, *Dance and Drama in Bali*, London 1938.

14 Artaud, *The Theatre and its Double*, p. 54.

15 The codification is in some ways similar to western ballet, which is perhaps why anthropologists have classified Balinese theatre under dance rather than drama.

16 A. F. Ansimov, in *Studies in Siberian Shamanism*, ed. Henry N. Michael, Toronto 1963, pp. 101–2.

17 For a fuller discussion of primitivism in twentieth-century western culture, see Marianna Torgovnick, *Gone Primitive*, Chicago 1990.

3 DREAMS, ARCHETYPES AND THE IRRATIONAL

1 For instance Pierre Quillard's *La Fille au mains coupées*, or Lugné-Poe's production of *Les Aveugles* at the Théâtre d'Art on 19 March and 11 December 1891.

2 Maurice Maeterlinck, *Théâtre II*, Paris 1904, p. 56.

3 Antonin Artaud, *The Theatre and its Double* (trans. Mary Richards), New York 1958, pp. 37 and 80–1.

4 Preface to Amiel, *Le Voyageur*, Paris 1925, p. 11. Compare Harold Pinter, programme note for *The Room* and *The Dumb Waiter*, Royal Court Theatre 1960: 'The desire for verification is understandable but cannot always be satisfied.... A character on the stage who can present no convincing argument or information as to his past experience, his present behaviour or his aspirations, nor give a comprehensive account for his motives, is as legitimate and as worthy of attention as one who, alarmingly, can do all these things. The more acute the experience the less articulate the expression.'

5 *L'Ermitage*, vol. 2 (1893), p. 120, and *La Plume*, vol. 4, no. 82 (1892), p. 395.

6 Paul Margueritte, *Le Petit Théâtre (Théâtre de Marionettes)*, Paris 1889, pp. 7–8.

7 *The Autobiographies of W.B. Yeats*, New York 1958, pp. 233–4.

8 According to Lugné-Poe, 'Gémier ... imposed silence by a wild and startling jig which he danced without a break until he collapsed into the prompter's box with his legs quivering in the air' (*Acrobaties*, Paris 1931, p. 177); while Yeats recorded that 'the audience shake their fists at one another' and that

'the most spirited party' were those who 'shouted for the play' (*Autobiographies*, pp. 233–4).

9 Programme note for *Ubu roi, Selected Works of Alfred Jarry*, London 1969, p. 80.

10 See George Wellwarth, who analyses Jarry as 'rebelling not only against the outmoded conventions of the current drama . . . but against absolutely everything' (*The Theatre of Protest and Paradox*, New York 1964, p. 3).

11 Guillaume Appollinaire, *Il y a*, Paris 1949, p. 176.

12 *Selected Works of Alfred Jarry*, pp. 192–3.

13 *Ibid.*, pp. 77–9.

14 Alfred Jarry, *The Ubu Plays*, London 1968, p. 106.

15 *Selected Works of Alfred Jarry*, pp. 72–3 and 83, 86.

16 G. de Pawlowski, in *Nouvelles Littéraires*, 3 September 1912.

17 André Therive, in *Revue Critique*, vol. 24, no. 197 (February 1922).

18 *Six Plays of Strindberg*, New York 1955, pp. 65ff.

19 12 November 1887. *Brev*, vol. 7, p. 218 (also cited in *The Plays of Strindberg* (trans. Michael Meyer), vol. 1, New York 1964, pp. 21–2).

20 See *Strindberg: The Plays* (trans. Michael Meyer), London 1975, vol. 2, pp. 82, 85 and 88.

21 *Ibid.*, p. 58.

22 *Ibid.*, pp. 258 and 259.

23 *Ibid.*, p. 94. In *To Damascus* this symbolic pattern is varied. Within the street scene 'frame' there are indeed seven scenes leading to the Golgotha of the asylum, but since another seven follows to repeat the structural pattern in reverse, the Unknown could be said to go through the full fourteen Stations of the Cross.

24 *Strindberg: The Plays*, p. 150.

25 *Ibid.*, p. 621.

26 *Ibid.*, p. 564.

27 *Strindberg: The Plays*, vol. 2, pp. 628ff, and letter to Carl Larson, 2 November 1901, cit. *ibid.*, p. 547.

28 *Myths, Rites, Symbols*, vol. 1, pp. 2–3.

29 What is relevant here is not the validity of this idea but its vogue. It was also accepted by Freud who defined myths as 'the distorted vestiges of the wish phantasies of whole nations – the age-long dreams of young humanity' (*Collected Papers*, vol. 4, London 1925, p. 182), even though it is based on dubious assumptions: that a 'people' has a collective mind, and that a race passes through the same sort of mental development as an individual, growing from infancy to adulthood.

4 THERAPY AND SUBLIMINAL THEATRE

1 Strindberg, *Open Letters to the Intimate Theatre*, Washington 1966, p. 294.

2 *Ibid.*, pp. 21 and 76.

3 Lugné-Poe, *Nouvelles Littéraires*, 3 February 1923.

4 Abbé Louis Bethléhem, *Les Pièces de théâtre*, Paris 1935 (3rd edn), p. 397.

5 Artaud, cit. in *Paris-Midi*, 5 June 1928.

6 'Das Theater von Morgen: I. Vom Geist des Theaters . . . II. Die Förderung einer geistigen Bühne . . . III. Entstehung', *Die Schaubühne*, 11, 18, 25 May 1916, pp. 453ff, 474ff and 499ff. As a term for describing painting, of course, 'expressionism' antedates Hasenclever's essays, and is usually attributed to Julien-Auguste Hervé in 1901.

7 Hasenclever, *Humanity*, in *An Anthology of German Expressionist Drama*, ed. Walter Sokel, New York 1963, p. 179.

8 *Ibid.*, pp. 196 and 186.
9 *Seven Plays by Ernst Toller*, New York 1936, p. 105.
10 *Humanity*, pp. 199–201.
11 *Ibid.*, p. 172, and Fritz von Unruh, *Ein Geschlecht*, Leipzig 1918, p. 8.
12 *Seven Plays by Ernst Toller*, pp. 57 and 115ff.
13 *Humanity*, p. 189.
14 Reinhard Sorge, *Der Bettler*, Berlin 1912, p. 156.
15 This was one of the first complaints. See Julius Bab's attack on expressionism as 'a kind of *horror vacui*, a vertigo in the face of the void, of this abstract space where only the ghosts of emotive exclamation marks move about', *Die Weltbühne*, 22 August 1918, p. 176. Significantly the terms in which Kenneth Tynan attacked Ionesco (*The Observer*, 22 June 1958) are precisely the same, which indicates how comparable the absurd and expressionism actually are.
16 Paul Kornfeld, epilogue appended to *Die Verführung*, reprinted in *An Anthology of German Expressionist Drama*, ed. Walter Sokel, p. 7.
17 Kasimir Edschmid, *Über Lyrischen Expressionismus*, Berlin 1917, pp. 59–60.
18 Edschmid, *Über den Expressionismus in der Literatur und die neue Dichtung*, Berlin 1919, p. 57.
19 Erwin Kalser, Programme note to *Von Morgens bis Mitternacht*, Lessingtheater 1916.
20 See Strindberg, *Open Letters to the Intimate Theatre*, p. 23, and Felix Emmel, *Das ecstatische Theater*, Prien 1924, pp. 35 and 37, where Friedrich Kayssler's acting notes are cited. These subjective feelings could hardly be transferred to the audience without loss of intensity. Indeed it is arguable that the more self-preoccupied an actor is, the less he communicates; but the general response does seem to have been qualitatively different from that evoked by the conventional theatre, at least according to critics at the time, even though there are (naturally) no 'transfigured' audiences on record. See Günther Rühle, *Theater für die Republik*, Frankfurt 1967.
21 'Das neue Pathos', in *Das Neue Pathos* I, 1913, pp. 1ff.
22 Georg Kaiser, *From Morn to Midnight*, New York 1922, p. 154.
23 Antonin Artaud, *The Theatre and its Double* (trans. Mary Richards), New York 1958, p. 82, and Artaud's lecture on 'Post war theatre in Paris' (1936), in *Cahiers Renaud-Barrault*, vol. 71 (1970), p. 7.
24 Adolphe Appia, 'Eurythmics and the Theatre', t/s in the Appia Collection, Beinecke Library, Yale University, p. 71; and *The Work of Living Art*, Coral Gables, Fla. 1960, pp. 64–5.
25 Paul Claudel, quoted by Richard Beecham in *Adophe Appia*, Cambridge 1987, p. 78.
26 Jacob Levy Moreno, *Das Stegreiftheater*, Potsdam 1924, cit. in Paul Pörtner, *Theater Heute*, September 1967, pp. 11 and 12.
27 *Ibid.*
28 See Charles Dullin, *Souvenirs et notes de travail d'un acteur*, Paris 1946, p. 60.
29 See Artaud, *The Theatre and its Double*, pp. 57 and 95–7.
30 *Ibid.*, p. 108.
31 Artaud, *Oeuvres complètes*, Paris 1961–74, vol. 3, pp. 22–3.
32 Oskar Kokoschka, *My Life*, London 1974, pp. 26–7.
33 *Ibid.*, p. 28.
34 *Ibid.*, pp. 22–3 and 28.
35 Kokoschka, cit. in Ludwig Goldscheider, *Kokoschka*, London 1963, p. 14.
36 *Neue Freie Presse*, 5 July 1909.
37 Kokoschka, *My Life*, p. 29.

38 Tzara, in *The Dada Painters and Poets*, ed. Robert Motherwell, New York 1951, pp. 237–8.

5 ANTONIN ARTAUD AND THE THEATRE OF CRUELTY

1 Antonin Artaud, 'Post war theatre in Paris', *Cahiers Renaud-Barrault*, vol. 71 (1970), pp. 6 and 17. It should be stressed again that Artaud's statements about Balinese theatre were based on fundamental misconceptions, since the only performance he saw was out of context, and therefore lacked the cultural and religious significance that would have allowed a proper estimate of its qualities.

2 Artaud, *The Theatre and its Double* (trans. Mary Richards), New York 1958, pp. 82 and 86.

3 *Ibid.*, pp. 15 and 23.

4 See Jacques Derrida, 'Le Théâtre de la Cruauté et la clôture de la représentation', *Critique*, vol. 230 (July 1966), pp. 609ff; Bernard Dort, *Théâtre public*, Paris 1967, p. 245; George Hangher, 'When is a play not a play?', *TDR* (*The Drama Review/Tulane Drama Review*), vol. 5, no. 2, pp. 54ff; and Paul Arnold, 'The Artaud experiment', *TDR*, vol. 8, no. 2, pp. 15ff.

5 See André Franck, commentary to *Lettres d'Antonin Artaud à Jean-Louis Barrault*, Paris 1952; Ross Chambers, ' "La Magie du réel": Antonin Artaud and the experience of theatre', *Australian Journal of French Studies*, vol. 3, no. 1 (January–April 1966), pp. 51ff; and Eric Sellin, *The Dramatic Concepts of Antonin Artaud*, Chicago 1968, *passim*.

6 Artaud, *The Theatre and its Double*, p. 42.

7 Cit. in Sellin, *The Dramatic Concepts ... Artaud*, p. 101.

8 Romain Weingarten, 'La force d'un peu plus vivre', *Cahiers Renaud-Barrault*, vol. 22, no. 3 (May 1958), p. 149.

9 Artaud, *The Theatre and its Double*, p. 12.

10 Letter to Jean Paulhan, 25 January 1936, *Oeuvres complètes* (hereafter *OC*), Paris 1961–74, vol. 5, pp. 272–3.

11 Marginal note to a letter dated 17 June 1936, *Lettres ... à Jean-Louis Barrault*, p. 105.

12 *To Have Done With the Judgement of God*, *TDR*, vol. 9, no. 3, pp. 81–2.

13 '*Marat/Sade* Forum', *TDR*, vol. 10, no. 4, p. 226. See also Michael Kustow, 'Sur les traces d'Artaud', *Esprit*, May 1965, pp. 958ff; and Charles Marowitz, 'Notes on the Theatre of Cruelty', *TDR*, vol. 11, no. 2, pp. 161ff.

14 16 October 1934, *OC*, vol. 3, p. 308.

15 'Théâtre Alfred Jarry ... saison 1926–7', *OC*, vol. 2, p. 15.

16 *The Theatre and its Double*, p. 111, and letter to Louis Jouvet, 29 April 1931, *OC*, vol. 3, p. 206.

17 Raymond Rouleau, Letter on Artaud's *Dream Play* production, in A. Swerling, *Strindberg's Impact in France 1920–1960*, Cambridge 1971, p. 175. See also Tania Balachova, in *From Script to Stage*, ed. R. Goodman, San Francisco 1971, p. 150.

18 In the possession of Roger Blin. Act I, sc. iii has been published in *Cahiers Renaud-Barrault*, vol. 51, November 1965.

19 Artaud, *The Theatre and its Double*, pp. 55 and 58.

20 *OC*, vol. 2, p. 27.

21 'Théâtre Alfred Jarry ... saison 1928', *OC*, vol. 2, p. 29.

22 *OC*, vol. 2, p. 13. My italics.

23 See *Artaud Anthology*, ed. Jack Hirschman, San Francisco 1965, pp. 82, 111 and 171; also Artaud, *The Theatre and its Double*, pp. 102–3.

24 *The Cenci* (trans. S. Watson Taylor), London 1969, p. 8; and *OC*, vol. 5, p. 303.

25 *The Cenci*, pp. 38, 47–8, and *The Theatre and its Double*, p. 102.
26 *The Theatre and its Double*, p. 130.
27 'Après *Les Cenci*', *OC*, vol. 5, pp. 58–9.
28 See the letter of 16 November 1932, reprinted in *The Theatre and its Double*, p. 103, and 'Les Cenci', *La Bête Noire*, no. 2 (1 May 1935), reprinted in *The Cenci*, p. 7.
29 'Théâtre Alfred Jarry . . . 1929', *OC*, vol. 2, p. 34.
30 Ross Chambers, ' "La Magie du réel": Antonin Artaud . . .', p. 58, and *Lettres . . . à Jean-Louis Barrault*, p. 90.
31 *OC*, vol. 2, p. 38.
32 In the *Revue des deux mondes* of 1 November 1893: 'M. Strindberg is not a true realist; rather his harsh and acrid eloquence, his indictments against society, the taste which leads him to depict the ugliness of life and the soul without restraint . . . without shame, epitomize the literature of cruelty.
33 *Lettres . . . à Jean-Louis Barrault*, p. 96.
34 *OC*, vol. 2, p. 38.
35 Letter to Roger Vitrac (undated), cit. in Henri Béhar, *Roger Vitrac*, Paris 1966, p. 290. In the same letter Artaud defines his approach as 'the point of view of a stage director . . . theatre is essentially everything that relates to staging'. For a fuller treatment of Artaud's relationship with the surrealists, see J.H. Matthews, *Theatre of Dada and Surrealism*, Syracuse 1974.
36 *OC*, vol. 2, p. 16.
37 Roger Vitrac, *Victor, ou les enfants au pouvoir*, in *Théâtre*, Paris 1946, p. 63.
38 Artaud, letter to *Paris Soir*, 12 December 1928, reprinted in the programme to *Victor*.
39 *Comœdia*, 27 January 1938.
40 Vitrac, *Poison*, in *Théâtre III*, Paris 1964, p. 54.
41 Tristan Tzara (1918), in *The Dada Painters and Poets*, ed. Robert Motherwell, New York 1951, p. 81. For the links between the Parisian dadaists and surrealists see Barrault, *Memories for Tomorrow*, New York 1974, p. 77; and for the ideological implications of the Berlin dadaists see my book on *Erwin Piscator's Political Theatre*, Cambridge 1972, pp. 13ff.
42 Tzara, cit. in René Lacôte, *Tristan Tzara*, Paris 1952, p. 68; and his introduction to Georges Huguet, *L'Aventure Dada*, Paris 1975, p. 7.
43 *OC*, vol. 2, pp. 78–9.
44 *Six Plays of Strindberg*, New York 1955, p. 293.
45 Artaud, Lecture on 'Post war theatre in Paris', *Cahiers Renaud-Barrault*, vol. 71, p. 17; and pp. 10–11.
46 *OC*, vol. 2, pp. 117, 121 and 124.
47 *The Cenci*, pp. 45 and 55.
48 Pierre Jean Jouvé, *Nouvelle Revue Française*, vol. 23, no. 281 (June 1935), p. 94.
49 Interview, 6 June 1935, cit. in Jean-Pierre Faye, 'Artaud vu par Blin', *Lettres Françaises*, 21 January 1965, p. 4; *Comœdia* and *Le Journal*.
50 *Il n'y a plus de firmament*, *OC*, vol. 2, p. 92.
51 *OC*, vol. 2, pp. 131–4.
52 *Ibid.*, pp. 185–6. My italics.
53 André Bellessort, *Le Gaulois*, cit. in Artaud, 'Théâtre Alfred Jarry . . . saison 1929', *OC*, vol. 2, p. 262.
54 Virmaux comments that 'the two media [film and theatre] appear more like twins than opposites in Artaud's mind', but limits his illustration to a brief consideration of the relationship between words and images in *La Révolte du boucher* and *Le Jet de sang* ('Artaud and film', *TDR*, vol. 11, no. 1, pp. 164–5).

Bounoure and Caradec simply state 'it was precisely [Artaud's] long frequentation of the cinema which led to those scenic concepts . . .', but do not elaborate ('Antonin Artaud et le cinéma', *K Revue de la Poésie*, no. 1–2 (June 1948), p. 49. Hayman includes a chapter on 'Film actor and surrealist' in *Artaud and After* (Oxford 1977), but disappointingly it refers to Artaud's film acting hardly at all and makes no mention whatsoever of any possible film influence on his stage work.

55 See Letters to Yvonne Allendy, 21 and 26 March 1929, *OC*, vol. 3, pp. 150ff. Bounoure and Caradec even go so far as to claim that 'it was the introduction of talking-films which determined [Artaud] to drive the theatre into a new road' (*K Revue de la Poésie*, no. 1–2, p. 53).

56 Herbert Jhering, *Drama von Reinhardt bis Brecht*, vol. 1, Reinbeck 1967, pp. 374–5. See also Artaud, 'Sorcellerie et cinéma' and the draft of a letter to Steve Passeur, 12 December 1921, *OC*, vol. 3, pp. 81 and 240.

57 See *OC*, vol. 3, p. 74; 'La Coquille et le clergyman', *Cahiers de Belgique*, no. 8 (October 1928); and *OC*, vol. 2, p. 34.

58 *OC*, vol. 2, p. 91.

59 *OC*, vol. 3, p. 47.

60 *Cinémagazine*, 9 September 1927.

61 Valentin Hugo, 'La Passion de Jeanne d'Arc', *Ciné-Miroir*, 11 November 1927. Falconetti played Joan.

62 Artaud, *The Theatre and its Double*, pp. 79, 116 and 123.

63 Interview for *Cinémonde*, reprinted in *K Revue de la Poésie*, no. 1–2, p. 59.

64 See Artaud, *The Theatre and its Double*, pp. 87 and 94.

65 André Breton, *Anthologie de l'humour noir*, Paris 1966, p. 347.

66 C. G. Jung and K. Kerényi, *Essays on a Science of Mythology*, Princeton 1973, p. 73, and Ernst Cassirer, *The Philosophy of Symbolic Forms*, New Haven 1955, p. 38.

67 Letters to André Gide, 10 February 1935, *OC*, vol. 5, p. 241, and to Germain Dulac, 25 September 1927, cit. in Virmaux, 'Artaud and film', *TDR*, vol 11, no. 1, p. 157.

68 Artaud, *The Theatre and its Double*, pp. 87 and 94–5.

69 *Ibid.*, p. 76, and Letter to Yvonne Allendy, 25 November 1929, *OC*, vol. 3, p. 182.

70 Letter to Louis Jouvet, 1 March 1935, *OC*, vol. 5, p. 252.

71 *Les Dix-huit secondes*, *OC*, vol. 3, pp. 11ff, *La Coquille et la clergyman*, *OC*, vol. 3, pp. 25ff, *Les 32*, *OC*, vol. 3, pp. 30ff, *La Révolte du boucher*, *OC*, vol. 3, p. 50.

72 Martin Esslin, *Artaud*, London 1976, p. 88; Jean-Louis Barrault, cit. in Jean Louis Brau, *Antonin Artaud*, Paris 1971, p. 97; F. Porché, *La Revue de Paris*, vol. 42, no. 10 (May 1935), p. 480.

73 Charles Dullin, 'Lettre à Roger Blin', *K Revue de la Poésie*, no. 1–2, p. 23.

74 Porché, *La Revue de Paris*, vol. 42, no. 10 (May 1935).

75 *OC*, vol. 3, p. 285, and vol. 5, p. 51.

76 *The Jet of Blood*, in *Modern French Theatre* (trans. George Wellwarth), New York 1966, pp. 223 and 226.

77 Artaud, in *Cahiers Renaud-Barrault*, vol. 71, p. 17.

78 *Ibid.*, p. 124.

79 Letter to Yvonne Allendy, 15 April 1929, *OC*, vol. 3, p. 160; note (December 1935) to *Vie et mort de Satan le Feu*, Paris 1953, p. 106. See also 'Après *Les Cenci*', *OC*, vol. 5, p. 54.

80 See Artaud, *The Theatre and its Double*, pp. 27, 30, 35 and 81; *OC*, vol. 2, pp. 186–7 and vol. 4, p. 96.

81 Jean Prudhomme, *Le Matin*; Pierre Audiat, *Paris soir*, 7 May 1935; Jouvé, *Nouvelle Revue Française* (1 June 1935), pp. 914–15.

82 This viewpoint is put forward by Bernard Dort, *Théâtre public*, p. 245, and Jacques Derrida, 'La Parole souffle', *Tel Quel*, no. 20 (Winter 1965), p. 64, though both make the mistake of assuming that Artaud's theoretic statements about an 'elemental theatre' represent his actual stage aims.

83 See *OC*, vol. 2, pp. 38, 42 and 269–70, and Paul Claudel, cit. in Henri Peyre, *Yale French Studies*, vol. 14, p. 95.

84 *OC*, vol. 3, pp. 46–7.

85 *OC*, vol. 2, p. 39 and vol. 5, pp. 241 and 358. In spite of Artaud's insistence that *Les Cenci* was 'an original play . . . not what is called an adaptation' (*OC*, vol. 5, p. 248) this central theme is taken straight from Shelley's version of the story.

86 Max Joly, cit. in Robert Maguire, 'Le "Hors-Théâtre" ', unpublished Ph.D. thesis, Paris, p. 347; *OC*, vol. 5, pp. 241 and 329.

87 Cit. in Maguire, p. 392; *Lettres . . . à Jean-Louis Barrault*, pp. 69–70.

88 Porché, *La Revue de Paris*, vol. 42, no. 10. See also Joly's comment that the first evening of the Théâtre Alfred Jarry 'troubled and disappointed' Artaud because 'the reaction of the audience was not violent' (cit. Maguire, p. 346).

89 *OC*, vol. 2, pp. 185 and 187.

90 *OC*, vol. 5, p. 50.

91 Arnold argues this point. See 'The Artaud experiment', *TDR*, vol. 8, no. 2, pp. 15ff. So does Sellin, who argues that interest in a theatrical form cannot constitute an 'influence' without practical experience in it (*The Dramatic Concepts of Antonin Artaud*, Chicago 1968, p. 51).

92 *OC*, vol. 3, p. 216.

6 RITUAL AND ACTS OF COMMUNION

1 Barrault, *Cahiers Renaud-Barrault*, vols. 22–3.

2 Artaud, 'Post war theatre in Paris' (Mexico 1936), *Cahiers Renaud-Barrault*, vol. 71 (1970), p. 18.

3 Jean-Louis Barrault, *Memories for Tomorrow*, New York 1974, p. 74; *Cahiers Renaud-Barrault*, vol. 69, p. 18; and interview in Bettina Knapp, *Off-Stage Voices*, New York 1975, pp. 41–2.

4 Breton, *Anthologie de l'humour noir*, Paris 1966, p. 347; Barrault, *Theatre Quarterly*, vol. 3, no. 10 (1973), p. 5.

5 Barrault, *Memories for Tomorrow*, p. 297; *Télé-Médecine*, 25 October 1975; *Theatre Quarterly*, vol. 3, no. 10, p. 3.

6 Artaud, *The Theatre and its Double* (trans. Mary Richards), New York 1958, p. 145.

7 *Autour d'une mère*, production script in *Cahiers Renaud-Barrault*, vol. 71, pp. 23ff.

8 Barrault, *Memories for Tomorrow*, p. 67.

9 *Ibid.*, p. 101.

10 Barrault, *Cahiers Renaud-Barrault*, vol. 69, p. 18, Dullin, *Souvenirs et notes de travail d'un acteur*, p. 60. It is also significant that Claudel's work, which formed the basis of Barrault's 'total theatre', was originally linked to the symbolist movement, *L'Annonce fait à Marie* and *L'Otage* being first performed by Lugné-Poe (1912 and 1914).

11 Paul Claudel, 'Modern drama and music' (1930), reprinted in *Total Theatre*, ed. E.T. Kirby, New York 1969, pp. 202 and 206. In Barrault's 1953 production of *Christopher Colombus* some approximation to this ideal was achieved by his acting out the whole play to Milhaud 'square by square, and I would hum to

him whatever came into my head at the exact places where I "heard" music. He would measure this to the second, and we would then discuss the spirit, the human content required of this piece of music' (*Memories for Tomorrow*, p. 190).

12 See Barrault, *Memories for Tomorrow*, pp. 243–4 and 248.
13 Artaud, *The Theatre and its Double*, p. 125; Barrault *Memories for Tomorrow*, p. 191.
14 'L'Acteur: athlète affectif,' *Cahiers Renaud-Barrault*, vol. 29, p. 89.
15 *Memories for Tomorrow*, pp. 89, 208 and 248.
16 Barrault, interview in *France Nouvelle*, 28 October 1970, and Preface to *Rabelais* (trans. Robert Baldick), London 1971, pp. 13 and 16.
17 *Memories for Tomorrow*, p. 328.
18 *Rabelais*, pp. 57–8.
19 Barrault, interview in *Combat*, 30/31 October 1970.
20 *Rabelais*, pp. 118–19; 'An actor's eye view . . .' in *Theatre Quarterly*, vol. 1, no. 3 (1971), p. 83.

7 BLACK MASSES AND CEREMONIES OF NEGATION

1 Bernard Frechtman, Showbill for *The Blacks*, New York 1961.
2 See Norman Mailer, *The Village Voice*, 18 May 1961, p. 14; Lucien Goldmann, *Cahiers Renaud-Barrault*, vol. 57 (1966), pp. 90ff.
3 Jean Genet, *The Balcony* (revised edn), New York 1966, pp. 7, 57 and 73–5; and *The Blacks*, New York 1960, pp. 8 and 10.
4 *The Blacks*, pp. 84, 109–10, 99 and 38–9.
5 Roger Blin, in *Off-Stage Voices*, New York 1975, p. 27.
6 *The Maids, Two Plays by Jean Genet*, New York 1962, p. 86; *The Balcony*, pp. 15 and 19.
7 *The Balcony*, p. 82; *The Maids*, p. 63; *The Blacks*, pp. 24, 106 and 107.
8 *Off-Stage Voices*, p. 22, and Genet, *Letters to Roger Blin*, New York 1969, p. 66.
9 Artaud, *The Theatre and its Double* (trans. Mary Richards), New York 1958, p. 103.
10 *The Balcony*, pp. 87–8; Genet, *Miracle de la rose*, Paris 1946, p. 215.
11 Strindberg, *Coram Populo!* (trans. David Scanlan), *TDR (The Drama Review/ Tulane Drama Review)*, vol. 6, no. 2, pp. 128ff.
12 *Letters to Roger Blin*, p. 21, and *The Screens*, New York 1966, p. 190.
13 *Letters to Roger Blin*, p. 14, and *Off-Stage Voices*, pp. 38–9.
14 Genet, 1954 preface to *The Maids, TDR*, vol. 7, no. 3, p. 40; Blin in *Off-Stage Voices*, pp. 28–9.
15 *Letters to Roger Blin*, pp. 13, 27, 29 and 61.
16 *TDR*, vol. 7, no. 3, pp. 37–9.
17 See Rose Zimbardo, *Modern Drama*, no. 8 (1965), p. 247; Oreste Pucciani, *TDR*, vol. 7, no. 3, p. 44; Robert Kanters, in *The Theatre of Jean Genet*, ed. Richard Coe, New York 1970, p. 120.
18 See Frantz Fanon, *The Wretched of the Earth: Black Skins, White Masks* (trans. Charles Markman), New York 1967, p. 31.
19 *The Balcony*, p. 10; *Letters to Roger Blin*, p. 51; *The Screens*, pp. 179 and 190.
20 *The Maids*, pp. 41, 42, 43, 62 and 84.
21 *The Screens*, p. 86.
22 *The Blacks*, p. 12.
23 Blin, in *Off-Stage Voices*, pp. 25–6.
24 1954 preface to *The Maids, TDR*, vol. 7, no. 3, p. 39.
25 Fernando Arrabal, interview in Swerling, *Strindberg's Influence in France*, p. 167.
26 Arrabal, in *Off-Stage Voices*, pp. 85 and 93.

27 Arrabal, 'Auto-Interview', *TDR*, vol. 13, no. 1, pp. 74–5, and 'Dialogue with Arrabal', *Evergreen Review*, no. 15 (November/December 1960), p. 71.
28 *Arrabal: Plays III*, London 1970, pp. 24, 88 and 92.
29 *Ibid.*, pp. 30 and 71.
30 Jacques Lemarchand, *Figaro Littéraire*. See *Off-Stage Voices*, p. 87; *Arrabal: Plays III (The Grand Ceremonial)*, pp. 104–5.
31 Lindsay Kemp, interview with the author, Toronto 1978.
32 *Ibid.*

8 MYTH AND THEATRE LABORATORIES

1 Jean Cocteau, in *Modern French Theatre*, pp. 96–7. See also Peter Brook, introduction to Jean Anouilh, *Ring Around the Moon* (trans. Christopher Fry): 'Anouilh . . . conceives his plays as ballets, as patterns of movements . . . he is a poet of words-acted, of scenes-set, of players-performing' (p. vii).
2 Peter Brook, *Encore*, November 1960, p. 11, and *Encore*, July–August 1961, pp. 8–10.
3 See Peter Brook, *The Empty Space*, Harmondsworth 1972, pp. 97–8 and 151; and interview in *Theatre Quarterly*, vol. 3, no. 10 (1973), p. 16.
4 Brook and Charles Marowitz, *Sunday Times*, 12 January 1964; Marowitz, *TDR (The Drama Review/Tulane Drama Review)*, vol. 11, no. 2, p. 156, and LAMDA programme note.
5 *The Empty Space*, p. 55; *TDR*, vol. 11, no. 2, p. 155.
6 Clive Barker, cit. in Geoffrey Reeves and Albert Hunt, *Peter Brook*, Cambridge 1993.
7 Tom Milne, in *Encore*, July–August 1964, pp. 23–4.
8 For a detailed discussion of the various productions of Peter Weiss' *Marat/Sade*, see my *Modern German Drama*, Cambridge 1979, pp. 157f.
9 Brook, *Plays and Players*, February 1964, p. 21.
10 John Kane (Puck in Brook's *Dream* production), *Sunday Times*, 13 June 1971.
11 Marowitz, 'Lear log,' *TDR*, vol. 8, no. 2, p. 103.
12 Brook, *Theater Heute*, no. 2 (1965) p. 9.
13 These were derived from a radio series, assembled by A. L. Lloyd, called (significantly) 'The Voice of the Gods'.
14 David Turner, programme note, National Theatre, March 1968; and Director's Notes, National Theatre archives.
15 Marowitz, *TDR*, vol. 11, no. 2, p. 156.
16 Colin Blakely (Creon), *TDR*, vol. 13, no. 3, p. 121.
17 Brook, interview in *TDR*, vol. 17, no. 3 (1973), p. 47.
18 *Ibid.*, p. 50.
19 See Brook, *The Empty Space*, p. 106.
20 Marowitz, *Plays and Players*, February 1964, pp. 20–2; and *TDR*, vol. 11, no. 2, p. 157.
21 Blakely, *TDR*, vol. 13, no. 2, pp. 120–1.
22 Ted Hughes, interview in *The Times Literary Supplement*, 1 October 1971.
23 *Ibid.*; and A.C.H. Smith, *Orghast at Persepolis*, London 1972, pp. 43–4.
24 See Ilia Zdanévitch, *Ledentu le Phare, poème dramatique en Zaoum*, editions du 41, 1922; Tristan Tzara, *Oeuvres complètes*, vol. 1 (1912–1924), Paris 1975, p. 77; *Orghast*, cit. in A. C. H. Smith, *Orghast at Persepolis*, p. 50.
25 Claude Lévi-Strauss, *The Raw and the Cooked*, New York 1969, vol. 1, p. 12.
26 A. C. H. Smith, *Orghast at Persepolis*, p. 119; and Geoffrey Reeves, cit. on p. 181.
27 See John Heilpern, *Conference of the Birds: The Story of Peter Brook in Africa*, London 1979, *passim*.

28 Brook, interview with Michael Gibson, *The Drama Review*, vol. 17, no. 3 (September 1973), p. 50.

29 Colin Turnbull, *The Mountain People*, London 1974, pp. 11 and 294.

30 Benedict Nightingale, *The New Statesman*, 23 January 1976, p. 110.

31 Brook, Introduction to *The Mahabharata*, New York 1987, pp. xvi, xiv and xv.

32 *Ibid.*, p. xiii.

33 *The Mahabharata*, pp. 3 and 41, 167, 189–91.

34 *Ibid.*, pp. 3, 19–20, 119 and 238.

35 *Ibid.*, pp. 34, 136, and 158–61.

9 SECULAR RELIGIONS AND PHYSICAL SPIRITUALITY

1 Jerzy Grotowski, *TDR* (*The Drama Review*/*Tulane Drama Review*), vol. 17, no. 2, p. 133.

2 Grotowski, *Towards a Poor Theatre*, New York 1968, p. 19.

3 *Ibid.*, pp. 41 and 63; and *TDR*, vol. 14, no. 1, p. 176.

4 Eugenio Barba, in *Towards a Poor Theatre*, p. 84.

5 Grotowski, *Theatre Quarterly*, vol. 3, no. 10, p. 24; *Towards a Poor Theatre*, p. 46.

6 *Towards a Poor Theatre*, pp. 16 and 131.

7 See Serge Ouaknine, *Les Voies de la création théâtrale*, Paris 1970, vol 1, p. 115, and Raymonde Temkine, *Grotowski*, New York 1972, p. 60.

8 Eugenio Barba, *TDR*, vol. 9, no. 3, p. 155.

9 *Towards a Poor Theatre*, pp. 119–20; Artaud, *The Theatre and its Double* (trans. Mary Richards), New York 1958, p. 58. Another point of similarity is in Grotowski's use of 'resonators' in different parts of the body, channelling the voice through diaphragm, stomach, back, shoulders and the top of the skull to develop the actor's whole body into an expressive instrument – a concept outlined by Artaud in 'An affective athleticism': 'The important thing is to become aware of the localization of emotive thought. One means of recognition is effort or tension; and the same points that support physical effort are those which also support the emanation of emotive thought: they serve as a springboard for the emanation of a feeling' (*The Theatre and its Double*, p. 138).

10 See Emile Copfermann and Michael Kustow, cit. in Temkine, *Grotowski*, pp. 21 and 143.

11 Grotowski, *TDR*, vol. 13, no. 1, pp. 33 and 36.

12 Barba, programme notes to *Dr Faustus*, in *Towards a Poor Theatre*, pp. 79 and 86.

13 Grotowski, *Towards a Poor Theatre*, p. 34.

14 Barba, *TDR*, vol. 9, no. 3, p. 154.

15 Grotowski, *Towards a Poor Theatre*, p. 37, and *TDR*, vol. 13, no. 1, p. 44.

16 Barba, *TDR*, vol. 9, no. 3, p. 163; Grotowski, cit. *ibid.*, p. 159.

17 Serge Ouaknine, *The Constant Prince*, text and extended stage directions, *Theater Heute*, no. 8 (1971), pp. 34ff. (The lines are Fernando's speech to Muley in scene 3 of the original.) For a full eyewitness description of the rehearsal process and performance, see Ouaknine, *Les Voies de la création théâtrale*, vol. 1.

18 Programme note, in *Towards a Poor Theatre*, p. 97.

19 Grotowski, *Towards a Poor Theatre*, p. 257.

20 *Ibid.*, p. 22.

21 See Josef Kelera, cit. in *Towards a Poor Theatre*, p. 109; Temkine, *Grotowski*, pp. 27, 31 and 136; Ouaknine, *Theater Heute*, no. 8 (1971), p. 33.

22 Interview in *Tygodnik Demokratyczny*, no. 13 (1970), cit. in Jennifer Kumiega, *The Theatre of Grotowski*, London 1985, p. 99.

23 Grotowski, *TDR*, vol. 14, no. 1, p. 177.

24 Grotowski, Conference in New York, 12 December 1970, cit. in *TDR*, vol. 17, no. 2, p. 120; and *TDR*, vol. 14, no. 1, p. 177.
25 Grotowski, in *Dialectics and Humanism*, Warsaw Spring 1980, p. 19; and interview in *Trybuna Ludu*, no. 252 (1976), cit. in Kumiega, *The Theatre of Grotowski*, p. 201.
26 Grotowski, Press conference in New York, 15 October 1973, cit. in *TDR*, vol. 19, no. 4, p. 61. For a detailed acount of the different versions of *Apocalypsis cum Figuris*, see Kumiega, *The Theatre of Grotowski*, pp. 98–105.
27 See Grotowski, *Towards a Poor Theatre*, p. 40.
28 Grotowski, Press conference in New York, 15 October 1973.
29 See Richard Mennen, *TDR*, vol. 19, no. 4, p. 66.
30 Descriptions have been published by Mennen, *TDR*, December 1975, p. 68, by Dan Ronnen, *TDR*, vol. 22, no. 4, p. 75, and by Kumiega, *The Theatre of Grotowski*, pp. 160ff. Compare Arnold Van Gennep, *The Rites of Passage*, Chicago 1960, pp. 89ff and Jane Harrison, *Prolegomena to the Study of Greek Religion*, Cambridge 1903, pp. 151ff. For an anthropologist's analysis of Grotowski's 'special projects', see Ronald L. Grimes, 'Route to the Mountains', *New Directions in Performing Arts*, December 1976.
31 Grotowski, *TDR*, vol. 17, no. 2, pp. 133–4, and *TDR*, vol. 22, no. 4, p. 68.
32 Group declaration, *Gazeta Robotnicza*, 28 January 1984, cit. in Kumiega, *The Theatre of Grotowski*, p. 214; and Ryszard Cieślak, cit. in Richard Mennen, *TDR*, December 1975, p. 69 (my italics).

10 ANTHROPOLOGY, ENVIRONMENTAL THEATRE AND SEXUAL REVOLUTION

1 See Frédéric Baal, *TDR* (*The Drama Review/Tulane Drama Review*), vol. 16, no. 4, p. 102.
2 See Grotowski, *TDR*, vol. 14, no. 1, pp. 173 and 177.
3 See *TDR*, vol. 14, no. 1, p. 54; and Barba, *A Dictionary of Theatre Anthropology* (E. Barba and N. Savarese), London 1991, p. 5.
4 Barba, *TDR*, vol. 14, no. 1, p. 56.
5 An outline of the scenario for *Kaspariana* has been published in *TDR*, vol. 13, no. 1, pp. 46ff.
6 Barba, *TDR*, vol. 9, no. 3, p. 164; and *TDR*, vol. 19, no. 4, p. 57.
7 Eugenio Barba, *Beyond the Floating Islands*, New York 1986, pp. 182, 187, 263, and 267.
8 *Ibid.*, pp. 184 and 263.
9 See Richard Schechner, *TDR*, vol. 5, no. 4, pp. 124ff.
10 These were three of the subjects that Schechner identified as areas which would be particularly fruitful for the main thrust of avant garde theatre. Others were the analysis of 'performance' in everyday activities (Goffman) and aspects of psychotherapy that emphasize person-to-person interaction and body awareness, both of which relate to his later work. See *TDR*, vol. 17, no. 4, pp. 5ff. This is also reflected in his *Ritual, Play and Performance* (New York 1976), a collection of essays by anthropologists and sociologists (with the avant garde represented only by Grotowski and himself!), that covers five areas listed as 'Ethology', 'Play', 'Ritual and performance in everyday life', 'Shamanism, trance, meditation' and 'Rites, ceremonies, performances'.
11 See Schechner, *Theatre Quarterly*, vol. 1, no. 20 (1971), pp. 51ff, and *Environmental Theatre*, New York 1973, pp. 55, 82, 101, 114 and 176.
12 See *Rites of Passage*, p. 185, and Schechner, *Environmental Theatre*, p. 253.
13 See *Environmental Theatre*, pp. 44 and 206. See also Julian Beck's comment on the standard of performance in the Living Theatre, p. 190 in this volume.

14 All quotations from the script are taken from The Performance Group, *Dionysus in 69*, New York 1970, unpaginated.
15 *Environmental Theatre*, p. 83.
16 For a more detailed discussion of Peter Stein's work, see my book on *Modern German Drama, A Study in Form*, Cambridge 1979, pp. 145ff.
17 The few remaining members of Schechner's 'commune' continued to perform as the Wooster Group.
18 Richard Schechner, *Between Theatre and Anthropology*, Philadelphia 1985, pp. 265, 270, 272, 286 and 281.
19 For a full discussion of the Open Theatre's work, see Eileen Blumenthal, *Joseph Chaikin*, Cambridge 1984.
20 See *Environmental Theatre*, pp. 191, 219, 222 and 223. More recently Schechner has developed his 'subjective' theatre in a way that concentrates solely on 'the psychology of perception', producing plays like David Gaard's *The Marilyn Project* in which the action is 'consciously made multivocal and ambivalent', with two sets of actors playing the same scenes simultaneously on a split stage – an extension of the 'mirror exercise' that both he and Peter Brook developed independently to 'raise the consciousness' of the performer and to act as a paradigm of the feed-back between performer and spectator. In Schechner's view this corresponds to the stucturalism of Lévi-Strauss.
21 *TDR*, vol. 17, no. 4, p. 4, and *Environmental Theatre*, p. 236.
22 Artaud's theory of 'cruelty' was reinterpreted to correspond to their own pre-occupations: 'Artaud believed that if we could only be made to feel, really feel anything, then we might find all this suffering intolerable, the pain too great to bear, we might put an end to it, and then being able to feel we might truly feel the joy, the joy of everything else, of loving, of creating, of being at peace, and of being ourselves' (Julian Beck, introduction to Kenneth H. Brown, *The Brig*, New York 1965). Beck in *We, The Living Theatre*, ed. Aldo Rostagno, New York 1970, p. 81.
23 Judith Malina and Julian Beck, *Paradise Now*, New York 1971, pp. 16 and 77.
24 See *We, The Living Theatre*, pp. 9 and 23–4, *Paradise Now*, p. 20, 'Notes to *Paradise Now*', *TDR*, vol. 13, no. 3, pp. 97 and 103.
25 Beck, cit. in William Glover, *Theatre Arts*, December 1961, and *TDR*, vol. 13, no. 3, pp. 25 and 42.
26 *Paradise Now*, pp. 27, and 79–80. Other examples were the so-called, 'revolutionary slogans' in *Mysteries*, 'Abolish money, Abolish police, Change the world, Fuck for peace . . .', *We, the Living Theatre*, p. 80.
27 *The Brig*, pp. 45–6.
28 *Paradise Now*, p. 75.
29 Beck, cit. in Pierre Biner, *The Living Theatre*, New York 1972, p. 89.
30 *Paradise Now*, pp. 3 and 75–6.
31 Cit. in Biner, *The Living Theatre*, p. 48, and cit. in Jan Kott, *TDR*, vol. 14, no. 1, p. 23. However, their production of *The Maids* was an exception, completely conventional in staging.
32 'Notes to *Paradise Now*,' *TDR*, vol. 13, no. 3, p. 91.
33 *Paradise Now*, p. 105, and Beck, cit. in Biner, *The Living Theatre*, p. 93. See also *TDR*, vol. 13, no. 3, p. 43, where Beck proposes the systematic use of psychedelic drugs to 'enable one to begin to associate differently in the head, remember differently, learn time differently'.
34 Beck, introduction to *The Brig*, p. 31.
35 *TDR*, vol. 13, no. 3, p. 41.
36 *Paradise Now*, p. 15.

37 See Malina, cit. in Biner, *The Living Theatre*, p. 181; Van Gennep, *Rites of Passage*, p. 170.

38 *Paradise Now*, pp. 27, 61, 65, 95–6, 125–7 and 140.

39 Eliade (citing material collected by Negelein, Frazer and Frobenius), *Myths, Rites, Symbols*, vol. 1, pp. 234ff, 242–3 and 240.

40 *Paradise Now*, pp. 63–4 and 111.

41 Malina, *TDR*, vol. 13, no. 3, pp. 30–1. (In the opening scene of *Frankenstein* the actors seriously attempted to make one of their number levitate, though in fact the whole play was predicated on the failure of this mystical attempt to defy physical laws.)

42 *Paradise Now*, pp. 23, 44, 125.

43 Beck and Malina, interview in Biner, *The Living Theatre*, pp. 92–4, and *TDR*, vol. 13, no. 3, p. 42.

44 Scripts of these productions and comments by Beck and Malina have been published in *TDR*, vol. 19, no. 3, pp. 80ff and 94ff.

11 INTERCULTURALISM AND EXPROPRIATING THE CLASSICS

1 See Ruby Cohn, *Modern Shakespearean Offshoots*, Princeton, New Jersey 1976, p. 7.

2 Edward Bond, interview in *Gambit*, no. 17, p. 24. See also Shaw's preface to *Caesar and Cleopatra*: 'Better than Shakespeare?' or Brecht's rationale for adapting Marlowe: 'We wanted a production that would break with the Shakespeare tradition of the German theatre – that plaster-monument style so dear to the bourgeoisie' (*Gesamte Werke*, vol. 17, p. 951).

3 Marowitz, *Theatre Quarterly*, vol. 1, no. 3 (1971), pp. 48–9; Schechner, *Makbeth*, New York 1978, pp. xvi, xiv.

4 Marowitz, *Theatre Quarterly*, vol. 1, no. 3 (1971), p. 49, *A Macbeth*, London 1971, p. 15, and *TDR* (*The Drama Review/Tulane Drama Review*), vol. 11, no. 2, p. 156.

5 Schechner, Paul Epstein, Brooks McNamara, *Makbeth*, pp. vii, xii, xxii and 25.

6 Ionesco, *Macbett*, London 1973, pp. 91, 21–2 and 23.

7 Ionesco, interview, *New York Times*, 18 January 1972.

8 Heiner Müller, *Theater der Zeit*, no. 8 (1975), pp. 58 and 59; interview in *Theater Heute*, Sonderheft 1975, p. 120.

9 Müller, *Macbeth*, in *Theater Heute*, June 1972, pp. 40, 45, 46 and 47.

10 Müller, in *Schauspiel*, Frankfurt September 1975, pp. 23–4; Wilson, cit. in *New York Times*, 20 May 1990, p. 36; and in *Practice*, vol. 5, no. 2 (1987), pp. 4 and 8. (Wilson tends to reuse the same illustrations and repeat the same points, in very similar words, in interview after interview during the 1980s: for instance, many of the exact phrases here recur in the 1985 programme for the ART *CIVIL warS*.)

11 Müller, *Die Schlacht*, in *Theater Heute*, Sonderheft 1975, p. 131.

12 Müller, *Theater Heute*, Jahrbuch 1988, pp. 26 and 27.

13 Robert Wilson, in *TDR*, vol. 20, no. 1, p. 109: note the correspondence between this and Wilson's 1987 definition of 'meaning' *per se*, cited on p. 199 of this volume.

14 Wilson, in *The New York Times*, 16 March 1975; and in *Practice*, vol. 5, no. 2 (1987), p. 116.

15 Excerpts from the text for *KA MOUNTAIN AND GUARDenia Terrace* were printed as part of the 1972 Shiraz Festival programme.

16 Müller in conversation with Wilson, in *Modern Drama*, March 1988, pp. 455

and 457; Wilson, in *Practice*, vol. 5, no. 2, p. 127; Müller, programme note for *Quartette*, ART 1987–8 season.

17 Wilson, in *Practice*, vol. 5, no. 2, p. 126; Müller, programme note to the ART 1985 production, p. 23.

18 Wilson, interview in ART programme for *CIVIL warS*, 1985, pp. 16–17.

19 See, for example, *NewsWeek*, 18 March 1985, *The New York Review*, 11 April 1985.

20 Insert to ART programme for *CIVIL warS* III E and IV A, Boston 1985; and programme note for *CIVIL warS* Act V, Brooklyn Academy 1987.

21 *Ibid.*, p. 18.

22 Wilson, cit. in Arthur Holmberg, *The Antioch Review*, vol. 44, no. 2 (1986), p. 228.

23 Ariane Mnouchkine, cit. in Marie-louise and Denis Bablet, *Le Théâtre du Soleil ou la quête du bonheur*, Ivry 1979, p. 46b.

24 *Théâtre du Soleil, L'Age d'or, Première ebauche, Texte program*, Paris 1975, p. 13.

25 Mnouchkine, cit. *Le Soir*, 20–22 July 1984.

26 Mnouchkine, cit. in *Theatre/Public*, July-October 1982, p. 82.

27 For a more extensive discussion of these and other Théâtre du Soleil productions, see Adrian Kiernander, *Ariane Mnouchkine*, Cambridge 1993, to whose interpretation much of this analysis is indebted.

28 For an analysis of the process of orientalization, see Edward Said, *Orientalism*, London 1978.

29 Hélène Cixous, interviewed by Kiernander, 22 January 1988; Mnouchkine, in *Marie Claire*, April 1986, p. 100.

12 FROM THE MARGINS TO MAINSTREAM

1 Eugène Ionesco, in *Cahiers Renaud-Barrault*, vol. 69 (1969), pp. 22–23 and 27.

2 Ionesco, *Present Past, Past Present*, New York 1971, pp. 150–1 and 154; *Notes and Counter Notes*, New York 1964, pp. 164–5.

3 *Notes and Counter Notes*, pp. 257 and 131; *Present Past Past Present*, pp. 54–5.

4 Ionesco, in *Theater Heute*, November 1968, pp. 8–9.

5 *Notes and Counter Notes*, pp. 16, 92 and 219–20; *Plays III*, London 1960, p. 150.

6 Ann Jellicoe, Preface to *The Sport of My Mad Mother*, London 1964, p. 5, and *Some Unconscious Influences in the Theatre*, Cambridge 1967, pp. 18 and 21.

7 Sam Shepard, in *Rolling Thunder Logbook*, New York 1978, pp. 31–2.

8 Sam Shepard, *Seven Plays*, New York 1981, pp. 226 and 251.

9 Sam Shepard, *Fool for Love and Other Plays*, New York 1984, pp. 147, 156–7 and 164–5.

10 Shepard, *Four Two Act Plays*, New York 1980, pp. 179, 211, 214 and 217–18.

11 *Fool for Love and Other Plays*, pp. 72, 74, 97 and 108.

12 John Juliani, cit. in *Theatre Quarterly*, vol. 5, no. 20 (1975), p. 160.

13 The one and only performance of *The Sky is Falling* was documented, with excerpts from the scenario, by Richard Schechner in *Theatre Quarterly*, vol. 1, no. 2, pp. 59ff.

14 A descriptive commentary on the performance, by its author, was published in *TDR (The Drama Review/Tulane Drama Review)*, vol. 14, no. 4, pp. 53ff.

15 David Rudkin, in *Plays and Players*, February 1964, p. 17.

16 David Rudkin, *The Sons of Light*, London 1981, p. 31; *The Triumph of Death*, London 1981, pp. 1 and 29.

17 *The Sons of Light*, pp. 9, 57, 66, 76–7 and 78.

18 *Plays and Players*, May 1976, pp. 25 and 26; Antonin Artaud, *The Theatre and its Double* (trans. Mary Richards), New York 1958, pp. 82f.

19 Peter Shaffer, *The Royal Hunt of the Sun*, London 1964, pp. viii and 79.
20 Shaffer, *Equus and Shrivings*, New York 1975, p. 9. Compare with p. 152 in this volume.
21 Shaffer, interview in *The Sunday Times*, 29 July 1973.
22 For a discussion of the links between avant garde theatre and Meredith Monk or Ann Halprin, see Christopher Innes, *Holy Theatre*, Cambridge 1984, pp. 247–51.
23 R. Murray Shafer, *Canadian Theatre Review*, vol. 47 (Summer 1986), pp. 5 and 14.
24 Shafer, *Canadian Theatre Review*, vol. 55 (Summer 1988), p. 37.
25 Shafer, *Canadian Theatre Review*, vol. 47, pp. 23, 24, 25 and 26.

SELECT BIBLIOGRAPHY

Complete bibliographical references are provided in the notes to each chapter. This bibliography is therefore limited to selected primary texts that occupy a significant place in the discussion, and to general critical studies, including those which were of use in preparing this book, but which are not cited in the text.

PRIMARY SOURCES

Dramatic scripts

Arrabal, Fernando, *Plays, 3 vols* (trans. Barbara Wright), London 1962.
Artaud, Antonin, *The Jet of Blood in Modern French Theatre* (trans. George Wellwarth), New York 1966.
—— *The Cenci* (trans. S. Watson Taylor), London 1969.
Attar, Farid Ud-din, *The Conference of the Birds* (adaptation by Jean-Claude Carrière and Peter Brook), Connecticut 1982.
Barrault, Jean-Louis, *Rabelais* (trans. Robert Baldick), London 1971.
Beck, Julian, *Paradise Now: Collective Creation of the Living Theatre*, New York 1971.
Brown, K. *The Brig, a Concept for Theatre or Film*, New York 1965.
Cannan, Denis and Higgins, Colin, *The Ik* (with introduction by Colin Turnbull), Connecticut 1982.
Carrière, Jean-Claude, *The Mahabharata* (trans. with an introduction by Peter Brook), New York 1987.
Cixous, Hélène, *L'Indiade, ou, L'Inde de leurs rêves; et quelques écrits sur le théâtre*, Tours 1987.
—— *L'histoire terrible mais inachevée de Norodom Sihanouk, roi du Cambodge*, Paris 1987.
Genet, Jean, *The Balcony* (trans. Bernard Frechtman), New York 1966.
—— *The Screens* (trans. Bernard Frechtman), New York 1966.
Hughes, Ted, *Oedipus* (adapted from Seneca), London 1969.
Hunt, Albert, Kustow, Michael and Reeves, Geoffrey (eds), *US*, London 1968.
Ionesco, Eugène, *Plays*, vols 1–3 (trans. Donald Watson), London 1958–60.
—— *Macbett* (trans. Charles Marowitz), New York 1973.
Jarry, Alfred, *Selected Works of Alfred Jarry* (trans. R. Shattack and S. Watson Taylor), London 1965.
—— *The Ubu Plays* (trans. Cyril Connolly and S. Watson Taylor), London 1968.
—— *Ubu aux Bouffes* (adapted by Peter Brook), Paris 1977.
Kaiser, George, *From Morn to Midnight* (trans. Ashley Dukes), New York 1922.
Kornfeld, Paul, *Anthology of German Expressionist Drama* (trans. and ed. W. H. Sokel), New York 1963.

Maeterlinck, Maurice, *Théâtre II*, Paris 1904.
Müller, Heiner, *Macbeth*, in *Theatre Heute*, June 1972.
—— *Die Schlacht*, in *Theater Heute*, Sonderheft 1975.
Ouaknine, Serge, *The Constant Prince*, in *Theater Heute*, no. 8, 1971.
Performance Group, The, *Dionysus in 69*, New York 1970.
Ritchie, J. M. and Garten, H. F. (eds), *Seven Expressionist Plays: Kokoschka to Barlach*, London 1980.
Rudkin, David, *The Sons of Light*, London 1981.
—— *The Triumph of Death*, London 1981.
Shaffer, Peter, *The Royal Hunt of the Sun*, London 1964.
—— *Equus and Shrivings*, New York 1975.
Schechner, Richard, *Makbeth*, New York 1978.
Shepard, Sam, *Four Two Act Plays*, New York 1980.
—— *Seven Plays*, New York 1981.
—— *Fool for Love and Other Plays*, New York 1984.
Sokel, Walter (ed.), *An Anthology of German Expressionist Drama*, New York 1963.
Sorge, Richard, *Der Bettler*, Berlin 1912.
Strindberg, August, *The Plays of Strindberg*, vols 1–4 (trans. Michael Meyer), London 1964–75.
Toller, Ernst, *Seven Plays by Ernst Toller*, New York 1936.
Unruh, Fritz von, *Ein Geschlect*, Leipzig 1918.
Vitrac, Roger, *Théâtre*, Paris 1964.

Theoretical writings (by the artists discussed)

Appia, Adolphe, *Die Musik und die Inscenierung*, Munich 1899.
Artaud, Antonin, *Vie et Mort de Satan le Feu*, Paris 1953.
—— *The Theatre and its Double* (trans. Mary Richards), New York 1958.
—— *Artaud: Anthology* (ed. Jack Hirschman), San Francisco 1965.
—— *Les Tarahumaras*, Paris 1987.
Barba, Eugenio, *Beyond the Floating Islands*, New York 1986.
—— and Savarese, Nicola, *A Dictionary of Theatre Anthropology*, London 1991.
Barrault, Jean-Louis, *Memories for Tomorrow* (trans. Jonathan Griffin), New York 1974.
Beck, Julian, *The Life of the Theatre: The Relation of the Artist to the Struggle of People*, San Francisco 1972.
Brook, Peter, *The Empty Space*, Harmondsworth 1968.
—— *The Shifting Point*, New York 1987.
Franck, André (ed.), *Lettres d'Antonin Artaud à Jean-Louis Barrault*, Paris 1952.
Genet, Jean, *Letters to Roger Blin* (trans. Richard Seaver), New York 1969.
Grotowski, Jerzy, *Towards a Poor Theatre*, New York 1968.
Hirschman, Jack (ed.), *Artaud Anthology*, San Francisco 1965.
Ionesco, Eugène, *Notes and Counter Notes* (trans. Donald Watson), New York 1964.
—— *Present Past Past Present: A Personal Memoir* (trans. Helen R. Lane), New York 1971.
—— *Entre la vie et la rêve: entretiens avec Claude Bonnefoy*, Paris 1977.
—— *Fragments of a Journal* (trans. Jean Stewart), London 1987.
Jacques-Dalcroze, Emile, *Rhythm, Music and Education*, London 1921.
Jellicoe, Anne, *Some Unconscious Influences in the Theatre*, Cambridge 1967.
Kokoschka, Oskar, *My Life* (trans. David Britt), London 1974.
Malina, Judith, *The Diaries of Judith Malina*, New York 1984.
Marowitz, Charles, *Confessions of a Counterfeit Critic*, London 1973.
—— *The Art of Being*, London 1978.

Miesel, Victor H., *Voices of German Expressionism*, New Jersey 1970.

Rostagno, Aldo, with Beck, Julian and Malina, Judith, *We, The Living Theatre*, New York 1970.

Schechner, Richard, *Environmental Theatre*, New York 1978.

—— *Between Theatre and Anthropology*, Philadelphia 1985.

—— *Performance Theory*, New York 1988.

—— *By Means of Performance: Intercultural Studies of Theatre and Ritual*, New York 1990.

Strindberg, August, *Open Letters to the Intimate Theatre*, Washington 1966.

Documentation

Barrault, Jean-Louis, *Cahiers Renaud-Barrault*, Paris 1953-.

—— *Les Voies de la Création Théâtral*, Paris 1970-.

Beck, Julian, *The Living Book of the Living Theatre*, Connecticut 1971.

Heilpern, John, *Conference of the Birds: The Story of Peter Brook in Africa*, London 1979.

Kirby, E. T. *Total Theatre*, New York 1969.

Motherwell, Robert (ed.), *The Dada Painters and Poets*, New York 1951.

Raabe, Paul (ed.), *The Era of German Expressionism* (trans. J. M. Ritchie), Woodstock, NY 1974.

Rockwell, John (ed.), *Robert Wilson and the Theatre of Images*, New York 1984.

Rubin, William (ed.), *'Primitivism' in 20th Century Art: Affinity of the Tribal and the Modern*, New York 1984.

Selbourne, David, *The Making of* A Midsummer Night's Dream, London 1982.

Smith, A. C., *Orghast at Persepolis*, London 1972.

Williams, David, *In Search of a Lost Theatre: The Story of Peter Brook's Centre*, Paris 1986.

—— *Peter Brook: A Theatrical Casebook*, London 1988.

SECONDARY SOURCES

General

Allen, Roy, *Literary Life in German Expressionism and the Berlin Circles*, Michigan 1983.

Ansimov, A. F., *Studies in Siberian Shamanism*, Toronto 1963.

Baas, George, *Essays on Primitivism and Related Ideas*, New York 1986.

Bakhtin, Mikhail, *Rabelais and his World* (trans. Helene Iswolsky, Cambridge, Mass. 1968.

Benson, Timothy, *Berlin Dada*, Michigan 1987.

Calmesco, Matei, *Five Faces of Modernity*, Durham 1987.

Cassirer, Ernst, *Language and Myth*, New York 1949.

Dobrez, A. C., *The Existential and its Texts*, London 1986.

Edschmid, Kasimir, *Uber den Expressionismus in der Literatur*, Berlin 1917.

—— *Uber Lyrischen Expressionismus*, Berlin 1917.

Eliade, Mircea, *Myths, Rites, Symbols*, vol. 1, New York 1971.

Fachereau, Serge, *Expressionisme, dada, surréalisme et autres issues*, Paris 1976.

Freud, Sigmund, *Collected Papers vol. 4*, London 1925.

Goldwater, Robert John, *Primitivism in Modern Art*, Massachusetts 1986.

Hedges, Inez, *Languages of Revolt: Dada and Surrealist Literature and Film*, Durham, NC 1983.

Huguet, George, *L'aventure Dada*, Paris 1975.

Jung, C. G. and Kerényi, K., *Essays on a Science of Mythology*, Princeton 1937.

Kayser, Wolfgang, *The Grotesque in Art and Literature* (trans. Ulrich Weisstein), Bloomington 1963.
Poggioli, Renato, *The Theory of the Avant Garde*, Massachusetts 1968.
Said, Edward, *Orientalism*, London 1978.
Sokel, Walter, *The Writer in Extremis*, California 1959.
Togorovnick, Mariania, *Gone Primitive*, Chicago 1990.
Van Gennep, Arnold, *The Rites of Passage*, Chicago 1960.

Theatrical

Behar, Henri, *The Théâtre Dada et Surréaliste*, Paris 1979.
Benson, Renata, *German Expressionist Drama: Ernst Toller and Georg Kaiser*, London 1984.
Braun, Edward, *The Director and the Stage*, London 1982.
Daniels, May, *The French Drama of the Unspoken*, Edinburgh 1953.
Dugdale, John, *File on Shepard*, London 1989.
Dullin, Charles, *Souvenirs de travail d'un acteur*, Paris 1946.
Emmel, Felix, *Das Ecstatische Theatre*, Prien 1924.
Esslin, Martin, *The Theatre of the Absurd*, Harmondsworth 1968.
Grace, Sherrill, *Regression and Apocalypse*, Toronto 1989.
Innes, Christopher, *Erwin Piscator's Political Theatre*, Cambridge 1972.
—— *Holy Theatre*, Cambridge 1981, pbk 1984.
Knowles, Dorothy, *French Drama of the Inter-War Years, 1918–39*, London 1967.
Matthews, J. H., *Theatre in Dada and Surrealism*, New York 1974.
Pronko, Leonard, *Avant-Garde: The Experimental Theatre in France*, Berkeley 1962.
—— *Theatre East and West: Perspectives Towards a Total Theatre*, Berkeley 1967.
Richie, James MacPherson, *German Expressionist Drama*, Boston 1977.
Rose, Mark V., *The Actor and his Double: Mime and Movement for the Theatre of Cruelty*, Chicago 1986.
Wellarth, George, *The Theatre of Protest and Paradox*, New York 1964.
Wiles, Timothy, *The Theatre Event: Modern Theories of Performance*, Chicago 1980.
Zoete, Beryl de, *Dance and Drama in Bali*, London 1938.

SUPPLEMENTARY STUDIES OF INDIVIDUAL ARTISTS

Adamov, Arthur, *August Strindberg*, Paris 1955.
Auerbach, Doris, *Sam Shepard and the Off-Broadway Theatre*, Boston 1982.
Bablet, Marie-Louise and Denis, *Le Théâtre du Soleil ou la quête du bonheur*, Ivry 1979.
Beaumont, Keith, *Alfred Jarry: A Critical and Biographical Study*, Leicester 1984.
Beecham, Richard, *Adolphe Appia*, Cambridge 1987.
Besnier, Patrick, *Alfred Jarry*, Paris 1990.
Biner, Pierre, *The Living Theatre*, New York 1972.
Blumenthal, Eileen, *Joseph Chaikin: Exploring the Boundaries of Theatre*, Cambridge 1984.
Borie, Monique, *Antonin Artaud: Le théâtre et le retour aux sources: une approche anthropologique*, Paris 1989.
Braun, Edward, *The Theatre of Meyerhold*, London 1979.
Brecht, Stefan, *The Theatre of Visions: Robert Wilson*, New York 1978.
Coe, Richard (ed.), *The Theatre of Jean Genet*, New York 1970.
Damerval, Gerrard, *Ubu roi: La Bomb Comique de 1896*, Paris 1984.
Dittman, Reidar, *Eros and Psyche: Strindberg and Munch in the 1890s*, Michigan 1982.
Esslin, Martin, *Artaud*, London 1976.
Halls, W. D., *Maurice Maeterlinck*, Oxford 1960.

Hart, Lynda, *Sam Shepard's Metaphysical Stages*, Connecticut 1987.

Hayman, R., *Artaud and After*, Oxford 1977.

Hoffmann, Edith, *Kokoschka: Life and Work*, London 1947.

Kiernander, Adrian, *Ariane Mnouchkine*, Cambridge 1992.

Kumega, Jennifer, *The Theatre of Grotowski*, London 1985.

Lennon, Nigel, *Alfred Jarry: The Man with the Axe*, Los Angeles 1984.

Little, J. P., *Genet: Les nègres*, London 1990.

Neff, Renfrew, *The Living Theatre*, USA 1970.

Schumacher, Claude, *Alfred Jarry and Guillaume Appolinaire*, London 1984.

Sellin, Eric, *The Dramatic Concepts of Antonin Artaud*, Chicago 1968.

Shyer, Laurence, *Robert Wilson and his Collaborators*, New York 1989.

Stewart, Harry E., *Jean Genet: A Biography of Deceit*, New York 1989.

Swerling, Anthony, *Strindberg's Impact on France 1920–60*, Cambridge 1971.

Temkine, Raymond, *Grotowski*, New York 1972.

Tornquist, Peter, *Strindbergian Drama: Themes and Structures*, New Jersey 1982.

Trewin, John C., *Peter Brook: A Biography*, London 1971.

Virmaux, Alain, *Antonin Artaud et le Théâtre*, Paris 1970.

Weighaus, Georg, *Heiner Müller*, Munich 1981.

White, Kenneth, *Le Monde d'Antonin Artaud, ou, pour une culture cosmopoetique*, Brussels 1989.

INDEX